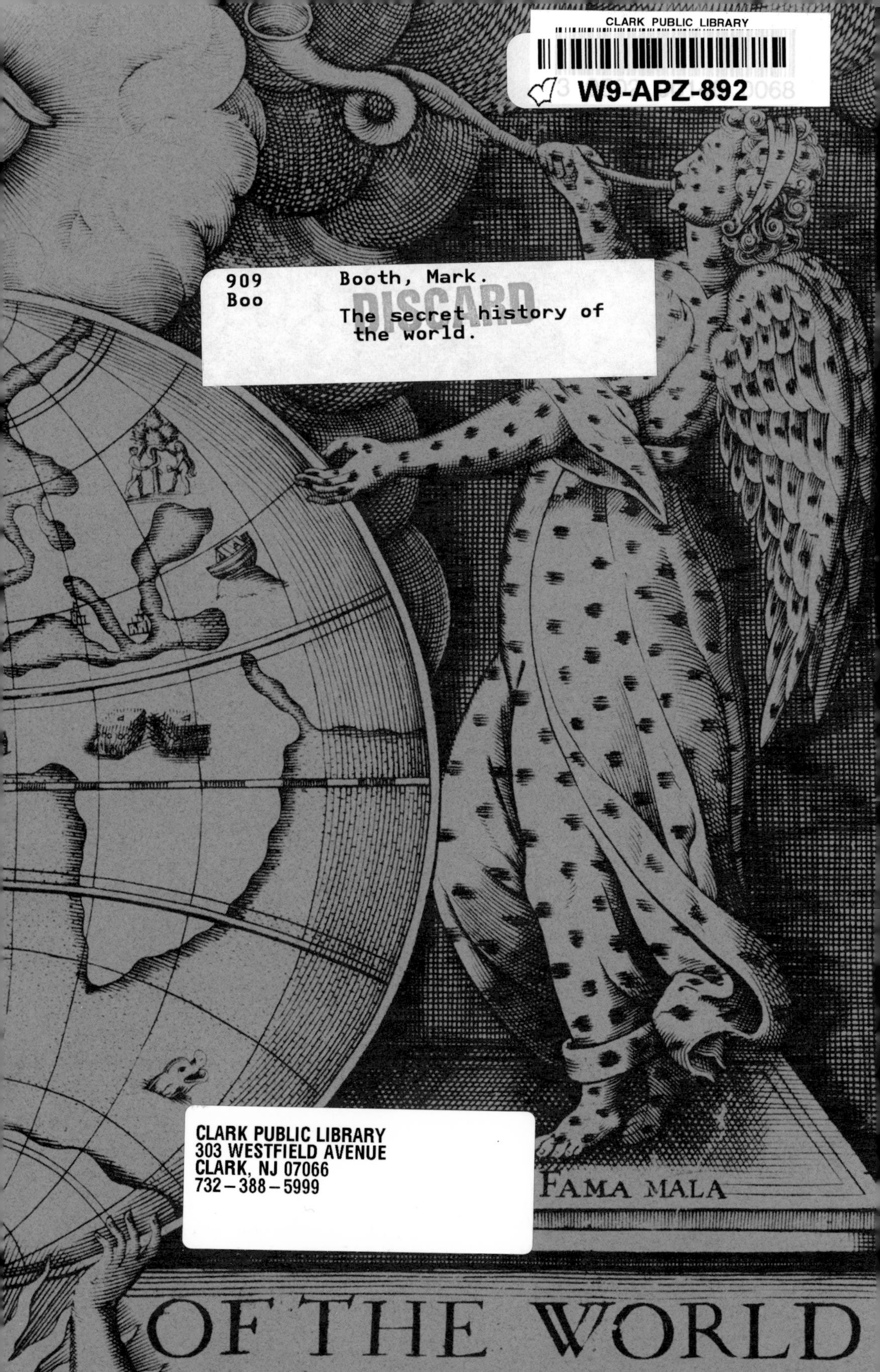
FAMA MALA
OF THE WORLD

THE SECRET HISTORY OF THE WORLD

THE SECRET HISTORY OF THE WORLD

AS LAID DOWN BY THE SECRET SOCIETIES

Mark Booth

THE OVERLOOK PRESS
Woodstock & New York

This edition first published in the United States in 2008 by
The Overlook Press, Peter Mayer Publishers, Inc.
Woodstock & New York

WOODSTOCK:
One Overlook Drive
Woodstock, NY 12498
www.overlookpress.com
[for individual orders, bulk and special sales, contact our Woodstock office]

NEW YORK:
141 Wooster Street
New York, NY 10012

Cataloging-in-Publication Data is available from the Library of Congress

Manufactured in the United States of America
ISBN 978-1-59020-031-5
10 9 8 7 6 5 4 3 2 1

Contents

Frontispiece of Sir Walter Raleigh's *The History of the World*, 1614

Introduction

THIS IS A HISTORY OF THE WORLD that has been taught down the ages in certain secret societies. It may seem quite mad from today's point of view, but an extraordinarily high proportion of the men and women who *made* history have been believers.

Historians of the ancient world tell us that from the beginnings of Egyptian civilization to the collapse of Rome, public temples in places like Thebes, Eleusis and Ephesus had priestly enclosures attached to them. Classical scholars refer to these enclosures as the Mystery schools.

Here meditation techniques were taught to the political and cultural elite. Following years of preparation, Plato, Aeschylus, Alexander the Great, Caesar Augustus, Cicero and others were initiated into a secret philosophy. At different times the techniques used by these 'schools' involved sensory deprivation, breathing exercises, sacred dance, drama, hallucinogenic drugs and different ways of redirecting sexual energies. These techniques were intended to induce altered states of consciousness in the course of which initiates were able to see the world in new ways.

Anyone who revealed to outsiders what he had been taught inside the enclosures was executed. Iamblichus, the neoplatonist philosopher, recorded what happened to two boys who lived at Ephesus. One night, lit up by rumours of phantoms and magical practices, of a more intense, more blazingly real reality hidden inside the enclosures, they let their curiosity get the better of them. Under cover of darkness they scaled the walls and dropped down the other side. Pandemonium followed, audible all over the city, and in the morning the boys' corpses were discovered in front of the enclosure gates.

In the ancient world the teachings of the Mystery schools were guarded as closely as nuclear secrets are guarded today.

Then in the third century the temples of the ancient world were closed down as Christianity became the ruling religion of the Roman Empire. The danger of 'proliferation' was addressed by declaring these secrets *heretical,* and trafficking in them continued to be a capital offence. But as we shall see, members of the new ruling elite, including

Church leaders, now began to form secret societies. Behind closed doors they continued to teach the old secrets.

This book contains an accumulation of evidence to show that an ancient and secret philosophy that originated in the Mystery schools was preserved and nurtured down the ages through the medium of secret societies, including the Knights Templar and the Rosicrucians. Sometimes this philosophy has been hidden from the public and at other times it has been placed in plain view – though always in such a way as to remain unrecognized by outsiders.

To take one example, the frontispiece of *The History of the World* by Sir Walter Raleigh, published in 1614, is on display in the Tower of London. Thousands file past it every day, missing the goat's head hidden in its design and other coded messages.

If you've ever wondered why the West has no equivalent to the tantric sex on open display on the walls of Hindu monuments such as the temples of Khajuraho in central India, you may be interested to learn that an analogous technique – the cabalistic art of *karezza* – is encoded in much of the West's art and literature.

We will see, too, how secret teachings on the history of the world influence the foreign policy of the present US administration regarding Central Europe.

Is the Pope Catholic? Well, not in the straightforward way you might think. One morning in 1939 a young man aged twenty-one was walking down the street when a truck drove into him and knocked him down. While in a coma he had an overwhelming mystical experience. When he came round he recognized that, although it had come about in an unexpected way, this experience was what he had been led to expect as the fruit of techniques taught him by his mentor, Mieczlaw Kotlorezyk, a modern Rosicrucian master.

As a result of this mystical experience the young man joined a seminary, later became Bishop of Cracow, then later still Pope John Paul II.

These days the fact that the head of the Catholic Church was first initiated into the spirit realm under the aegis of a secret society is perhaps not as shocking as it once was, because science has taken over from religion as the main agent of social control. It is science that decides what it is acceptable for us to believe – and what is beyond the pale. In both the ancient world and the Christian era, the secret philosophy was kept secret by threatening those who trafficked in it with death. Now in the post-Christian era the secret philosophy is still surrounded by dread, but the threat is of 'social death' rather than execution. Belief in key tenets, such as prompting by disembodied beings or that the course of history is materially influenced by secret cabals, has been branded as at best crackpot, at worst the very definition of what it is to be mad.

In Mystery schools candidates wishing to join were made to fall down a well, undergo trial by water, squeeze through a very small door and hold logic-chopping discussions with anthropomorphic animals. Ring a bell? Lewis Carroll is one of the many children's writers – others are the Brothers Grimm, Antoine de Saint-Exupéry, C.S. Lewis and the creators of *The Wizard of Oz* and *Mary Poppins* – who have believed in the secret history and the secret philosophy. With a mixture of the topsy-turvy and child-like literalness these writers have sought to undermine the common sense, materialistic view of life. They want to teach children to think backwards, look at everything upside down and the other way round, and break free of established, fixed ways of thinking.

Other kindred spirits include Rabelais and Jonathan Swift. Their work has a disconcerting quality in which the supernatural is not made a big issue of – it is simply a given. Imaginary objects are seen as at least as real as the mundane objects of the physical world. Satirical and sceptical, these gently iconoclastic writers are undermining of readers' assumptions and subversive of down-to-earth attitudes. Esoteric philosophy is nowhere explicitly stated in *Gargantua and Pantagruel* or *Gulliver's Travels*, but a small amount of digging brings it into the light of day.

In fact this book will show that throughout history an astonishing number of famous people have secretly cultivated the esoteric philosophy and mystical states taught in the secret societies. It might be argued that, because they lived in times when even the best educated did not enjoy all the intellectual benefits that modern science brings, it is only natural that Charlemagne, Dante, Joan of Arc, Shakespeare, Cervantes, Leonardo, Michelangelo, Milton, Bach, Mozart, Goethe, Beethoven and Napoleon all held beliefs that are discredited today. But then isn't it rather surprising that many in modern times have held the same set of beliefs, not just madmen, lone mystics or writers of fantasies, but the founders of the modern scientific method, the humanists, the rationalists, the liberators, secularizers and scourges of superstition, the modernists, the sceptics and the mockers? Could the very people who have done most to form today's scientifically oriented and materialistic world-view secretly have believed something else? Newton, Kepler, Voltaire, Paine, Washington, Franklin, Tolstoy, Dostoyevsky, Edison, Wilde, Gandhi, Duchamp: could it be true that they were initiated into a secret tradition, taught to believe in the power of mind over matter and that they were able to communicate with incorporeal spirits?

Recent biographies of some of these personalities hardly mention the evidence that exists to show that they were interested in these sorts of ideas at all. In the present intellectual climate where mention is made, they are usually dismissed in terms of a hobby, a temporary aberration, amusing ideas the personalities may have toyed with or used as metaphors for their work but never taken seriously.

However, as we shall see, Newton was undoubtedly a practising alchemist all his adult life and regarded it as his most important work. Voltaire participated in ceremonial magic through all the years he dominated the intellectual life of Europe. Washington invoked a great spirit in the sky when he founded the city that would bear his name. And when Napoleon said he was guided by his star, this was no mere figure of speech; he was talking about the great spirit who showed him his destiny and made him invulnerable and magnificent. One of the aims of this book is to show that, far from being passing fads or unaccountable eccentricities, far from being incidental or irrelevant, these strange ideas formed the core philosophy of many of the people who made history – and perhaps more significantly, to show that *they shared a remarkable unanimity of purpose*. If you weave together the stories of these great men and women into a continuous historical narrative, it becomes apparent again and again that at the great turning points in history, the ancient and secret philosophy was there, hiding in the shadows, making its influence felt.

In the iconography and statuary of the ancient world, starting from the time of Zarathustra, knowledge of the secret doctrine of the Mystery schools was denoted by the holding of a rolled scroll. As we shall see, this tradition has continued into modern times, and today the public statues of the world's towns and cities show how widely its influence has spread. There's no need to travel as far as sites like Rennes-le-Château, Rosslyn Chapel or the remote fastnesses of Tibet to find occult symbols of a secret cult. By the end of this book the reader will be able to see that these traces lie all around us in our most prominent public buildings and monuments, in churches, art, books, music, films, festivals, folklore, in the very stories we tell our children and even in the names of the days of the week.

TWO NOVELS, *FOUCAULT'S PENDULUM* and *The Da Vinci Code*, have popularized the notion of a conspiracy of secret societies that seeks to control the course of history. These novels concern people who hear intriguing rumours of the ancient and secret philosophy, set themselves on the trail of it and are drawn in.

Some academics, for example Frances Yates at the Warburg Institute, Harold Bloom, Sterling Professor of Humanities at Yale, and Marsha Keith Suchard, author of the recent groundbreaking *Why Mrs Blake Cried: Swedenborg, Blake and the Sexual Basis of Spiritual Vision*, have researched deeply and written wisely, but their job is to take a measured approach. If they have been initiated by men in masks, taken on journeys to other worlds and shown the power of mind over matter, they are not letting on.

The most secret teachings of the secret societies are transmitted only orally. Other parts are written in a deliberately obscure way that makes it impossible for outsiders to understand. For example, it *might* be possible to deduce the secret doctrine from Helena Blavatsky's prodigiously long and obscure book of the same name, or from the twelve volumes of G.I. Gurdjieff's allegory *All and Everything: Beelzebub's Tales to his Grandson*, or from the six hundred or so volumes of Rudolf Steiner's writings and lectures. Similarly you might – in theory – be capable of decoding the great alchemical texts of the Middle Ages or the esoteric tracts of high-level initiates of later periods such as Paracelsus, Jacob

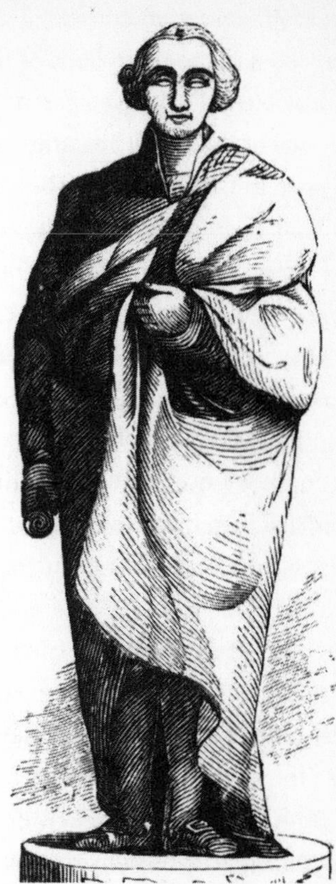

LEFT *Statue of Roman statesman.*

RIGHT *Statue of George Washington, by Sir Francis Chantrey, engraving from 1861.*

Boehme or Emmanuel Swedenborg, but in all these cases the writing is aimed at people already in the know. These texts aim to conceal as much as they reveal.

I have been looking for a concise, reliable and completely clear guide to the secret teachings for more than twenty years. I have decided to write one myself because I am convinced that no such book exists. It is possible to find self-published books and web sites that claim to do it, but, like collectors in any field, those who browse in bookshops on a spiritual quest soon develop a nose for 'the real thing', and you only have to dip into these books and sites to see there is no guiding intelligence at work, no very great philosophical training and very little hard information.

This history, then, is the result of nearly twenty years' research. Books such as *Mysterium Magnum*, a commentary on Genesis by the mystic and Rosicrucian philosopher Jacob Boehme, together with books by his fellow Rosicrucians Robert Fludd, Paracelsus and Thomas Vaughan have been key sources, as well as modern commentaries on their work by Rudolf Steiner and others. These are referenced in the notes at the back, rather than considered in the main body of the text, for reasons of conciseness and clarity.

But, crucially, I have been helped to understand these sources by a member of more than one of the secret societies, someone who, in the case of one secret society at least, has been initiated to the highest level.

I had been working for years as an editor for one London's largest publishers, commissioning books on a wide range of more or less commercial subjects and sometimes also indulging in my interest in the esoteric. In this way I have met many leading authors working in the field. One day a man walked into my office who was clearly of a different order of being. He had a business proposition, that we should reissue a series of esoteric classics – alchemical texts and the like – to which he would write new introductions. We quickly became firm friends and spent a lot of time together. I found I could ask him questions about more or less anything and he would tell me what he knew – amazing things. In retrospect I think he was educating me, preparing me for initiation.

On several occasions I tried to persuade him to write these things down, to write an esoteric theory of everything. He repeatedly refused, saying that if he did 'the men in white coats would come and take me away', but I also suspected that for him to publish these things would be to break solemn and terrifying oaths.

So in a sense I have written the book I wanted him to write, based in part on the Rosicrucian texts he helped me to understand. He guided me, too, to sources to be found in other cultures. So as well as the cabalistic, hermetic and neoplatonic streams that lie relatively close to the surface of Western culture, there are also Sufi elements in this book and ideas flowing from esoteric Hinduism and Buddhism, as well as a few Celtic sources.

I have no wish to exaggerate the similarities between these various streams, nor is it within the scope of this book to trace all the ways that these myriad streams have merged, separated then merged again down the ages. But I will focus on what lies beneath the cultural differences and suggest that these streams carry a unified view of a cosmos that contains hidden dimensions and a view of life as obeying certain mysterious and paradoxical laws.

By and large the different traditions from around the world illumine one another. It is rather wonderful to see how the experiences of a hermit on Mount Sinai in the second century or of a medieval German mystic fit with those of a twentieth-century Indian swami. Because esoteric teachings are more deeply hidden in the West, I often use oriental examples to help understand the secret history of the West.

I do not intend to discuss potential conflicts between different traditions. Indian tradition places far more emphasis on reincarnation than the Sufi tradition, which speaks of only a few. So for the sake of the narrative I have compromised by including only a small number of reincarnations of famous historical personalities.

I have also made cavalier judgements as to which schools of thought and which secret societies draw on authentic tradition. So the Cabala, Hermeticism, Sufism, the Templars, the Rosicrucians, esoteric Freemasonry, Martinism, the theosophy of Madame Blavatsky and Anthroposophy are included, but Scientology, the Christian Science of Mary Baker Eddy, together with a whole slew of contemporary 'channelled' material, is not.

This is not to say that this book shies away from controversy. Previous attempts to identify a 'perennial philosophy' have tended to come up with collections of platitudes – 'we are all the same under the skin', 'love is its own reward' – which are difficult to disagree with. To anyone expecting something similarly agreeable, I must apologize in advance. The teaching I will be identifying as common to Mystery schools and secret societies from all over the world will outrage many people and fly in the face of common sense.

One day my mentor told me I was ready for initiation, that he would introduce me to some people.

I'd been looking forward to this moment, but to my surprise, I refused. No doubt fear played a part. I knew by then that many initiation rituals involved altered states of consciousness, even what are sometimes called 'near-death' experiences.

But it was partly also because I didn't want to have all this knowledge given to me all of a piece. I wanted to continue enjoying trying to work it out for myself.

And neither did I want to take an oath that forbad me to write.

THIS HISTORY OF THE WORLD IS structured in the following way. The first four chapters will look at what happened 'in the beginning' as taught by the secret societies, including what is meant in the secret teaching by the expulsion from Eden and the Fall. These chapters will aim, too, to provide an account of the world-view of the secret societies, a pair of conceptual spectacles – so readers may the better appreciate what follows.

In the following seven chapters many figures from myth and legend are treated as historical figures. This is the history of what happened before written records began, as it was taught in the Mystery schools and is still taught in the secret societies today.

Chapter 8 includes the transition into what is conventionally thought of as the historical period, but the narrative continues to tell stories of monsters and fabulous beasts, of miracles and prophecies and historical figures who conspired with disembodied beings to direct the course of events.

I hope that throughout the reader's mind will be pleasurably bent equally by the strange ideas presented and by the revealing of the names of the personalities who have entertained these ideas. I hope, too, that some of the strange claims will strike a chord, that many readers will think ... yes, that explains why the names of the week run in the order they do ... That's why the image of the fish, the water-carrier and a serpent-tailed goat are everywhere ascribed constellations that don't really resemble them ... That's what we're really commemorating at Halloween ... That explains the bizarre confessions of demon-worship by the Knights Templar ... That is what gives Christopher Columbus the conviction to set out on his insanely perilous voyage ... That is why an Egyptian obelisk was erected in New York's Central Park in the late nineteenth century ... That is why Lenin was embalmed ...

Through all this the aim is to show that the basic facts of history can be interpreted in a way which is almost completely the opposite of the way we normally understand them. To prove this would, of course, require a whole library of books, something like the twenty miles of shelves of esoteric and occult literature said to be locked away in the Vatican. But in this single volume I will show that this alternative, this mirror image view, is a consistent and cogent one with its own logic that has the virtue of explaining areas of human experience that remain inexplicable to the conventional view. I will also cite authorities throughout, providing leads for interested readers to follow.

Some of these authorities have worked within the esoteric tradition. Others are experts in their own disciplines – science, history, anthropology, literary criticism – whose results in their specialist fields of research seem to me to confirm the esoteric world-view, even where I have no way of knowing whether their personal philosophy of life has any spiritual or esoteric dimension.

But above all – and this the point I want to emphasize – I am asking readers to approach this text in a new way – *to see it as an imaginative exercise.*

I want the reader to try to *imagine* what it would feel like to believe the opposite of what we have been brought up to believe. This inevitably involves an altered state of consciousness to some degree or other, which is just as it should be. Because at the very heart of all esoteric teaching in all parts of the world lies the belief that higher forms of intelligence can be accessed in altered states. The Western tradition in particular has always emphasized the value of imaginative exercises which involve cultivating and dwelling upon visual images. Allowed to sink deep into the mind, they there do their work.

So although this book can be read just as a record of the absurd things people have believed, an epic phantasmagoria, a cacophony of irrational experiences, I hope that by the end some readers will hear some harmonies and perhaps also sense a slight philosophical undertow, which is the suggestion that it may be true.

Of course, any good theory which seeks to explain why the world is as it is must also help predict what will happen next, and the last chapter reveals what that will be – always presuming, of course, that the great cosmic plan of the secret societies proves to be successful. This plan will encompass a belief that the great new impulse for the evolution will arise in Russia, that European civilization will collapse and that, finally, the flame of true spirituality will be kept burning in America.

TO HELP WITH THE ALL-IMPORTANT WORK of the imagination there are strange and uncanny illustrations integrated throughout, some of which have not previously been seen outside the secret societies.

There are also illustrations of some of the most familiar images from world history, the greatest icons of our culture – the Sphinx, Noah's Ark, the Trojan Horse, the Mona Lisa, Hamlet and the skull – because all of these are shown to have strange and unexpected meanings according to the secret societies.

Lastly there are illustrations from modern European artists such as Ernst, Klee and Duchamp, as well as from American outlaws such as David Lynch. Their work is also shown to be steeped in the ancient and secret philosophy.

INDUCE IN YOURSELF A DIFFERENT STATE of mind and the most famous and familiar histories mean something very different.

In fact if *anything* in this history is true, then everything your teachers taught you is thrown into question.

I suspect this prospect doesn't alarm you.

As one of the devotees of the ancient and secret philosophy so memorably put it:

You must be mad, or you wouldn't have come here.

I

In The Beginning

God Peers at His Reflection • The Looking-Glass Universe

ONCE UPON A TIME THERE WAS NO TIME AT ALL.

Time is nothing but a measure of the changing positions of objects in space, and, as any scientist, mystic or madman knows, *in the beginning there were no objects in space.*

For example, a year is a measure of the movement of the earth round the sun. A day is the revolving of the earth on its axis. Since by its own account neither earth nor sun existed in the beginning, the authors of the Bible never meant to say that everything was created in seven days in the usual sense of 'day'.

Despite this initial absence of matter, space and time, something must have happened to get everything started. In other words, *something must have happened before there was anything.*

Since there was noTHING when something first happened, it is safe to say this first happening must have been quite different from the sorts of events we regularly account for in terms of the laws of physics.

Might it make sense to say this first happening could have been in some ways more like a *mental* event than a physical event?

The idea of mental events generating physical effects may at first seem counter-intuitive, but in fact it's something we experience all the time. For example, what happens when I'm struck by an idea – such as 'I just *have* to reach out and stroke her cheek' – is that a pulse jumps a synapse in my brain, something like an electrical current burns down a nerve in my arm and my hand moves.

Can this everyday example tell us anything about the origins of the cosmos?

In the beginning an impulse must have come from somewhere – but where? As children didn't we all feel wonder when we first saw crystals precipitating in the bottom of a solution, as if an impulse were squeezing out of one dimension into the next? In this history we shall see how for many of the world's most brilliant individuals the birth of the universe, the mysterious transition from no-matter to matter has been explained in just such a way. They have envisaged an impulse squeezing out of another dimension into this one – and they have conceived of this other dimension as the mind of God.

WHILE YOU ARE STILL ON THE THRESHOLD – and before you risk wasting any more time on this history – I must make it plain that I am going to try to persuade you to consider something which may be all right by a mystic or a madman, but which a scientist will not like. A scientist will not like it at all.

To today's most advanced thinkers, academics like Richard Dawkins, the Charles Simony Professor of the Public Understanding of Science at Oxford, and other militant materialists who regulate and maintain the scientific world-view, the 'mind of God' is no better than the idea of a white-haired old man up above the clouds. It is the same mistake, they say, that children and primitive tribes make when they assume God must be like them – the anthropomorphic fallacy. Even if we allowed that God might conceivably exist, they say, why on earth should 'He' be like us? Why should 'His' mind be in any way like ours?

The fact is that they're right. Of course there is no reason at all ... unless it's the other way round. In other words, the only reason why God's mind might be like ours is if ours was made to be like His – that is, if God made us in His image.

And this is what happens in this book, because in this history everything is the other way round.

Alice enters the other-way-round universe.

Everything here is upside down and inside out. In the pages that follow you will be invited to think the last things that the people who guard and maintain the consensus want you to think. You will be tempted to think forbidden thoughts and taste philosophies that the intellectual leaders of our age believe to be heretical, stupid and mad.

Let me quickly reassure you that I'm not going to try to embroil you in academic debate, to try to persuade you by philosophical argument that any of these forbidden ideas are right. The formal arguments for and against can be found in the standard academic works referenced in the notes. But what I am going to do, is ask you to stretch your *imagination*. I want you to imagine what it would feel like to see the world and its history from a point of view that is about as far away from the one you've been taught as it is possible to get.

Our most advanced thinkers would be horrified, and would certainly advise you against toying with these ideas in any way at all, let alone dwelling on them for the time it will take to read this book.

There has been a concerted attempt to erase from the universe all memory, every last trace of these ideas. Today's intellectual elite believes that if we let these ideas slip back into the imagination, even briefly, we risk being dragged back into an aboriginal or atavistic form of consciousness, a mental slime from which we have had to struggle over many millennia to evolve.

SO IN THIS STORY, WHAT DID HAPPEN before time? What was the primal mental event?

In this story God reflected on Himself. He looked, as it were, into an imaginary mirror and saw the future. He imagined beings very like Himself. He imagined free, creative beings capable of loving so intelligently and thinking so lovingly that they could transform themselves and others of their kind in their innermost being. They could expand their minds to embrace the totality of the cosmos, and in the depths of their hearts they could discern, too, the secrets of its subtlest workings. Sometimes the love in them was almost snuffed out, but at other times they found deeper happiness the other side of despair, and sometimes, too, they found meaning the other side of madness.

Putting yourself into God's position involves imagining that you are staring at your reflection in a mirror. You are willing the image of yourself you see there to come alive and take on its own independent life.

As we shall see in the following chapters, in the looking-glass history taught by the secret societies this is exactly what God did, his reflections – humans – gradually and in stages, forming and achieving independent life, nurtured by Him, guided and prompted by Him over very long periods.

TODAY'S SCIENTISTS WILL TELL YOU THAT in the hour of your greatest anguish there is no point in crying out to the heavens with any expression of your deepest, most heartfelt

A nineteenth-century depiction of the cabalistic image of God reflecting on himself.

feelings, because you will find no answering resonance there. The stars can show you only indifference. The human task is to grow up, to mature, to learn to come to terms with this indifference.

The universe that this book describes is different, because it *was made with humankind in mind.*

In this history the universe is anthropocentric, every single particle of it straining, directed towards humankind. This universe has nurtured us through the millennia, cradled us, helped the unique thing that is human consciousness to evolve and guided each of us as individuals towards the great moments in our lives. When you cry out, the universe turns towards you in sympathy. When you approach one of life's great crossroads, the whole universe holds its breath to see which way you will choose.

Scientists may talk of the mystery and wonder of the universe, of every single particle in it being connected to every other particle by the pull of gravity. They may point out amazing facts, such as that each and every one of us contains millions of atoms that were once in the body of Julius Caesar. They may say we are stardust – but only in the slightly

LHOOQ – Manifeste DADA by Marcel Duchamp, reproduced in the book Surrealism and Painting *by André Breton. The notion that the physical world responds to our inner desires and fears is a difficult and perhaps somewhat troubling one that we will keep returning to in order to try to understand it better. In 1933 André Breton, a devotee of the philosophy of the secret societies, said something very wonderful that has illumined art and sculpture ever since – and never more so than in the case of the ready-mades of Duchamp: 'Any piece of flotsam or jetsam within our grasp should be considered as a precipitate of our desire.'*

disappointing sense that the atoms we are made of were forged from hydrogen in stars that exploded long before our solar system was formed. Because the important point is this: however they deck it out with the rhetoric of mystery and wonder, theirs is a universe of blind force.

In the scientific universe matter came before mind. Mind is an accident of matter, inessential and extraneous to matter – as one scientist went so far as to describe it, 'a disease of matter'.

On the other hand in the mind-before-matter universe that this book describes, the connection between mind and matter is much more intimate. It is a living, dynamic connection. Everything in this universe is alive and conscious to some degree, responding sensitively and intelligently to our deepest, subtlest needs.

In this mind-before-matter universe, not only did matter emerge from the mind of God, but *it was created in order to provide the conditions in which the human mind would be possible.* The human mind is still the focus of the cosmos, nuturing it and responding to its needs. Matter is moved by human minds perhaps not to the same extent but *in the same kind of way* that it is moved by the mind of God.

In 1935 the Austrian physicist Erwin Schrödinger formulated his famous theoretical experiment, Schrödinger's Cat, to describe how events change when they are observed. In effect he was taking the secret societies' teachings about everyday experience and applying them to the sub-atomic realm.

At some point in childhood we all wonder whether a tree falling really makes any sound if it takes place in a remote forest where no one is there to hear it. Surely, we say, a sound not heard by anyone can't properly be described as a sound? The secret societies teach that something like this speculation is true. According to them, a tree only falls over in a forest, however remote, so that someone, somewhere at some time is affected by it. Nothing happens anywhere in the cosmos except in interaction with the human mind.

In Schrödinger's experiment a cat sits in a box with radioactive material that has a 50 per cent chance of killing the cat. Both the cat's being dead and its being alive remain 50 per cent probabilities suspended in time, as it were, until we open the box to see what's inside, and only then does the actual event – the death or survival of the cat – happen. By looking at the cat we kill or save it. The secret societies have always held that the everyday world behaves in a similar way.

In the universe of the secret societies a coin flipped in strict laboratory conditions will still land heads up in 50 per cent of cases and tails up in 50 per cent of cases according to the laws of probability. However, these laws will remain invariable *only* in laboratory conditions. In other words, the laws of probability only apply when all human subjectivity has been deliberately excluded. In the normal run of things *when human happiness and hopes for self fulfilment depend on the outcome of the roll of the dice, then the laws of probability are bent. Then deeper laws come into play.*

These days we are all comfortable with the fact that our emotional states affect our bodies and, further, that deep-seated emotions can cause long-term, deep-seated changes, either to heal or to harm – psychosomatic effects. But in the universe that this book describes, our emotional states directly affect matter *outside* our bodies too. In this psychosomatic universe the behaviour of physical objects in space is directly affected by mental states without our having to *do* anything about it. We can move matter by the way we look at it.

In *Chronicles: Volume One,* Bob Dylan's recently published memoirs, he writes about what has to happen if an individual is to change the times in which he or she lives. To do this 'you've got to have power and dominion over the spirits. I had done it once ...' He writes that such individuals are able to '... see into the heart of things, the truth of things – not metaphorically either – but really see, like seeing into metal and making it melt, see it for what it is with hard words and vicious insight'.

Note that he emphasizes he is not talking metaphorically. He is talking directly and quite literally about a powerful, ancient wisdom, preserved in the secret societies, a wisdom in which the great artists, writers and thinkers who have forged our culture are steeped. At the heart of this wisdom is the belief that the deepest springs of our mental life are also the deepest springs of the physical world, because in the universe of the secret societies *all chemistry is psycho-chemistry*, and the ways in which the physical content of the universe responds to the human psyche are described by deeper and more powerful laws than the laws of material science.

It is important to realize that by these deeper laws are meant more than the mere 'runs of luck' that gamblers experience or accidents seeming to happen in sequences of three. No, by these laws the secret societies meant laws that weave themselves into the warp and weft of each individual life at the most intimate level, as well as the great and complex patterns of providential order that have shaped the history of the world. The theory of this book is that history has a deeper structure, that events we usually explain in terms of politics, economics or natural disaster can more profitably be seen in terms of other, more spiritual patterns.

ALL THE UPSIDE-DOWN, INSIDE-OUT, other-way-round thinking of the secret societies, all that is bizarre and mind-bending in what follows stems from the belief that mind preceded matter. We have almost no evidence to go on when we decide what we believe happened at the beginning of time, but the choice we make has massive implications for our understanding of the way the world works.

If you believe that matter came before mind, you have to explain how a chance coming together of chemicals creates consciousness, which is difficult. If, on the other hand, you believe that matter is precipitated by a cosmic mind, you have the equally difficult problem of explaining how, of providing a working model.

From the priests of the Egyptian temples to today's secret societies, from Pythagoras to Rudolf Steiner, the great Austrian initiate of the late nineteenth to early twentieth century, this model has always been conceived of as a series of thoughts emanating from the cosmic mind. Pure mind to begin with, these thought-emanations later become a sort of proto-matter, energy that becomes increasingly dense then becomes matter so ethereal that it is finer than gas, without particles of any kind. Eventually the emanations became gas, then liquid and finally solids.

Kevin Warwick is Professor of Cybernetics at Reading University and one of the world's leading creators of artificial intelligence. Working in friendly rivalry with his contemporaries at MIT in the United States, he has made robots able to interact with their environment, learn and adjust their behaviour accordingly. These robots exhibit a level of intelligence that matches that of the lower animals such as bees. Within five years, he says, robots will have achieved the level of intelligence of cats and in ten years they will be at least as intelligent as humans. He is also in the process of engineering a new generation

An alchemical engraving from the Mutus Liber, *published anonymously in 1677. In alchemy the precipitation of the morning dew is a symbol of the emanation of the Cosmic Mind into the realm of matter. As the Cabala puts it, the Ancient of Days shakes his shaggy head and a dew of divine white light falls. More particularly dew is a symbol of the spiritual forces that work on the conscience during the night. This is why a bad conscience may give us a sleepless night. Here initiates are seen collecting and working on the dew – in other words reaping the benefits upon waking of the spiritual exercises they performed when they went to bed.*

of robotic computers he expects to be able to design and manufacture other computers, each level generating the lesser level beneath it.

According to the cosmologists of the ancient world and the secret societies, emanations from the cosmic mind should be understood in the same way, as working downwards in a hierarchy from the higher and more powerful and pervasive principles to the narrower and more particular, each level creating and directing the one below it.

These emanations have also always been thought of as in some sense personified, as being in some sense also intelligent.

When I saw Kevin Warwick present his findings to his peers at the Royal Institute in 2001, he was criticized by some for suggesting that his robots were intelligent and so by implication conscious. But what is undeniably true is that these robots' brains grow in something like an organic way. They form something very like personalities, interreact with other robots and make choices beyond anything that has been programmed into them. Kevin argued that while his robots might not have consciousness with *all* the characteristics of human consciousness, neither do dogs. Dogs are conscious in a doggy way and his robots, he said, are conscious in a robotic way. Of course, in some ways – such as the ability to make massive mathematical calculations instantly – robots display a consciousness that is superior to our own consciousness.

We might think of the consciousness of the emanations from the cosmic mind in similar terms. We might also be reminded of the Tibetan spiritual masters who are said to be able to form a type of thoughts called *tulpas* by intense concentration and visualization. These beings – we might call them Thought-Beings – attain some sort of independent life and go off and do their master's bidding. Similarly Paracelsus, the sixteenth-century Swiss magus, wrote about what he called an 'aquastor', a being formed by the power of concentrated imagination which may obtain a life of his or her own – and in special circumstances become visible, even tangible.

At the lowest level of the hierarchy, according to the ancient and secret doctrine in all cultures, these emanations, these Thought-Beings from the cosmic mind, interweave so tightly that they create the appearance of solid matter.

Today if you wanted to find language to describe this strange phenomenon, you might choose to look to quantum mechanics, but in the secret societies the interweaving of invisible forces to create the appearance of the material world has always been conceived of as a net of light and colour or – to use an alchemical term – the Matrix.

TOP SCIENTIST ASKS: IS LIFE ALL JUST A DREAM?

THIS HEADLINE RAN IN THE *SUNDAY TIMES* in February 2005. The story was that Sir Martin Rees, Britain's astronomer royal, was saying, 'Over a few decades computers have evolved from being able to simulate only very simple patterns to being able to create virtual worlds with a lot of detail. If that trend were to continue, then we can imagine computers which will be able to simulate worlds perhaps even as complicated as the one we think we're living in. This raises the philosophical question: could we ourselves be in such a simulation and could what we think is the universe be some sort of vault of heaven rather than the real thing. In a sense we could ourselves be the creations within that simulation.'

The wider story was that leading scientists around the world are becoming increasingly fascinated by the extraordinary degree of fine-tuning that has been necessary for us to evolve. And this is making them question what is really real.

As well as these recent developments in science, novels and movies have gone some way to acclimatizing us to the idea that what we routinely take to be reality might be a 'virtual reality'. Philip K. Dick, who was perhaps the first writer to seed these ideas in pop culture, was steeped in initiatic wisdom regarding altered states and parallel dimensions. His novel *Do Androids Dream of Electric Sheep?* was filmed as *Blade Runner*. Other films with this theme include *Minority Report* – also based on a book by Dick – *Total Recall, The Truman Show* and *Eternal Sunshine of the Spotless Mind*. But the biggest has been *The Matrix*.

In *The Matrix* menacing, shade-wearing villains police the virtual world we call reality in order to control us for their own nefarious purposes. In part, at least, this is an accurate reflection of the teachings of the Mystery schools and secret societies. Although all the beings that live behind the veil of illusion are part of the hierarchies of emanations from the mind of God, some display a disturbing moral ambivalence.

These are the same beings that the peoples of the ancient world experienced as their gods, spirits and demons.

THE FACT THAT SOME LEADING SCIENTISTS are again beginning to see possibilities in this very ancient way of looking at the cosmos is an encouraging sign. Although modern sensibility has little patience with metaphysics, with what might look like high-minded, recherché abstractions piled up on each other, the cosmology of the ancient world was, as any fair historian of ideas will allow, a magnificent philosophical machine. In its account of interlocking, evolving dimensions, the clashing, morphing and intermingling of great systems, in its scale, complexity and awesome explanatory power it rivals that of modern science.

We cannot simply say that physics has replaced metaphysics and made it redundant. There is a key difference between these systems which is that they are explaining different things. Modern science explains how the universe comes to be as it is. Ancient philosophy of the kind we will be exploring in this book explains how our experience of the universe comes to be as it is. For science the great miracle to be explained is the physical universe. For esoteric philosophy the great miracle is human consciousness.

Scientists are fascinated by the extraordinary series of balances between various sets of factors that has been necessary in order to make life on earth possible. They talk in terms of balances between heat and cold, wetness and dryness, the earth being so far from the sun (and no further), the sun being at a particular stage of evolution (neither hotter nor cooler). At a more fundamental level, in order for matter to cohere, the forces of gravity and electromagnetism must each be of a particular degree (neither stronger nor weaker). And so on.

Looked at from the point of view of esoteric philosophy we can begin to see that an equally extraordinary series of balances has been necessary to make our subjective consciousness what it is, in other words to give our experience the structure it has.

By 'balances' I'm talking about more than having a balanced mind in the colloquial sense, that is to say of having emotions which are healthy and not too strong. I'm talking of something deeper, something essential.

What, for example, is needed to make possible the internal narrative, the collection of stories we string together to form our basic sense of self? The answer is, of course, memory. It is only by remembering what I did yesterday that I can identify myself as the person who did these things. The key point is that it is a particular degree of memory that is needed, neither stronger nor weaker. The Italian novelist Italo Calvino, one of the many modern writers who have followed the ancient and mystical philosophy, puts it precisely: 'Memory has to be strong enough to enable us to act without forgetting what we wanted to do, to learn without ceasing to be the same person, but it also has to be weak enough to allow us to keep moving into the future.'

Other balances are necessary in order for us to be able to think freely, to weave thoughts around that central sense of self. We have to be able to perceive the outside world through the senses, but it is equally important for us not to be overwhelmed by sensations which could otherwise occupy all our mental space. Then we could neither reflect nor imagine. That this balance holds is as extraordinary in its way as – for example – the fact that our planet is neither too far from, nor too close to, the sun.

We also have the ability to move our point of consciousness around our interior life – like a cursor on a computer screen. As a result of this, we have the freedom to choose what to think about. If we did not have the right balance of attachment and detachment from our interior impulses as well as from our perceptions of the outside world, then at this very moment you would have no freedom to choose to take your attention away from the page you are looking at now and no freedom to think about anything else.

And so, crucially, if the most fundamental conditions of human consciousness were not characterized by this set of exceptionally fine balances, it would not be possible for us to exercise free thought or free will.

When it comes to the very highest points of human experience, what the American psychologist Abraham Maslow usefully called 'peak experiences', even finer balances are necessary. For example, we may be required to make decisions at the great turning points of our lives. Again, it is the common, if not universal human experience, that if we try to work out what is the right thing to do with our lives using all our intelligence, if we work at it with a good and whole heart, if we exercise patience and humility, we can – just – discern the right thing to do. And once we have made the right decision, the chosen course of action will probably require all the willpower we are capable of, perhaps for just as long as we are able to bear it, if we are to complete it successfully. This is right at the core of what it means to experience life as a human being.

There is no inevitability about our consciousness having the structure that makes possible these freedoms, these opportunities to choose to do the right thing, to grow and develop into good, perhaps even heroic people – unless you believe in Providence, that is to say unless you believe that it was *meant* to be.

Human consciousness *is* therefore a sort of miracle. If today we tend to overlook this, the ancients were stirred by the wonder of it. As we are about to see, their intellectual leaders tracked subtle changes in human consciousness with as much diligence as modern scientists track changes in the physical environment. *Their account of history – with its mythical and supernatural happenings – was an account of how human consciousness evolved.*

Modern science tries to enforce a narrow, reductive view of our consciousness. It tries to convince us of the unreality of elements, even quite persistent elements in experience, that it cannot explain. These include the shadowy power of prayer, premonitions, the feeling of being stared at, the evidence for mind-reading, out-of-body-experiences, meaningful coincidences and other things swept under the carpet by modern science.

And much, much more importantly, science in this reductive mood denies the universal human experience that life has a meaning. Some scientists even deny that the question of whether or not life has meaning is worth asking.

We will see in the course of this history that many of the most intelligent people who have ever lived have become devotees of esoteric philosophy. I believe it may even be the case that *every* intelligent person has tried to find out about it at some time.

It is a natural human impulse to wonder if life has a meaning, and esoteric philosophy represents the richest, deepest, most concentrated body of thought on this subject. Before we embark on our narrative, therefore, it is vital that we apply one more sharp philosophical distinction to the softer edge of modern scientific thought.

SOMETIMES THINGS GO WRONG, AND LIFE seems pointless. But then at other times our lives do seem to have meaning. For example, life sometimes seems to have taken a wrong turn – we fail an exam, lose a job or a love affair ends – but then we find our true métier or true love as a result of this seeming wrong turn. Or it happens that someone decides against boarding a plane, which then crashes. If something like this happens, we may feel as if 'someone up there' is looking after us, that our footsteps have been guided. We may have a heightened sense of the precariousness of life, how easily things could have turned out differently had it not been for an almost imperceptible, perhaps otherworldy nudge.

Similarly with the down-to-earth, science-oriented part of ourselves we may see a coincidence as a chance coming together of related events, but sometimes deep down we suspect that a coincidence is not a matter of chance at all. In coincidences we sometimes feel we catch a hint, albeit an elusive one, of a deep pattern of meaning hidden behind the muddle of everyday experience.

And sometimes people find that just when all hope seems lost, happiness *is* discovered the other side of despair, or that inside hatred hides the growing germ of love. For reasons we'll look at later, questions of happiness are these days closely connected with notions of sexual love, so that it is often the experience of falling in love that gives us the sense that 'this was MEANT to be'.

RECENTLY LEADING SCIENTISTS HAVE been widely quoted as boasting that science is on the brink of discovering the explanation for – or the meaning of – everything in life and the universe. This is usually in relation to 'string theory', a theory, they say, shortly to be formulated, of all the forces of nature, which will combine the laws of gravity with the physics of the quantum world. We will then be able to relate the reasonable laws that govern objects we can sense with the very different behaviour of phenomena in the sub-atomic realm. Once this has been formulated we will understand everything there is to be understood about the structure, origin and future of the cosmos. We will have accounted for everything there is, because, they say, there *is* nothing else.

Before we can learn the secrets of the initiates and begin to understand their strange beliefs about history it's important to be clear about the distinction between 'meaning' as it is used in connection with questions about the meaning of life and 'meaning' as scientists use it.

A boy arranges to meet his girlfriend for a date, but she stands him up. He's hurt and angry. He wants to understand the painful thing that's happened to him. When he tracks her down, he interrogates her. His repeated question is WHY?

... because I missed my bus, she says,

... because I was late leaving work

... because I was distracted and didn't notice the time

... because I'm unhappy about something.

And so he presses and presses until he gets what he's after (sort of):

... because I don't want to see you any more.

When we ask WHY, it can be taken in two ways: either as in the girl's first, evasive answers, as meaning the same as HOW, that is to say requiring answers which give an account of a sequence of cause and effect, of atom knocking against atom; – or, alternatively,

WHY can be taken in the way the boy wanted to be answered, which is a matter of trying to winkle out INTENTION.

Similarly when we ask about the meaning of life and the universe we're not really asking HOW it came about in the cause-and-effect sense of how the right elements and conditions came together to form matter, stars, planets, organic matter and so on. We're asking about the intention behind it all.

So the big WHY questions – WHY life? WHY the universe? – as a matter of quite elementary philosophical distinction, cannot be answered by scientists, or more accurately not by scientists acting in their capacity as scientists. If we ask 'WHY are we here?' we may be fobbed off with answers which – like the girl's early answers– are perfectly valid, in the sense of being grammatically correct answers to the question, but which leave a twist of disappointment in the pit of the stomach, because they don't answer the question in the way that deep down we want it answered. The fact is that we all have a deep-seated, perhaps ineradicable longing for such questions to be answered at the level of INTENTION. The scientists who don't grasp this distinction, however brilliant they are as scientists, are philosophical morons.

Obviously we can choose to *give* parts of our lives purpose and meaning. If I choose to play soccer, then kicking the ball into the back of the net *means* a goal. But our lives as a whole, from birth to death, cannot have meaning without a mind that existed beforehand to give it meaning.

The same is true of the universe.

So when we hear scientists talk about the universe as 'meaningful', 'wonderful' or 'mysterious', we should bear in mind that they may be using these words with a certain amount of intellectual dishonesty. An atheistic universe can only be meaningful, wonderful or mysterious in a secondary and rather disappointing sense – in the same sense that a stage conjuror is said to be 'magic'. And, really, when it comes to considering the great questions of life and death, all the equations of science are little more than difficult and long-winded ways of saying 'We don't know'.

TODAY WE ARE ENCOURAGED TO PUT aside the big questions of life and death. Why are we here? What is the meaning of life? Such questions are strictly meaningless, we are told. Just get on with it. And so we lose some of the sense of how strange it is to be alive.

This book has been written in the belief that something valuable is in danger of being snuffed out altogether, and that as a result we are less alive than we used to be.

I am suggesting that if we look at the basics of the human condition from a different angle, we may appreciate that science doesn't really know as much as it claims to know, that it fails to address what is deepest and highest in human experience.

In the next chapter we will begin to imagine ourselves into the minds of the initiates of the ancient world and to see the world from their perspective. We will consider ancient wisdom we have forgotten and see that from its perspective even those things which modern science encourages us to think of as most solidly, reliably true, are really just a matter of interpretation, little more than a trick of the light.

A 'perspected' picture, which may be seen either as a witch or a young woman in a feathered hat, depending on your predisposition.

2

A Short Walk in the Ancient Woods
Imagining Ourselves into the Minds of the Ancients

CLOSE YOUR EYES AND IMAGINE A TABLE, a good table, the table you'd ideally like to work on. What size would it be? What wood would it be made of? How would the wood be joined? Would it be oiled or polished or planed bare? What other features would it have? Imagine it as vividly as you can.

Now look at a real table.

Which table can you be sure of knowing the truth about?

What *can* you be more sure of – the contents of our mind or the objects you perceive with your senses? Which is more real, mind or matter?

The debate springing from these simple questions has been at the heart of all philosophy.

Today most of us choose matter and objects over mind and ideas. We tend to take physical objects as the yardstick of reality. Contrariwise Plato called ideas 'the things that really are'. In the ancient world the objects of the mind's eye were taken as the eternal realities we can really be sure of, as opposed to the transitory, external surfaces *out there.* What I want to suggest now is that people did not formerly believe in a mind-before-matter universe because they had carefully weighed up the philosophical arguments on either side and come to a reasoned decision, but because *they experienced the world in a mind-before-matter way.*

While *our* thoughts are pale and shadowy in comparison with our sense impressions, in the case of ancient man it was the other way round. People then had less of a sense of physical objects. Objects were not as sharply defined and differentiated to them as they are to us.

If you look at depiction of a tree on the walls of an ancient temple, you will see that the artist has not really looked to see how branches are joined to the trunk.

In ancient times no one really *looked* at a tree in the way we do.

An irritating thing that tour guides on ancient sites like to say goes something like this: 'Look at this carving of women washing clothes in the river, or men sowing crops – you can still see exactly the same scene very near here.' There are two types of history, one being the modern, commonsensical approach that assumes that human nature has not substantially changed. This history belongs to the other type. In this history consciousness changes from age to age, even from generation to generation. Note the anatomically inaccurate and somewhat perfunctory depiction of a tree from an 8th Dynasty tomb. The artists who painted these walls were less interested in these physical objects than in the gods depicted only a few paces away in the inner sanctum of the temple. What they looked at in detail and with their greatest powers of concentration were the objects of the mind's eye. These they portrayed in golden, bejewelled and highly detailed images. The contention of this history, therefore, is that, contrary to what our tour guide might say, any similarity between women washing today and women washing four or five thousand years ago is little more than a matter of appearances.

THESE DAYS WE TEND TO THINK VERY reductively about our thoughts. We tend to go along with the prevailing intellectual fashion that sees thoughts as nothing more than words – perhaps with a penumbra of other stuff, such as feelings, images and so on – but with only the words themselves having any real significance.

However, if we dwell on this fashionable view, even only briefly, we will find that it flies in the face of everyday experience. Take an apparently mundane and insignificant thought such as 'I mustn't forget to phone my mother this evening'. If we now try to examine a thought like this as it weaves through our field of consciousness, if we try to hold it back in order to throw a little light on it, we can perhaps see that it carries a loose cluster

Signet ring from Mycenae with poppy-bearing priestess. Experience of a thought in all its constantly mutating, multi-dimensional glory may well be familiar to people who experiment with drugs such as marijuana or hallucinogens such as LSD. William Emboden, Professor of Biology at California State University, has published convincing evidence to show that in ancient Egypt the blue lily was used, along with opium and the mandrake root, to induce a trance state.

of word associations, such as might come to light in a psychoanalyst's word association test. If we then concentrate harder, it may well become apparent that these associations are rooted in memories that bring with them feelings – and may even carry with them their own impulses of will. The guilt I feel at not having phoned my mother earlier, as we now know from psychoanalysis, has roots in a complex knot of feelings that go back to infancy – desire, anger, feelings of loss and betrayal, dependency and the desire for freedom. As I contemplate my feelings of failure, other impulses arise – nostalgia for when things were better perhaps, when my mother and I were one – and an old pattern of behaviour is reanimated.

As we continue to try to pin this thought down, it will twist this way and that. The very act of looking at it changes it, causes reactions, perhaps sometimes even contradictory reactions. A thought is never still. It is a living thing that can never be identified definitively with the dead letter of language. This is why Schopenhauer, another proponent of the mystical philosophy at the heart of this book, said that 'as soon as you try to put a thought into words it ceases to be true'. Words can never convey or capture the complexity of an image or of the feelings.

Whole dimensions lie glistening on the dark side of even the most dull and commonplace thought.

The wise men and women of the ancient world knew how to work with these dimensions, and over many millennia they created and refined images which would perform just this function. As taught in the Mystery schools, the very early history of the world unfolds in a series of images of this type.

Before considering these powerful and evocative images I now want to ask the reader to begin to take part in an imaginative exercise: to try to imagine how someone in ancient times, a candidate who hoped for initiation into a Mystery school, would have experienced the world.

Of course it is a way of experiencing the world that is completely delusional from the point of view of modern science, but as this history progresses we will see more and more evidence that many of the great men and women of history have deliberately cultivated this ancient state of consciousness. We will see that they have believed that it gives them a view of the way the world really is, the way it works, that is in some ways superior to the modern way. They have brought back into 'the real world' insights that have changed the course of history, not only by inspiring works of art and literature of the greatest genius, but by prompting some of history's greatest scientific discoveries.

THEREFORE LET US NOW TO TRY IMAGINE ourselves into the mind of someone about two and a half thousand years ago, walking through woodland to a sacred grove or a temple such as Newgrange in Ireland, or Eleusis in Greece ...

To such a person the wood and everything in it was alive. Everything was watching him. Unseen spirits whispered in the movements of the trees. A breeze brushing against his cheek was the gesture of a god. If the buffeting of blocks of air in the sky created lightning, this was an outbreak of cosmic will – and maybe he walked a little faster. Perhaps he sheltered in a cave?

When ancient man ventured into a cave he had a strange sense of being inside his own

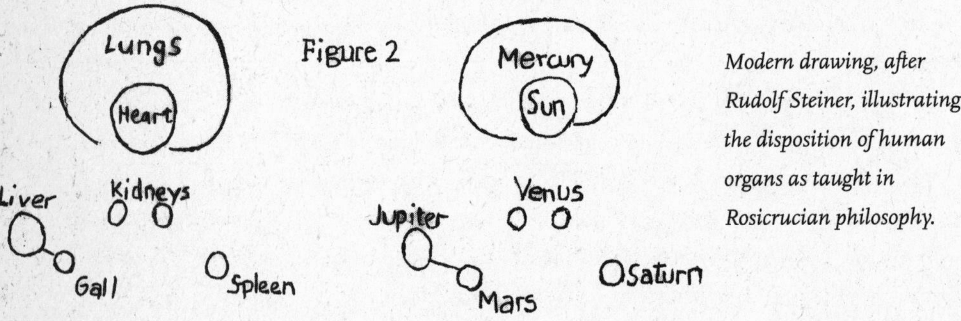

Modern drawing, after Rudolf Steiner, illustrating the disposition of human organs as taught in Rosicrucian philosophy.

skull, cut off in his own private mental space. If he climbed to the top of a hill, he felt his consciousness race to the horizon in every direction, out towards the edges of the cosmos – and he felt at one with it. At night he experienced the sky as the mind of the cosmos.

When he walked along a woodland pathway he would have had a strong sense of following his destiny. Today any of us may wonder, How did I end up in this life that seems to have little or nothing to do with me? Such a thought would have been inconceivable to someone in the ancient world, where everyone was conscious of his or her place in the cosmos.

Everything that happened to him – even the sight of a mote in a sunbeam, the sound of the flight of a bee or the sight of a falling sparrow – was *meant* to happen. Everything spoke to him. Everything was a punishment, a reward, a warning or a premonition. If he saw an owl, for example, this wasn't just a symbol of the goddess, this *was* Athena. Part of her, a warning finger perhaps, was protruding into the physical world and into his own consciousness.

It's important to understand the particular way in which human beings have affinities with the physical world according to the ancients. They believed in a quite literal way that nothing inside us is without a correspondence in nature. Worms, for example, are the shape of intestines and worms process matter as intestines do. The lungs that enable us to move freely through space with a bird-like freedom are the same shape as birds. The visible world is humanity turned inside out. Lung and bird are both expressions of the same cosmic spirit, but in different modes.

To the teachers of the Mystery schools it was significant that if you looked down on to the internal organs of the human body from the skies, their disposition reflected the solar system.

In the view of the ancients, then, *all biology is astrobiology*. Today we know full well how the sun gives life and power to living things, drawing the plant out of the seed, coaxing it to unravel upwards, but the ancients also believed that the forces of the moon, by contrast, tend to flatten and widen plants. Bulbous plants such as tubers were thought to be particularly affected by the moon.

More strikingly, perhaps, the complex, symmetric shapes of plants were believed to be caused by the patterns that the stars and planets make as they move across the sky. As a heavenly body takes a path that sees it curving back on itself like a shoelace, so that same shape is traced in the curling motion of a leaf as it grows, or a flower. For example, they saw Saturn, which traces a sharp pattern in the sky, forming the pine needles of conifers. Is it a coincidence that modern science shows that pine trees contain unusually large traces of lead, the metal believed by the ancients to be inwardly animated by the planet Saturn?

In the ancient view the shape of the human body was similarly affected by the patterns made in the sky by stars and planets. The movements of the planets, for example, were inscribed in the human body in the loop of the ribs and the lemniscate – bootlace shape – of the centripetal nerves.

Science has coined the word 'biorhythms' to describe the way the relationship of the earth with the moon and the sun, marked by the sequence of the seasons and day following night, is built biochemically deep into the function of every living being, for example in sleep patterns. But beyond these more obvious rhythms, the ancients recognized how other, more mathematically complex rhythms that involve the outer reaches of the cosmos work their way into human life. Humans breathe on average 25,920 times per day, which is the number of years in a great Platonic year (i.e. the number of years it takes the sun to complete a full cycle of the zodiac). The average or 'ideal' human life – seventy-two – also has the same number of days in it.

This sense of interconnectedness was not just a matter of *bodily* interconnectedness. It extended to consciousness too. When our man on a walk saw a flock of birds turn as one in the sky, it seemed to him as if the flock were one moved all together by one thought – and indeed he believed that this was the case. If the animals in the wood moved altogether in a sudden, violent way, if they panicked, they had been moved by Pan. Our man knew that this was exactly what was happening, because he commonly experienced great spirits thinking through himself *and through other people at the same time*. He knew that when he reached the Mystery school and his spiritual master introduced astonishing new thoughts to him and his fellow pupils, they would all be experiencing the very same thoughts, just as if the Master were holding up physical objects for them all to see. In fact he felt closer to people when sharing their thoughts than he ever did through mere physical proximity.

Today we tend to be very proprietorial about our thoughts. We want to take credit for originating them, and we like to think that our private mental space is inviolate, that no other consciousness can intrude on it.

However, we don't need to dwell on these assumptions long to see they don't always fit experience. If we are honest we must admit we do not invariably construct our thoughts. It's not just that geniuses like Newton, Kepler, Leonardo, Edison and Tesla talk of inspiration coming to them, as if in a dream and sometimes literally in a dream. For all of us it is the case that everyday thoughts naturally just *come* to us too. In common parlance we say 'It strikes me that ...' and 'It occurs to me that ...' If you're lucky it may happen now and then that a perfectly phrased quip comes to you that sets the table aroar. Then of course you're happy to bask in the glory – but the unvarnished truth is that the quip probably just jumped up and out of your mouth before you had any time consciously to phrase it.

The reality of everyday experience is that thoughts are quite routinely introduced into what we like to think of as our private mental space from somewhere else. The ancients understood this 'somewhere else' as being some-*one* else, the someone being a god, an angel or a spirit.

And an individual is not always prompted by the same god, angel or spirit. While today we like to think of ourselves as each having one individual centre of consciousness located inside the head, in the ancient world each person experienced him or herself as having *several different centres of consciousness originating outside the head.*

We saw earlier that gods, angels and spirits were believed to be emanations from the great cosmic mind – Thought-Beings in other words. What I am asking you to consider now is that these great Thought-Beings expressed themselves through people. If today we naturally think of people thinking, in ancient times they thought of Thoughts peopling.

As we shall see later on, gods, angels and spirits can bring about great changes in a nation's fortunes. The focus of these changes will often be an individual. For example, Alexander the Great or Napoleon were vehicles for a great spirit, and for a while carried all before them in a remarkable way. No one could oppose them and they succeeded in everything they did – until the spirit left them. Then quite suddenly everything began to go wrong.

We see the same process in the case of artists who become vehicles for the expression of a god or spirit for a certain period of their lives. Then they seem to 'find their voice' and create masterpiece after masterpiece with a sure hand, sometimes transforming the consciousness of a whole generation, even changing the whole direction of a culture in history. But when the spirit leaves, an artist never again creates with the same genius.

Similarly if a spirit weaves through an individual to create a work of art, the same great spirit may once again be present whenever that work of art is contemplated by others. One of his contemporaries said: 'When Bach plays the organ, even God comes to Mass.'

Today many Christians believe that God is present in the blood and wine at the climax of the Mass, albeit in a rather elusive way which centuries of theological debate have never quite managed to pin down. On the other hand if you read liturgies that have survived from ancient Egypt, notably *The Book of the Opening of the Mouth*, or consider chronicles kept in the temple of the Vestal Virgins in Rome that record the regular 'epiphanies', or appearances of the gods, it is quite clear that in those days the gods' presence was expected at the climax of religious ceremonies – and in a far more imposing way than in Christian services today. The people of the ancient world experienced the gods' presence as awe-inspiring.

When a thought came to the man walking through the woods, he felt as if he had been brushed by the wing of an angel or by the robe of a god. He sensed a presence even if he could not always perceive it directly and in detail. But once inside the holy precinct, he could perceive not just the wing, not just the swirling waves of light and energy that made up the robe. In the midst of the light he saw the angel or god itself. On these occasions he would have believed that he really was perceiving a being from the spiritual realm.

Today we experience moments of illumination as interior events, while the ancients experienced them as impinging on them from outside. The man we have been following expected the Thought-Being he saw to be visible to others – what today we would call a collective hallucination.

We don't know how to go about having such an experience. We don't know how to go about meeting a disembodied spirit. We don't know who they are. Today it often seems that we search and search for a genuine spiritual experience but are seldom sure we've had one that genuinely deserves the name. In the ancient world experience of spirits was so strong that to deny the existence of the spirit world would not have occurred to them. In fact it would have been almost as difficult for people in the ancient world to deny the existence of spirit as it would for us to decide not to believe in the table, the book, in front of us.

Paucity of experience makes belief in disembodied spirits difficult today. In fact the Church teaches that belief is admirable *because* it is difficult. The more your belief is out of proportion to the evidence the better, it seems. This teaching would have seemed absurd to people in the ancient world.

IF YOU BELIEVE IN A MIND-BEFORE-MATTER universe, if you believe that ideas are more real than objects as the ancients did, collective hallucinations are, of course, much easier to accept than if you believe in a matter-before-mind universe – in which case they are almost impossible to explain.

In this history gods and spirits control the material world and exercise power over it. We will see, too, how sometimes disembodied beings break through, unbidden. Sometimes whole communities are possessed by a convulsion of uncontrollable sexual savagery.

This is why commerce with the spirits was always considered highly dangerous. In the ancient world *controlled* communion with the gods and spirits was the preserve of the Mystery schools.

ROBERT TEMPLE, WHOSE CURRENT affiliations include Visiting Professor of Humanities, History and Philosophy of Science, University of Louisville, USA, and Visiting Professor of the History and Philosophy of Science, Tsinghua University, Beijing, has demonstrated that ancient cultures such as the Chinese and the Egyptians had an understanding of the universe that was in some ways in advance of our own. For example, he has shown that the Egyptians, far from being primitive or backward in these matters, knew that Sirius is a three-star system – something which modern science only 'discovered' in 1995 when French astronomers, using powerful radio telescopes, detected the red dwarf, subsequently named Sirius C. The point is that the ancient Egyptians were neither ignorant nor childlike, even though we may be tempted to consider them so.

First-century Roman relief of a candidate being led to an initiation ceremony.

One of the stupid beliefs we are fond of attributing to the ancients is that they worshipped the sun, as if they believed the physical object were a sentient being. Robert Temple's commentary on key texts by Aristotle, Strabo and others shows they saw the sun as a sort of lens through which the spiritual influence of a god rayed from the spiritual into the earthly realm. Other gods rayed their influences through the other planets and constellations. As the positions of the heavenly bodies changed, so the various patterns of influence give history direction and shape.

Returning to the man walking through the ancient wood, we see now that he experienced the spirits behind the sun, the moon and the other heavenly bodies as working on different parts of his mind and body. He felt his limbs move like flowing Mercury and he felt the spirit of Mars raging inside him in the fierce river of molten iron that was his blood.

The state of his kidney was affected by the movement of Venus. Modern science is only just starting to understand the role the kidney plays in sexuality. At the beginning of the twentieth century it discovered the kidney's role in the storing of testosterone. Then in the 1980s the Swiss pharmaceuticals giant Weleda began to conduct tests which showed that the movements of the planets affect chemical changes in metal salt solutions that are dramatic enough to be seen with the naked eye, even when these influences are too subtle to be measured by any scientific procedure so far devised. What is even more remarkable is that these dramatic changes come about when a solution of metal salt *is examined in relation to the movement of the planet with which it has traditionally been associated.* Thus copper salts contained in the kidney are affected by Venus, copper being the metal traditionally associated with Venus. Modern science may be on the verge of confirming what the ancients knew well. It really is true to say that Venus is the planet of desire.

The Mystery schools taught that as well as head-consciousness we each have, for example, a heart-consciousness which emanates from the sun then enters our mental space via the heart. Or to put it another way, the heart is the portal through which Sun god enters our lives. Likewise a kind of kidney-consciousness beams into us from Venus, spreading out into our mind and body via the portal of our own kidneys. The working together of these different centres of consciousness makes us variously loving, angry, melancholy, restless, brave, thoughtful and so on, forming the unique thing that is human experience.

Working through our different centres of consciousness in this way, the gods of the planets and constellations prepare us for the great experiences, the great tests that the cosmos means us to have. The deep structure of our lives is described by the movements of the heavenly bodies.

I am moved to desire by Venus and, when Saturn returns, I am sorely tested.

IN THIS CHAPTER WE HAVE ALREADY BEGUN to use some of the imaginative exercises used in the esoteric teaching. In the next chapter we will cross the threshold of the Mystery school and begin to follow the ancient history of the cosmos.

3

The Garden of Eden

The Genesis Code • Enter the Dark Lord • The Flower People

SCIENCE AND RELIGION AGREE THAT IN the beginning the cosmos moved from a state of nothingness to the existence of matter. But science has very little to say about this mysterious transition, all of it highly speculative. Scientists are even divided on whether matter was created all at once or whether it continues to be created.

By contrast, there was remarkable unanimity among the initiate priests of the ancient world. Their secret teachings are encoded in the sacred texts of the world's great religions. In what follows we will see how a secret history of creation is encoded in Genesis, that a few overfamiliar phrases can be opened up to reveal extraordinary new worlds of thought, mighty vistas of the imagination. And we shall see, too, that this secret history chimes with the secret teachings of other religions.

IN THE BEGINNING THERE PRECIPITATED out of the void nothing but a matter that was finer and more subtle than light, then an exceptionally fine gas. If a human eye had been looking at the dawn of history it would have seen a vast cosmic mist.

This gas or mist was the Mother of All Living, carrying everything needed for the creation of life. The Mother Goddess, as she was sometimes also called, will metamorphose in the course of this history and assume many different forms, many different names, but for now 'the earth was without form and void'.

Now for history's first great reversal of fortune. The Bible narrative continues: 'Darkness was upon the face of the earth.' According to biblical commentators working within the esoteric tradition, this is the Bible's way of saying that the Mother Goddess was attacked by a searing dry wind that almost extinguished the potential for life altogether.

Again, to a human eye it would have looked as if the gently interweaving mists that had first emanated from the mind of God were suddenly overtaken by a second emanation.

There was a violent storm like some rare and spectacular phenomenon observed by astronomers – the death of a massive star, perhaps – except that here 'in the beginning' it would have been on a completely overwhelming scale that filled the entire universe.

So this it what it would have looked like to a physical eye, but to the eye of the imagination this great cloud of mist and the terrible storm that attacked it can be seen to cloak two gigantic phantoms.

BEFORE WE TRY TO MAKE SENSE OF THIS ancient history of the cosmos, or to understand why so many brilliant people have believed in it, it is important to try to absorb it in the form it would have been presented in ancient times – as a series of imaginative images. It is important to let these images work on our imaginations in the same way that initiate priests intended them to work on the imagination of the candidate for initiation.

A few years ago I found myself falling into conversation with one of the legendary figures of London's gangland, a man who had helped spring a villain called Frank 'the Mad Axeman' Mitchell from a psychiatric prison and then, according to the stories, gone a bit mad himself. He killed the Mad Axeman in the back of a van with a sawn-off shotgun, then bathed in his blood, laughing. But his most vivid memory, the one he personally found the most chilling, was also his earliest. He remembered a fight he must have seen when he was perhaps just two or three years old.

His grandmother was bare-knuckle fighting on the cobbles outside her home among the Victorian terraces of the old East End. He remembered the gaslight on the wet cobbles and flying spittle, and how his grandmother resembled a giantess, lumbering but supernatural in strength. He remembered, too, that her massive forearms, built up and rubbed raw by the washing she took in to help feed him, thudded again and again into the other woman, even as she lay on the ground unable able to defend herself.

We must try to imagine something similar as we contemplate the two titanic forces locked in combat at the beginning of time. The Mother Goddess would often be remembered as a loving, life-giving and nurturing figure, comfortingly round and soft looking, but she also had a terrifying aspect. She was warlike when needs be. Among the people of ancient Phrygia, for instance, she was remembered as Cybele, a merciless goddess who rode on a chariot pulled by lions and who required devotees to work themselves into such a wild and savage delirium that they would castrate themselves.

Her opponent was, if anything, more frightening. Long, bony, his skin was a scaly white and he had glowing, red eyes. Swooping low over Mother Earth, the Dark Lord was armed with a deadly scythe – giving away his identity to anyone who hasn't already guessed it. For if the first emanation from the mind of God would metamorphose into the goddess of the earth, the second emanation would become the god of Saturn.

Saturn would trace the limits of the solar system. In fact he was the very principle of limitation. What Saturn's intervention introduced into creation was the potential for *individual objects* to exist and therefore the transition from formlessness to form. In other words because of Saturn there is a law of identity in the universe by which something exists and *is* nothing else and neither is anything else it. Because of Saturn an object occupies a certain space at a certain time and no other object can occupy that space, and neither can that object be in more than one place at one time. In Egyptian mythology Saturn was Ptah who moulds the earth on a potter's wheel, and in many mythologies Saturn's title is *Rex Mundi*, King of the World or 'Prince of this world', because of his control of our material lives.

If an individual entity can exist through time, then by implication *it can cease to exist too*. This is why Saturn is the god of destruction. Saturn eats his own children. He is sometimes portrayed as Old Father Time and sometimes as Death himself. Because of Saturn's influence everything that lives contains the seeds of its own end, and it is because of Saturn that what feeds us also destroys us. Death is in everything in the cosmos – woven into the bright blue sky, a blade of grass, the pulse of a baby's fontanel, the light in a lover's eye. Because of Saturn our lives are hard. Because of Saturn every sword is double-edged and every crown a crown of thorns. If we sometimes feel our lives almost too hard to bear, if we bruise and if we do cry out to the stars in despair, it is because Saturn pushes us to our limits.

And it could have been worse. The potential for life in the cosmos could have been extinguished even before birth. The cosmos would have remained through all eternity a place of the endless sifting of dead matter.

In the course of this history we will see that Saturn has returned at different times and in different guises to pursue his aim of mummifying humanity and squeezing the life out of it. At the end of this history we will also see that his most decisive intervention, an event long predicted by the secret societies, is expected to take place shortly.

In Genesis the Evil One's attempt to nullify God's plans at birth, this first act of rebellion of a Thought-Being against the Mind that emanated it, is dealt with in just one short phrase, but, as we have already suggested, the Bible is not here dealing with a scale of time we would recognize today. Saturn's tyranny over Mother Earth, his murderous attempt to squeeze all potential for life out of the cosmos, continued over vast periods immeasurable to the human mind.

His tyranny was eventually overthrown, and Saturn, if not entirely defeated, was kept in check and confined to his proper sphere. Again, Genesis tells us how this came about: 'And God said Let there be light, and there was light.' Light was pushing back the darkness that had been brooding over the waters.

How was this victory achieved? Of course there are two accounts of creation in the

Bible. The second, at the start of the Gospel of St John, is in some respects fuller and it can help us to decode Genesis.

But before we can continue to decode the biblical story of the creation, we must deal with a sensitive issue. We have already started to interpret Genesis in terms of the Earth goddess and Saturn. Anyone brought up in one of the great monotheistic religions will naturally feel some resistance to this. Surely this polytheistic belief in the gods of stars and planets is characteristic of more primitive religions like those of the ancient Egyptians, Greeks or Romans?

Conventionally minded Christians may wish to stop reading now.

TODAY'S CHURCH PREACHES AN EXTREME and radical monotheism. This is perhaps partly because of the dominance of a science that leaves little room for God. In science-friendly Christianity God has become an undifferentiated and undetectable immanence in the universe, and spirituality is nothing more than a vague and fuzzy feeling of at-oneness with this immanence.

But Christianity has roots in older religions of the region in which it arose and all of these were naturally polytheistic and astronomical. The beliefs of early Christians reflected this. For them spirituality meant commerce with actual spirits.

Christian churches from the cathedral at Chartres and St Peter's in Rome to small parish churches all over the world have been built on the sites of ancient holy wells, sacred caves, temples and Mystery schools. Throughout history certain sites like these have been regarded as portals for the spirits, cracks in the normal fabric of the space-time continuum.

The science of astro-archaeology has demonstrated that these portals are aligned with astronomical phenomena, intended to funnel influx from the spirit worlds at propitious times. At Karnak in Egypt at sunrise on the summer solstice a thin ray of sunlight would enter the portals of the temple and travel five hundred yards through courtyards, halls and passageways until it penetrated the darkness of the Holy of Holies.

It may surprise some Christians to learn how far this tradition has continued. All Christian churches are astronomically aligned, normally due east on the saint's day to

Christian chapel of the Seven Sleepers, built over a dolmen neat Plouaret, France.

Beautiful astronomical symbolism on the exterior of Notre-Dame Cathedral, Paris.

which the Church is dedicated. Great cathedrals from Notre Dame in Paris to the Sagrada Familia in Barcelona are covered with astronomical and astrological symbols.

Modern churchmen are often quick to condemn astrology, but none can deny, for example, that the great Christian festivals are all astronomically derived – Easter being the first Sunday following the full moon that falls on or follows the vernal equinox, or that Christmas is the first day after the winter solstice when the rising sun begins to move visibly back in the reverse direction along the horizon.

Even a glance at the biblical texts reveals that today's radically monotheistic reading of the scriptures is out of step with what the writers of these texts believed. The Bible refers to many disembodied spiritual beings, including the gods of rival tribes, angels, archangels, as well as devils, demons, Satan and Lucifer.

All religions believe that mind came before matter. All understand creation as taking place by a series of emanations, and this series is universally visualized as a hierarchy of spiritual beings, either gods or angels. A hierarchy of angels, archangels and so on has always been a part of Church doctrine, alluded to by St Paul, elucidated by his pupil St Dionysus, codified by St Thomas Aquinas and vividly imagined in art and also in literature by Dante and others.

These doctrines are often overlooked and disregarded by modern Christianity, but what Church leaders have been actively determined to suppress – what has been reserved for *esoteric* teaching – is that *different orders of angels are to be identified with the gods of the stars and planets.*

Though it hasn't filtered down to the wider congregation, modern biblical scholarship acknowledges that the Bible contains many passages that should be understood as referring to astronomical deities. For example, Psalm XIX says: 'He set a tabernacle for the Sun, Which is as a bridegroom coming out of his chamber, His going forth is from the end of heaven, And his circuit unto the ends of it.' Study of this passage in conjunction with

LEFT *The Four Cherubim in Ezekiel's dream in Raphael's painting.*
RIGHT *The combination of the Cherubim – the 'Tetramorph' – in Hindu mythology.*

comparative texts from neighbouring cultures reveals that it describes the marriage of the sun to Venus.

A passage like this might be dismissed as incidental to the main theological thrust of the Bible. You might suspect it of being an interpolation from a foreign culture. But the reality is that after layers of mistranslation and other types of obfuscation have been removed, the most important passages in the Bible can be seen to describe the deities of the stars and planets.

The four Cherubim are among the most powerful symbols in the Bible, appearing in key passages in Ezekiel, Isaiah, Jeremiah and Revelation. Popular in Hebrew and Christian iconography, prominent in Church art and architecture everywhere, they are symbolized by the Ox, the Lion, the Eagle and the Angel. In esoteric teaching these four Cherubim are the great spiritual beings behind four of the twelve constellations that make up the zodiac. The proof of their astronomical identities lies in the imagery associated with them: Ox = Taurus, Lion = Leo, Eagle = Scorpio, and Angel = Aquarius.

This fourfold pattern of symbolism regarding the constellations is repeated in all the world's great religions. But for the most important and telling example of polytheism in Christianity we must return to the story of the creation as it is told in Genesis and the Gospel of St John.

Genesis 1:26 is usually translated as 'In the beginning God made heaven and earth', but in fact any biblical scholar will admit, even if only when pressed, that the word 'Elohim' here translated as 'God' is *plural*. The passage properly reads 'In the beginning *the gods* made heaven and earth'. This is a rather puzzling anomaly that clergymen outside the esoteric tradition tend to turn a blind eye to, but inside this tradition it is well known that what is being referred to here are astronomical deities

We can discover their identity, as I have suggested, by matching the passage in Genesis with the parallel passage in the Gospel of St John. 'In the beginning was the Word, and the Word was with God and the Word was God ... All things were made by him ... And the light shineth in the darkness and the darkness comprehended it not.'

This parallel is helpful because John did not newly mint the phrase [the Word]. He was referring to a tradition already ancient in his lifetime, and which he evidently expected his readers to understand. Some four hundred years earlier Heraclitus, a Greek philosopher, had written 'the Logos [i.e. the Word] was before the Earth could be'. The important point here is that according to ancient tradition the Word that shone in the darkness in John's gospel – and so we now see, the gods who 'let there be light' in Genesis – are the seven great spirits who work together as the great spiritual influence emanating from the sun.

Thus both Old and New Testaments allude to the role of the Sun god in creation as it was generally understood in the religions of the ancient world.

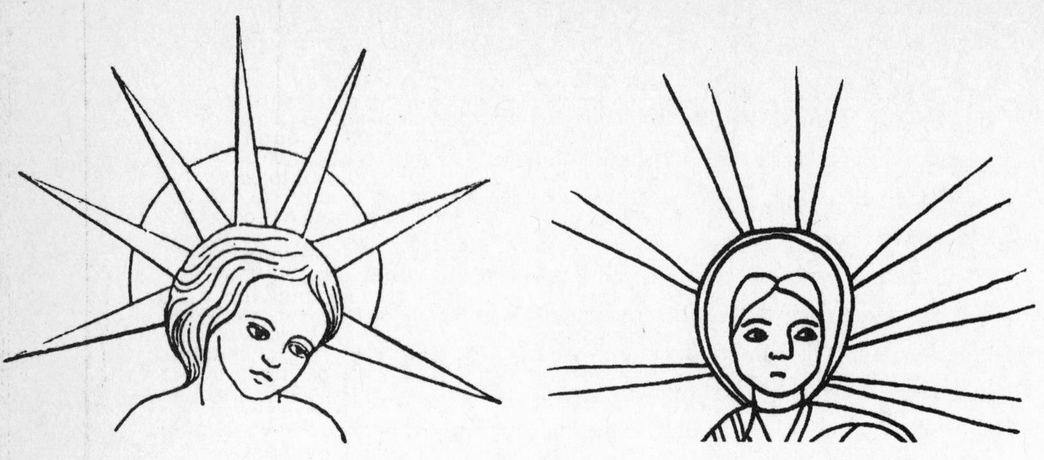

Depiction of Apollo from a Roman sculpture. In the ancient world the Sun god was typically depicted emanating seven rays, as a mark of the seven sun spirits that make up his nature. In the Egyptian Book of the Dead *they are called the Seven Spirits of Ra and in ancient Hebrew tradition as the Seven Powers of Light. Exactly the same Sun-god imagery is used to depict Christ in the very earliest Christian art, here in a mosaic of the third century in the Vatican grottes.*

THE SECOND GREAT ACT IN THE DRAMA of creation comes about when the seven-fold Sun god arrives in order to rescue Mother Earth from Saturn.

In the eye of imagination the Sun is a beautiful and radiant young man with a leonine mane. He rides a chariot and he is a musician. He has many names – Krishna in India, Apollo in Greece. Arising in splendour in the midst of the storm, he pushes back the darkness of Saturn until Saturn becomes like a giant dragon or serpent encircling the cosmos.

The Sun then warms Mother Earth into new life, and as he does so, he gives vent to a great, triumphal roar that reverberates to the outer limits of the cosmos. The roar causes matter in the cosmic womb to vibrate, to dance and form patterns. In inner group esoteric circles this process is sometimes known as 'the dance of the substances'. After a while it causes matter to coagulate into a variety of strange shapes.

What we are seeing here, then, is the sun singing the world into existence.

The Sun-Lion is a common image in ancient art. Whenever it appears it refers to this early stage in the mind-before-matter account of creation. A magnificent re-telling of the history of the Sun-Lion in the act of creation was written as late as the 1950s. It comes in the prequel to *The Lion, the Witch and the Wardrobe*, called *The Magician's Nephew*. Something that non-esoteric schools of literary criticism have missed is that the work of C.S. Lewis is steeped in Rosicrucian lore. In his story the Sun-Lion is called Aslan:

> In the darkness something was happening at last. A voice had begun to sing. It was very far away and Digory – *the first child to explore Narnia* – found it hard to decide from what direction it was coming. Sometimes it seemed to come from all directions at once. Sometimes he almost thought it was coming out of the earth beneath them. There was hardly even a tune. But it was, beyond comparison, the most beautiful voice he had ever heard. It was so beautiful he could hardly bear it ... The eastern sky changed from white to pink and from pink to gold. The Voice rose and rose, till the air was shaking with it ... The Lion was pacing to and fro about that empty land and singing his new song. And as he walked and sang the valley grew green with grass. It spread out from the Lion like a pool. It ran up the sides of the hills like a wave.

What the teachers of the Mystery schools meant to indicate by the victory of the Sun god was the momentous transition from a purely mineral cosmos to a cosmos burgeoning with plant life.

In the earliest and most primitive form of plant life according to the Mystery tradition, single germs were joined together in vast floating structures like webs that filled the whole universe. In the *Vedas*, the sacred books of India, this stage of creation is described as 'the net of Indra', an infinite net of luminous, living threads, perpetually interweaving, coming together like waves of light then dissolving again.

Time passed and some of these threads began to weave together more permanently, the light streams dividing into tree-like forms. An imaginative impression of what this was like can perhaps be got by remembering what it was like, as a small child, to visit a great hothouse like the ones that Alice Liddell, the girl who inspired *Alice in Wonderland*, liked to visit at Kew Gardens. Great tendrils stretch everywhere. Here are humid mists and a sunny, luminous greenness.

If you were able to land in the midst of all of this and if you sat on one of the great green branches stretching out of sight, and if this great branch on which you were sitting suddenly stirred, you would have an experience like a hero in a fairy story sitting on a rock that moves and reveals itself to be a giant. Because the vast vegetable being at the heart of the cosmos, whose soft and luminous limbs stretched to all four corners of it, was Adam.

This was Paradise.

Because there was as yet no animal element to the cosmos, Adam was without desire and so without care or dissatisfaction. Needs were satisfied before they could even be felt. Adam lived in a world of endless springtime. Nature yielded an unending supply of food in

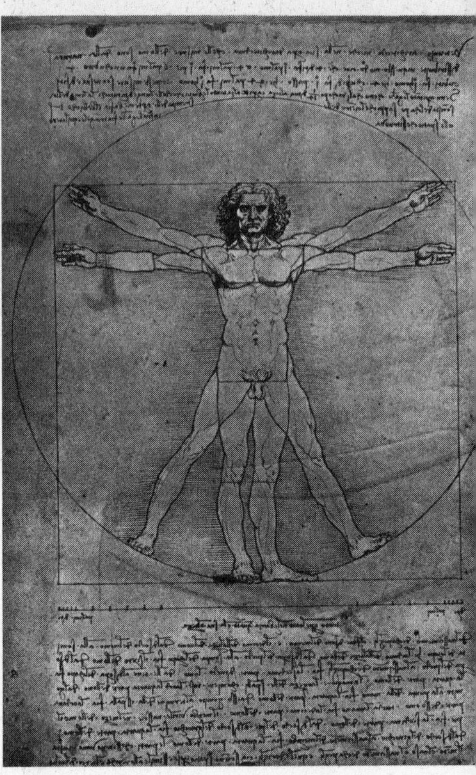

LEFT *From a thirteenth-century manuscript. Adam stretched to the corners of the cosmos.*

RIGHT *A comparison of this with the famous drawing by Leonardo reveals a layer of meaning often missed. Adam literally occupied the whole cosmos.*

the form of a milky sap, similar to that which we find in dandelions today. Memorials to this blissful satiation have come down to us in statues of the many-breasted Mother Goddess.

As time went on the plant forms became more complex, more like the plants of today. Again, if you had been able to see this time in the history of the cosmos with the physical eye, you would have been struck by the myriad fluttering, palpitating flowers.

We have suggested that the secret history of the creation shadows the scientific history of creation in intriguing ways. We have just seen, for example, how a purely mineral stage of existence has been followed by a primitive plant stage, followed by an era of more complex plants. But there is a vital difference I must draw to your attention. In the secret history not only is it true to say that what eventually evolved into human life passed through a vegetable stage, but *the vegetable element remains an essential part of the human being today*.

If you removed the sympathetic nervous system from the body and stood it up on its own, it would look like a tree. As one of Britain's leading homeopathic healers put it to me, in a rather beautiful phrase: 'The sympathetic nervous system is the gift of the vegetable kingdom to the physical body of man.'

Esoteric thought all over the world is concerned with the subtle energies that flow round this vegetable part of the body and also with the 'flowers' on this tree, the chakras which operate, as we shall see, as its organs of perception. The great centre of the vegetable component of the human body, feeding on the waves of light and warmth radiating from the sun, is the chakra of the solar plexus – called 'solar' because it was formed in this, the era controlled by the sun.

Awareness of this vegetable element in the human body has remained greatest among the peoples of China and Japan. In Chinese medicine the energetic flow of this vegetable life force, called *chi*, is understood to animate the body, and disease arises when the delicate network of energies becomes blocked. The fact that the flow of this energy is undetectable by modern, materialistic science, the fact that it seems to operate in some elusive realm between the human spirit and the meat of the animal body, does

Germanic sun-idol. Engraving of 1596. J. B. van Helmont, an important alchemist and scientist who will feature later in this history, called the stomach 'the seat of the soul'.

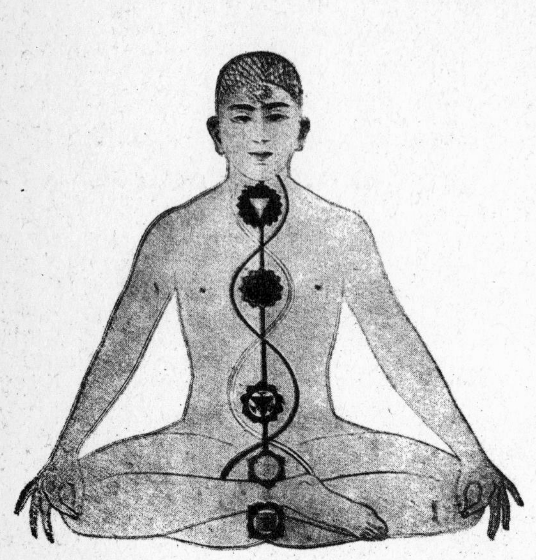

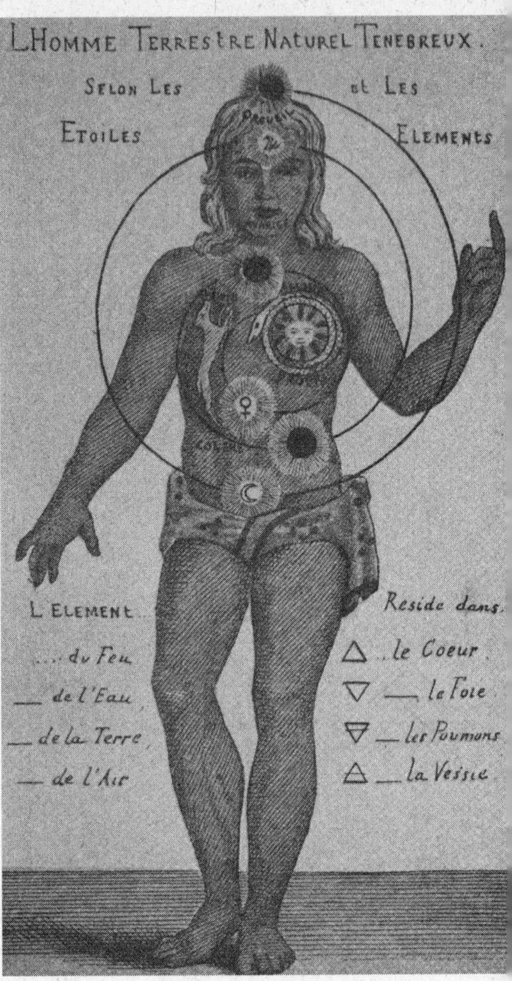

Hindu illustration of the seven major chakras and, for comparison, illustration by Johann Gichtel to the writings on chakras by the seventeenth-century Christian mystic Jacob Boehme.

not make the medicine any the less effective, as generation upon generation of patients attest.

As well as in medicine, the Chinese and Japanese tend to lay great emphasis on the role of the solar plexus in spiritual practice. If you contemplate a statue of a meditating Buddha, you will see someone who has gathered himself inward, and that the centre of this meditation, his centre of mental and spiritual gravity, is his lower belly. This is because he has withdrawn from the rigid, deadly mentality of the brain and sunk down into the centre within himself – sometimes called the *hara* – that is connected with *all* life. He is concentrating on becoming more aware of being alive, of his unity with all living things.

ALTHOUGH THE IDEA OF CHAKRAS HAS become popular in the West because of an influx of oriental esoteric thought, the chakras are also central to the Western esoteric tradition and can be seen in both Egyptian and Hebrew thought. And just as Christianity contains a hidden tradition of gods of the stars and planets, so it also contains a hidden tradition of the chakras.

The organs of the vegetable body are situated in nodes up and down its trunk. They are made up of different numbers of petals – the solar plexus chakra, for example, having ten petals and the brow chakra having two petals. The seven major chakras – situated at the groin, solar plexus, kidneys, heart, throat, brow and crown – feature in the seventeenth-century writings of Jacob Boehme and, as we will see later, in those of his near-contemporary, the Catholic Saint, Teresa of Avila, where they are called 'the eyes of the soul'.

Moreover, on closer inspection the Bible itself can be seen to contain many coded references to the chakras. The 'horns' with which Moses has traditionally been depicted are explained away by conventionally minded Christians as the result of a misunderstanding based on a mistranslation. But in the esoteric tradition these horns

The almond shape that surrounds this vision of Jesus, called the vesica piscis, *is derived from the Egyptian hieroglyph called the Ru, which symbolized the birth-portal and also the Third Eye, or brow chakra. What is intended by the masons who carved this device on a church at Alpirsbach, Germany, is that you can have direct experience of and communication with the great spiritual beings by activating the Third Eye. It is extraordinary to consider that Christian art and architecture all over the world commonly features a representation of the Third Eye, unrecognized by the great majority of Christians.*

represent the two petals of the brow chakra, sometimes called the Third Eye. The flowering rod of Aaron refers to the activation of the chakras, the opening of the subtle flowers up and down the subtle tree. In the final chapter we will see how in Revelation the account of the opening of the seven seals is in fact a way of talking about the enlivening of the seven chakras, and predicting the great visions of the spiritual world that will result.

THE PINEAL GLAND IS A SMALL GREY gland, the size of an almond, which is situated in the brain where the spinal chord reaches up into it. In esoteric physiology, when we have a hunch, our pineal gland begins to vibrate, and if spiritual disciplines are used to increase and prolong this vibration, this may lead to the opening of the Third Eye, situated, of course, in the middle of the brow.

The Third Eye as a uraeus snake in an Egyptian wall carving.

Man meditating on the pineal gland, taken from a drawing by Paul Klee with Hindu depiction of the same for comparison.

Modern anatomists only 'discovered' the pineal gland in 1866, when two monographs were published almost simultaneously by H.W. de Graaf and E. Baldwin Spencer. Later it was discovered that the pineal gland is large in children and when the crystallization of various body parts happens around puberty – that is to say when we naturally become less imaginative – the pineal gland begins a process of calcification and also shrinks. Scientists now know that melatonin is a hormone, most of which is produced by the pineal gland, mostly at night. Melatonin is essential for the rhythm of waking and sleeping and the maintenance of the immune system.

If modern science discovered the pineal gland relatively late, the ancients certainly knew of it very early on, and also believed they understood its function. They knew, too, how to manipulate it to achieve altered states. The Egyptians clearly depicted it as a uraeus snake and in Indian literature it is shown as the Third Eye of Enlightenment, or the Eye of Siva. It was depicted as the pine-cone-topped wand of the followers of Dionysius, and a fourth-century BC Greek anatomist described it as 'the sphincter which regulates the flow of thought'.

They saw the pineal gland as an organ of perception of higher worlds, a window opening on to the brightness and wonder of the spiritual hierarchies. This window could be opened systematically by meditation and other secret practices which gave rise to visions. Recent research at the University of Toronto has shown that meditating on the pineal gland using methods recommended by Indian yogis causes it to release a rush of melatonin, the secretion that causes us to have dreams and, in sufficient dosages, can also cause waking hallucinations.

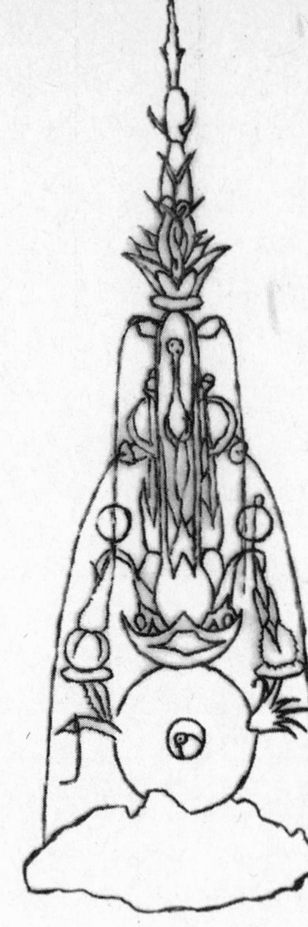

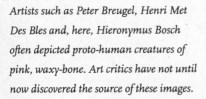

Artists such as Peter Breugel, Henri Met Des Bles and, here, Hieronymus Bosch often depicted proto-human creatures of pink, waxy-bone. Art critics have not until now discovered the source of these images.

RETURNING TO THE CREATION NARRATIVE and the great imaginative images encoded within Genesis, we see that Adam's body had at first been very soft and amorphous, his skin almost as delicate as the skin on a pond, but now it began to harden. As the great Christian mystic and Rosicrucian philosopher Jacob Boehme wrote in *Mysterium Magnum*, his commentary on Genesis, 'what would in time become bone now hardened and became something closer to wax'. Warmed by the sun, his green limbs also began to become tinged with pink.

As Adam solidified he also began to divide into two, that is to say he was an hermaphrodite who reproduced in an asexual way. When pressed, any scholar of biblical Hebrew will have to admit that Genesis 1.27, the passage usually translated 'Male and female He created them', properly reads 'Male and female they [i.e. the Elohim] created him [singular]'.

So, it was by this plant-like method of reproduction that Eve was born out of Adam's body, moulded from the waxy cartilage which served Adam for bone.

The progeny of Adam and Eve also reproduced asexually, procreating by using sounds in a way that was analogous to the creative activity of the Word. This episode in history is related to Freemasonic lore pertaining to 'the Word that has been lost', the esoteric

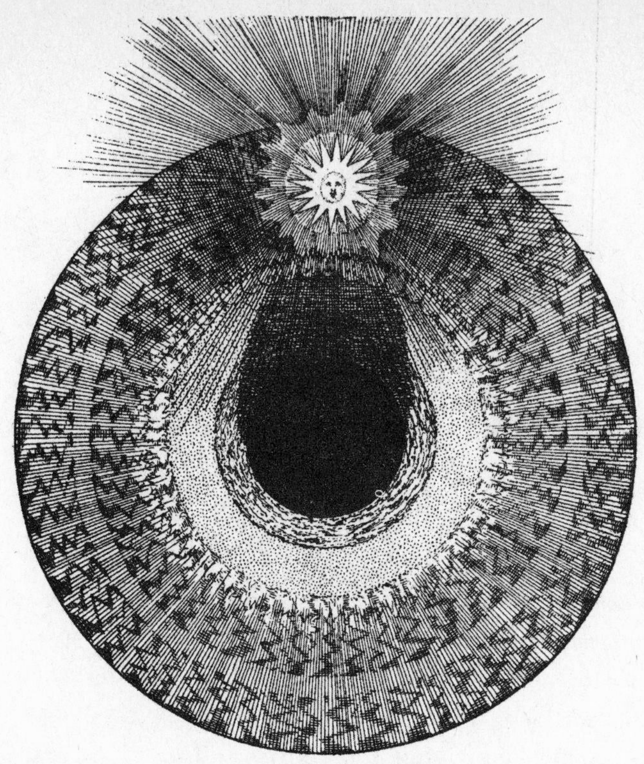

The separation of the earth and sun in a seventeenth-century English print, illustrating the writings of Robert Fludd, an eminent Rosicrucian scholar traditionally believed to have been one of the board employed to translate the King James Bible.

belief when in the far future this Word is rediscovered, it will be possible to impregnate using only the sound of the human voice.

Adam, Eve and their progeny did not die, but now and then they merely went to sleep in order to refresh themselves. But the lotus-eating state of the Garden of Eden could not go on forever. If it had done, humanity would never have evolved beyond the vegetable stage.

It was always intended that the Sun god would separate from the earth ... for a while.

OF COURSE NO ARTEFACTS HAVE SURVIVED from the time when gods and proto-humans lived in plant form, but there is at least a reliable record of such artefacts.

Herodotus, the Greek writer of the fifth century BC is sometimes called the father of history, because he was the first to try to research and piece together a coherent and objective account of history.

In approximately 485 BC Herodotus visited Memphis in Egypt. There in vast underground vaults, he was shown rows of statues of former kings stretching back as far as

Mandrake men in nineteenth century engraving. Mandrake roots have always played a prominent part in esoteric lore because their shapes often seem to represent a vegetable striving towards the human form. Might the colossi Herodotus saw have looked something like this?

the eye could see into almost unimaginably distant times. Walking with the priests along the rows, he came to a series of 345 colossal wooden carvings of beings who had reigned before Menes, their first human king. These beings, said the priests, were 'born one from the other', that is to say without need of a sexual partner, by the plant-like method of parthenogenesis. Each carrying a plaque giving name, history and annals, the wooden monuments were a record of a long lost era of the vegetable life of humankind.

4

Lucifer, The Light of the World

The Apple of Desire • A War in Heaven • The Secrets of the Days of the Week

CREATION WAS RE-ENACTED IN THE Mystery schools, a drama in three acts.

The first act dramatized Saturn's oppression of Mother Earth. This was called the Age of Saturn.

The second act dramatized the birth of the Sun and his protection of Mother Earth. This, the paradise time of the flower people, was remembered as the Age of the Sun.

During the re-enactment of these great events the candidate for initiation found himself in the middle of what was partly a play with special effects, and partly a séance. In an altered state, perhaps drugged and with little ability to distance himself from events, the candidate was guided by the priests on a shaman-like journey through the spirit worlds. Drama as we know it today would eventually move out of the Greek Mystery centres to become *public* performances, but in the early days of the Mystery schools at least, candidates would never have seen anything like this before.

We now come to the third act, the subject of this chapter. At the start of it, there is the momentous event we alluded to at the end of the last chapter. Earth and sun separate. From now on the sun's life-giving rays, rather than illuminating it from inside, shine down upon the earth from the sky. As a result the earth cools and becomes denser. It becomes less gaseous and more liquid. It shrinks and the whole of its watery surface is covered by Adam and Eve and their flowery, gently fluttering progeny.

Suddenly, at the climax of the third act, the candidate for initiation into the Mystery school watching this drama would have caught a whiff of sulphur, maybe even been half-blinded by a flash like lightning, as the peaceful pastoral scene was invaded by a glistening alien life-form, horrifyingly livid and horned. The picture that was being presented to his imagination was of a snake seemingly endlessly long, millions of miles of it weaving its way into the cosmos, a snake with a perverse kind of beauty. 'Thou hast been in Eden, the garden of God,' says Ezekiel 28:13, 'every precious stone was thy covering, the sardius, topaz, and the diamond, the beryl, the onyx and the jasper, the sapphire, the emerald and carbuncle and gold.'

The candidate for initiation would have watched with horror as it coiled itself ever more tightly around Adam's vegetable trunk. He would have understood that what he was watching was the series of events by which life on earth moved painfully to the next stage of evolution. Because *the story of the serpent entwined around the tree contains the clearest possible image of the earth's transition from vegetable to animal life.*

Since the eighteenth century when a matter-before-mind world-view began to take over from the ancient, mind-before-matter world-view, the Church has tried to reconcile the Genesis account of creation with the findings of science. This has been a doomed enterprise because it is based on a modern, anachronistic reading of Genesis.

Genesis does not consider evolution objectively as a modern scientist does, piecing together bits of geological, anthropological and archaeological evidence impartially and objectively evaluated. The story of Genesis is a *subjective* account of the way humanity evolved, what it felt like. In other words *the story of the entwining of snake and tree is a picture of the formation of the spine and central nervous system characteristic of animals as it has been retained in the human collective subconscious.*

Again and again we will see that the esoteric account is not necessarily inconsistent with the scientific one. As we suggested by the perspected picture, it views the same facts from a very different point of view.

WE SAW IN THE LAST CHAPTER HOW MATTER had in a sense prepared the ground in which vegetable life could be born. Now vegetable life as it were formed a cradle into which animal life could be born. To put it another way, vegetable life formed a seed bed into which the seeds of animal life fell.

This is the beginning of the momentous episode in history called the Fall.

The candidate for initiation would be made to feel the terrible sense of crisis and danger involved in the Fall in a quite literal way. Suddenly and as if impelled by an earth tremor, he found himself falling down into a black hole, pitched into what he immediately discovered to be a snake pit. In the esoteric tradition the rough-hewn chamber that lies underneath the Great Pyramid at Gizah, known as the Chamber of Ordeal, performed just this function. Recent excavations at Baia in Italy, where a system of caves, part natural and part man-made were believed by the Romans to be the actual entrance to the Underworld, have actually revealed the site of a trap door which would have flung the candidate for initiation down into the snake pit below.

The candidate experienced for himself how Lucifer and his legions infested the whole earth with a plague of glistening serpents. He saw how, according to the secret history,

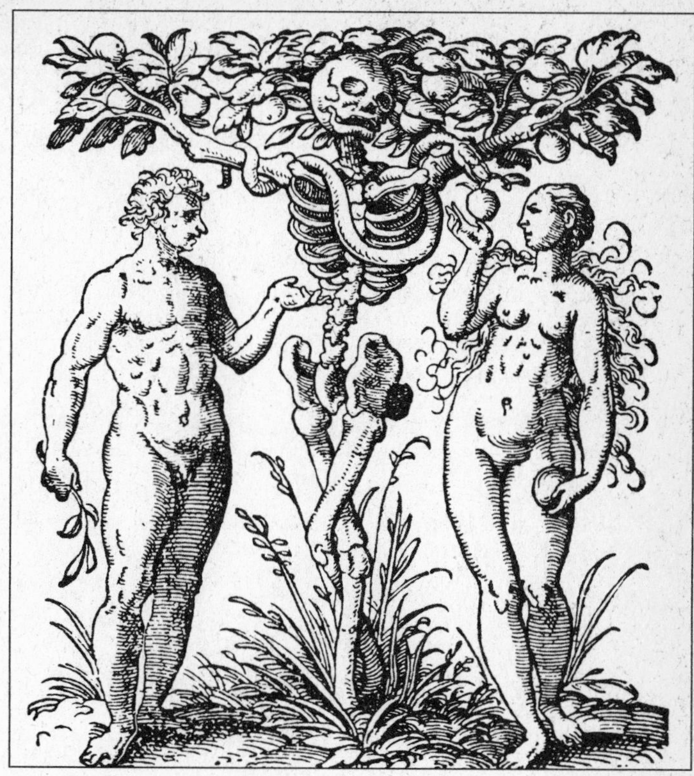

LEFT *Adam, Eve and the serpent by Masaccio.*

RIGHT *Renaissance engraving of the tree in the Garden of Eden as a skeleton, after Sebald Beharne.*

the whole earth had once begun to seethe with primitive animal life. He saw, too, how desire tormented the very ground, making it heave, and he realized traces of this torment could be seen in expressive rock formations.

But why *should* the translation from vegetable to animal life be marked by such torment? The account of the catastrophe in Genesis certainly emphasizes this tormented aspect in some of the most sonorous phrases on the Old Testament: 'Unto the woman He said, I will greatly multiply thy sorrow and thy conception; in sorrow shalt thou bring forth children ... And unto Adam He said ... cursed is the ground for thy sake; in sorrow shalt thou eat it all the days of thy life; Thorns also and thistles shall it bring forth to thee.' It seems that as a result of the Fall, humans have to suffer, to strive, *and to die* – but why?

Wrapped up in this ancient language are more truths modern science would recognize. Plants reproduce by a method called parthenogenesis. A part of the plant falls off and grows into a new plant. This new plant is in a sense a continuation of the old one, which

Loki, the Norse equivalent to Lucifer, is usually portrayed as a beautiful and fiery god but also evil, quick-witted and cunning. Ninteenth-century illustration by R. Savage

therefore – in a sense – does not die. *The evolution of animal life and its characteristic method of reproduction – sex – brought death with it.* As soon as hunger and desire were felt so too were dissatisfaction, frustration, sorrow and fear.

WHO IS IT WHO TEMPTS EVE? WHO IS the serpent who inflames the world with desire?

We probably all feel we know the answer to this question – but naively. The problem is that those in charge of our spiritual development have kept us at a nursery level of understanding.

We began to see in the last chapter how the Church has covered up its astronomical roots, how the beginning of Genesis contains hidden within it stories of the same gods of the planets we know from other, more 'primitive' religions – the god Saturn, the Earth goddess and the Sun god. As we now move further into the Genesis account of history we can see again how this covering up of astronomical roots, the radical monotheism of the modern Church, can stop us from understanding clearly what the ancient text is trying to tell us.

Most people would naturally assume that Christianity allows the existence of only one Devil – *the* Devil – in other words that Satan and Lucifer are the same entity.

In fact we need only a quick, fresh look at the texts to see that the authors of the Bible intended something quite different. Again, this is something biblical scholars accept, but which hasn't filtered down to congregations.

We have seen that Satan, the Dark Lord, the agent of materialism, is to be identified with the god of the planet Saturn in Greek and Roman mythology. Is Lucifer, the snake, the tempter who inflames humanity with animal desire also to be identified with Saturn – or perhaps with a different planet?

There is a vast, erudite body of literature comparing biblical texts to older and contemporary texts from neighbouring cultures, which shows that the two main representatives of evil in the Bible, Satan and Lucifer, are not the same entity. Fortunately we do not need to immerse ourselves in this literature, because there is a quite explicit statement in the Bible itself: Isaiah 14.12, 'How thou art fallen from heaven, O Lucifer, son of the morning.'

The Morning Star is, of course, Venus. *The Bible, therefore, identifies Lucifer with the planet Venus.*

It might at first seem counter-intuitive to equate the goddess of Venus in Greece and Rome – Aphrodite to the Greeks – with Lucifer in the Judeo-Christian tradition. Venus/Aphrodite is female and seems more life-enhancing. But in reality there are key points of similarity.

Both Lucifer and Venus/Aphrodite are bound up with animal desire and sexuality.

The correlation between Lucifer and Venus can also be seen in the mythology of the Americas, where he appears in the figure of the horned and feathered snake god Quetzal Coatl.

The snake sometimes found coiled round the body of the goddess was called 'the minister of the goddess' by the Greeks.

The apple is the fruit associated with both. Lucifer tempts Eve with an apple and Paris hands Venus an apple in a gesture that precipitates the abduction of Helen and the Great War of the ancient world. The apple is universally the fruit of Venus because if you slice an apple in two, the path that Venus traces in the sky over a forty-year period is a five-pointed star, pinpointed by the position of the pips.

Lucifer and Venus are also ambiguous figures. Lucifer is evil, but he is a necessary evil. Without Lucifer's intervention, proto-humanity would not have evolved beyond a vegetative form of life. As a result of Lucifer's intervention in history we are animated, both in the sense that we can move about the surface of the planet and also in the sense that we are moved by desire. An animal has a conscious awareness of itself as a distinct entity that is denied to plants. *To say that Adam and Eve 'knew they were naked' is to say that they became aware that they had bodies.*

Many beautiful representations of Venus have come down to us from the ancient world, but there were terrifying representations too. Behind the image of a woman of matchless beauty lurked the terrifying serpent woman.

IN ORDER TO DELVE DEEPER INTO THIS ambiguity and to understand better the next great event in the secret history of the world, we now turn to an early German version of Venus/Lucifer tradition which appeared in medieval poetry and would enter the mainstream of world literature when it was taken up and adapted by Wolfram von Eschenbach in *Parzifal*.

> See! Lucifer, there he is!
> If there are still master-priests

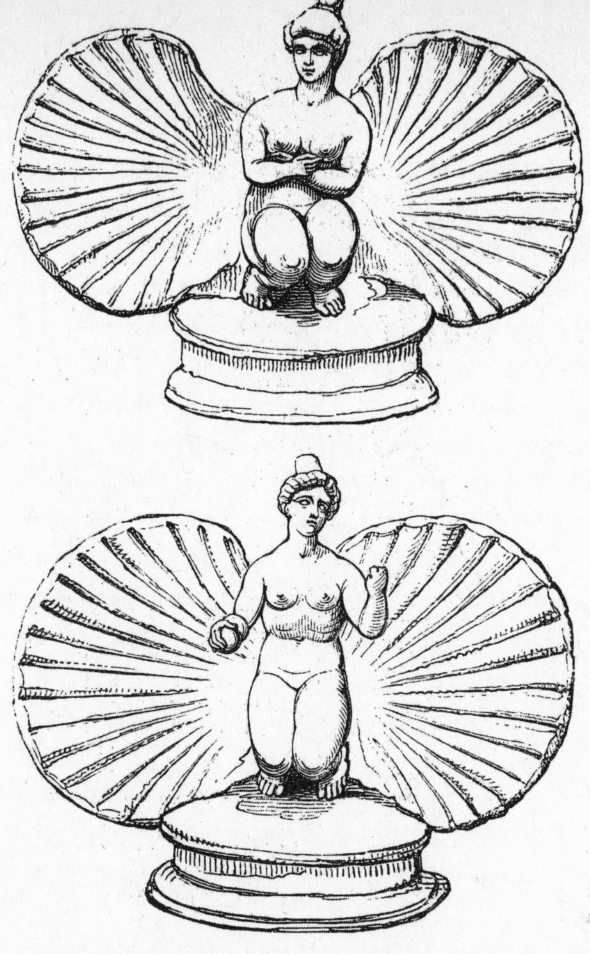

These small Greek statues capture something of the joy the Greeks took in the pleasures of desire, their joy in the material world. In Greek creation stories the birth of Venus is brought about by an act of rebellion by Saturn, who takes his sickle and slices at the testicles of Uranos, the Sky god, castrating him. As the sperm of Uranos falls into the sea, the beautiful goddess Venus springs into being, fully formed, and floats ashore on a sea shell. The ancients believed that shells were precipitated out of water, just as matter is precipitated out of spirit, hence their symbolizing emanation from the cosmic mind, both here and in the iconography of St James of Compostela.

Then you know well that I am saying the truth.
Saint Michael saw God's anger ...
He took Lucifer's crown from his head
In such a way that the stone jumped out of it
Which on earth became Parsifal's stone.

Tradition tells us that as Lucifer fell a great emerald dropped from his forehead. This signals that humanity would increasingly suffer a loss of vision in the Third Eye, the brow chakra.

While the result of the influence of Satan is that life is often hard to bear, it is as a result of the influence of Venus that life is often *hard to understand*. The influence of Venus brought a paradoxical, tricky quality to the heart of the universe.

In other words, delusion entered the world. Lucifer endowed matter with a glamour that would dazzle humankind, and blind people to higher truths.

Why is it that the way forward sometimes looks like the way backwards? Why is it that the thing we most ought not to do looks almost indistinguishable from the thing we ought to do? In my heart of hearts I know what I ought to do, but I have another, alien element entwined inside me that wants to lead me astray. The Luciferic element is infused into my very physiology. Desire and delusion combine in me dangerously. Because of Lucifer's influence, 'the good that I would do I not; but the evil which I would not, that I do'. (Romans 7.19.) St Paul, who as we shall see was an initiate of the Mystery tradition, is saying that part of me always knows what is right, but that it is often overruled by a part that is in thrall to Lucifer.

MODERN SCIENCE NEVER FRAMES THE questions, How did delusion come into the world? Or imagination? Or willpower? But to the ancients delusion, imagination and will were among the greatest forces in the universe, living out there in three-dimensional space as well as in our own minds. For them the history of creation was an account of how these things came to be.

Friedrich Nietzsche said, 'Unless you have chaos inside you, you cannot give birth to a dancing star.' Humans would never have been able to become freely creative, brave or loving if they had not been able to make mistakes, to see things as other than they are and to believe things to be other than they are. Because of Lucifer it is the case that we do not always believe in proportion to the evidence. We can often believe what we *want* to believe. For instance, the life of someone we know can appear a miserable failure or a heart-warming success *depending on how we choose to look at it*, whether good-heartedly or mean-spiritedly. And when the harsh fire, the primeval sulphur burns in the pit of our stomachs, it is difficult for us to choose to be good-hearted.

When in the very beginning the Earth goddess had been attacked by the god of Saturn, the young Sun god had arrived to protect her, and, fighting a great battle in heaven, had defeated Saturn. The candidate for initiation who was being shown the secret history of the world had therefore already watched one great battle. He now had to watch another one in which the enemy was the great snake that had slithered into Paradise in order to corrupt it.

Who was to be the new champion to fight this second battle?

As with the Church's conflation of Satan and Lucifer in order to disguise its astronomical roots, we must now disentangle another deliberately created confusion.

In the early chapters of Genesis telling the story of creation, the word usually translated as 'God' is, as we have seen, 'Elohim'. Later Genesis ceases to refer to Elohim and instead the word usually translated as 'God' is 'Jehovah'. Biblical scholars working outside the esoteric tradition have tended to explain what appears to them as two different names for the same God as the result of two different literary strands, the Elohim strand and the Jehovah strand, probably dating from different periods and woven together by a later redactor.

However, scholars working within the esoteric tradition have a much simpler explanation. Elohim and Jehovah are not different names for the same entity but *different entities.* Elohim is, as we have seen, a collective name for the Seven Spirits working together as the god of the Sun, while Jehovah came into being when one of these seven broke away to defend the Earth from Venus.

In order to discover Jehovah's true, astronomical identity, we must look again at the iconography of his opponent, Venus. We must also remember that for the ancients the history of the origins of the cosmos was as much about how human experience was put together, how experience gained its characteristic structure, as it was about how the physical universe was put together. In other words, it was as much about the principles of human nature as about the laws of the natural world.

Human nature is so formed that any power I may have to resist my animal desires – indeed what stops me from becoming a mere animal – derives from my capacity for thought and reflection. Venus was traditionally depicted holding a mirror, but not out of vanity as is nowadays supposed. The mirror was a symbol of the power of *reflection* to modify desire.

Depicted here on the back of a Greek mirror from the first century BC *is the story of Semele, goddess of the Moon, and a beautiful youth called Endymion. In the story Semele falls in love with Endymion and casts a spell that leaves him in perpetual dreamy sleep. Here is an explicit depiction of the moon working on the pineal gland in the form of the wand of Dionysus.*

Medieval depiction of Jehovah as a war god.

The god of reflection was the god of the great reflector in the sky – the moon. In all ancient cultures the moon regulated not only fertility but thought.

In fact the initiate priests believed that in order to create the conditions in which human thought would be possible, the cosmos had had to arrange itself in a particular way. In order for human reflection to be possible, the sun and the moon had had to arrange themselves in the sky so that the moon reflected the light of the sun down to earth.

They also believed that this arrangement in the sky had to be reproduced on a smaller scale inside the human head. There the pineal gland represented the sun, and the gland which could modify and reflect on the visions that the pineal gland received from the spirit worlds was the pituitary gland.

This might seem one of the madder things that anyone has ever believed, but to the ancients it corresponded to their everyday, lived experience. They tracked small changes in their consciousness, which seemed to them to mutate with the changing positions of the sun and moon. Readers are invited to check their own experience to see whether their dreams are more vivid when the moon is big and full.

If you observe oysters in a tray for a month, you will see that they wax and wane with the moon. Modern science has confirmed that the pituitary gland behaves like an oyster.

THE GOD OF THE MOON WOULD BECOME known to the Hebrews as Jehovah and to the Muslims as Allah, *the great god of thou-shalt-not.*

So at the climax of this great cosmic drama of creation, with the earth in danger of

Perseus, the wielder of the Moon-shield.

becoming a living Hell, a new force arose to meet Lucifer. Just as the seven Elohim had acted to hold Saturn/Satan in check, now one of these seven broke away to become the god of the Moon, and from there directed operations to hold Venus/Lucifer in check.

This great cosmic battle against Venus was remembered in cultures around the world, for example in the story of Krishna's battle with the snake-demon Kaliya, and the stories of Apollo's battle with the Python and of Perseus combating the sexually ravenous dragon that threatened Andromeda by using his shield as a mirror.

The Jehovah of the Old Testament is a jealous, angry and warlike god. In Hebrew tradition, Jehovah's forces are led by Archangel Michael. As the Book of Revelation has it: 'And there was a war in heaven. Michael and his angels fought against the dragon, and the dragon fought against his angels ... and the great dragon was cast out, that old serpent which deceiveth the whole world, he was cast out into the earth.'

WE HAVE SEEN, THEN, THAT IN THE THIRD great act of the drama of creation, the god of the Moon won a great victory.

So began the era of the moon. *The first three epochs of the cosmos, the mineral, vegetable and animal eras – Saturn-day, Sun-day and Moon-day – are remembered in the names of the first three days of the week.* These days of the week are named after these three heavenly bodies in this particular order for this reason alone.

Here we see a sun god's battle against a snake or dragon in an engraving taken from the painting by Raphael.

5

The Gods who Loved Women

The Nephilim • The Genetic Engineering of Humankind • The Fish Gods • The Original History of the Origin of the Species

WE ARE NOW ABOUT TO LOOK INTO ONE of the murkier and more shameful episodes in the history of the world. Even within the secret societies a veil is sometimes drawn.

A priest in Babylon at the time of Alexander the Great was one of the first historians. It is clear from the few remaining fragments that Berosus, like Herodotus before him, had studied the king lists inscribed on temple walls and delved into the secret priestly archives.

The few fragments of Berosus that survive contain teachings on the history of the origins of the earth and the sky and of the race of hermaphrodites, the pre-sexual humans who reproduced by means of parthenogenesis.

Berosus goes on to describe how the land came to be inhabited by a primitive race. Then one day a monster emerged on the seashore, an animal called Oannes '... whose whole body was that of a fish; under the fish's head he had another head with feet also below similar to those of a man, subjoined to the fish's tail. His voice and language were articulate and human; and representation of him is preserved even to this day ...'

'This monster was accustomed to pass the day among men, but took no food then; and he gave them an insight into letters and sciences and arts of every kind. He taught them to construct cities, to found temples, to compile laws, and explained to them the principles of geometrical knowledge. He made them distinguish the seeds of the earth and showed them how to collect fruits; in short, he instructed them in everything which could soften manners and humanize their lives ...'

'And when the sun had set this being Oannes retired again into the sea, and passed the night in the sea, for he was amphibious ... '

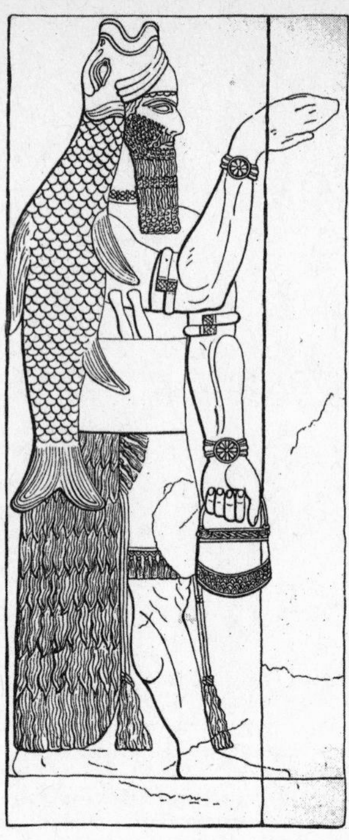

Oannes: nineteenth-century engraving taken from the walls of Nineveh – original now in the British Museum.

'After this appeared other animals like Oannes ... '

Similar stories of fish gods who suddenly appear and become the teachers of mankind can be found in other traditions, for example the Indian stories about Matsya, the first avatar of Vishnu, and the stories of the ancient Phoenicians of the Dagon, who taught humankind the art of irrigation, and the ancient fish gods of the Dagon tribe in West Africa. We even know from Plutarch that the earliest representations of Zeus were of a man with a fish tail, an image which survived in Greek mythology in the form of his brother Poseidon.

Some modern writers outside the esoteric tradition have seen in this fish imagery evidence for an alien invasion in ancient times. It's even been suggested that the human race was genetically engineered by alien invaders, which is a good illustration of the way that esoteric traditions are misinterpreted by people trying to impose a materialistic interpretation on them.

If our candidate for initiation had been initiated to a high enough level, he would have been taught the truth of the matter, something very like the following ...

In Genesis there is a passage which may at first not seem to refer to exactly the same fishy events, though it is also about invasion by beings from another realm:

Genesis, 6:1-5. 'And it came to pass when men began to multiply on the face of the earth, and daughters were born unto them, That the sons of God saw the daughters of men that they were fair: and they took wives which they chose ... when the sons of God came in unto the daughters of men, and they bare children to them, the same became mighty men which were of old, men of renown. And God saw that the wickedness of man was great in the earth, and that every imagination of the thoughts of his heart was only evil continually.'

What on earth are we to make of this passage? The phrase here translated as 'sons of God' is elsewhere in the Bible a phrase used to mean angels, messengers coming down from heaven. But in this context 'coming down' also seems to carry with it moral opprobrium. By saying that the angels had sex with women is Genesis perhaps saying that these angels *lowered* themselves to participate in the material world? And perhaps they had become too enamoured with it?

As I say, we are now trying to penetrate one of the murkier episodes in the secret history, and indeed these five verses in Genesis might well remain completely impenetrable were it not for the fact that this episode is treated rather more fully in ancient Hebrew traditions – particularly the *Book of Enoch.*

This book disappeared from mainstream, exoteric history in AD 300–400, but traditions regarding its existence, its contents and teachings were preserved in Freemasonry. Then in 1773 some very tattered scripts of it were tracked down in Ethiopian monasteries by the Scottish explorer James Bruce, and in this way the old Freemasonic traditions were vindicated.

Never part of the canon of Christian scripture as it was put together in the fourth century, the *Book of Enoch* was nevertheless sufficiently esteemed by writers of the New Testament for them to quote from it, evidently viewing it as an authority with a status something like sacred scripture. It is a measure of the status of this book that Jesus Christ evidently recognized its notions of a coming kingdom and the judgement of the world. Moreover the phrase used at his Transfiguration, 'This is my Son, the Elect One', is meant to show that Jesus Christ is the One promised by the *Book of Enoch.*

This is what the *Book of Enoch* has to say about the angels who loved women:

Enoch 6.1–4. 'And it came to pass when the children of men had multiplied that in those days were born unto them beautiful and comely daughters. And the Angels, the children of heaven, saw and lusted after them, and said to one another: "Come, let us choose ourselves wives from among the children of men and beget us children." ... And all the others together with them took unto themselves wives, and each chose for himself one, and they began to go in unto them and to defile themselves with them, and they taught them charms and enchantments ... and they became pregnant.'

Later Enoch is given a tour of the Heavens, where the rebel angels – or Watchers – ask Enoch to intercede with God on their behalf. But when Enoch tries to do so, God only repudiates them, sending Enoch back:

'And go say to the Watchers, who have sent thee to intercede for them: You should intercede for men, and not men for you ... '

The story of the rebellious angels is then retold, as it were, in God's own words with additional details:

Enoch 6. 15–16. 'Wherefore have ye left the high, holy and eternal Heaven, and lain with women, and defiled yourselves with the daughters of men and taken to yourselves wives, and done like the children of the Earth, and begotten giants as your sons. And though you were spiritual beings living the eternal life, you have defiled yourselves with the blood of women, and have begotten children with the blood of flesh and blood as those also who die and perish ... And now as to the Watchers who have sent thee to intercede for them, who have been aforetime in Heaven, say to them: "You have been in Heaven, but all the mysteries had not yet been revealed to you, and you knew worthless ones, and these in the hardness of your hearts you have made known to women, and through these mysteries women and men work much evil on earth." Say to them therefore: "You have no peace."'

The Epistle of Jude 6:6 describes the Watchers as having 'not kept their own appointed habitations'. A third century Christian writer, Commodorius, wrote: 'The women who seduced the angels were of such lewdness that their seducers could not now desire to return to heaven.'

But beyond these few, strange fragmentary hints lies a set of characters very familiar to us all.

When the Epistle to Jude describes the Watchers as not having kept to their appointed seasons, it seems to be referring to them in some way as timekeepers. But the final, telling clue to revealing the hidden identity of these 'fallen angels' lies in their number, given in one of the versions the *Book of Enoch* as seven.

In all traditions seven is the number of the great gods of the solar system. Again we see that the biblical narrative has encoded within it stories of the same astronomical gods as those of Greece and Rome.

The angels who became sexually attracted to human women are none other than the gods of Olympus.

WE HAVE SEEN THAT THE BIBLE CONTAINS encoded within it an account of creation in which key roles have been played by Saturn, earth, the sun, Venus and the moon. We have followed the story from the purely material to the vegetable to the first stirrings of animal life. The age that followed would be marked by the arrival of the gods of the solar system; Jupiter – or Zeus, as he was known to the Greeks – became the king of all the gods. The gods of Mars and Mercury would fly into view during this age too.

The infant Jupiter had to be hidden from his father, Saturn. Mother Earth kept

Jupiter on the island of Crete in a cave deep underground. Isolated from the other gods, the boy Jupiter lived on the milk of a goat-nymph and ate the honey of sacred bees.

Mother Earth hid Jupiter in this cave because she was afraid that Saturn and the Titans, the elder sons and daughters of Saturn, would come to destroy him. She knew that the birth of Jupiter showed that the reign of Saturn was coming to an end, but the transition from one age to another is always a painful one. The old order always tries to stay on beyond its allotted time.

The Titans were Saturn's enforcers. They were the consciousness eaters. They wanted to swallow up the new life and create what Milton, who knew all about the secret history, called 'a universe of Death'.

The Titans would always be the enemies of Jupiter. They failed to kill him while he was still an infant, but they did not cease to wage war on him, sporadically and in great battles, until finally and decisively Jupiter defeated them and imprisoned them underground. There these great forces of materialism became part of the very structure of the earth, and whenever volcanoes rumbled and threatened to erupt the ancients heard their discontent.

With the Titans imprisoned, Jupiter became for a while the undisputed ruler of Mount Olympus, king of the gods and god of a new age. He shook his magnificent locks and the whole earth trembled. He was the only god strong enough to throw the thunderbolt.

In his masterpiece *The Marriage of Cadmus and Harmony*, the great Italian scholar and writer Roberto Calasso, who has done much to bring esoteric lore regarding the historical reality behind myths to a wider public, put it like this: 'Olympus is a rebellion of lightness against precision.' In other words the Olympic gods – Jupiter, Apollo, Mars, Mercury, Diana, Athena and the others – rebelled against the limitations imposed by Saturn. The Olympians flew through the air to perform magical deeds and defeat terrible monsters. It was a splendid, spectacular era that thrashes and writhes in the mind, inspiring some of history's most imaginative art, sculpture and literature.

But it was also somewhat sinister, an age charged with moral ambiguity. The thunderbolt of Jupiter struck through a dense fug of testosterone, the feral reek of animal passion, the fell heartlessness of animal ferocity.

Jupiter raped Callisto and she was turned into a bear. He raped Io, turning her into a cow. He punished Lycaon for cannibalism by turning him into a wolf. Apollo's lust for Hyacinth caused the beautiful youth to metamorphose into the flower and his rape of Daphne ended in her morphing into the laurel bush.

We should take note that all these myths are concerned with is the proliferation of natural forms, the cramming of every square inch of our planet with the almost infinite variety of plants and animals, the biodiversity that is its great natural glory. Zeus is not moral in a sense that Moses would have recognized, but he and his fellow Olympians direct the galvanizing fecundity, the myriad creativity of the biological world.

Telamones depicted being forced to hold up the earth in a nineteenth-century engraving of recent discoveries at Pompeii. The Telamones were Titans forced to become a part of the earth's structure. Their progeny were earth-demons, or goblins. As late as the nineteenth century they were still feared in some remote rural regions in southern Europe. These red-eyed creatures with skin made of scales like dead grey fingernails were said to pursue you in spirit even after you had died.

BUT WHAT OF THE STORY OF THE FISH GODS? How does that fit in?

We have seen that many mythologies around the world tell the strange story of the arrival of the fish gods, and we have touched on the fact that even Jupiter in his earliest representations was one of them. We have seen, too, that the myths of Jupiter and the other Olympian gods are an account of the proliferation of animal forms. Bringing these two things together gives rise to an astonishing possibility.

Could it be that the ancient myths anticipated the modern, scientific insight that *the animal life that would eventually evolve into the human form began life as a fish?*

If this were true, it would be an astonishing revelation

DARWIN'S DISCOVERY OF THE EVOLUTION of the species is one of history's great scientific discoveries, ranked alongside Galileo's, Newton's and Einstein's. Could it be that the priests of the Mystery schools knew of the evolution of species many thousand of years earlier? We shall now discover how evidence for this claim, which may, initially at least, sound implausible, is written across the sky in blazing lights for all to see.

We are cracking the code of the cosmos. We saw how the earliest episodes in history are to be understood in terms of the ordered creation of the solar system. One after the other

Saturn, the Sun, Venus, the Moon and Jupiter joined in the work of weaving together the basic conditions that made possible the evolution of life on earth. Following this sequence has brought us to the dawn of animal life and of consciousness and the beginning of the proliferation of animal forms.

In order to understand the history of the development of these animal forms, we must turn again to astronomy, and following on from the sequence in which the ancients believed the planets were created we turn to an interlocking sequence – the constellations of the zodiac.

TO ANCIENTS THE FORCES OF NATURE WERE asleep during winter and then reawakened, exerting their influence anew in the spring. The constellation in which the sun rose in the spring was therefore very important to them. The sun vivified that constellation, energizing it and increasing its power to shape the world and its history.

Because of a slight wobble in the earth as it spins on its axis, the sun seems to us to fall slowly backwards against the backdrop of stars. Over a period of some 2160 years the sun rises in the same constellation. It then moves on to the next one. We are currently in the Age of Pisces and famously awaiting the dawn of the Age of Aquarius. As constellation follows constellation, and age follows age, the symphonic variations of the Music of the Spheres signal a new movement. The cycle of animating powers, of instinctual drives sweeping through the cosmos, moves on to a new plane.

We think of the twelve constellations of the zodiac following in a sequence according to months of the year, Aries followed by Taurus, then Gemini and so on. In the larger cycle measured by the appearances of these constellations at the spring equinox, the constellations move 'backwards', Gemini is followed by Taurus, then Aries and so on.

This phenomenon is known as precession. There is some dispute among academics as to when the ancients first became aware of it. The breakthrough book on this subject was *Hamlet's Mill*, written by MIT Professor of the History and Philosophy of Science Giorgio de Santillana and Hertha von Dechend, Professor of Science at Frankfurt University, and published in the late 1950s. Tremendously erudite, it began a process of rediscovering an astronomical dimension of myths that had long been forgotten outside the secret societies. Their thesis is that one of the stories central to all mythology, indeed all literature from *Oedipus Rex* to *Hamlet*, the story of the dispossessed son who defeats his uncle to regain his father's throne, is a description of an astronomical event: of one precessional epoch succeeding another.

But *Hamlet's Mill* provides an essentially static model. It shows *that* precession is encoded on one particular archetype, not *how* the succession of ruling constellations allows us to organize different layers of myth in their proper chronological sequence.

Let us now look at this sequence in terms of the historical reality that lies behind the myths of Jupiter and the other gods, according to esoteric tradition.

Because we have been looking at history as it has been remembered in myths, particularly the myths of the gods of Olympus, we have naturally been picturing for ourselves anatomically modern humans. However, we should continue to bear in mind that these myths represent what these things would have looked like to the eye of the imagination. But to a physical eye, if any such had existed, it would all have looked very different.

Because *what these imaginative pictures represent is the beginning and development of primitive life-forms.*

If the age of the first marine life was marked by the rulership of the planet Jupiter, then in terms of the precession of the constellations it was marked by Pisces. When the sun first began to rise in the constellation of Pisces, a new form condensed out of the semi-liquid substance on the earth's surface. This was the earliest embryonic form of the fish – somewhat like a modern jellyfish.

The ancients conceived of this evolutionary impulse as a god. If primitive life on earth – the life that would eventually evolve into human life – took on a primitive fish form, that was because a god took on this form and, as it were, pulled life on earth with him.

In Egypt this miraculous event, the birth of animal life, was known as the birth of Horus, and the earliest representations of Horus, like those of Jupiter, were half-man, half-fish.

So we again see that the Greeks and Egyptians, like the Greeks and the Hebrews, worshipped the same god in different cultural clothing.

The next precessional age was the first Age of Aquarius. This was the era of the evolution of amphibians, giant floating creatures, somewhat like the modern dolphins but with webbed limbs and lantern-like foreheads. This lantern was the pineal gland; protruding from the top it still holds in some reptiles, such as the *Tuatara* species of lizard, from New Zealand.

The 'Lantern of Osiris' is an ancient record of this late vegetable protuberance from the animal form.

The 'lantern' was still these proto-human creatures' main organ of perception. Sensitive to warmth and coolness in other living beings, both in the vicinity and in the distance, the lantern could intuit their inner nature. These proto-humans could intuit, too, the nature of plants, assessing their suitability as food or medicine – in the way that some animals can. And because the laws of natural growth were not yet completely fixed, humans could also speak to plants in a way which might, as the ancient sagas of the Jews have it, make 'a tree yield fruit or ears of wheat grow as tall as the cedars of Lebanon'. We must imagine the speech made by these amphibian-humans as sounding something like the bellow of a stag.

Lantern-headed humans were later idealized as unicorns. The Earth goddess still told them what to do clairvoyantly, so that the natural law and the moral law were the same thing. This historical truth is beautifully portrayed in the famous tapestry in the Musée de Cluny in Paris, where the unicorn lays its head in the lap of a virgin.

Our collective memory of the unicorn is, of course, of a hunted creature. Humans might seek sanctuary in the lap of Mother Earth, but the world was becoming a dangerous place. We saw that desire had originally existed independently of humankind, and desires continued to exist independently, unintegrated into the proto-human form. These desires running wild were the dragons of mythology. They terrorized the rest of creation.

As the marshy surface of the earth began to harden into something like dry land, the next stage of the development of human form began. This was the beginning of the Age of Capricorn, when proto-humans developed calves and limbs to crawl on to land to pursue their burgeoning animal desires.

According to the ancient wisdom it was the arrival of Mars that led to the evolution of warm-blooded animals. Mars arrived at the time of the transition from the lizard-like amphibians of the Age of Capricorn to the land animals of the Age of four-footed Sagittarius.

The iron of Mars yielded red blood and provided the conditions that would make egotism possible – and not only in the sense of a healthy drive to survive. As the earth continued to harden and become denser and drier, it shrank further, with the result that one being could only prosper at another's expense. It became part of the human condition that I can hardly move without harming, even killing, another living creature. Because of Mars there is also a cruel part of human nature that rejoices in this, exults in forcing a fellow human being to submit, and experiences euphoria when it is dominant over others, when it is able to exercise willpower without restraint.

As proto-humans became wholly land creatures, it also became necessary to create new ways for humans to communicate. It was as the result of the influence of Mercury that the thorax evolved. Mercury also fashioned leaner and fitter limbs, the better for humans to move towards each other and live and work together. He was, of course, the messenger and scribe of the gods, known as Hermes to the Greeks and Thoth to the Egyptians.

He was also the god of tricks and thieving.

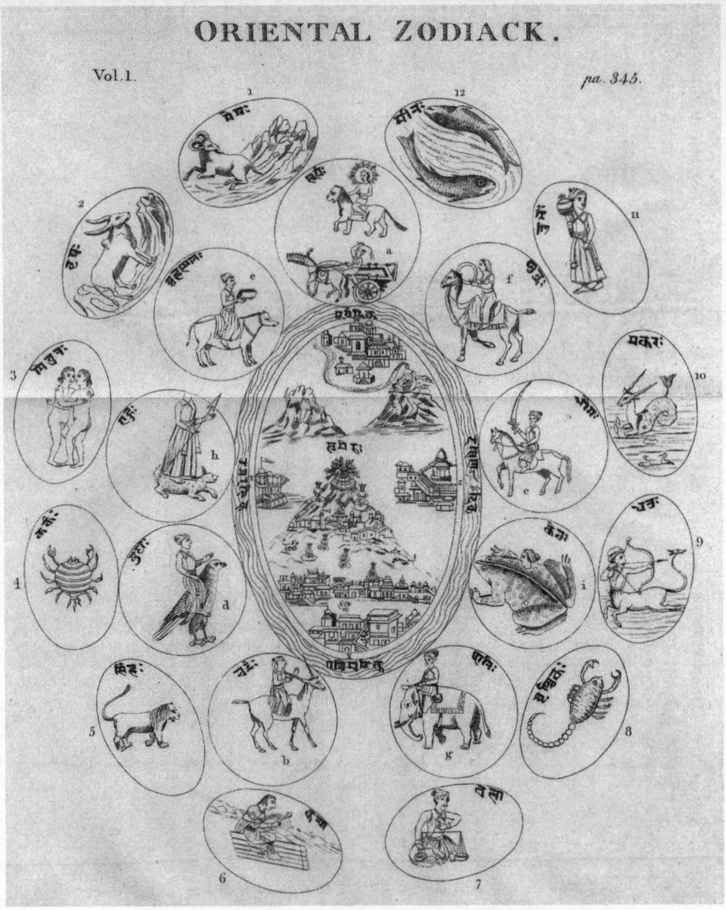

ORIENTAL ZODIACK.

Vol.1. pa. 345.

Zodiacs from Egypt, India and Greece showing an extraordinary similarity of imagery.

THIS CHAPTER HAS BEEN A COMMENTARY on Genesis, taking into account parallel traditions, such as the Egyptian and the Greek. This way of interpreting or decoding the Bible surfaced among the Neoplatonists and early Cabalists and was exposed by groups like the Rosicrucians. Much of what we have been considering can be found, for example, in the seventeenth-century writings of Robert Fludd (highly influential on Milton's *Paradise Lost*) and, slightly later, Jacob Boehme's commentary on Genesis, already mentioned, *Mysterium Magnum*. The work of elucidating these commentaries and reframing the wisdom of the Rosicricians in modern times was carried out by the great Austrian scholar and initiate Rudolf Steiner, whose Anthroposophical Society perhaps has the best claim to be a genuine survivor of the true Rosicrucian stream.

However, even outside the esoteric tradition, it is acknowledged that the ancient civilizations around the world showed remarkable agreement when it came to the images associated with the sequence of the constellations of the zodiac. This agreement is all the more remarkable, you might think, when you consider how little the arrangements of the stars as seen from the surface of the earth suggest these images.

The reality is that the ancients saw in this sequence of the constellations the history of the evolution of humanity and the world, as it was collectively remembered and understood. For them *the history of the world was written in the stars.*

The head of the Medusa, on a Greek gem. The night sky was a living history, because the heavenly bodies were seen as the material bodies of spiritual beings or gods. The ancients believed they had the ability to communicate with these beings and felt their influence. For instance, it is no coincidence that the star Algol – associated with the head of the Gorgon Medusa in Greek tradition – was felt to be a malignant influence in all *the cultures of the ancient world. The Hebrew astrologers named it after the dark spectre Lilith, and even before this Hebrews of the desert had called it the Head of Satan, while the Chinese named it by a phrase meaning 'piled up corpses'. Diverse cultures were experiencing the same spiritual reality when they looked up at the same area of the sky.*

THEREFORE, WHAT IS GENERALLY REGARDED as a modern idea that put paid to ancient superstition is in fact itself an ancient idea. An understanding of the ordered evolution of the species originated thousands of years before Darwin set sail in HMS *Beagle.*

This secret history was encoded in the zodiac, written down by initiates such as Jacob Boehme and Robert Fludd, and preserved into modern times by esoteric groups such as the Freemasons and various Rosicrucian groups, but always and very deliberately in a way that was hard for outsiders to understand.

Then in the nineteenth century, when the sacred texts of Hinduism were first translated into European languages and openly published, much esoteric knowledge which had previously been carefully managed and controlled, now leaked into the public consciousness. Fascination with these ideas also led to a renewed interest in the Cabala and other Western traditions and helped fire the craze for spiritualism. Many of the great intellectuals of the period became interested in trying to apply scientific methodology to spiritual and spiritualist phenomena. In 1874 Charles Darwin attended séances with the novelist George Eliot. Darwin's rival A.E. Wallace took part in several controlled experiments into spiritualism, believing its phenomena could be measured and verified just as well as other types of phenomena were measured and verified by the other sciences. As we shall see later, many leading intellectuals, including scientists, believed that there was something in esoteric philosophy, and that science and the supernatural would eventually come together.

Friedrich Max Müller was a young German scholar, employed by the East India Company in the 1840s to translate the *Rig Veda*, before being awarded a professorial chair at Oxford. He went on to translate the sacred books of the East in fifty volumes, making oriental esoteric doctrines widely available for the first time. He was also very friendly with Darwin with whom he kept up a regular correspondence. *The Origin of Species* was published in 1859.

IN THE SECRET HISTORY THE EVOLUTION of the species was not the even progress that science supposes. There were twists and turns that have important implications for the way we understand our own physiology and mental make-up. There were dead ends, false starts and even deliberate attempts at sabotage.

Snakes, spiders, beetles and parasitic creatures, on the other hand, were formed under the malignant influence of Dark Side of the Moon.

According to the secret doctrine the animals we know today evolved into the forms we are familiar with today, influenced by the stars and planets, lions by the constellation of Leo, for instance, bulls by the constellation of Taurus. Centaurs, mermaids, sirens, fauns and satyrs were predecessors of anatomically modern humans, representing the impulse to create anatomically modern humans in various transitional stages.

The cosmic plan was that all the world's biological forms would gradually be incorporated into humankind, which was intended to be the crown of all creation. As the gods led humanity closer and closer to human anatomy as we know it, they assumed the part-animal, part-human forms remembered by the Sumerians, the Egyptians, the Persians and the Babylonians, until they finally assumed anatomically perfect forms remembered by the last great civilizations of the ancient world, the Greeks and Romans. For example, the goddess of the planet Venus was cow-headed Hathor and the god of the planet Mercury was dog-headed Anubis on the walls of Egyptian temples. According to the secret tradition, these same gods, the same living beings, were remembered by the classical Greeks in a later, more evolved form.

The ancient texts describing this era also lay great emphasis on its giants. The author of the *Book of Enoch* writing in the Hebrew tradition and Plato writing in the Greek tradition agree that in these early pre-Flood times there arose a race of giants. In fact, traditions of an antediluvian race of giants can be found all over the world from the Danavas and

Daityas of India to the Miaotse of China. In a *Dialogue between Midas the Phrygian and Silenus* that has survived in fragmentary form from the time of Alexander the Great, Silenus says that 'men grew to double the size of the tallest men in his time, and they lived to twice the age'. In the secret tradition, the gigantic Bamyan statues recently destroyed in Afghanistan were not three giant statues of buddhas but three life-sized statues of giants of 173, 120 and 30 feet high. The drapery that made them look like buddhas was made of plaster, said to have been added to the stone later. In the nineteenth century it was recorded that the locals believed them to be statues of the Miaotse, the giants of Chinese tradition. The famous statues of Easter Island are also supposed to record the real heights of historical giants.

Then there were the dead-end freaks – the one-legged men, the bat-men, the insect-men and the men with tails. Manetho, an Egyptian historian of the third century BC, also recorded traditions of the progency of the Watchers, writing 'they ... brought double-winged human beings, also others with four wings and two faces, human beings with one body and two heads, still other human beings had thighs of goats and horns upon their heads; others had the feet of horses behind and men in front; there were also others said to have been man-headed bulls and four-headed dogs, whose tails emerged like fish-tails from their backs ... and other monsters, such as all kinds of dragon-like beings.'

This, then, is the era remembered in the great myths and finds echoes in great fantasy literature, such as J.R.R. Tolkien's *The Lord of the Rings* or the Narnia books of C.S. Lewis. This fantasy literature represents a welling up into the present of a collective memory of this period when humans lived on the earth with giants, dragons, mermaids, centaurs, unicorns, fauns, satyrs. Legions of dwarves, sylphs, nymphs, dryads and other lesser spiritual beings served the gods and humans rubbed shoulders with them, fought battles with them and sometimes fell in love with them.

IN THE SECRET HISTORY, THE LAST CREATURES to incarnate before humans were the apes. They came about because some human spirits rushed into incarnation too early, before human anatomy had been perfected.

In the secret history, therefore, it is not right to say that humans are descended from apes, rather that *apes represent a degeneration of humankind.*

Of course none of the fabulous creatures have left any trace in the fossil record. So why have the great men and women of history who were initiates of the secret societies believed in them? Why should any intelligent person even begin to toy with the idea?

6

The Assassination of the Green King
Isis and Osiris • The Cave of the Skull • The Palladium

IN THE PERIOD DESCRIBED BY THE MYTHS of Olympus, gods walked among humans. But the history of the *last* god to rule as king of the earth is recorded in its fullest version in Egyptian rather than Greek tradition. The Egyptians unquestioningly believed that their most important god had once walked among them, led them into battle and ruled them wisely and well.

Herodotus described a visit to the shrine where Osiris was said to be buried. 'Gigantic stone obelisks stand in the courtyard and there is a circular artificial lake next to it. It is on this lake at night that the Egyptians act out the Mysteries, the Black Rite that celebrates the death and resurrection of a being whose name I dare not speak. I know what goes on but ... say no more.'

Fortunately we can supplement this teasing account with the history of Osiris as told by Herodotus's near-contemporary Plutarch, an initiate priest of the Oracle at Delphi. In the following I have used Plutarch's account as a basis, weaving in additional material from other sources ...

We have to start by imagining a world at war, ravaged by roaming monsters and wild animals. Osiris was a great hunter, a 'Beast Master' – remembered as Orion the Hunter in Greek mythology and Herne the Hunter in Norse mythology – and a great warrior. He cleared the land of predatory beasts and defeated invading armies.

But this great warrior's downfall came not in combat with monsters or on the battlefield, but because of the enemy within.

Returning from another military campaign, Osiris was welcomed back by cheering crowds, by the populace who loved him. The reign of Osiris, though constantly under attack from outside the country, would be remembered as a golden age. And it was an age of domestic as well as civil bliss. His name is connected with insemination, 'ourien' meaning semen, and what we today call the belt of Orion is a euphemism. In ancient times it was a penis that became erect as the new year progressed. These things should alert us to the fact that there is a strong sexual current in the history that follows.

Osiris accepted an invitation from his brother Seth to a gala dinner to celebrate victory.

Some said Osiris had been sleeping with beautiful dark-skinned Nepthys, wife of Seth and sister of his own wife, Isis. Did this provide Seth with a motive for murder? He may not have needed one. The clue to Seth's animosity is contained in his name. He was an envoy of Satan.

After dinner Seth announced a game. He had made a beautiful chest, something like a coffin but fashioned out of cedar and inlaid with gold, silver, ivory and lapis lazuli. Whoever fitted most neatly into this chest, he said, could take it away.

One by one the guests tried but they were too fat, to thin, too tall, too short. Finally Osiris stepped in and lay down. 'It fits!' he cried. 'Fits me like the skin I was born in!'

But his pleasure at winning was cut short as Seth slammed down the lid. Seth hammered in nails and filled every crack with molten lead – the metal of Satan. Then Seth and his followers carried the chest down to the banks of the Nile and cast it on the waters.

Osiris was an immortal, and Seth knew he couldn't kill him, but he could, he believed, get rid of him for good.

The chest floated down the Nile for several days and nights, eventually washing ashore on the coast of what we now call Syria. A tender young tamarisk tree growing there wrapped the chest in its branches, and eventually grew all around it, enclosing it lovingly and protectively in its trunk. In time this tree became famous for its splendour, and the king of Syria had it chopped down and fashioned into a pillar that stood in the centre of his palace.

In the meantime Isis, separated from her man and deposed from her throne, cut her hair, blackened her face with cinders and wandered the surface of the earth, searching, tearfully, for her beloved husband. After a while she took a job as a servant girl at the court of a foreign king. (Readers will readily appreciate how this story, originally a sacred drama in the temples of Egypt, has come down to us in slightly garbled form as the pantomime *Cinderella*.)

But Isis never gave up hoping to find her man, and one day her magic powers led her to see Osiris clairvoyantly in the chest inside the tree in the middle of the very palace where she was working, the palace of the Syrian king. Isis revealed her true identity as a queen and persuaded the king to chop down the pillar and let her take the chest away.

She left by boat and landed on the island of Chemmis in the Nile delta. There she intended to use her magic arts to revive her husband.

But Seth had magic powers too. He and his evil cohorts were hunting by moonlight, and in a vision Seth suddenly saw Isis cradling Osiris. While she lay sleeping, he swooped down upon the loving couple.

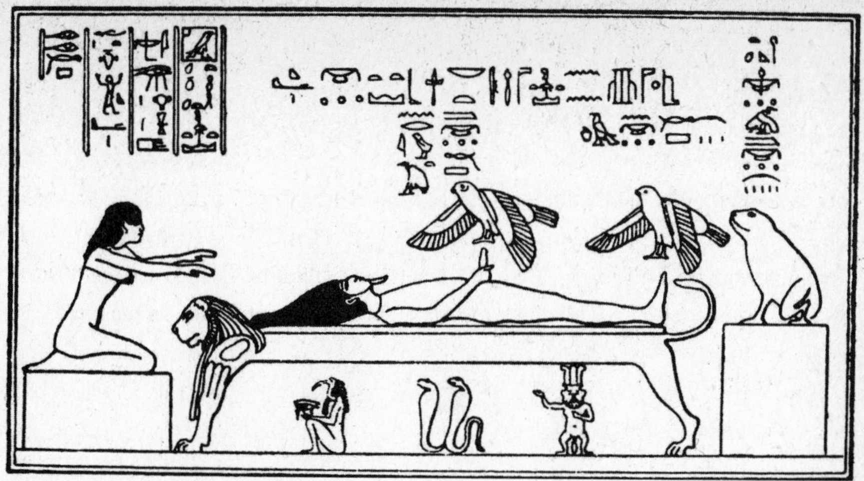

Wall-carving from the temple at Philae.

Determined to make sure this time, he attacked Osiris with savage glee, hacking him into fourteen different pieces that he then had hidden in secret in different corners of the land.

So the widowed Isis had to set out on her travels again. (Freemasonic readers will perhaps be aware that they call themselves 'Sons of the Widow' partly as a mark of their participation in her quest.)

Isis wore seven veils to disguise herself from Seth's minions and was aided by Nepthys. She also loved Osiris and now turned herself into a dog to help find and dig up the parcels of Osiris's corpse. They retrieved all of them except the penis, which had been eaten by fish in the Nile.

They arrived at an island in Abydos in southern Egypt and there at night Isis and Nepthys bandaged all the remaining parts together using a long, winding piece of white linen.

The first mummy.

Finally, Isis fashioned a penis out of gold and attached it. She was not able to bring him wholly back to life, but she revived Osiris sexually so that she was able to hover, touching him gently and delicately as she enveloped his penis in the form of a bird until he ejaculated. In this way she impregnated herself on him, and in this same way Horus, the new Master of the Universe, was conceived.

Horus grew up to avenge his father's death by killing his Uncle Seth. Osiris meanwhile lived in the Underworld as its king and Lord of the Dead. It is in this role that he was most often depicted by the Egyptians, usually with a green face, heavily swathed and apparently immobile, but emanating a power that is symbolized in his royal regalia, and carrying the crook and flail.

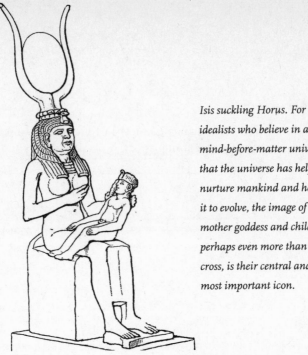

Isis suckling Horus. For idealists who believe in a mind-before-matter universe, that the universe has helped nurture mankind and helped it to evolve, the image of the mother goddess and child, perhaps even more than the cross, is their central and most important icon.

WHAT THE HELL DOES ALL THIS MEAN? How can we decode it?

On one level it seems to represent the succeeding of one constellation by another in the precession of the equinoxes. Horus deposes Seth and supplants him.

On another level, perhaps the most obvious one, it is a fertility myth about the yearly cycle of the seasons. The appearance of the star Sirius on the horizon after months of being hidden was a sign to the ancient Egyptians that Osiris would arise again shortly afterwards and that the inundation of the Nile was due. Myths of the resurrected god-king were told all around the world from Tammuz and Marduk to the Fisher King stories associated with Parsifal and the King Arthur cycle. They follow this same pattern. The king is fatally wounded in the genitals and while he lies suffering the land stays barren. Then in the spring a magical operation is performed and he rises again, both sexually and in a way that fertilizes the whole world.

This is why Osiris came to be worshipped in Egypt as a god of crops and summer fertility. The longed-for yearly appearance in the east of Orion and his consort Isis, known to us as Sirius, the brightest star in the heavens, heralded the inundation of the Nile that revived the vegetable and so also the animal and human world – literally a matter of life and death. The Egyptians made small mummies out of linen bags stuffed with corn – corn dollies. When it was watered the corn sprouted through the bag, showing that the great god was being reborn.

I am the plant of life, says the Osiris of the pyramid texts.

I WILL NOT DWELL ON THIS ASPECT OF OSIRIS because the level of meaning in myths that relates to fertility has become widely appreciated in the hundred or so years since Sir James Frazer's *The Golden Bough*.

The trouble is that it is has tended to be appreciated at the expense of everything else.

If the Egyptian populace thronging the outer courtyards of the temples understood the story of Osiris on this level of the fertility myth, there was another, higher level known only to the priests of the inner sanctum, the Black Rite whose secrets Herodotus claimed to know.

This secret was a *historical* secret.

To get at the truth of it, we now need to look at a similarly bizarre and disturbing story from the Greek myths. We know from Plutarch that in antiquity Osiris, the last god-king to rule the earth, was equated with Dionysus, the last of the Olympic gods.

The sources disagree on the subject of Dionysus's parentage. Some say his father was Hermes, others Zeus. All agree that the little god's mother was Mother Earth and that, as with Zeus, she hid the infant Dionysus in a cave.

Dionysus, like Zeus, represents the evolution of a new form of consciousness, and again the Titans were determined to nip it in the bud. Again we see that the Titans are the consciousness eaters.

They smeared their faces white with gypsum to conceal their identity as the black-faced sons of the crow god. They didn't want to frighten him as they lured Dionysus from a cradle hidden in a niche in the back of the cave.

Suddenly the Titans fell on Dionysus, tearing him into pieces. They flung these pieces into a boiling cauldron of milk, then tore the meat from his bones with their teeth.

Meanwhile, Athena had stolen into the cave unnoticed and she snatched away the goat-boy's heart before it was cooked and eaten. She took this to Zeus, who cut open a hole in his thigh, inserted the body part and sewed it up again. After a while, just as Athena had sprung fully formed from the head of Zeus, the reborn Dionysus sprang fully grown from Zeus's thigh.

IN ORDER TO UNDERSTAND THE HISTORICAL reality behind this mysterious story and the parallel story of Osiris, it is necessary to remind ourselves that in this account of the history of the universe matter was only precipitated out of the cosmic mind over very long periods and was only very gradually developing towards the sort of solidity we are familiar with today.

It is also as well to remind ourselves again that although we may view many of the great figures of myths, both gods and human, as having an anatomy like our own, this is only how they appear in the eye of imagination.

The world looked very different to the physical eyes that were evolving at this time. This was still the world recorded in the *Metamorphoses* of the initiate-poet Ovid, when the anatomical forms of humans and animals were not fixed as they are now, a world of giants, hybrids and monsters. The most anatomically advanced humans were evolving the two eyes we have today, but the Lantern of Osiris still protruded from the middle of the forehead, where the bone of the skull had not yet hardened.

Gradually, though, matter became denser. And the important point to bear in mind here is that, despite the fact that matter was precipitated from mind, it was alien to mind. To the extent that matter hardened, it became a greater barrier to the free flow of the cosmic mind. What gradually happened, then, was that as matter hardened to something approaching the solid objects we know today, two parallel dimensions evolved, the spirit world and the material world, the former viewed by the Lantern of Osiris and the latter by the two eyes.

The story of Osiris/Dionysius is the next and perhaps the most decisive stage in this process, when parts of the great cosmic mind, the universal consciousness, became parcelled off and absorbed into individual bodies. The bony roof of the skull hardened, closing over the Lantern of Osiris, so filtering out the great cosmic mind above.

According to the ancient wisdom, so long as there had been no barrier to the spirits, gods and angels ranged up above them, there had been no possibility of humans enjoying the individual free thought or will that distinguishes human consciousness. If we were not cut off from the spirit worlds and from the great cosmic mind, if our bodily make-up did not filter it out, our minds would be completely dazzled and overwhelmed.

Humans would now have some space for themselves in which to think.

The archetypal image of this model of the human condition is Plato's Allegory of the Cave. Prisoners are chained in cave so that they face a wall and cannot look round. Events taking place outside the mouth of the cave throw shadows on to the wall that the prisoners take for reality.

This is an exposition of the philosophy academics call idealism, which holds that the cosmic mind and the thoughts or Thought-Beings emanating from it (*ideas*) are the higher reality. Physical objects, on the other hand, are mere shadows or reflections of this higher reality.

Because we are remote from the time when people believed in idealism, it is difficult for us to appreciate it as a living philosophy of life, rather than just as a dry as dust theory. But people who believed in idealism experienced the world in an idealistic way and also understood idealism as a historical process.

Academics tend to miss the surprisingly literal layer of meaning in Plato's Allegory. The cave here is the bony roof of the skull. The skull is a dark, bony room covered in flesh.

Plato was an initiate and would have been well aware of the delicate mechanism of shadowing and reflecting that takes place inside the human skull, the occult physiology and psychology of the secret doctrine.

The defining characteristic of human life, its crowning achievement, and also the crowning achievement of the cosmos, is the capacity for thought. The brain is the most complex, the most subtle, altogether the most mysterious and miraculous physical object in the known universe.

According to the secret doctrine *the cosmos created the human brain in order to be able to think about itself.*

IT IS VITAL, IF WE ARE TO UNDERSTAND WHAT is happening here, to snap out of a materialistic way of thinking, to look at things, as it were, through the other end of the telescope. If you are an idealist, you believe that the universe was created by Mind for minds.

More particularly, you believe that the cosmic Mind created the material universe in order to give human minds the form they have.

The idealist history of creation is the history of this process, and the great events in this history have been the putting into place of the sun, moon, the planets and the stars. *Our consciousness now has the structure it has because the heavenly bodies are ranged above us in the way they are.*

With the moon in place to reflect the light of the sun down to earth and with this process reproduced in microcosm within the human skull, with matter having at last become sufficiently dense that the human mind is 'closed off', we have reached the point where human anatomy and human consciousness have achieved a form we would recognize today. The basic conditions making it possible for humans to reflect, that is to say, to think, were now in place.

There is, however, one more issue to consider.

IN THE SECRET HISTORY THERE IS ALSO A specifically *sexual* dimension to this development.

The Mystery priests believed that as the Lantern of Osiris withdrew underneath the bony covering of the skull and begun to occupy the position where we know it today as the pineal gland, the fleshly penis protruded. According to the ancient wisdom, the penis was the last part of the human body to assume its present, fleshly form, which is why artists in the secret societies, such as Michelangelo and, Signorelli, Leonardo's brother initiate, often depicted the penis of the men of mythology as plant-like.

At this great turning point in history, then, just as the penis became flesh, humans could no longer propagate themselves by the old plant-like method of parthenogenesis. Humanity gave itself entirely over to animal sexuality.

And from this opens up a third and terrible dimension.

The Companions of Pan *by Luca Signorelli. This engraving is a rare record of a painting destroyed during World War Two.*

Human bones were hardening and becoming material. A human skull became something half-living and half-dead.

This is why it is an axiom of the secret doctrine that *the beginning of death was the birth of thought.*

According to the secret doctrine, there is a fundamental opposition between life and thought. The life processes in humans – digestion, respiration and the processes of growing, for example – are largely unconscious. The conscious, thoughtful dimension in humans is only made possible by a partial suppression of these life processes. The human organism 'steals' forces which in animals are used for growth and biological structuring, and channels them to create the conditions necessary for thought. It is said that this is one of the reasons why humans are, comparatively, sickly animals.

Human thought is a deadly process, restricting both growth and longevity.

When proto-humans were vegetable creatures, they did not experience death. When they began to take on animal characteristics, they began to experience a foretaste of death. This was an experience like dream-filled sleep. After a while they would 'awake' again into the material world. This sleep, even when it was very deep sleep, no longer gave humans the refreshment they craved. As human bones and the body of the earth hardened and rigidified to something near to what they are today, humans moved less freely, indeed painfully. The call of death grew louder and louder until it became almost overwhelming.

Sleep deepened until it became like death, and then it became death.

Now humans were finally entangled in the savage cycles of life, death and rebirth, cycles in which creatures must die in order to make way for a new generation. They now lived in a place where fathers must die to make way for sons, where the king must die to give way to a younger, more vigorous successor. Scholars have managed to piece together textual references with carvings at the Step Pyramid complex at Saqqara near Cairo in order to understand something of what must have happened at the 'Heb-Sed' rituals that took place there. Having undergone a Mystery school ceremony of death and rebirth in an underground chamber, the newly regenerated pharaoh would emerge into a more public courtyard. There he had to undergo a series of trials of strength and potency, including running with a bull, to try to prove that, as he would ritually cry, 'I am free to run through the land'. If the pharaoh failed these tests he would suffer the same bloody death as the bull. The following eyewitness account, of a bull god sacrifice in India, comes from a nineteenth-century British traveller: 'When the stroke is given which severs the head of the victim from his body, the cymbals strike up, the tom-toms beat, the horn is blown and the whole assembly, shouting, smear their bodies with blood, they roll themselves in it, and, dancing like demons, accompany their dances with obscene songs, allusions and gestures.'

Herodotus must have witnessed something very like this if he was allowed see the Black Rite of the Egyptians. At the climax of the initiation ceremony we have been following, the candidate would also have seen something similar – the death of a great god.

In Northern Europe the god who became entangled in the cycles of nature was portrayed as the Green Man. A leaf-clad god, fierce like nature but also a victim of it, Osiris stares down at the congregation from the walls of countless Christian churches.

THE HUMAN CONDITION WAS CHANGING on many different levels. We have reached a pivotal time in the secret history of the world when matter had precipitated out of mind and hardened to such a degree that the human skull was finally formed into a shape very like it is today. But the Third Eye was still much more active than it is today and had not become vestigial. *Perceptions of the material world were equally as vivid as perceptions of the spiritual world.*

A human being ushered into a throne room might look at another human being sitting in front of him, or at least what appeared to be very like a human being. Although humans no longer had unlimited access to the spirit worlds, the man might then be permitted to look at the king again with his Third Eye, and, if he did, he might see a god sitting there.

The greatest historical record of humanity's lost ability to exercise this double mode of perception comes in the Hindu sacred text the *Bhagavad Gita*. A charioteer called Arjuna has been full of doubts on the eve of battle. So Krishna, the leader he is about to drive into the fray, allows Arjuna to see him as he looks to the eye of vision, in his supreme, divine form. Trembling with awe and wonder he sees Krishna's eyes as the sun and moon, sees that Krishna fills all of heaven and earth with radiance as if with the light of a thousand suns, that he is worshipped by countless other gods and that he contains within himself all the wonders of the cosmos. Afterwards Krishna shrinks into his human form again, and shows his gentle human face to reassure terrified Arjuna.

Osiris might equally have given this experience to someone who had walked into his throne room at Thebes. Jacob Boehme described the world of cut stone, carved wood, of royal robes and flesh and blood as 'Outworld'. He intended to be a bit disparaging. He knew that the inner world, accessible to the Third Eye, is the real one, and in the midst of the bloody, painful, death-drenched world in which the followers of Osiris now found themselves, this is what they clung on to.

THE MYTH OF OSIRIS, THEREFORE, HAS many layers of meaning, but it is above all a myth about consciousness.

It informs us that we must all die – but in order to be reborn. The key point in this story is that Osiris is reborn not into ordinary life but into a higher state of consciousness. 'I shall not decay,' he proclaims in the *Book of the Dead*, 'I shall not rot, I shall not putrefy, I shall not turn into worms, I shall have my being, I shall live, I shall live.' Again we come across a phrasing, an idea of being born again that may seem strangely familiar to Christians. Osiris is here discovering that he has what Christians call 'eternal life'.

IN THE STORY OF OSIRIS WE HAVE SEEN how the forces of sex, death and thought became ever more tightly entwined in order to create the unique thing that is human consciousness. The wise men and women of antiquity understood how death and sexuality are necessary for thought to arise, and because they understood how these forces had been woven together in a historical process, they also understood how conscious thought could be used to manipulate the sexual and the death forces in order to achieve higher states. Since ancient times these techniques have been among the best kept secrets of the Mystery schools and secret societies.

We will look into these techniques in some detail later, but all this is a difficult area for us because our understanding of sexuality tends to be on a very materialistic level.

For instance, it is very difficult for us today to look at paintings and carvings of the erect phallus adorning the walls of Hindu or Egyptian temples and to imagine how they would have been intended to be 'read', because in the modern world spirituality has for the most part been removed from sex.

In the ancient world sperm was understood to be an expression of the cosmic will, the hidden generative power in things, the ordering principle of all life. Each particle of sperm was held to contain a particle of the *prima materia* out of which everything was made, a particle which could explode with incredible burning heat to form a whole new macrocosm. Adolescents in our era may catch some reverberation of the ancient feeling, when the first stirrings of sexuality bring on feelings of keen, new intensity and an aching desire, felt in the breast, to embrace the whole world.

Desire is always open to corruption, though. What we desire, we *possess* in our imagination. Desire hardens. When we desire someone we 'reify' them to borrow Jean-Paul Sartre's phrase. We want to bend them to our will, which is the influence of the Spirit of Opposition.

In the mind-before-matter view this diminishing of other people by the way we perceive them can be literally true. The way you look at people affects their internal physiological and chemical constitution.

Modern science has taught us to think of the sexual urge as something impersonal, something that has a will apart from our own, as an expression of the will to survive of the species. For the ancients, too, the sexual urge was an expression of a will beyond the individual. They saw sexuality impelling us towards the great moments of our lives, because they saw how sex controls who we are born to, as well as determining the people we are attracted to.

A man in the ancient world might see a woman he desired and be overcome by a quite frightening, overwhelming desire. He would know that the rest of life would be shaped by her response. He would also know that the roots of his desire lay very, very deep, having their origins long before his present lifetime. He would know that the sexual desire that drove him towards that woman was not merely biological – as in the modern account – but had other dimensions, spiritual and sacred. If the planet of love had been steering them towards this meeting, then so, too, had the other great gods of the sky been preparing

Melancholia I *by Dürer and opposite* The Death Posture *by Austin Osman Spare. In the same way that in the secret societies techniques are taught to control sexual forces as a way of achieving higher forms of consciousness, so there are also teachings on channelling the closely intertwined death forces. Osman Spare developed a practice which involved closing off mouth, nostrils, ears and eyes. In India adepts including Bhagavan Shri Ramana and Thakur Haranath have achieved long, death-like trances which have even led to their being prepared for burial, then been reborn into a new, higher form of consciousness.*

this experience for them over many, many millennia and through many incarnations.

Today we know that when we look at a distant star we are seeing something that happened a very long time ago, because of the time it has taken for the light from that star to reach the earth. The ancients knew another truth, which is that when they contemplated their own will, they were also looking at something which they had formed long before they were born. The ancients knew that every time they felt themselves merging with another human being in the sexual act, the flight of whole

constellations was involved. They knew, too, that *how* they made love would have an effect on the cosmos for millennia to come.

When we make love we are interreacting with great cosmic powers, and if we choose to do so *consciously* we may participate in this magical act. It was this magical element in the sexual act that Rilke was referring to when he wrote that 'two people coming together in the night summon up the future'.

THERE IS ONE FURTHER TWIST TO THE STORY of Osiris, a dark shadow to an already dark story. We saw that Isis had a sister, Nepthys, and there was a suggestion of sexual impropriety with Osiris, some sexual fall from grace perhaps. But later Nepthys used her magic powers to help Isis in her search for the body parts of Osiris and helped, too, to bind them together again.

Nepthys, then, is a figure representing some dark form of wisdom, fallen but capable of redemption.

In Christian mythology this same figure, this same spiritual impulse, reappears as

Mary Magdalene. We have been following the history of the Fall. We have seen that the Fall was not the fall of human spirits into a pre-existing material world – it is a very easy and common mistake to imagine it like this – but a Fall in which human bodies became denser as the material world became denser.

We live in a Fallen world. Just as myriad spirits help us to grow and evolve, so too others, just as numerous, work to destroy both us and the very fabric of our world. In Christian mythology – and in the secret doctrine of the Church – the earth suffered and was punished for having fallen by having her own spirit imprisoned deep in the underworld inside her. Sometimes called Sophia, notably in the Christian tradition, this wisdom is only reached when we travel down through the dark and demonic places of the earth and also of ourselves. It is because of Nepthys – because of Sophia – that we all have need to touch rock bottom, to experience the worst that life has to offer, to wrestle with our demons, to test our intellect to its limits and journey to the other side of madness.

We know from Plutarch that in antiquity Isis was identified with Athena, the Greek goddess of wisdom. Athena had a half-sister, a dark-skinned girl called Pallas, whom she loved more than anyone. Carefree, they used to play on the plains of Anatolia, running games, wrestling and mock fights with spears and shields. But one day Athena was distracted. She slipped and accidentally speared Pallas to death.

From then on she called herself Pallas Athena, to acknowledge the dark side of herself, just as in a sense Nepthys represents the dark side of Isis. She also carved a statue of Pallas out of black wood to memorialize her.

This statue, called the Palladium, carved by the hand of a goddess and washed by her tears was revered as an object of world-changing power in antiquity. When the people of Anatolia kept it in their capital, Troy was the greatest city in the world. The Greeks wanted to know what the Trojans knew. When they carried it off triumphantly, the leadership of world civilization passed to them. It was later buried beneath Rome in all its glory, until the Emperor Constantine moved it to Constantinople, when it became the centre of world spirituality. Today it is said to be hidden somewhere in Eastern Europe, which is why in recent times, the great powers, the Freemasonic ones, have sought to control this region.

The cult of Nepthys together with its Greek and Christian equivalents, forms one of the darkest and most powerful streams in occultism. Great forces like these shape the history of the world even now.

7

The Age of Demi-Gods and Heroes
The Ancient Ones • The Amazons • Enoch • Hercules, Theseus and Jason

WHEN HERODOTUS WAS PUZZLING OVER the strange wooden statues of the kings who had reigned before any human king, the Egyptian priests told him that no one could understand this history without knowing about 'the three dynasties'.

If Herodotus had been an initiate of the Mystery schools, he would have understood that the three dynasties were, first, the oldest generation of creator gods – Saturn, Rhea, Uranos – the second generation made up of Zeus, his siblings and their children, such as Apollo and Athena – and lastly the generation of demi-gods and heroes. This last generation is the subject of this chapter.

ALL THE WHILE MATTER WAS GROWING denser, and because matter and spirit are inimical, the gods became less and less a constant presence. The higher, the more ineffable, the god, the harder it became to squeeze down into the tightening net of physical necessity that covered the earth. Great gods such as Zeus or Pallas Athena seemed to make their presence felt and intervene directly in human affairs only at times of crisis.

In the Mystery schools it was taught that a decisive change in this direction came

Medallion showing Isis on the moon. In The Golden Asse *by Apuleius, Isis is described in the following terms: 'Just above her brow was a disk in the form of a mirror, or resembling the light of the Moon, in one of her hands she bore serpents, in the other, blades of corn.'*

about in 13,000 BC. From then on the higher gods would find it difficult to descend further than the moon. Their visits to the surface of the earth became infrequent and fleeting. It was believed that on these visits they accidentally left behind the strange and unearthly mistletoe, a plant which cannot grow in the soil of the earth, but which grew naturally on the moon.

Without the presence of the greater gods to keep them down, the crab-like progeny of Saturn that had been imprisoned in underground caves began to creep up into the daylight again, infesting the surface of the earth and preying on humankind. Sea monsters also leapt on to the shore to drag off members of the tribe who had strayed too close. Giants carried off cattle and sometimes preyed on human flesh, too.

Full-scale wars took place between humans and armies of other creatures, stragglers from the previous epoch. The war between the Lapiths – a tribe of Neolithic flint-knappers – and the Centaurs is recorded on the Parthenon frieze. The Centaurs had been invited to the wedding of the leader of the Lapiths, but were inflamed by the sight of the white,

Drawing by the nineteenth-century Swiss-born artist Henry Fuseli of a demon sometimes called the Hanon-Tramp. Moon demons inhabit the 'Dark Side of the Moon', where they play a legitimate role in the spiritual economy of the cosmos, helping to tear corruption from human spirits after death. However, if they break through into the earthly realm, they appear as malevolent dwarves. The height of a six- or seven-year old child with large, hypnotic eyes, they sometimes emit an ear-splitting yell that can freeze a human with fear. More powerful when the moon is waning, these demons may account for some modern encounters with 'aliens', which in a physical form at any rate play no part in esoteric cosmology.

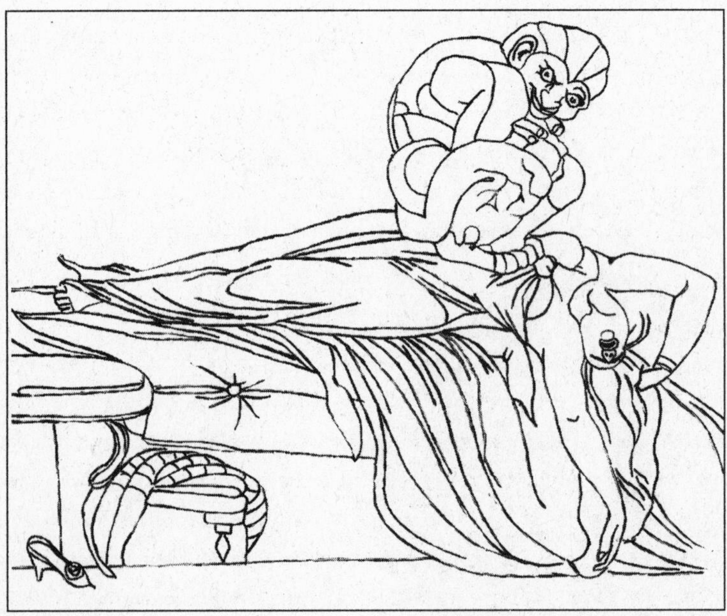

Battle of Lapiths and Centaurs in the Parthenon frieze.

hairless bodies of the Lapith women. They dragged off the bride and raped her – and her bridesmaids and page boys, too. In the ensuing fight a Lapith king was killed, and so began a feud that lasted for generations.

As bones thickened, the animal world began to feel its weight. Creation grew tired and animals grew vicious, as they had to struggle to survive. As humanity continued to fall, so too did nature. It became red in tooth and claw. Lions and wolves began to attack humans. Plants grew thorns to scratch and make the gathering of fruit difficult, and poisonous plants evolved, like wolfsbane.

The Parthenon frieze also records battles against the Amazons, a race of warrior women, who were the first to ride horses into battle. An Amazon had to kill a man before she was allowed to marry. Wearing armour of fur and carrying shields in a half-moon shape, their cavalry scythed down row upon row of foot soldiers. They were magnificent, and they represented a new form of human behaviour, because hard on the heels of the possibility of death had come the possibility of killing and of murder. Cut us and we would bleed. Cut us hard or often enough and we would die. Some humans began to delight in this. The *Book of Enoch* describes how the surface of the earth became covered with warring armies, and says that 'human flesh itself had become perverse'.

Because of the encasing, bony skull and the enmeshing of the organs of spiritual perception, humans were now shut off not only from the gods ranged above them, but also from each other. A shadow was falling over human relations. It became possible for one centre of consciousness to believe itself cut off from another. 'Am I my brother's keeper?' asked Cain, who represents the evolution of the new form of consciousness. This question would have meant nothing to Adam and Eve, who were like branches on the same tree.

In the same way that we would be overwhelmed by the spirit worlds if they were not filtered out, if there were no filter on empathy we would feel everyone's pain as our own and so be completely overwhelmed by the suffering of others. Without a degree of isolation no human could experience him or herself as an individual, no one could feel the burning fire in the forehead that drove Cain onwards. But of course there were pitfalls in this ...

History shows that humans have a horror of humans with other forms of consciousness, which they often find hard to tolerate. Sometimes they feel the need to eradicate it from the face of the earth. We need only think of the treatment by Europeans of the Aztecs, the near genocide of the Aborigines of Australia or the attempt to wipe out gypsies by the Nazis. Later we will see that since the time of Moses, the Jews have often been at the forefront of forging new forms of consciousness.

Humans were now free to make mistakes, to choose the bad and to enjoy it. It was no longer the case that humans received all their spiritual nourishment from the milky sap-filled breasts of Mother Earth. The natural law and the moral law were no longer the same thing.

The earth grew colder, harder and more dangerous in many different ways. People struggled to survive and would sometimes find themselves stretched to the limits of endurance. They discovered that the road ahead would always be fraught with the danger of death, but unless they took that road they would die anyway. From now on they would have to put at risk what they valued most or they would lose it. Beyond a certain point, there is no return. That point, they discovered, must be reached.

They discovered uncomfortable things about themselves, too – that they had become brutalized by this new world, and had grown a hard, protective carapace of habit. To break open this carapace and expose the sensitive part of themselves, the better part that brought them fully alive again, was a bloody and painful process that few could face.

The world became darker, a place of paradox where opposites meet and where it is painful to be human, a world calling out for heroism.

THE LARGEST AND MOST TERRIFYING OF the monstrous, progeny of Saturn came last. Typhon emerged out of the sea, heading straight for Olympus, spitting fire from his mouth and blocking out the sun with his bat-like wings. He had the head of an ass, and when he emerged from the sea, the gods saw that below the waist he was nothing but a coiling mass of thousands of snakes. Zeus tried to fell him with thunderbolts, but Typhon only shrugged them aside. As Typhon bore down upon him, Zeus then snatched the flint scythe that Cronos had used to castrate Uranos. But the monster's snake-like limbs wrapped themselves around the limbs of Zeus, holding them fast and snatching the scythe from him. Then keeping the king of the gods pinned down, Typhon cut out all his sinews. Zeus is immortal and could not be killed, but without his sinews he was completely helpless.

Typhon took the sinews away with him and retired to a cave to recuperate from his own wounds. Apollo and Pan then emerged from the shadows and hatched a plan. They went to find Cadmus, the dragon-slaying hero, who was wandering the earth looking for his sister Europa. She had been carried away by Zeus, disguised as a white bull. Now Apollo and Pan promised Cadmus that if he helped them, his quest would be over.

Pan gave Cadmus his pipes, and, disguised as a shepherd, the hero went to play for the wounded Typhon. Never having heard music before, Typhon was entranced by this strange new sound. Cadmus told him that it was nothing compared to the music he could make with a lyre, but sadly the sinews on his lyre were broken. Typhon handed over the sinews of Zeus, and Cadmus told him he needed to go back to his shepherd's hut to string his lyre. So it was that Zeus regained his sinews and was able to surprise the monster, overpower him and bury him under Mount Etna.

The important point to note here is that Zeus was only saved with the help of a hero. The gods now *needed* humans.

THE MYTHS OF THE GREEK HEROES – Cadmus, Hercules, Theseus and Jason – are some of the most famous stories in human history. It might seem as if they are entirely missing from the biblical account, but according to the ancient tradition preserved in the secret societies Cadmus is to be identified with Enoch, the first human in Hebrew tradition to whom the gods turn for help.

The Old Testament contains only a few enigmatic words on Enoch. Genesis 5.21–24. 'And Enoch lived sixty and five years, and begat Methuselah, And Enoch walked with God after he begat Methuselah three hundred years and begat sons and daughters; And all the days of Enoch were three hundred and sixty-five years; And Enoch walked with God and he was not: for God took him.'

There is little to go on here but, as we have already seen, there is a literary tradition about Enoch in Hebrew literature, including, as we have seen, some books which are widely quoted in the New Testament. In one of these, the *Book of Jubilees,* Enoch is described as discovering the writings of the Watchers, but this is a clumsy translation. What is meant is that he discovered, which is to say invented, language itself.

Hebrew tradition presents Enoch as a strange figure. His shining countenance was uncomfortable to look at and he was evidently an uncomfortable presence. In this he may remind us of the Jesus of the Gospels, captivating vast crowds but feeling that he wants to withdraw in order to be alone with the great spiritual beings who are showing themselves to him.

In solitude Enoch was able to commune with the gods and angels with a clarity that humankind was fast losing.

Initially Enoch would spend one day teaching the multitude, then spend three days alone. Then he spent only one day a week, then one day a month and finally one day a year. The crowds yearned for his return, but when he did so his face shone so brightly it was so uncomfortable for them to look at that they had to avert their eyes.

What was Enoch doing on his solitary vigils? We will see repeatedly that great turning points in history are caused by two types of thought. First, turning points arise when great thinkers like Socrates, Jesus Christ and Dante think for the first time something that nobody has ever thought before. Second, turning points arise when thoughts are set down and inscribed indelibly, because they preserve some ancient wisdom that is in danger of being lost forever.

The generation of Jared, Enoch's father, had been the last to experience an uninterrupted vision of the successive waves or generations of gods, angels and spirits emanating from the mind of God. What Enoch was preserving in the first language and the first stone monuments, the oldest stone circles, was this vision of the hierarchies of spiritual beings ranged above. Enoch is one of the great figures in the secret history of the world because he gave a complete account of what we might call, in today's terms, the ecosystem of the spirit worlds. For this, he is remembered not only as Cadmus in the Greek tradition, but as Idris in the Arabian tradition and Hermes Trismegistus in the esoteric Egyptian tradition. He knew that, just as thought processes weaken health, language weakens memory. He also looked forward to an approaching catastrophe which would destroy everything made by mankind, except what he carried in his head and the sturdiest stone monuments.

He memorialized the heavenly hierarchies not only in stone monuments but in the invention of language itself. Because according to the secret doctrine *all language originated with the giving of names to the heavenly bodies.*

Indeed, the earliest art, such as is found at the famous caves at Lascaux in France and Altamira in Spain is likewise really a depiction of these same heavenly bodies. These heavenly bodies are the thoughts of the great cosmic mind, weaving through everything in the cosmos. Language and art now enabled humans to appropriate these cosmic thoughts in some way and to make them their own.

Enoch retreated further and further into the mountains, where the ground was inhospitable and the weather stormy. Fewer and fewer were able to follow him. He said: 'And my eyes saw the secrets of the lightning and of thunder, and the secrets of clouds and the dew, and there I saw from whence they proceed and where they come from to soak the Earth. And there I saw closed chambers out of which the winds are divided, and the chamber out of which came the mist and the cloud that has hung over the earth from its beginning. And I saw the chambers out of which come the Sun and the Moon, where they go to.'

The *Book of Enoch* relates that in his final, ecstatic vision he was given a tour of the heavens, of the different spheres of heaven and the different orders of angels who live there and the whole history of the cosmos.

Finally, Enoch addressed the last ragged band of followers who had been able to keep up with him on his mountain trek. As he was speaking they looked up and saw a horse descend from the sky in a whirlwind. Enoch mounted the horse and rode into the sky.

WHAT THIS STORY OF ENOCH'S ASCENSION into heaven tells us is that he did not die as humans do – because he was not properly human. Like the other demi-gods and heroes of Greek tradition, Enoch/Cadmus was an angel occupying the body of a human.

The stories of Hercules, Theseus and Jason are too well known to need retelling here, but aspects of them have special significance for the secret history.

In the stories of the man-god Hercules we see just how deeply into matter humankind had fallen. Hercules wanted to be left alone to get on with his material life, to enjoy worldly pleasures – getting drunk, feasting, brawling – but he was repeatedly interrupted by his duty to follow his spiritual destiny. A stumbling, bungling, sometimes laughable figure, Hercules was torn between opposing cosmic forces.

Ovid also shows how, as the gods withdrew, Eros began to make mischief. Hercules was hag-ridden by desire as much as by the spirits who try to control him.

Today if we fall in love with a beautiful person, we may well see beauty as a sign of great spiritual wisdom. When we look into beautiful eyes, we may perhaps hope to find there the very secret of life itself. The story of Hercules's love for Deianira, Ariadne's love for Theseus, or Jason's love for Medea, show that the spiritual connection between people was already becoming clouded. It was now possible to gaze into the eyes of a beauty and be deceived about what you saw there. Sexuality had become tricky.

The danger of delusion was made worse, by the *love of delusion*. What is best for me and what is worst for me, the thing I most ought to do and the thing I most ought not to do, look very much alike. In my heart of hearts I may know which is which – but then a spirit of perversity makes me want to choose wrongly. Great psychic perturbation always surrounds great beauty.

The twelve labours of Hercules show him moving through a series of trials each set for him by the successive spirits who rule the constellations. It is a series of trials which all humans take, and by and large they take them unwittingly, like Hercules. The life of Hercules, then, illustrates the pain of being a man. He is Everyman, trapped in a cycle of pain.

To modern sensibility the fact of a story's being allegorical makes it less likely to be an accurate depiction of real events. Modern writers try to drain their texts of meaning, to flatten them out in order to make them more naturalistic.

To the ancients, who believed that every single thing that happened on earth was guided by the motions of the stars and planets, the more a narrative brought out these 'poetic' patterns, the truer and more realistic the text.

So, it may be tempting to view the journeys into the Underworld made by Hercules, Theseus and Orpheus as mere metaphor. It is true that on one level their adventures represent the beginning of humanity's coming to terms with the reality of death. But as we try to imagine the adventures underground of Hercules, Theseus and the others, we must not imagine these to be purely internal or mental journeys such as we might contemplate today. When they battled with monsters and demons, they were confronting forces that infested their own beings, the corrupted human flesh, the dark labyrinth of the human brain. But they were also fighting real monsters of flesh and blood.

IF WE COMPARE THE STORY OF THESEUS and the Minotaur with a much earlier myth such as Perseus and the Gorgon Medusa, we can see that by the time of Theseus the rate of metamorphosis seems to have slowed down. In the Perseus story every episode involves supernatural powers or magical transformation. On the other hand, the bull-man Minotaur is apparently a rare survivor or straggler from an earlier epoch.

THE LAST ADVENTURE THAT THE demi-gods and heroes took together should also be interpreted as history. Wars were fought to try to steal the 'inner sanctum' knowledge of rival tribes, and on one level Jason's quest for the Golden Fleece was an example of just such a raid.

Isaac Newton revealed some of the secret wisdom of his brotherhood when he showed that the quest for the Fleece, like the labours of Hercules, shows the progress of the sun though the signs of the zodiac. What he did not reveal, though he undoubtedly would have been aware of it, was that the Fleece represents animal spirit that has been totally purified by *catharsis*, so that it shines like gold.

Curled round the tree is a snake that intends to prevent Jason from taking the Fleece. The snake is a descendant of the Luciferic serpent that originally worked this corruption into the physiology of humankind, coiled around the tree in the Garden of Eden.

But if Jason can wrest the Fleece from him, he will win great powers for himself. He will be able to ask his spirit to leave his body at will, to communicate freely with gods and angels like the people of earlier epochs. He will be able to control his own physiology, influence the minds of others telepathically, even transform matter.

So the text of Jason's quest by Apollonius should be read as a manual of initiation as well as a true historical account. We will see later how alchemists of the Middle Ages and later Newton himself acted on this insight.

IF YOU LOOK AT THIS PERIOD OF ENOCH, Hercules and Jason with the eye of science, you will see none of the great events that have been described in this chapter. You will not see heroes or monsters arising from the sea or phantasmal deities like Zeus or black

The Labours of Hercules. The neoplatonist philosopher Porphyry decoded these twelve labours to reveal the signs of the zodiac that lie behind them. According to modern thinking, if a narrative is allegorical in form, this is a good reason for believing it cannot be an accurate account of historical events. But if you believe, as the ancients did, that all events on earth are governed by the movements of the heavenly bodies, then the opposite is true. All accounts of real historical events must inevitably mirror astronomical events like the passage of the sun through the constellations. Hercules is here depicted on a sarcophagus relief journeying through the constellations of Leo, represented by the Nemean Lion, Scorpio represented by the Hydra and the Erymanthian Boar, representing Libra – by taming the Wild Boar Hercules is balancing animal spirits with a measured intelligence.

magic causing the fall of empires. You will see only wind and rain on a dreary, natural landscape whose only human features are at best some fairly unimpressive dwellings and primitive stone tools.

But perhaps science only shows us what happened on the surface. Perhaps more important things were happening underneath? What the secret history preserves is a memory of subjective experience, of the great experiences that transformed the human psyche during this period. So which is more real? Which tells us more about the reality of being human in this period, the scientific one or the esoteric one encoded in the ancient myths?

Might there be levels of truth or reality in today's events that are missed by the science-oriented common-sense consciousness we use to navigate our way through traffic jams, supermarkets and e-mails?

8

The Sphinx and the Timelock
Orpheus • Daedalus, the First Scientist • Job • Solving the Riddle of the Sphinx

WHEN JASON SET OFF ON THE *ARGOS* ON what proved to be the last hurrah of the demi-gods and heroes, his boat contained many of the great figures of the age, including Hercules and Theseus. But among these muscle-bound super-heroes, there was one with very different powers, a transitional figure who looked forward to life after the demi-gods and heroes had left, when humans would have to fend for themselves.

Orpheus had travelled down from the north, bringing with him the gift of music. His music was so beautiful that it could not only charm humans and animals, it could make trees, even rocks move.

On the voyage with Jason he helped the heroes when brute force could not. Singing and accompanying himself on his lyre, he charmed the great clashing rocks that threatened to crush the *Argos* and he sent the dragon that guarded the GoldenFleece to sleep.

On his return he fell in love with Eurydice, but on the day of their wedding she was bitten on the ankle by a snake and died. Half-blinded by grief, Orpheus descended into the Underworld. He was determined not to accept the new order of life and death, determined to win her back.

Death was now a terrible thing, no longer a welcome rest when the spirit recuperated and refreshed itself in preparation for its next incarnation. It was a painful separation from those you love.

Descending deeper and deeper, Orpheus encountered the grim old ferryman Charon, who at first refused to row him across the River Styx to the land of the dead. But Charon was charmed by the lyre, as was Cerberus, the three-headed dog whose job was to guard the way to the Underworld. Orpheus charmed, too, the terrible demons whose task was to tear from the spirits of the dead the unregenerate animal lusts and savage desires that still clung to them.

Finally, he reached the place where the King of the Underworld held his love captive. The King was not unequivocally charmed by Orpheus, because the release he granted was not unconditional. There was just one, small condition. Eurydice could return to the world of the living if Orpheus could lead her up there without ever once turning round to make sure she was following.

But of course Orpheus, at the last moment, as the sunlight hit his face, perhaps worried he was being tricked by the King, *did* turn round. He saw the love of his life suddenly pulled back down away from him, down the stone passageways, out of sight, fading into the Underworld like a wisp of smoke. The other, more muscle-bound heroes had succeeded in their quests by fighting the good fight to the limits of their strength and endurance, by being brave and never giving up. But times were changing. The great initiates who preserved this story for us wanted us to understand that Orpheus *failed* because he tried to do what every good hero had done – *he tried to make sure.*

It may also be that his music lost some of its charm, because it did not stop a band of maenads, the female followers of Dionysus, throwing themselves upon him and tearing him limb from bloody limb. They threw his head into the river, and it floated downstream, still singing. As it floated by, the weeping willows crowded the banks. Finally the head of Orpheus was rescued and set on an altar in a cave, where crowds came to consult it as an oracle.

IF CADMUS/ENOCH NAMED THE PLANETS and the stars, it was Orpheus who measured them, and by measuring them, invented numbers. There are eight notes in an octave, but in a sense really only seven, as the eighth always represents elevation to the next octave. The octaves, then, refer to ascent through the seven spheres of the solar system, which in antiquity were central to all thought and experience. By giving a system of notation, Orpheus was originating mathematics. Concepts could be manipulated, paving the way for the scientific understanding of the physical universe.

Orpheus is a transitional figure because on the one hand he is a magician with the power to move stones with music, but on the other he is a forerunner of science. Later we will see a similar ambiguity in many great scientists, even in modern times, but the other representative of the transition taking place at the time of Orpheus was Daedalus. (We know he was a contemporary because he was the keeper of the Minotaur, killed by Theseus, who joined in the quest for the Golden Fleece.)

Daedalus is famous for making wings out of wax and feathers to help him and his son, Icarus, to escape from Crete. He also designed the labyrinth and is credited with inventing the saw and the sail. So he was an inventor, an engineer, an architect in ways we would recognize today. He did not use magic.

If science was an innovation of the age, so too was magic. Magic was the application of a scientific way of thinking to the supernatural. In this age we no longer see the seemingly effortless shape shiftings of earlier ages or the turning of those who have offended into spiders, stags or plants. Instead we see Jason's wife Medea and Circe, to whom Medea went for help, advice and magical protection. Circe and Medea had to work in order to achieve their supernatural effects, using potions, spells, incantations. If the invention of words and numbers enabled humans to begin to manipulate the natural world, it also gave them the idea of being able to manipulate the spirit world. Medea offered Jason a blood-red potion, made from the juice of the crocus, to soothe the dragon that guarded the Fleece. She used chants and sprigs of juniper to spray the dragon's eyelids. She dealt in magic elixirs and knew the secrets of the snake-charmer.

As the material world continued to become denser and as the beings of the spirit worlds were increasingly squeezed out, even the lowest level of spirits, the nature spirits, the sylphs, dryads, naiads and gnomes, became elusive. They seemed to disappear into the streams, trees and rocks, fleeing the first light of dawn. But they still seemed tantalizingly close, and it was these spirits – then as now – that magicians found easier to manipulate.

Some magicians tried to bend the great gods to their will, too, to draw them down from the moon. The myths of the original werewolf, Lycaon, who prompted the flood of Deucalion, of Poseidon's flooding of the Thracian plain, causing Athena to move her city to the present site of Athens, and of the terrible storms that pursued Medea wherever she went are depictions of the environmental catastrophes that were resulting from the practice of black magic.

At the end of this period humanity is sick and so, too, is nature.

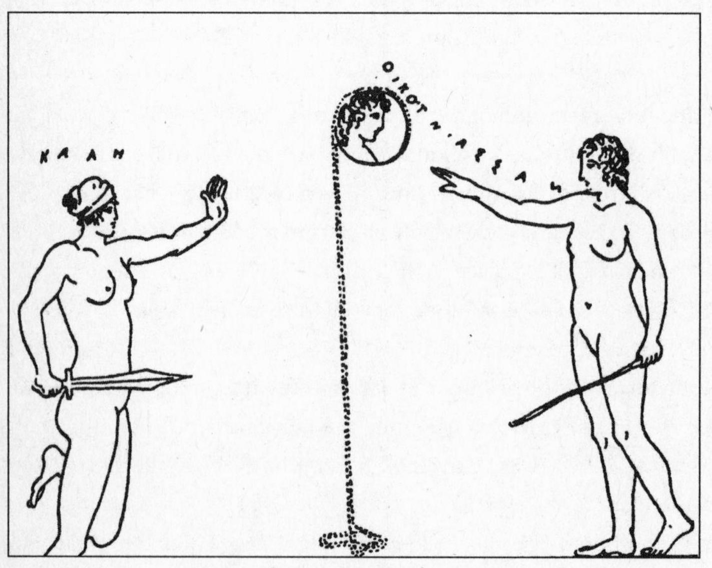

Magicians drawing down the moon. Greek drawing.

ORPHEUS MIGHT HAVE FAILED BY THE standards of the conventional hero, but his influence on history was greater and more long-lasting than that of Hercules, Theseus and Jason. The music Orpheus originated would be a balm for healing the sick and troubled spirit of humanity down the millennia.

If people were becoming isolated not only from the gods but from one another, if they were worn down by an always harsh and sometimes hostile environment, and if their imaginations were infected by the perverse and bestial impulses of magic, all of this would now be countered by the aesthetic influence on the imagination, not only through music but also literature, painting and sculpture. Inspiring images of beauty, truth and love worked on humanity at a level below that of the conscious mind. They were more powerful than any explicit, abstract moral teaching.

Orpheus was the mythical founder of the Greek mysteries that would light up and inspire ancient Greece.

PERHAPS THE MOST POWERFUL ARTISTIC expression of the spiritual crisis at the end of the age of the heroes comes in the Bible.

In the written form it has come down to us, the story of Job is one of the later texts of the Old Testament, but in its origins it is one of the oldest parts.

Job was a good man, yet he lost all his money. His sons and daughters died. Left all alone he was covered with a plague of boils. Meanwhile, the wicked prospered. The story of Job has come down to us, not because he was a great leader or doer of great deeds, but because he was the first human being ever to think a very important and deeply true thought: '*life is unfair*'. Hercules had been the sport of the gods, but it was Job who cried out to the heavens in defiance. Unlike Hercules, Job had the language to do this.

Today we take it for granted that we have enough mental manoeuvrability to choose what to think about. However, before the invention of language, which was the great achievement of this age, this manoeuvrability would not have been possible.

Language enables us to distance ourselves from the world. It helps us to withdraw from what is physically present, and can enable us to break down experience, whether present or not, into bits we can manipulate. To some degree we can put experience into order as we wish.

There is an alienating element to this process. As well as the advantages it brought, language made the world a colder, darker and trickier place. We saw earlier how thinking is itself a deadening process. Language, too, makes us unhealthy, less vividly alive and less sure-footed in our wanderings in the world.

So language brought with it a new form of consciousness. Before Job people fel that everything that happened to them was meant to happen to them, that there was a divine purpose behind everything. They did not – could not – question. Now

Blake's Job.

language enabled Job to step back. He began to notice inconsistencies. Life *is* unfair.

But God rebuked Job for understanding so little. 'Where were you when I laid the foundations of the Earth? When the morning stars sang together and all the angels shouted for joy? Have you entered the springs of the sea or walked the depths of the deep? Have the gates of death been opened to you? Do you know where the Sun lives and where the darkness comes from? Can you bind the chains of the Pleiades or loose the belt of Orion?'

What saved Job was that he had that sense we all have when we awake from a wonderful dream, when we try to bring it back but cannot. He was aware that the range of human experience was in some way diminishing. 'Oh that I was as in the times of old, when God watched over me, when his lamp shone on my head' (Job 29:2–4).

Job refers, of course, to the 'Lantern of Osiris'.

Today the word 'apocryphal' carries pejorative associations, but really it means hidden – or esoteric. In the apocryphal Testament of Job, he was rewarded for being conscious of what he did not know, conscious of what he had lost. Job's sons and daughters were returned to him, his daughters wearing golden girdles. One belt gave Job the ability to understand the language of the angels, the second the secrets of creation and the third the language of the Cherubim.

MUSIC, MATHEMATICS AND LANGUAGE were invented in the age of the heroes and so too was astronomy – another achievement attributed to Enoch. The first stone circles not only marked out the dispositions of the hierarchies of the gods and angels, they marked out the positions of the stars and planets.

In the secret history, therefore, it also now becomes possible for the first time to begin to fix the dates of great events.

BETWEEN THE LION PAWS OF THE SPHINX at Giza, gazing eastwards, is a large stone that carries the inscription 'This is the Splendid Place of the First Time'. The mysterious First Time, or *Zep Tepi,* was a phrase the Egyptians used to allude to *the beginning of time.* In their mythology Zep Tepi was marked by the rising of the primordial mound out of the waters and the alighting on it of the Phoenix.

By a remarkable feat of reconstruction, which he made while standing between the paws of the Sphinx, Robert Bauval has managed to determine the date of Zep Tepi. In Egyptian mythology the Phoenix arrived to mark the beginning of a new age. In Egyptian mythology the Phoenix, or Bennu bird, is the symbol of the Sothic cycle of 1,460 years, (which is the time it took the Egyptians' 365-day calendar to resynchronize with the beginning of the yearly cycle, marked by the heliacal rising of Sirius). The synchronization of these two cycles, the yearly and the Sothic, took place in 11,451, 10,081, 7160, 4241, and 2781 BC. Bauval noticed immediately that these dates coincided with the commencement of some of the great building projects up and down the Nile. Clearly the starting of this cycle was very important to the ancient Egyptians ...

Trying to figure out which cycle might have been the 'first' one, he was initially attracted by the idea that it might be 10,081 BC, because of an esoteric tradition that the Sphinx had been built at this time or even earlier.

Then Bauval worked out that on the earlier date of 11,451 BC the Milky Way, which had immense significance in ancient cultures around the world as the 'river of souls', was lying directly over the course of the Nile, so that they mirrored each other. Moreover, it also struck him that on this very early date of 11,451 the Sothic and yearly cycles coincided with a *third cycle,* the Great Year – the 25,920-year-long complete cycle of the zodiac – in a most meaningful way. Because on that date the Lion-bodied Sphinx's eastwards gaze would have taken in the dawning of the Age of Leo.

The Sphinx embodies the four cardinal constellations of the zodiac, the four corners of the cosmos – Leo, Taurus, Scorpio and Aquarius, the Four Elements that work together to make the material world. The Sphinx, according to the secret history, is a monument to the first time the Four Elements locked into place and matter finally became solid.

When in the *Timaeus* Plato famously wrote of the World Soul being crucified on the World Body, he was not prophesying the crucifixion of Christ, as some Christian apologists have supposed. He was recalling this crucial moment in world history as idealism conceives it, when consciousness was finally fixed in solid matter.

The Sphinx, therefore, has a very special place in history as idealism tells it. It marks that point when, after wave upon wave of emanations from the cosmic mind, solid matter as we know it today was finally formed. That is why it is perhaps the greatest icon of the ancient world. The laws of physics as we know them today were only then set in motion, and from that point on the dates can be firmly fixed, because the great clock of the cosmos was finally set in its complex pattern of orbits.

If this late solidification of matter were what actually happened, it would, of course, invalidate dating methods, such as Carbon-14, conventionally used to try to establish early chronologies. Modern science makes an assumption in its calculations that the ancients did not, namely that the natural laws have held true in all places and at all times.

THE SPHINX ASKS OEDIPUS A RIDDLE: 'What walks on four legs, then two legs, then three legs?' If he cannot answer it, the Sphinx will kill him, but he correctly interprets it as a riddle concerning the ages of man. A baby walks on four legs, grows up to walk on two legs, until so old that a third leg, or walking stick, is needed. But 'ages' here is also another way of evoking the evolution of humanity. The form of the Sphinx is a monument to this evolution.

The Sphinx is defeated by the acumen of Oedipus, and casts itself into the precipice or abyss. The Sphinx's dying is a way of showing that the gods of the elements, these organizing principles of the universe, became successfully absorbed inside the human body at this time.

Central to the Oedipal legend is the terrible fate he hoped – but failed – to avoid. He duly kills his father and becomes his mother's lover. As the laws of nature become fixed and mechanical, humans are trapped in them.

So the Sphinx also marks the end of the Age of Metamorphosis, the fixing of the biological forms we know today. It also bars the way back. In Genesis it is one of the Cherubim who bars the way back into Eden, and the Egyptians called the Sphinx, made up of four Cherubim, 'Hu', meaning protector. By this they meant that he guarded against any slide back into the old ways of procreation.

It's a common misconception that in 1650, when Bishop Usher famously calculated the date of the creation as humankind as 4004 BC, this was some last vestige of an ancient superstition. In fact Usher's calculation was the product of a time when materialism was gaining ground – and so, too, was a narrow, literal interpretation of the Bible that would have seemed absurd to the ancients. They believed that human souls had existed for vast, immeasurable eras before 11,451 BC, and only then did the human *body* as we know it today fully materialize around the human spirit.

It is interesting to note that, according to the calculations of Manetho in the third century BC, this is almost exactly the time when the reign of the demi-gods came to an end.

WE WILL SEE LATER THAT, ACCORDING TO esoteric doctrine, not only was matter only precipitated out of mind a short while ago, but that it exists only for a brief interval. It will dissolve again in just over nine thousand years, when the sun rises again to meet the gaze of the Sphinx in the constellation of Leo.

In the teachings of the secret societies we live on a small island of matter in a vast ocean of ideas and imagination.

The Sphinx, which showed the Four Elements locked into place at the four cardinal points. In modern times the eminent Egyptologist R.A. Schwaller de Lubicz – protégé of Henri Matisse – was the first to reveal to a wider public that the Sphinx might have been carved before 10,000 BC. *He pointed to the fact that the walls surrounding the monument show signs of water erosion that could not have been made after that time. The Sphinx, according to the secret history, is a monument to the first time the Four Elements locked into place and matter finally became solid. In 11,451* BC *east, west, north and south were then locked with the Four Elements that make up the physical world.*

9

The Neolithic Alexander the Great

Noah and the Myth of Atlantis • Tibet • Rama's Conquest of India • The Yoga Sutras of Pantanjali

IF YOU HAVE A PASSING ACQUAINTANCE with the myth of Atlantis, you may well have been left with the impression that there is only one ancient source for this legend – Plato.

The Platonic account goes like this. Egyptian priests told Solon, a statesman and lawyer of the generation of Plato's great grandfather, about a great island in the Atlantic that had been destroyed some nine thousand years earlier – in about 9600 BC.

The civilization on this island had been founded by the god Poseidon, and peopled by the descendants of his coupling with a beautiful woman called Cleito. (As we saw in Chapter 5, this intervention by a fish god is a coded account of evolution, common to mythologies all around the world.)

As well as the main island, this Atlantean civilization also ruled over several lesser islands in the region.

The largest island was dominated by a beautiful and fertile plain and a large hill. Here Cleito lived, and the people enjoyed food which grew abundantly on the island. Two streams of water came up through the earth, one of hot water and one of cold.

To keep Cleito for himself, Poseidon had a series of circular canals dug around the hill. In time a sophisticated civilization grew up, taming wild animals, mining metals and building – temples, palaces, racecourses, gymnasiums, public baths, government buildings, harbours and bridges. Many walls were coated with metals – with brass, tin and a red metal, unknown to us, called orichalcum. The temples had roofs of ivory and pinnacles of silver and gold.

The islands of Atlantis were ruled over by ten kings each with his own kingdom, the nine others being subservient to the ruler of the largest island.

The central temple, dedicated to Poseidon, had statues of gold, including one of the god standing in a chariot pulled by six-winged horses and flanked by hundreds of Nereids riding dolphins. Live bulls roamed freely around the forest of columns in this temple, and every five or six years the ten kings who ruled the islands between them were left alone in the temple to hunt these bulls without weapons. They would capture one, lead it up to the great column of orichalcum, inscribed with laws of Atlantis, and there behead it.

Life on the islands of Atlantis was generally idyllic. In fact life was so good that eventually people could not bear it any longer and began to become restless, decadent and corrupt, searching after novelty and power. So Zeus decided to punish them. The islands were flooded until only small islets remained, like a skeleton sticking out of the sea. Then finally a great earthquake engulfed all that was left in the course of one day and one night.

YES, IT WOULD MAKE THIS ACCOUNT OF the destruction of Atlantis unlikely to be true, if Plato were the only classical writer on the subject. Aristotle said of it, 'Plato alone made Atlantis rise out of the sea, and then he submerged it again', which has been taken to mean that Plato simply made the whole thing up. However, a little research shows that classical literature is packed with references to Atlantis, for example in the works of Proclus, Diodorus, Pliny, Strabo, Plutarch and Posidinus, and they include many elements which are not in Plato and seem to come from earlier sources – assuming, that is, that they haven't been made up too.

Proclus says that three hundred years after Solon, Crantor was shown columns by the priest of Sais covered with a history of Atlantis in hieroglyphic characters. A near-contemporary of Plato's, now known as pseudo-Aristotle, wrote about a similar island paradise in his book *On Marvellous Things Heard.*

The Greek historian Marcellus, also a near contemporary of Plato's, is clearly relying on ancient sources when he writes that 'in the Outer Ocean [the Atlantic] there are seven small islands and three larger ones, one of which was dedicated to Poseidon'. This ties in with Plato's account in terms of the number of kingdoms. A Greek historian of the fourth century BC, Theopompus of Chios, retells a story told two hundred years before Plato by Midas of Phrygia, that 'besides the well-known portions of the world – Europe, Asia, Libya (Africa) – there is another which is unknown, of incredible immensity where vast blooming meadows and pastures feed herds of various huge and mighty beasts and where the men are twice the height and live to twice the age of men'. As we have already seen, Enoch and the myths and legends of many cultures around the world recorded the prevalence of giants before the Great Flood.

Then, of course, there is the Greek myth of the Great Flood. The story of Deucalion is much older than Plato. As in both Plato's account and the biblical one there is an implication here that the Great Flood was intended to destroy the greater part of humankind, because the development of humankind had gone wrong. Rudolf Steiner has pointed out that the stories of the demi-gods and heroes, Cadmus, Theseus, Jason – all involve journeys eastwards. We should read them, he says, as stories of migrations which took place as conditions on the Atlantean islands deteriorated and before the final catastrophe.

When Plato writes about Poseidon, the first god-king of Atlantis, this should remind us of what we saw in Chapter 5 – that Poseidon was the original half-fish form of Zeus/Jupiter. Poseidon was also god of the raging sea, god of subterranean, volcanic depths, whose bull-bellowing roar signalled climatic catastrophe. Poseidon was at work at both the beginning and end of Atlantis's history.

Other ancient cultures cross-reference Plato's account. The South American Aztecs recorded that they came from 'Aztlan', 'the land in the middle of the water'. Sometimes this land was called 'Aztlan of the Seven Caves'. It was depicted as a central, large step pyramid surrounded by six smaller pyramids. According to traditions collected by the invading Spaniards, humanity had nearly been wiped out by a vast flood, and would have been but for a priest and his wife who constructed a boat made out of a hollow log, in which they also rescued seeds and animals. The complex and sophisticated astronomy of these South American tribes has allowed one modern researcher to deduce that they dated this flood to about 11,600 BC.

This might seem a long way from Plato's date of around 9600 BC, but the crucial point here is that both dates agree in setting the Flood at the end of the Ice Age. Modern geology tells us that as the ice caps melted, a series of floods swept down from the north. We have already noted the suggestion that the islands of Atlantis suffered several catastrophic floods over a long period before the last island was finally, completely, submerged.

Underwater archaeologists are today discovering in many parts of the world the remains of civilizations which were covered by floods caused by the melting of ice at the end of the Ice Age. In April 2002 divers stories told by local fishermen were used to help locate the lost city of the Seven Pagodas off the coast of Mahabalipuram in India. The temple-like structures that have been found are much grander and more complex than we would expect for the end of the Ice Age – the Neolithic, or New Stone Age. Author and investigator Graham Hancock, who has done so much to question our academic assumptions about ancient history, was quoted at the time as saying, 'I have argued for many years that the world's flood myths deserve to be taken seriously, a view that most Western academics reject. But here in Mahabalipuram, we have proved the myths right and the academics wrong.'

I myself have seen artefacts retrieved from the sea bed off the American Atlantic coast – the so-called Scott stones – which I am persuaded it would very difficult for technology to reproduce today, let alone eleven thousand years ago when the area in question went under the sea. In design terms the Scott stones show features which are remarkably similar to Egyptian artefacts. This is not my secret to reveal, but I hope that perhaps by the time this book is published Aaron du Val, President of the

Miami Museum Egyptological Society, may have chosen to show the world what he has.

No detailed description of the events that put such artefacts under the sea has survived in the Greek myths that have come down to us, and the biblical account is characteristically brief, but these can be supplemented and illumined by accounts from other cultures, particularly the Sumerian and other Near Eastern accounts. No scholars dispute that some of these accounts from older cultures provided source material for the biblical story. Elements familiar to us from the biblical account, such as the ark, the doves and the olive branch, appeared in the earlier Sumerian account, where Noah is called Ziusudra. He appears, too, in the Mesopotamian account where he is called Atrahasis and in the Babylonian account which names him Upnapishtim. Weaving these different versions together creates an amplified version of the biblical story:

> One day Noah was standing in a reed hut, when he heard a voice coming through the wall that warned him of a rainstorm that would wipe out mankind. Tear down your reed hut and build a boat, he was told. Noah and his family set about building a great vessel made out of reeds, finally daubing it with bitumen in order to make it watertight. Everything growing out of the ground, everything grazing on it, the birds of the sky, the cattle and the wild animals roaming open country, he put in. Then for six days and nights the storm blew and their boat was tossed about by the waves. The downpour, the storm and the flood overwhelmed the surface of the earth. On the seventh day, hearing the winds begin to fall, Noah opened a window and light fell on his face. The world was silent, because all humanity had been returned to clay ...

The catastrophic deluge that nearly destroyed humankind is remembered every year by both the living and the dead on the Day of the Dead or Halloween. In England as late as the nineteenth century villagers would dress up as the dead, wear masks and make a mum-mumming sound with closed lips to imitate the sound made by the walking dead – hence the word 'mummers'.

WHEN NOAH AND HIS FAMILY DISEMBARKED to set foot on dry land, something rather odd happened. 'And Noah began to be a husbandman and he planted a vineyard, and he drank of the wine, and was drunken, and he was uncovered within his tent. And Ham saw the nakedness of father and told his two brethren without.' (Genesis 9.20–22)

It is entirely fitting that Noah should become a husbandman, because archaeology tells us that agriculture began during this period, the Neolithic. But what are we to make of the strange story of his drunken nakedness?

In order to make sense of it, we must turn to the tradition that identifies Noah with the legendary Greek figure Dionysus the Younger.

We need to disentangle two different strands of stories concerning two figures with the same name. Dionysus is the name of two distinct individuals, a god and later a demi-god. These two make very different contributions to human history in two different eras. The Dionysus who should be identified with Noah is very different from the earlier Dionysus Zagreus, the Elder Dionysus, the story of whose dismemberment we told in Chapter 6.

After the Flood, Dionysus the Younger, often depicted in a boat, travelled from Atlantis via Europe to India, with the aim of teaching the whole world the arts of agriculture, the sowing of crops, the cultivation of the vine and writing. This latter had of course been taught by Enoch, but was now in danger of being lost in the devastation brought by the Flood.

Dionysus and his followers carried the thyrsus, a pole wrapped with ivy-like snakes and topped with a pine cone like a pineal gland. This shows that Dionysus also taught the secret evolution of the human form, the development of the spine topped by the pineal gland we have just been considering.

The fauns and satyrs and the whole rout of Dionysus represent stragglers from Atlantis. They are the last remnant of a process of metamorphosis of forms. The curious story in Genesis of Noah's sons uncovering his genitals while he was drunkenly sleeping also refers to the petering out of this process. We saw that the genitals were the last parts of human anatomy to evolve into their present form, and his sons were curious to find

Noah's ark. Legend has it that the only animal that missed the ark was the unicorn, which therefore became extinct. This is an obvious depiction of the diminishing of the powers of the Third Eye. As the waters of the deluge closed over Atlantis, the era of Imagination ended. The subconscious was formed.

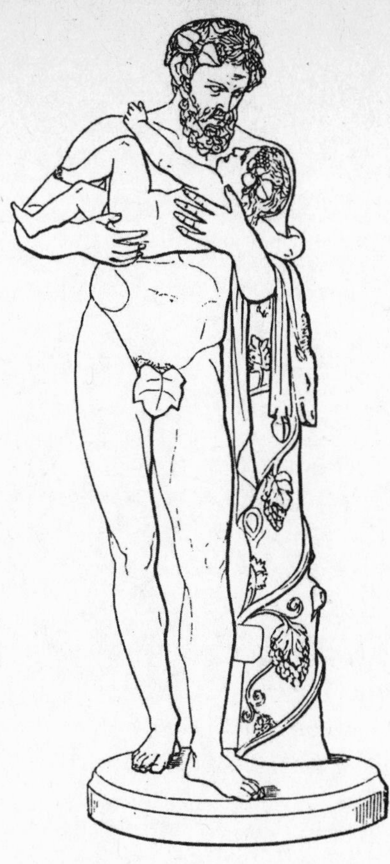

Dionysus the Younger was educated by the satyr Silenus.

out about their origins. Were they the sons of a human or a demi-god, a man or an angel?

Stories about this individual in the Greek and Hebrew traditions – Dionysus the Younger and Noah – are both connected with the grape and intoxication. We have already met followers of Dionysus. The wild and savage maenads tore Orpheus limb from limb with tooth and nail. In a state of ecstatic drunkenness the maenads were possessed by a god.

PRIMITIVE PEOPLES HAVE ALWAYS LIVED in tune with the vegetable part of their natures. One of the results of this is that they have understood how different plants have different effects on human biology, physiology and consciousness.

What we see in these Greek and Hebrew traditions of the beginnings of agriculture is a depiction of a new, more thoughtful form of consciousness. What greater outward symbol of the impact of orderly human thought on nature could there be than fields of wheat?

The task of the leaders of humanity would now be to forge the new thought-directed consciousness.

In the *Zend-Avesta*, the sacred literature of Zoroastrianism, the Noah/Dionysius figure is called Yima. He tells the people how to build a settlement – a 'var'– a fenced-in place, a

The invasion of Ceylon by Rama, the 'shepherd of the peoples'.

kind of stronghold 'taking in men, cattle, dogs, birds and blazing fires'. He instructs people that when they arrive at the place where they are to settle, they must 'drain off water, put up boundary posts, then make houses from posts, clay walls, matting and fences'. He urges his people to 'expand the earth by tilling it'. There was to be 'neither suppression nor baseness, neither dullness nor violence, neither poverty nor defeat, no cripples, no long teeth, no giants, neither any of the characteristics of the evil spirit'.

Again, we see an anxiety about a reversion to anomalous forms of the previous epoch such a giants.

The Greek epic poet Nonnus described Dionysus's migration to India, and the same journey is also described in the *Zend-Avesta* as 'the march of the Ram on India'. But the fullest description comes in the great Indian epic, the *Ramayana*.

Something that is clear from these accounts is that the great migrations eastwards were not moving into uninhabited territories. While the peoples of Atlantis had been all but eliminated, the emigrants travelled to new lands still occupied by aboriginal tribes. We see Dionysius's reaction to what he found in these new lands in his forbidding of cannibalism and human sacrifice. Native priests would sometimes keep enormous snakes or pterodactyls, rare survivors from antediluvian times, which were worshipped as gods and fed the flesh of captives. The *Ramayana* describes how Rama and his followers suddenly invaded these temples with torches, driving out both priests and monsters. He would appear without warning among enemies, sometimes with bow drawn, sometimes defenceless except that he was able to petrify them with his pale lotus-blue gaze.

Rama was dispossessed, a nomad. His kingdom lay beneath the seas. He did not live the life of a king, but camped out in the wild with his beloved Sita.

Then Sita was abducted by the evil magician Ravana. The *Ramayana* tells of the completion of Rama's journey with the conquest of India and the taking of Ceylon, the last refuge of Ravana. Rama formed a bridge over the sea between mainland India and Ceylon with the help of an army of monkeys, which is to say hominids, the descendants of human spirits who had rushed into incarnation too early and were doomed to die out. Finally, after a battle that lasted thirteen days, Rama killed Ravana by showering fire down on him.

We might see Rama as a Neolithic Alexander the Great. Following the conquest of India, he had the world at his feet. He also had a dream.

He was walking in the forests on a moonlit night, when a beautiful woman came towards him. Her skin was as white as snow and she was wearing a magnificent crown. He didn't recognize her at first, but then she said, 'I am Sita, take this crown and rule the world with me.' She knelt humbly and offered him a glittering crown – the kingship which had been denied him. But just then his guardian angel whispered in his ear: 'If you place that crown on your head, you will see me no more. And if you clasp that woman in your arms, she will experience such happiness that it will kill her instantly. But if you refuse to love her she will live out the rest of her life free and happy on earth, and your invisible spirit will rule over her.' As Rama made up his mind, Sita disappeared amongst the trees. They would never see each other again, leading the remainder of their lives apart.

Stories about Sita's later life suggest it was by no means obvious that she was as happy as the guardian angel had promised. In its ambiguity and uncertainty there is something very modern about this story.

We can also see in it a paradox that lies at the heart of the human condition. All love, if it is true love, involves a letting go.

With his prowess with the bow, his handsome face, blue eyes and lion chest, Rama is in many ways like the heroes that Greek myths describe, such as Hercules, but in the story of Rama there is, as I say, something new. Hercules was required to choose between virtue and happiness, and unsurprisingly chose the former. Rama's story, on the other hand, contains an element of *moral surprise*. The reader of the story will probably agree with Sita as she argues with Rama that it is only right and fitting that he now accept the crown he has been cheated of since birth. But then Rama's surprising choices – deciding not to take the crown that is rightfully his, not to marry the woman he loves – these dilate the moral imagination and quicken the moral intelligence. The story of Rama encourages us to see beyond the conventional, to imagine ourselves into the mind of others and also, ultimately, to think for ourselves. Esoteric thinking has always sought to undermine and subvert conventional, habitual, mechanical modes of thought. Later we will see how storytellers, dramatists and novelists steeped in esoteric thought, from Shakespeare and Cervantes to George Eliot and Tolstoy, would quicken the moral imagination, one of the distinguishing characteristics of the very greatest literature. If great art and literature give a sense of patterns, of laws operating beyond conventional thought, great esoteric art brings these laws near to the surface of consciousness.

The story of Rama also brings us back to the notion that according to the secret history the cosmos has been formed in order to create the conditions in which people could experience free thought and free will. Rama could have enforced what is good and right on his people by ruling them with a rod of iron, but he instead let them *decide* for themselves. Rama is thus the archetype of the exiled or 'Secret King' or 'Secret Philosopher' who influences the course of history not from the throne but by mingling incognito among the people. Rama tried to help humans to evolve freely.

Rama is a demi-god, but declines to be ruler of the world. No longer will gods or even demi-gods sit on thrones in bodies of flesh and bone.

AT JOURNEY'S END THE EMIGRANTS FOUNDED Shambala, a great spiritual fortress in the mountainous region of Tibet. The roof of the world, Tibet is the world's biggest, highest plateau surrounded by high mountain ranges. Some traditions say the Tibetan population is directly descended from the people of Atlantis.

Some say that Shambala can only be reached via an underground tunnel, others that it exists in another dimension into which a secret portal opens somewhere in the region. St Augustine was the greatest Christian theologian after St Paul and, like St Paul, was an initiate of a Mystery school. He wrote about the place where Enoch and the saints lived, a terrestrial paradise so high up that the Flood could not reach it. Emmanuel Swedenborg, the eighteenth-century Swedish theologian, diplomat and inventor – and also the leading esoteric Freemason of the age – wrote that 'the "Lost Word" must be sought among the sages of Tibet and Tartary'. Anne-Catherine Emmerich, the nineteenth-century German Catholic mystic wrote similarly of a Mount of Prophets where live Enoch, Elijah and others who did not die in the ordinary way but 'ascended', and where unicorns which survived the Flood may also be found.

From the mountain fastnesses of Tibet flowed streams of living spirituality which joined together, gathered force, depth and width and became a mighty river like the Ganges, feeding the whole of India.

IN THIS HISTORY OF THE WORLD WRITTEN in the stars, the next era began as the sun began to rise in the constellation of Cancer in 7227 BC and the first great Indian civilization, the earliest and most deeply spiritual of post-Flood civilizations, was founded. The founders felt little for the newly created material world, which they saw as 'maya', an illusion threatening to obscure the higher realities of the spirit worlds. They looked back with nostalgia to the time before this veil of matter had been drawn between humankind and the spiritual hierarchies.

The icy baths and other forms of self-torture of the ascetics can be looked on as part of the effort to stay awake to the spirit worlds. A conscious effort was made by them, while the veil was still relatively translucent, to remember the lineaments of the spirit world, and to impress them indelibly on human consciousness.

The success of this enterprise has meant that India is still the world's greatest storehouse of spiritual knowledge, particularly as regards occult physiology. As a high level initiate recently said to me, 'If you visit India today, you cannot help feeling how the air still just *crackles* with astrality.'

Great Western teachers such as Pythagoras, Apollonius of Tyana and St Germain have travelled to India in search of this astrality. The Gospels contain quotes from older, Indian sources and more ideas that originated there.

Sir John Woodruffe, the Sanskrit scholar who first translated the tantric texts in the nineteenth century, has written how even the venerable Sufi tradition leant on Hindu wisdom for teachings on the chakras, for example.

In the 1960s onwards, Indian religion was felt by many people in the West to offer a working spiritual knowledge, including practical spiritual disciplines and guides through the spirit worlds, which they could not find in church. A bookshop in the West is still likely to stock more books on mysticism derived from the Eastern than from the Western tradition.

FOLLOWING RAMA'S REFUSAL TO TAKE THE crown, no great single personality dominates this period. If Rama was an all-action hero who fought monsters, went on long, dangerous adventures and founded cities, his successors, sometimes called the Seven Wise Ones, or the Rishis, had a stillness, an inactivity about them. They built no stone buildings. They lived in buildings of mud or simple shelters twisted into shape from roots and tendrils. Nothing of the Rishis has lasted except what they *knew.*

There is a simple saying in the Cabala: 'Everything you have seen, every flower, every bird, every rock will pass away and turn to dust, but that you have seen them will not pass away.' This is a saying that would have seemed sympathetic to the Rishis. Seated with legs folded so that the soles of their feet turned upwards, they had no desire to feel gravity, the downward, reductive pull of the material world, but headed instead for the spirit worlds. They were able to see spiritual beings at work on the earth, how they help seeds to germinate in spring, flowers to blossom in summer, trees to bear fruit in autumn – and how seeds are preserved through winter by these same spiritual beings. The Rishis experienced the ebb and flow of spiritual influence like a giant breath. Ancient Indian civilization was like the lowest realm of Heaven.

Earlier we talked about the way materialists misappropriate words and phrases such as 'the meaning of life', using them in a secondary and slightly dishonest sense. The same is true of 'spiritual', often used by people to puff themselves as good-hearted or moral in a warm, fuzzy, perhaps pseudo-mystical way. What it really means is the ability to see, hear and communicate with the spirits like the Indian adepts.

They were also able to communicate in occult ways. Other people were felt by them to be sympathetic or not by their breathing. By breathing in someone else's air, they could sense that person's inner life.

Adepts were able to pour their knowledge into the souls of others in an unceasing flow of pictures. Much later this knowledge would be put into words and passed from generation to generation orally until it was finally written down as the *Vedas*.

Their gaze could drive away serpents and calm lions and tigers. Nothing could deflect the adepts from their contemplation. They wandered freely, building only the flimsiest shelters, eating fruit and drinking the milk of their flocks. They would eat only vegetable matter, never any meat. To do so, they believed, was to absorb the animal's death agony.

They immersed themselves in vegetable consciousness, in the physical processes – waking, sleeping, breathing, digesting – which we have seen are the gift of the vegetable kingdom to the human body. By learning to control the *ens vegetalis*, or etheric body, they could control, too, breathing, the rate of digestion, even heart rate and the flow of blood, leading to the amazing feats for which Indian adepts are famous – the ability to stop the heart altogether just by thinking about it, for example.

The adepts understood, too, how sinking deep into contemplation of the solar plexus chakra enabled them to perceive clairvoyantly. And they knew how to wrap others in a protective beam of love emanating from the heart chakra.

In addition to the sixteen petals of the heart chakra, the adepts saw 101 subtle and luminous arteries issuing from the same area like spokes from a wheel. Three of these, larger ones they saw rising to the head. One rises to the right eye and corresponds to the sun and the future. Another rises to the left eye and corresponds to the moon and the past. They understood how it was by a combination of these two organs that humans are enabled to perceive the movements of material objects in relation to one another in space and so also to have a sense of time passing.

The middle of the three arteries ran up from the heart and through the crown of the head. By this route, the way upwards is illumined from below, by means of a

The Neolithic 'swastika' carved on a boulder on Keighley moor in Yorkshire, England, is a symbol of the revolving two-petalled lotus and above – the same device – in a Celtic sun brooch found in Sweden. The Rig Veda *says, 'Behold the beautiful splendour of Savitva the Sun-God of the swastika to inspire our visions.'*

radiant heart. And it was by the route of this middle artery, too, that the spirit would depart up through the crown and out of the body at death.

To the ancients *all* life was involved in a pulse, rhythm or breath. They saw all human lives as breathed temporarily into the world of *maya*, or illusion, then breathed out again, a process repeated through the ages. They saw great flocks or shoals of souls being breathed in and out of material life together.

This ancient Indian civilization was in some ways an echo of the sun-filled, watery, vegetable world of the period before the sun and earth separated. In some ways it too was a lotus-eating period that would have to end if progress was to take place.

We saw how great beings from the higher hierarchies could no longer appear in physical bodies as they had earlier on Atlantis. They could still appear as semi-material spectres or phantoms, but even this was happening less frequently. By the end of the age people might only *see* them with their physical eyes once or twice in a lifetime. As the gods withdrew, people would have to find ways to follow them.

In this way yoga was born.

At the height of their meditations a rush of energy from the base of the spine would travel upwards through the middle artery via the heart to the head. Sometimes this energy was thought of as being like a snake, which rose through the spine up into the skull and bit at a point just behind the bridge of the nose. This bite released an ecstatic lace-like flux of luminous currents, seven hundred thousand lightning flares sounding like millions of bees. Adepts would find themselves in another dimension that appeared at first to consist of a mighty ocean of giant weaving waves of light and energy – the preliminary mystical experience in all traditions. As they became more accustomed to the spiritual world, these apparently impersonal forces would begin to resolve themselves into outer garments of the gods, and finally the faces of the gods themselves would emerge from the light, the same faces of the gods of stars and planets that have become familiar to us over the last few chapters.

One of the shortest books in the world, but one of the most powerful, is called the *Yoga Sutras of Pantanjali*. It was written down in its final form in about 400 BC, but originated in the teachings of the Rishis.

Pantanjali tells the reader to concentrate on the strength of the elephant and by this means attain that strength. He says it is possible to know past lives by concentrating on the past. It would be wishful thinking to believe you or I might be able to perform these feats just like that. These are things that now, as then, only the most advanced, the highest initiates, can attain. The rest of us will only be able to do them in future incarnations.

The Rishis taught that the evolution of the whole cosmos is the goal of existence, and that the seeds of all this transformation lie in the human body.

In 5067 BC these gods were moving the cosmos towards the next stage of human evolution as the sun entered the sign of Gemini. Just as, earlier, the impulse for the evolution of humankind had moved eastwards from drowning Atlantis to India, now it began to move westwards, as it continues to do today.

10

The Way of the Wizard

Zarathustra's Battle Against the Powers of Darkness • The Life and Death of Krishna the Shepherd • The Dawn of the Dark Age

IN 5067 BC IN THE REGION WE NOW call Iran, the birth of a great new leader was foretold. We should picture his mother living in a small agricultural community, like the one unearthed at Çatal Hüyük

It was in the depths of an exceptionally harsh winter when the plague struck. Tongues were wagging in the community, accusing the young woman of witchcraft, claiming the storms, the plague, were her doing.

Then in the fifth month of her pregnancy she had a nightmare. She saw an immense cloud and from it emerged dragons, wolves and snakes that tried to tear her child from her body. But as the monsters approached, the child spoke from inside her womb to comfort

Zarathustra with rolled scroll. The carrying of a rolled scroll in the right hand is always a sign that the subject is an adherent of the secret philosophy. Look around the streets of London, Paris, Rome, Washington DC or any of the great cities of the world, and you may be surprised how many statues of the great and the good carry rolled scrolls.

her, and as his voice died away, she saw a pyramid of light descending from the sky. Down this pyramid came a boy holding a staff in his left hand and a scroll in his right. His eyes shone with inner fire, and his name was Zarathustra.

There are different schools of thought about the dates of Zarathustra. Some writers of the ancient world placed him at approximately 5000 BC, while others, such as Plutarch, at 600 BC. Again, this is because there was more than one Zarathustra.

The birth of the first Zarathustra unleashed storms of hatred. The king was in thrall to a circle of sorcerers who persuaded him the boy must die. He went to the young mother's house and found the baby alone in his crib. The king was determined to stab the baby, but as he raised his hand, it became mysteriously paralyzed. Later he sent one of his servants to kidnap the child and abandon him in a wolf-ridden wilderness. But the pack of wolves the king hoped would tear the child in pieces saw something in his eyes and ran away terrified. The child grew to be the youth of his mother's dream.

But the forces of evil knew their greatest enemy had come down to earth. They were just biding their time.

The Age of Gemini was one of division. It was no longer possible to live safely in Paradise, as people had lived in the Indian epoch. If the Indian epoch had been a

Etruscan depiction of a demon in the form of a Persian Asura. The name Asura literally means not-god, 'a' meaning 'not' and Sura being the Persian name for a god or angel. Demons in all traditions are often shown gnawing the viscera. This is because of the primordial understanding that consciousness and memory are not stored in the brain alone, but in the whole body. Things we have done that we would rather not confront, painful and undigested experiences, are stored in the viscera.

recapitulation of the heavenly time before the separation of earth and sun, this new, Persian epoch was a recapitulation of the fiery period when the dragons of Lucifer had infected life on earth. Now the forces of evil reasserted themselves, led by Ahriman (the Satan of Zoroastrian tradition). The cosmos was invaded by hoards of demons that darkened the heavens. Demons thrust themselves between humans and the higher echelons of the spiritual hierarchies. If the Indian epoch was the time when the secret physiology of humankind was imprinted on human memory, then this Persian epoch is the time we look to for knowledge of demonology.

The hosts of demons against which Zarathustra led his own followers were also classified by him. These form the basis of classifications that the secret societies use today.

At this turning point in history people began to feel insecure on a level that today we call the existential. They were less sure that they lived in a cosmos that was ultimately benevolent, where everything would turn out right in the end. They began to suffer for the first time the species of fear that Emile Durkheim named *anomie* – fear of the destructive chaos that creeps in at the margins of life, that may attack us from the darkness outside the encampment or from the darkness that overwhelms us when we are sleeping. It may also lie in wait for us when we are dead.

WHEN WE FALL ASLEEP WE LOSE ANIMAL consciousness. In the teachings of the secret societies animal consciousness – or spirit – is pictured floating out of the body in sleep. This has two main consequences. First, without the animal element our body returns to a vegetating state. No longer sapped by the agitations of animal consciousness or the wearying effect of thought, the bodily functions that the vegetable element controls are renewed. We wake up refreshed.

Second, detached from the sensory perceptions of the body, the spirit enters an alternative state of consciousness, which is an experience of the sub-lunary spirit world. In dreams we perceive the spirit worlds, where we are approached by angels and demons and the spirits of the dead.

Or at least that is what humans experienced in the time of the Rishis. By the time of Zarathustra human nature had become enmeshed in matter and so corrupted that dreams had become chaotic and difficult to interpret. They were fantastical now and full of strange, distorted meanings. Still, dreams might contain promptings by spirits, fragments of past lives, even memories of episodes from history.

In deepest sleep the Third Eye may open and peer into the spirit worlds, but on waking we forget.

AFTER YEARS IN EXILE, THE YOUNG ZARATHUSTRA felt the need to return to Iran. On the border he had a vision. A gigantic shining creature of spirit came to meet him and told him

Marble group of the second century BC. Mithras, archangel of the sun – St Michael in Hebrew tradition – is here slaying the cosmic bull of material creation. From the bull's spine sprouts the corn of vegetable life and from his blood the wine of animal life. Note that Mithras is wearing the 'Phrygian cap' which resurfaced into exoteric history when it was worn by initiates of the secret societies who led the French Revolution. The French Martinist Joseph de Maistre wove together from various sources an account of the Mithraic initiation ceremonies. A pit was dug, which the candidate stood in. A metal grille was placed over the opening to the pit, and on this stood a bull that was sacrificed. The candidate would become drenched by the blood of the bull raining down from above. In another part of the ceremony the candidate would lie in a tomb as if dead. Then the initiator would grasp him by the right hand and pull him up into 'new life'. There were seven grades of initiate: Raven, Nymphus, Soldier, Lion, Persian, Courier of the Sun and Father.

to follow. Zarathustra had to take ninety steps to the spirit's gigantic nine as the spirit swept over the stony ground, taking Zarathustra to a clearing, hidden by rocks and trees. There a circle of six other, similar spirits hovered above the ground. This shining company turned to welcome Zarathustra, and invited him to leave his physical body for a while in order to join them.

We have met these shining spirits before. They are the spirits of the sun called in Genesis the Elohim. They now prepared Zarathustra for his mission.

First, they told him he must pass through fire without being burned.

Second, they poured molten lead – the metal of Ahriman – on to his chest, which he suffered in silence. Zarathustra then took the lead from his chest and calmly gave it back to them.

Third, they opened up his torso and showed him the secrets of his inner organs, before closing him up again.

Zarathustra returned to court and preached what the great spirits had revealed. He told the king that the sun spirits who created the world were working to transform it, and that one day the world would be a vast body of light.

The king he was addressing was a new one, but, like his predecessor he was in thrall to evil ministers. He did not want to hear this good news and let his ministers persuade him to have Zarathustra thrown in prison.

But Zarathustra escaped from prison and also from attempts to murder him. He lived to fight many battles against the forces of evil, battles where he pitched his magic powers against the powers of evil sorcerers. Later he became the archetype of the wizard, with a tall hat, cloak of stars and an eagle on his shoulder. Zarathustra was a dangerous, somewhat disconcerting figure, prepared to fight fire with fire.

He led his followers to secluded grottoes, hidden in the forests. There in underground caverns he initiated them. He wanted to provide them with the supernatural powers needed to fight the good fight. We know about this early Mystery school, because it survived five millennia underground in Persia before resurfacing as Mithraism, an initiatory cult popular among Roman soldiers, and then again in Manichaeism, a late Mystery religion which included St Augustine among its initiates.

Zarathustra prepared his followers to face Ahriman's demons or Asuras by terrifying initiation ordeals. He who fears death, he said, is already dead.

It was recorded by Menippus, the Greek philosopher of the third century BC, who had been initiated by the Mithraic successors of Zarathustra, that, after a period of fasting, mortification and mental exercises performed in solitude, the candidate would be forced to swim across water, pass through fire and ice. He would be cast into a snake pit, and cut across the chest by a sword so that blood would flow.

By experiencing the outer limits of fear, the initiate was prepared for the worst that could happen, both in life *and after death.*

An important part of this preparation was inducing in the candidate conscious experience of the separation of the animal part of his make-up from the vegetable and material parts, as happens in sleep. Equally important was to experience the separation of the animal from the vegetable part, as happens after death. In other

Paracelsus said: 'It is as necessary to learn evil things as good, for who can know what is good without learning what is evil.' Meeting of a contemporary secret society in woods in West Sussex, England. It is sometimes supposed that all secret societies engage in commerce with evil spirits. However, the great, historically significant secret societies, such as the Rosicrucians and the Freemasons, acknowledge the dark side in order to combat it.

words initiation involved what we today sometimes call an 'after-death experience'.

By the act of leaving the body the candidate knew beyond any possibility of doubt that death was not the end.

People who learn how to dream *consciously*, that is to say with the ability to think and exercise willpower we normally only enjoy in waking life, may develop powers which are 'supernatural' by today's definitions. If you can dream consciously, then you are on the way to being able to move about the spirit worlds at will, communicating freely with the spirits of the dead and other disembodied beings. You may perhaps learn about the future in ways which might otherwise be blocked. You may be able to travel to other parts of the material universe and view things where you are not bodily present – so-called astral travel. The great sixteenth-century initiate Paracelsus, who, as we shall see, has some claims to be the father of both modern experimental medicine and homeopathy, said he was able to *visit other people in their dreams.*

We will also see that many great scientific discoveries have been revealed to initiates while in this alternative state of consciousness.

Supernatural means of influencing minds is another of the gifts that initiation may confer. Initiates I have met have undoubted gifts of mind-reading way beyond the abilities of sceptical scientists to reproduce in 'cold reading' experiments.

Similarly science has only the flimsiest, question-begging explanations for hypnosis. This is because, though it may be abused by popular entertainers, hypnosis was originally – and at root remains – an occult practice. Ultimately explicable only in mind-before-matter terms, it originated with the Rishis of India and in techniques practised during the process of initiation by the temple priests of Egypt. In the *Yoga Sutras of Pantanjali*, this power of influencing others' minds is one of the powers called *vibhuti*. Mind-influence was used for benevolent purposes, but as the world became a more dangerous place it would have to be used for both defence and attack.

We saw earlier how in a mind-before-matter philosophy the way you look at someone can affect them at a sub-atomic level. The coiled cobra representations of the Third Eye on the foreheads of Egyptian initiates shows that it can reach out and strike at what it perceives. In the seventeenth century the scientist and alchemist J.B. von Helmont said that 'a man may kill an animal by staring at it for fifteen minutes'. From the eighteenth century onwards European travellers in India were amazed by the ability of adepts to throw anyone into an immediate state of catalepsy, just by looking at them. The story of one nineteenth-century traveller was recorded by George Eliot's friend, the initiate Gerald Massey. This traveller had been mesmerized by the gaze of a serpent. He was sinking deeper and deeper into a 'somnambulic' sleep under its fascinating influence. Then someone else in the party shot the snake, breaking its power over him – and he felt a blow to the head as if he too had been struck by a bullet. Travellers in the twentieth century reported tales of wolves that were able to freeze their victims and prevent them from crying out, even when the victim was unaware that he was being watched. In living memory in a small town called Crowborough, less than six miles from where I write, lived a local wise man and healer called Pigtail Badger. The villagers were afraid of him, because it was said that this tall, heavy-set, fierce-looking man could stop others in their tracks just by looking at them. It was said that sometimes he would do this to farm labourers, then sit and eat their lunches in front of them.

THE MOST IMPORTANT INITIATION TEACHINGS concerned the way the spirit worlds are experienced after death. This was not because a candidate would have doubted there was life after death – such a thought would have been unthinkable then – but because they feared what their experience would turn out to be. In the first instance they feared that demons they had evaded in their lifetime were lying in wait. Initiation showed candidates how to navigate the after-death journey safely.

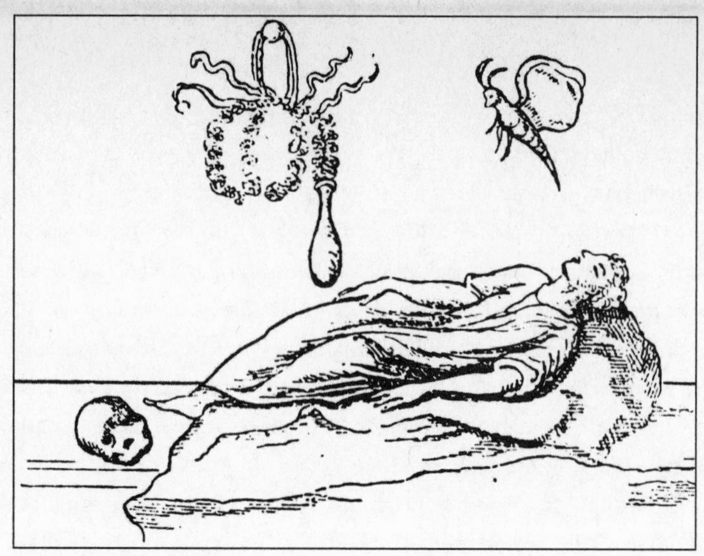

Iconography of the spirit leaving the body in Egyptian and Christian art (Didron's Christian Iconocraphy*). In the Egyptian depiction, the spirit is showing separating from the discarded soul-matter.*

In sleep the animal spirit leaves the vegetable and mineral parts of the body behind. In death, on the other hand, the vegetable part, which orders the basic life functions, leaves with the animal spirit.

The vegetable part of human nature has many functions, including storing memory. As the vegetable part detaches from the material body, both begin to disintegrate. This disintegration of the vegetable part causes the spirit to experience a review of the life just completed.

The vegetable part dissipates and detaches itself from the animal spirit in a matter of days. Then the spirit passes into the sub-lunar sphere. There it is attacked by demons who tear from it all impure, corrupt and bestial desires, all evil impulses of will. This region, where the spirit has to endure this painful process of purification for a period lasting approximately a third of the time spent on earth, is called Purgatory in Christian tradition. It is the same place as the Underworld of the Egyptians and Greeks. It is the *Kamaloca* (literally 'region of desire') of the Hindus.

Meister Eckhart, the thirteenth-century German mystic, said 'If you fight your death, you'll feel the demons tearing away at your life, but if you have the right attitude to death, you will be able to see that the devils are really angels setting your spirit free.' An initiate has the right attitude to death. He sees behind appearances and knows that demons in their proper place perform an invaluable role in what we might call the 'ecology' of the spirit world. Unless the spirit is purged in this way, it cannot ascend through the higher spheres and hear their music. Following its prodigal journey on earth, the spirit cannot be reunited with the Father until it has been purified.

It is important to continue to bear in mind that the knowledge gained in initiation is not dry or abstract, but existential. The initiate has an out-of-body experience which is shattering.

Illustration to Le Petit Prince *showing the ascent through the spheres.*

From the lunar sphere the disembodied spirit flies upwards to the realm of Mercury, from there to Venus and then on to the sun. Then the spirit experiences, as the Greek orator Aristides put it, 'a lightness which nobody who has not been initiated could either describe or understand'. It is important to continue to bear in mind that this teaching was common to Mystery schools of all cultures in the ancient world and has been perpetuated in the modern world by the secret societies. From the Egyptian *Book of the Dead*, through the Christian Cabala of the *Pistis Sophia* through Dante's *Commedia*, forward to modern works such as *Le Petit Prince* by the twentieth-century French writer Antoine de Saint-Exupéry, the secret doctrine is maintained, sometimes in books only initiates may read – and sometimes hidden in plain view.

In the ancient texts the initiate is told the secret names of the spirits who guard the entrance to every sphere and the sometimes secret handshakes and other signs and formulae needed to negotiate entry. In the *Pistis Sophia* these spheres are envisaged as made of crystal and the entrance keepers of these spheres as archons or demons.

In all the ancient religions, the being who guides the human spirit through the underworld and helps negotiate the way past the guardian demons is the god of the planet Mercury.

But the initiates of the Mystery schools kept a secret. Halfway on the journey through the spheres, there is a swap. The task of guiding the human spirit upwards is taken over by a great being whose identity may perhaps be a surprise. *In the latter part of the spirit's ascent through the heavenly spheres the guide who lights the way is Lucifer.*

In the spiritual ecology of the cosmos Lucifer is a *necessary* evil, both in this life – because without Lucifer humans could feel no desire – and in the afterlife. Without Lucifer the spirit would be plunged into total darkness and fail to understand the ascent. The second-century Roman writer Apuleius wrote that in the process of initiation the spirit confronts the gods of heaven in all their unveiled splendour – and with all their ambiguities removed.

The spirit ascends through the spheres of Jupiter and Saturn, passes through the sphere of the constellations and is finally reunited with the great Cosmic Mind. It has been a painful, confusing and tiring journey. Plutarch writes: 'But finally a wondrous light shines to greet us, beautiful meadows full of singing and dancing, the solemnity of sacred realms and holy appearances.'

Then the spirit must begin again the descent through the spheres, preparatory to the next incarnation. As it descends each sphere grants the spirit a gift which it will need when re-entering the material plane.

The following account has been compiled from fragments of ancient tablets, dating perhaps as far back as the third millennium BC, excavated in Iraq in the late nineteenth century:

The first gate he passed her out of, and he restored to her the covering cloak of her body.
The second gate he passed her out of and he restored to her the bracelets of her hands and feet.
The third gate he passed her out of, and he restored to her the binding girdle of her waist.
The fourth gate he passed her out of and he restored to her the ornaments of her breast.
The fifth gate he passed her out of and he restored to her the necklace of her neck.
The sixth gate he passed her out of and he restored to her the earrings of her ears.
The seventh gate he passed her out of and he restored to her the great crown of her head.

Even today every child is reminded of these gifts in the fairy story *Sleeping Beauty*. The human spirit still responds strongly and warmly to this story, experiencing it as true in a deep sense.

But in order to understand the esoteric content of *Sleeping Beauty* it is necessary to think in an upside down sort of way. The story relates that at the party to celebrate her birth, six fairies give the Princess gifts to help her have a happy and fulfilled life. The seventh fairy, who represents Saturn or Satan, the spirit of materialism, curses the child with death, which is commuted to a long period of sleep. These seven fairies are, of course, the seven gods of the planetary spheres.

What is upside down and the other way round about this story is that by the deathly, dreamless sleep which is the curse of the evil fairy is meant life on earth. In other words, because of the intervention by Satan, humans gradually lose any consciousness, and eventually any memory, of their time among the heavenly hierarchies: 'Our birth is but a sleep and a forgetting.' In this story, then, the party at the beginning of the narrative must be understood as taking place in the spirit world, and it is only when Beauty falls asleep that she is alive on the material plane. When she awakes, she dies!

In fact we have already seen a similar paradox in the story of Osiris, most of which takes place in the spirit world. When Osiris is nailed in the coffin that fits him like skin, it *is* his skin. He is only dead to Isis when he is alive on the material plane.

THESE STORIES SHOW HOW BOTH THIS life and the afterlife are ruled by the planets and stars. They should alert us to another very important dimension in initiatic teachings. Initiation prepares the candidate for meetings with the guardians of the different spheres both on the way up and on the way down. If these teachings are imprinted well

Rosicrucian beliefs about reincarnation are encoded in the story of Snow White and the Seven Dwarves. *Snow White 'dies' and is laid in a glass coffin – a legendary custom of the Rosicrucians. The whole idea of reincarnation may seem alien to people brought up in a modern, Christian culture. As we shall see, though, the New Testament contains ideas of reincarnation, the early Christians believed in it, and senior Christians have believed in it in secret ever since. Secret beliefs about reincarnation are encoded in art, architecture and literature here in Andrew Lang's* Red Fairy Book.

enough on the individual spirit, this will ultimately prepare the spirit for conscious participation with the higher spiritual beings in preparing for a new incarnation. The key word here is 'conscious'.

Initiation involves forging a conscious, working relationship with disembodied spirits and an existential knowledge of the way they work in our lives and our afterlives. It reveals the way they operate when we are awake, when we dream and *when we are dead.* We have seen that the histories we have been examining, such as the trials of Hercules, are structured according to different astronomical cycles – the journey of the sun through the months of the year and in the precession of the equinoxes. The point is that the same patterns that structure life on earth also structure the spirit worlds. Hercules and Job suffered trials in their earthly lives that have been recorded in the history of the world, but they will also have to suffer the same trials in the afterlife – unless they can learn to become conscious of them. And if they can't, they will also have to suffer them in their next incarnation.

This is the aim of initiation: to make more and more experience conscious, to roll back the boundaries of consciousness.

Initiation *by Renaissance master Andrea Mantegna. Compare this with the ancient Roman depiction of the process of initiation on p.43. The hooded acolyte is threatened and suddenly made to feel he has been pushed into a fatal fall. This is part of the process of inducing an out-of-body experience that enables the acolyte to achieve personal, existential knowledge of what will happen when the spirit leaves the body after death. The continuity in this process can also be seen in the account by the great eighteenth-century magus Cagliostro of his initiation into a Masonic Lodge in London. In the Esperance Lodge above a pub in Soho, he was asked to repeat an oath of secrecy then blindfolded. A rope was then tied round his waist, and he heard pulleys creak as he was winched up to the ceiling. Suddenly he fell to the floor, his blindfold was removed, and he saw a pistol being loaded with powder and a bullet. The blindfold was replaced and he was handed the pistol and asked to prove his obedience by shooting himself in the head. When he hesitated, his initiators shouted at him, accusing him of being a coward. He pulled the trigger, heard an explosion, felt a blow to the side of the head and smelled gunpowder. He had believed he was going to die – and now he was an initiate.*

In our individual lives – and collectively – we go round and round in the circles traced out for us by the planets and stars.

But if we can become conscious of these circles, if we can become conscious of the activity of the stars and planets in our lives in a most intimate way, then we are in a sense no longer trapped by them. We are no longer trapped by them, we rise above them, we are moving now not in a circle but in an upward spiral.

ZARATHUSTRA WORE A CLOAK COVERED with stars and planets as a mark of the knowledge that the great spirits of the sun had taught him. This was knowledge he passed on in initiation. When candidates re-entered the body, following their out-of-body experience, they were enabled by Zarathustra to explore the interior workings of their bodies in ways that thousands of years later people would only be able to rediscover though autopsies. Again the difference was that the ancients, according to their habit of seeing life as subjectively as possible, did not know human anatomy in an abstract, conceptual way, but rather they *experienced* it. This was how the ancients knew of the pineal gland long before it was 'discovered' by modern science.

At the transition from the sixth to the fifth millennium BC, humankind began to construct the great stone circles that survive to this day. In the same way that the withdrawal of the gods during the Indian period had forced humankind to think about ways of following them, now the obscuring of direct guidance from the gods made it necessary for humankind to discover new ways of seeking that guidance. Again humankind was being drawn out of itself.

As the initiator of these stone monuments, Zarathustra can be seen as a sort of post-Flood mirror image of Enoch.

The megalithic stone circles which began to spread throughout the Near East, Northern Europe and Northern Africa are intended to measure the movements of the heavenly bodies. In the 1950s Professor Alexander Thom of Cambridge University first realized that megalithic stone monuments across the world are constructed according to a common unit of measurement, which he called the 'megalithic yard'. This has since been verified by wide-ranging statistical analyses of monuments. Recently Dr Robert Lomas of Sheffield University has shown how it was that this unit of measurement was derived to such astonishing unanimity and accuracy in different parts of the world; a pendulum swinging 360 times during the time it takes for a star to move through one of the 360 degrees into which the sky's dome divides will be exactly 16.32 inches long, which is exactly one half a 'megalithic yard'.

Because the ancients looked to the stars and planets as the controllers of life on earth, they naturally defined their original mathematical measures of the physical world by reference to these heavenly – which is to say spiritual – bodies. Therefore mathematics in its origins was not only *holistic*, in the sense that it took into account the size, shape and movement of the earth and its relation to the heavenly bodies, but it was also the expression of a spiritual impulse.

EVIL POWERS ALWAYS THREATENED TO DESTROY Zarathustra. There are poignant reminders in the small mountainside shrines of Zoroastrianism today, where a flame is kept alight, but in permanent danger of being snuffed out. At the age of seventy-seven Zarathustra was murdered on his own altar.

SHORTLY BEFORE THE END OF THE FOURTH millennium Krishna was born. The year was 3228 BC. This shepherd and prophet was in some ways a forerunner of Jesus Christ. (We shall see shortly how Krishna, Osiris and Zarathustra are depicted attending the Nativity, albeit in disguise, in famous Renaissance paintings.)

He is not, of course, to be confused with the war god Krishna, the earlier Atlantean Krishna who fought in an epic battle to defeat the Luciferic forces of desire and delusion. Now these forces had sunk deeper into human nature, and degenerated into a desire for gold and for the spilling of blood.

His mother-to-be, the virgin Devaki, had been increasingly beset by strange visions. One day she fell into a deep ecstasy. She heard a heavenly music of harps and voices, and in the midst of a bright flashing of myriad lights saw the Sun god appear to her in human form. Overshadowed by him, she lost consciousness altogether.

In time Krishna was born. Devaki was later warned by an angel that her brother, Kansa, would try to murder the boy, so she fled the court to live among shepherds at the foot of Mount Meru.

Kansa was a child-killer, hunting down the children of the poor. He'd even done it while still a child himself. Now he sent a giant red-crested snake to kill his nephew, but Krishna was able to kill the snake by stamping on it. A female demon called Putana, whose breasts were full of poison, pulled him to her, but Krishna sucked on her breast with such force that she crumpled and fell down dead.

Kansa continued to persecute his nephew, trying to hunt him down like a wild animal, but as Krishna grew to manhood he was protected by shepherds and hid in the hills and the forests, where he preached a gospel of non-violence and love for all humanity: 'Return good for evil, forget your own suffering for another's', and 'Renounce the fruit of your works – let your work be its own reward'. Krishna was saying things no one had ever said before.

When these teachings reached Kansa, they enraged him further, tortured him in the very depths of his spirit.

Among Krishna's many titles are 'The Cowherd' and 'The Lord of the Milkmaids'. He enjoyed a simple country life, preaching but avoiding direct confrontation with Kansa.

Krishna is a god of transgression, whose numer – or sacred potency – takes him beyond conventional morality.

The local milkmaids were all madly in love with the slender youth. He liked to play the flute and dance the dance of love with them. On one occasion he watched them as they went to bathe in the Yumana River, then stole their clothes and climbed up a tree where they could not reach him. On another he was dancing with many milkmaids who all wanted to hold his hand, so he multiplied himself into many forms so that each could believe she held the hand of the true Krishna.

One day he and his brother entered Kansa's city of Mathura, disguised as poor country people, in order to take part in an athletics festival. They met a deformed girl called Kubja, carrying ointments and perfumes to the palace. When asked by Krishna she readily gave him some, though she could by no means afford it, and he cured her of her deformity and made her beautiful.

But Kansa had not been fooled by the brothers' disguise, and when they entered the wrestling competition he had primed two giants to kill them. If they failed, an enormous elephant was set to trample them to death. In the event Krishna and his brother turned the tables on all of them and escaped.

Finally Krishna decided to discard all disguise, to come out of hiding to confront Kansa. When he re-entered Mathura, Krishna was acclaimed as its saviour by a populace that showered him with flowers and garlands. Kansa was waiting with his retinue in the main square. 'You have stolen my kingdom,' said Kansa, 'Kill me!' When Krishna refused, Kansa had his soldiers seize him and tie him to a cedar tree. He was martyred by Kansa's archers.

With the death of Krishna in the year 3102 BC, the Kali Yuga – the Dark Age – began. A *yuga* is a division of a great year, there being eight yugas in a complete processional cycle.

In both Eastern and Western traditions, this great cosmic shift began in 3102 BC and it ended in 1899. As we shall see in Chapter 24, Freemasons commemorated the approaching end of the Kali Yuga by erecting gigantic monuments in the centre of every great city in the Western world. Most people pass by these familiar constructions unaware that they are beacons for the history and philosophy proposed in this book.

IN THE GATHERING DARKNESS A LIGHT appeared. As Krishna died another great personage was growing to adulthood, a light-bearer, who incarnated, just as three thousand years later Jesus Christ would incarnate.

We shall examine the life and times of the incarnated Lucifer in the next chapter.

II

Getting to Grips with Matter

Imhotep and the Age of the Pyramids • Gilgamesh and Enkidu • Abraham and Melchizedek

AS LONG AS SOCIETY HAS EXISTED THERE have been small groups within it which have practised secret techniques to work themselves into alternative states of consciousness. They have done this in the belief that this alternative state of consciousness lends the power to perceive things inaccessible to ordinary, everyday consciousness.

The problem is that from the point of view of *today's* everyday consciousness, which is commonsensical and down to earth in a quite unprecedented way, everything seen in the alternative state is, almost by definition, delusional. If initiates of secret societies work themselves into hallucinatory states in which they communicate with disembodied beings, see the future and influence the course of history, then these things are just that – hallucinations.

But what if they can be shown to yield results?

We have begun to see how these states have inspired some of history's greatest art, literature and music, but all of that might be dismissed by someone minded to do so as merely a matter of the life of the imagination, something without any relevance to life's practical aspects. A lot of art, even great art, has an element of fantasy, after all.

Our modern mind-set prefers to see more concrete results. What about great feats of engineering or great scientific discoveries? In this chapter we will be following the development of an age when great initiates of the Mystery schools led humanity to some unequalled feats of engineering, from the temple of Baalbeck in Lebanon, which includes in its construction a block of carved granite weighing about a thousand tons that even today's strongest crane could not lift, to the Great Pyramid at Giza and other lesser known pyramids in China.

At the start of this age the first great civilizations seemed suddenly to spring from nowhere – in the Sumerian civilization dominated by the bull hero Gilgamesh, in the

Egypt of the bull cult of Osiris and in bull-running Crete. The age of these civilizations is the Age of Taurus, beginning early in the third millennium BC. For no very good reason conventional history can determine, vast numbers of people now began to live together in highly organized cities of extraordinary size, technical brilliance and complexity.

A SHADOWY BUT MOMENTOUS EVENT took place in China. It is shrouded in mystery. Even great initiates are unable to see it with anything approaching total clarity.

In the third millennium BC the people of China lived a tribal, nomadic existence and, according to Rudolf Steiner, it was into one of their encampments that an extraordinary individual was born. Just as thousands of years later another exalted heavenly being would descend to earth in order to incarnate as Jesus Christ, so now Lucifer incarnated too.

The birth of Lucifer was the beginning of wisdom.

Of course I'm using 'wisdom' in a particular sense – in fact the same sense academic, biblical scholars use it when they talk about 'the wisdom books of the Bible'. The wisdom contained, for example, in the Book of Proverbs or Ecclesiastes, is a collection of rules for a happy and successful life, but unlike the teachings contained in other biblical books there is no moral or religious dimension here. This wisdom is entirely prudential and practical, advising you what you must do to look after your own best interests. There is no suggestion, for example, that good behaviour is likely to be rewarded or bad behaviour punished, except by human agency. There is no notion either of a providential order.

These books, compiled in the form we now have them in about 300 BC, were the fruits of a way of thinking which had developed approximately two and a half thousand years earlier. The secret history proposes that this form of wisdom became possible as a result of the incarnation and ministry of Lucifer.

For the most part initiations into spiritual disciplines have taken place between childhood and adulthood and after many years of preparation. For example, initiation into the Cabala has traditionally only been permitted at the age of forty, and candidates for initiation into the school of Pythagoras had to live in isolation and without speaking for years before their education could begin. But from birth Lucifer was raised entirely within the confines of a Mystery school. A circle of magi worked intensively on his education, allowing him to take part in the most secret ceremonies, moulding his soul, until at the age of forty he finally had a revelation. He became the first person ever to be able to think about life on earth in an entirely rational way.

WE SAW IN CHAPTER 8 HOW ORPHEUS invented numbers. But in the age of Orpheus it had been impossible to think of numbers without also thinking of their spiritual meaning. Now, because of Lucifer, it became possible to think of numbers without any symbolic connotations, to think of numbers purely as measures of quantity unencumbered by any notions of quality. People were now free to measure, to calculate and to make and build.

We know from Plutarch that Orpheus's son Asclepius equated with Imhotep, who lived in about 2500 BC. By then this great wave of change, this revolutionary way of thinking had swept over from the Far East.

Vizier to the Egyptian King Djoser, Imhotep was known as the builder, the sculptor, the maker of stone vases. He was also called Chief of the Observers, which would become the title of the high priest of Heliopolis. Sometimes represented as wearing a mantle covered in stars, and sometimes, too, represented holding a rolled scroll, Imhotep was famous in antiquity as both as the great master builder and architect of the Step Pyramid at Saqqara. In the nineteenth century archaeologists excavating beneath the Step Pyramid discovered a store of secret treasures, sealed there since the founding of the building, that became known as the 'impossible things of Imhotep'. Some of these are on display today in the Metropolitan Museum in New York. Nineteenth-century commentators were amazed above all by the vases, which they suggested would be impossible for the craftsmen of the day to reproduce. Giraffe-necked and pot-bellied as they are, it's still difficult today to see how the rock crystal of these vases was hollowed out.

Half an hour's drive north from Saqqara is the Great Pyramid. Arguably the most magnificent building ever, it stands four-square at this crossroads in history, oriented to the cardinal points with remarkable accuracy. The world does not need another description of its magnificence. Suffice to say that although it would in principle be possible to rebuild it today, this would be crippling for all but the world's richest economies. It would also stretch modern engineering to the limits of its abilities, particularly in the exactitude of its astronomical orientations.

But what makes the Great Pyramid even more extraordinary, almost miraculous according to the secret history, is that the fact that it was the *first* Egyptian building.

Conventional historians have assumed that the building ambitions of the Egyptians progressed from simple one-storey tombs called *mastabas*, through the relative complexity of the Step Pyramid and culminated in the massive complexity and sophistication of the Great Pyramid, conventionally dated to 2500 BC. In the absence of contemporary textual accounts, and because these buildings contain no organic material that can be carbon-dated, and because up till now there has been no method of dating cut stone, this has perhaps seemed an eminently commonsensical way of interpreting the evidence.

I suggested at the beginning of this book that this is an upside-down, other-way-round history, and in the secret doctrine the Great Pyramid was built in 3500 BC, before the founding of the great civilizations of Egypt and Sumeria, at a time when the only previously existing constructions were the stone circles and other 'cyclopean' monuments.

We must imagine Stone Age peoples wearing animal skins and carrying primitive stone tools gazing at the Great Pyramid in stupefaction.

According to the secret history, then, the Step Pyramid and the other lesser pyramids represent not an ascent but a decline.

The Great Pyramid has conventionally been seen as a tomb. As a variation on this theme, prompted by the narrow shafts which point from out of the so-called King's and Queen's Chambers towards particular stars, it has been seen as a sort of machine designed to aid the projection of the dead pharaoh's spirit out of this tomb towards its heavenly resting place. On this view, then, the Great Pyramid is a sort of gigantic *excarnation* machine.

From the point of view of the secret history this interpretation is anachronistic. It was the universal belief at this time that all human spirits travelled up through the planetary spheres to the stars after death. In fact, as we have seen, the living still had such vivid experience of the spirit worlds that it would have been as hard for them to decide to disbelieve in the reality of the after-death journey as it would be hard for us to decide to disbelieve in the reality of the book or table in front of us.

We should look elsewhere for an explanation of the function of the Great Pyramid. The whole tenor of ancient Egyptian civilization is that it was trying to get to grips with matter. We see this in its innovatory drive to cut and carve stone.

We also see the new relation to matter in the practice of mummifying. We are never more ready to ascribe stupid beliefs to the ancients than when we link Egyptian mummification and elaborate grave goods to a supposed belief that the spirit might actually want to *use* these grave goods in the afterlife. The point of these burial practices, according to esoteric thought, is rather that they exerted a sort of magnetic attraction on the ascending spirit that would help it attain speedy reincarnation. It was believed that if the discarded body were preserved, it would remain a focus for the spirit that had left it, exerting an attraction that pulled it down to earth again.

The esoteric explanation of the Great Pyramid is similar. We saw in Chapter 7 that the great gods, finding it increasingly difficult to incarnate, had retreated as far as the moon, visiting the earth increasingly rarely.

The Great Pyramid is a gigantic incarnation machine.

EGYPTIAN CIVILIZATION REPRESENTS A great new impulse in human evolution, very different from the oriental civilization which had taught that matter is *maya*, or illusion. The Egyptians initiated the great spiritual mission of the West, sometimes called in alchemy, Sufism Freemasonry, and elsewhere in the secret societies, *the Work*. The mission was to work on matter, to cut it, carve it, to imbue it with intention until every particle of matter in the universe has been worked on and spiritualized. The Great Pyramid was the first manifestation of this urge.

THIS HISTORY IS ABOUT CONSCIOUSNESS in different ways.

First, this history has been told in various groups who have made it their aim to work themselves into altered states of consciousness.

Second, this history supposes that consciousness has changed over time in a far more radical way than conventional historians allow.

Third, it suggests that the mission of these groups is to lead the evolution of consciousness. In a mind-born universe the end and aim of creation is always mind.

I want to focus now on the second of these ways, to show that some academics have recently written in support of the esoteric view that consciousness used to be very different from what it is today.

Contemporary with the rise of Egyptian civilization in about 3250 BC Sumerian civilization arose in the land between the Tigris and the Euphrates. In the early cities of Sumeria statues to ancestors and lesser gods stood in family homes. A skull was sometimes kept as a 'house' that a minor spirit could inhabit. Meanwhile, the much greater spirit who protected the interests of the city was held to live in the 'god house', a building at the centre of the temple complex.

As these cities grew, so too did the god houses, until they became ziggurats, great rectangular, stepped pyramids, built out of mud bricks. In the centre of each ziggurat was a large chamber in which the statue of the god resided, inlaid with precious metals and jewels, and wrapped in dazzling clothes.

According to the cuneiform texts, the Sumerian gods liked eating, drinking, music and dancing. Food would be put on tables, then the god left alone to enjoy it. After a time the priests would come in and eat what was left. The gods also needed beds to sleep in and for enjoying sex with other gods. They had to be washed for this and dressed and anointed with perfumes.

As with the grave goods in Egypt, the aim of these practices was to try to tempt gods to inhabit the material plane, by reminding them of the sensual pleasures denied them in the spirit worlds.

The bee is one of the most important symbols in the secret tradition. Bees understand how to build their hives with a sort of pre-conscious genius. Bee-hives incorporate exceptionally difficult and precise data in their construction. For example, all hives have built into them the angle of the earth's rotation. Sumerian cylinder seals of this time show figures with human bodies but bees' nests for heads. This is because in this period an individual's consciousness was experienced as made up of a collaboration of many different centres of consciousness, in the way we described in Chapter 2. These centres could be shared or even moved from one mind to another like a swarm of bees from one hive to another.

Bee-hive headed Sumerian goddesses.

A brilliant analysis of Sumerian and other ancient texts by Princeton Professor of History Julian Jaynes was published in 1976. *The Origin of Consciousness in the Breakdown of the Bi-Cameral Mind* argued that during this period humans had no concept of an interior life as we understand it today. They had no vocabulary for it, and their narratives show that features of mental life, such as willing, thinking and feeling which we experience as somehow generated 'inside' us, they experienced as the activity of spirits or gods in and around their bodies. *These impulses happened to them at the bidding of disembodied beings that lived independently of them, rather than arising inside themselves at their own bidding.*

It is interesting that the Jaynes analysis chimes with the esoteric account of ancient history given by Rudolf Steiner. Born in Austria in 1861, Steiner represents a genuine stream of Rosicrucian thinking, and he is the esoteric teacher of modern times who has given the most detailed account of the evolution of consciousness. Jaynes's researches are, as far I know, independent of this tradition.

It is perhaps easier to appreciate Jaynes's analysis in relation to the more familiar Greek mythology. In the *Iliad*, for example, we never see anyone in any sense sit down and work out what to do, in the way we see ourselves doing. Jaynes shows that for the people of the *Iliad* there is no such thing as introspection. When Agamemnon robs Achilles of his mistress, Achilles does not decide to restrain himself. Rather, a god accosts him by the hair, warning him not to strike Agamemnon. Another god rises out of the sea to console him, and it is a god who whispers to Helen of homesick longing. Modern scholars tend to interpret these passages as 'poetic' descriptions of interior emotions, in

LEFT *The most famous depiction of other worldly suggestion is the statue in the Cairo Museum which shows Horus whispering in the ear of the pharaoh Kefren.*

ABOVE *Here Athena restrains Achilies from striking Agamemnon, in a drawing by Flaxman, who was an initiate of the secret societies, and a demon sits on the shoulder of a saint.*

which the gods were symbols of the sort a modern poet might create. Jaynes's clear-sighted reading shows that this interpretation reads present-day consciousness back into texts written by people whose form of consciousness was very different. Neither is Jaynes alone in his view. The Cambridge philosopher John Wisdom has written: 'The Greeks did not speak of the dangers of repressing instincts but they did think of thwarting Dionysius or of forgetting Poseidon for Athena.'

We shall see in the concluding chapters of this history how the ancient form of consciousness continued to thrive very much later than even Jaynes posits. For the moment, though, I want to touch on a significant difference between Jaynes's analysis and the way the ancients themselves understood things. Jaynes describes the gods who control the actions of the humans as being 'aural hallucinations'. The kings of Sumeria and heroes of Greece are depicted by him as being, in effect, beset by delusions. In the ancient view, by contrast, these were not, of course, mere delusions but independent, living beings.

Jaynes believes that everyone in the Homeric era and earlier lived in a world of delusion until, as he sees it, the right side of the brain gained supremacy over the left. In Jaynes's view, then, each individual, although believing himself addressed by a god equally present to everyone else, was in fact trapped in a private delusion. The problem with this view is that, because hallucinations are, almost by definition, non-consensual, it would lead you to expect these people to live in a totally chaotic and barbaric state, characterized by complete mutual misunderstanding. Modern clinical psychiatrists define a schizophrenic as someone who cannot distinguish between externally and internally generated images and sounds. Clinical madness causes extreme, disabling distress together with impairment of domestic, social and occupational functioning. Instead the people of this era constructed the first post-Flood civilizations with separation between priestly, military, agricultural, trading and manufacturing orders. Organized labour forces engineered great public edifices, including canals, ditches and, of course, temples. There were complex economies and large, disciplined armies. In order for these peoples to have cooperated surely the hallucinations would have had to be *group* hallucinations? If the ancient world-view was a delusion, it had to have been a massive, almost infinitely complex and sophisticated delusion.

What I have tried to present so far is a history of the world as it was understood by ancient peoples who had a mind-before-matter world-view in which everyone collectively experienced gods, angels and spirits as interacting with them.

Thanks to Freud and Jung we are all familiar with the idea that our minds contain psychological complexes which are independent of our centres of consciousness and so to some degree may be thought of as autonomous. Jung described these major psychological complexes in terms of the seven major planetary deities of mythology, calling them the seven major archetypes of the collective unconscious.

Yet when Jung met Rudolf Steiner, who believed in disembodied spirits, including the planetary gods, Jung dismissed Steiner as a schizophrenic. We shall see in Chapter 27 how very late in life, shortly before he died, Jung went beyond the pale as far as the modern scientific consensus goes. He concluded that these psychological complexes were autonomous in the sense of being *independent of the human brain altogether*. In this way Jung took one step further than Jaynes. By no longer seeing the gods as hallucinations – whether individual or collective – but as higher intelligences, he embraced the ancient mind-before-matter philosophy.

The reader should beware of taking the same step. It is important you be on your guard against any impression that perhaps – to be fair – this version of history hangs together in some way, or that it feels true in some unspecific poetic or, worse, *spiritual* way. Important because a momentary lapse of concentration in this regard and you might, without at first noticing it and with a light heart and a spring in your step, begin to walk down the road that leads straight to the lunatic asylum.

A representation on a cylinder seal of two heroes hunting, said to be Gilgamesh and Enkidu.

GILGAMESH, THE GREAT HERO OF SUMERIAN civilization, was king of Uruk in approximately 2100 BC. His story is full of madness, extreme emotion, anxiety and alienation. The great poet Rainer Maria Rilke called it 'the epic of death-dread'.

The story as laid out here has largely been pieced together from clay tablets excavated in the nineteenth century, but it seems nearly complete.

At the start of his story the young king is called the 'butting bull'. He is bursting with energy, opening mountain passes, digging wells, exploring, going into battle. He is stronger than any other man, beautiful, courageous, a great lover from whom no virgin is safe – but lonely. He longs for a friend, someone who is his equal.

So the gods created Enkidu. He was as strong as Gilgamesh but was wild, with matted hair all over his body. He lived among wild beasts, ate as they did and drank from streams. One day a hunter came face to face with this strange creature in the woods and reported back to Gilgamesh.

When he heard the hunter's story, Gilgamesh knew in his heart that this was the friend he had been waiting for. He devised a brilliant plan. He instructed the most beautiful of the temple prostitutes to go naked into the woods, to find the wild man and tame him. When she made love to him he forgot, as Gilgamesh had known he would, about his home in the hills. Now when Enkidu came across wild animals they sensed the difference and no longer ran with him – they ran away from him.

When Gilgamesh and Enkidu met in the marketplace at Uruk there was a wrestling match of champions. The whole population crowded round to watch. Gilgamesh finally won, flinging Enkidu on to his back while still keeping his own foot on the ground.

So a famous friendship started a series of adventures. They hunted panthers and tracked down the monstrous Hawawa who guarded the way though the cedar forest. When they later slew the bull of heaven, Gilgamesh had the horns mounted on the walls of his bed chamber.

But then Enkidu fell dangerously sick. Gilgamesh sat by his bed six days and seven nights. Finally a worm fell out of Enkidu's nose. At the end Gilgamesh drew a veil across his old friend's face and roared like a lioness that has lost her cubs. Later he roamed the steppe, weeping, fear of his own death beginning to gnaw at his entrails.

Gilgamesh ended up at the tavern at the end of the world. He wanted to get out of his head. He asked the beautiful barmaid the way to Ziusudra, whom, we have seen, is another name for Noah or Dionysus. Ziusudra was a demi-god who had never really died.

Gilgamesh made a boat with punting poles topped with bitumen, such as are still used by marsh Arabs to this day, and went to meet the seer. Ziusudra said, 'I will reveal to you a secret thing, a secret of the gods. There is at the bottom of the sea a plant that pricks like the rose. If you can bring it back up to the surface, you can become young again. It is the plant of eternal youth.'

Ziusudra was telling him how to dive beneath the seas that covered Atlantis, how to find the esoteric lore that had been lost at the time of the Flood. Gilgamesh tied stones to his feet like the local pearl-divers, descended, plucked the plant, cut himself free of the stones and rose to the surface in triumph.

But while he was resting on the shore from his exertions, a snake smelled the plant and stole it.

Gilgamesh was as good as dead.

WHEN WE READ THE STORY OF GILGAMESH we may be intrigued to see how he fails the test that humanity's great leader has set him. There is a note of anxiety here that can then be heard spreading ever more widely in the Babylonian and Mesopotamian civilizations that grew up to dominate this region.

With the death of Gilgamesh we are in the time of the greatest ziggurats. The story of the Tower of Babel, the attempt to build a tower up to heaven and the resulting loss of a single language uniting all humanity, represents the fact that as nations and tribes began to become attached to their own tutelary spirits and guiding angels, they lost sight of the higher gods and the great cosmic mind beyond that gives all the different parts of the universe one destiny. The ziggurats represent a misguided attempt to scale the heavens by material means.

The Tower of Babel was built by Nimrod the Hunter. Genesis calls Nimrod 'the first potentate on earth'. The archaeologist David Rohl has convincingly identified Nimrod

llustration to The Wizard of Oz. *Frank Baum was a Theosophist who encoded esoteric wisdom in his most famous book. The animal, vegetable and mineral bodies are symbolized by the Cowardly Lion, the Scarecrow and the Tin Man respectively. 'Oz' is a cabalistic word with a geometric meaning of seventy-seven, illustrating the force of magic acting on matter.*

with the historical Enmer-kar ('Enmer the Hunter'), the first king of Uruk who wrote to the neighbouring king of Aratta, demanding tribute money in what is believed to be the earliest surviving letter.

Nimrod was the first man to seek power for its own sake. From this will to power came cruelty and decadence. In Hebrew tradition a prophecy of the imminent birth of Abraham prompted Nimrod to mass infanticide. We should understand by this that he practised infant sacrifice, burying the bodies in the foundations of his great buildings.

We join the secret story of Abraham in about 2000 BC wandering in between the sky scrapers of his native Ur (Uruk). He decided to go on a quest, to become a desert nomad to rediscover the sense of the divine that was in the process of being lost.

When he visited Egypt the pharaoh gave one of his daughters, Hagar, as a servant to Abraham's wife Sarai. Hagar bore Abraham his first son, Ishmael, who was to become the father of the Arab nations. We should understand by this that Abraham learned great initiatic knowledge from the Egyptian priests. Marriages of this time were usually within a tribe or extended family. Supernatural powers were connected with blood, and marriage between people of the same blood strengthened powers, something which used to be a part of the tradition of the gypsies, for example. Marriage of individuals from different tribes could involve an exchange of powers and knowledge.

WHAT FORM OF INITIATION MIGHT ABRAHAM have received in Egypt?

We should picture the candidate for initiation laid out in a granite tomb. He is surrounded by initiates who have sent him into a very deep sleep-like trance. When he is in this trance state they are able to raise his vegetable body – and with it his spirit or animal body – up out of his physical body, so that it hovers like a phantom over the mouth of the tomb. A witness of an initiation ceremony practised on the Irish poet W.B. Yeats described how

The weaving together of cosmic emanations to form the illusion of the material world is called the Matrix in the alchemical tradition. Still from the movie The Matrix, *in which the threshold between the material world and the 'real' world behind it is policed by menacing, supernatural figures wearing shades.*

None of the Surrealists recalled the vegetable age of the cosmos as often or as vividly as Max Ernst. His contemporary Gaudi also remembered the vegetable age in his architecture, in his daily devotions and even in his diet of milk and lettuce. This age still exists in a parallel dimension. W.Q. Judge, a Theosophist who was a contemporary of both artists, described this place as being 'as full of strange sights and sounds as an untrodden South American forest.'

The earliest matter was finer than gas or even light and only very gradually hardened into the solid matter we know today. Human bodies also passed through this process, bone passing through a pink waxy stage, written about by the Rosicrucian philosopher Jacob Boehme and illustrated here by Hieronymus Bosch.

LEFT *The Luciferic serpent entwined round the tree is the clearest possible image of the introducing of animal life into vegetable life – and also of the forming of the spine characteristic of animals. The serpent was necessary for the development of animal life, but also gave rise to the possibility of lust, rage, delusion – and evil.* Sin *by the nineteenth-century German artist Franz von Stuck.*

BELOW *Evil spirits find it hard to break out of the dimension in which they belong and into the mundane world, but sometimes uninitiated meddling can lead to this happening, so that entire communities become overrun and possessed by a terrifying and often sexual savagery. This is vividly portrayed in the films of David Lynch and in the TV series* Twin Peaks.

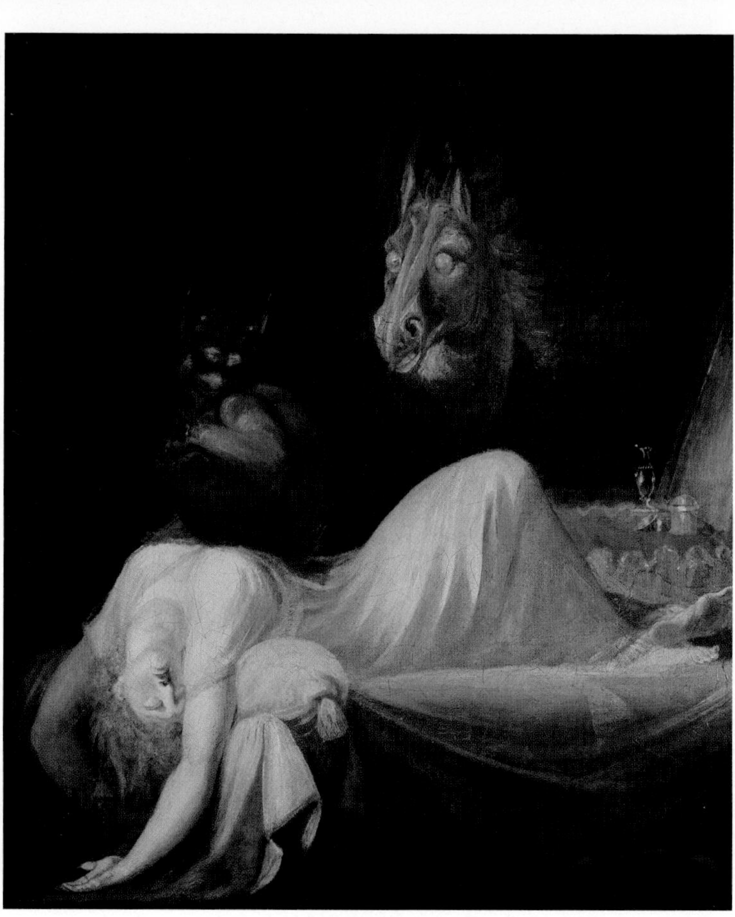

LEFT Nightmare. *Deeply knowledgeable about esoterica, the Swiss artist Henry Fuseli is here depicting a demon from the Dark Side of the Moon.*

ABOVE *Antique gem engraving by the Roman, Aspasius. In esoteric tradition myths of gods taking human lovers who are then transformed into plants and animals are an account of the proliferation of biological forms.*

BELOW *Before human anatomy developed into the form we are familiar with today, a 'Third Eye' protruded from the middle of the forehead. By means of this we were able to perceive Mother Nature and receive her wisdom. One of the famous tapestries in the Cluny Museum in Paris.*

ABOVE *This painting of* The Temptation of St Anthony *by the Dutch artist Domenicus van Wijnen has unusually explicit esoteric themes. All the great religions are idealist, in the sense of believing that matter was formed out of emanations from the cosmic mind. What distinguishes the esoteric element of these religions is seeing these emanations as spirits or angels associated with the Sun and Moon and the planets of the solar system.*

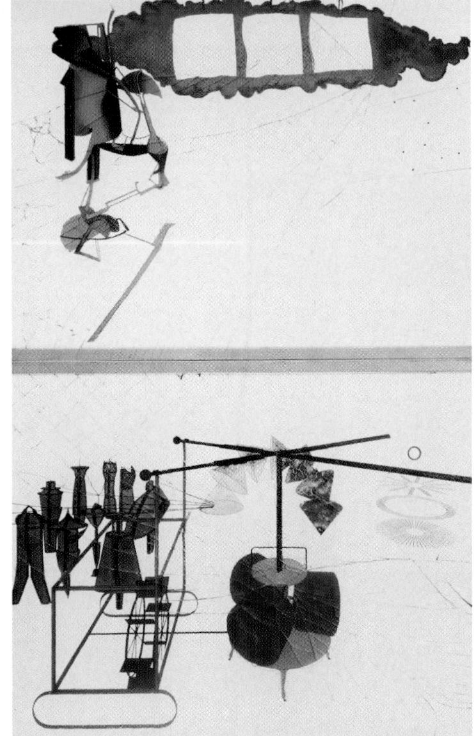

RIGHT A Bride Stripped Bare by her Bachelors, Even *by Marcel Duchamp. Stripped bare, the bride reveals herself to be Sophia, or esoteric wisdom, adored by the seven great spirits of the solar system. A cool, modern depiction of esoteric cosmology by a twentieth-century devotee of the Hermetica.*

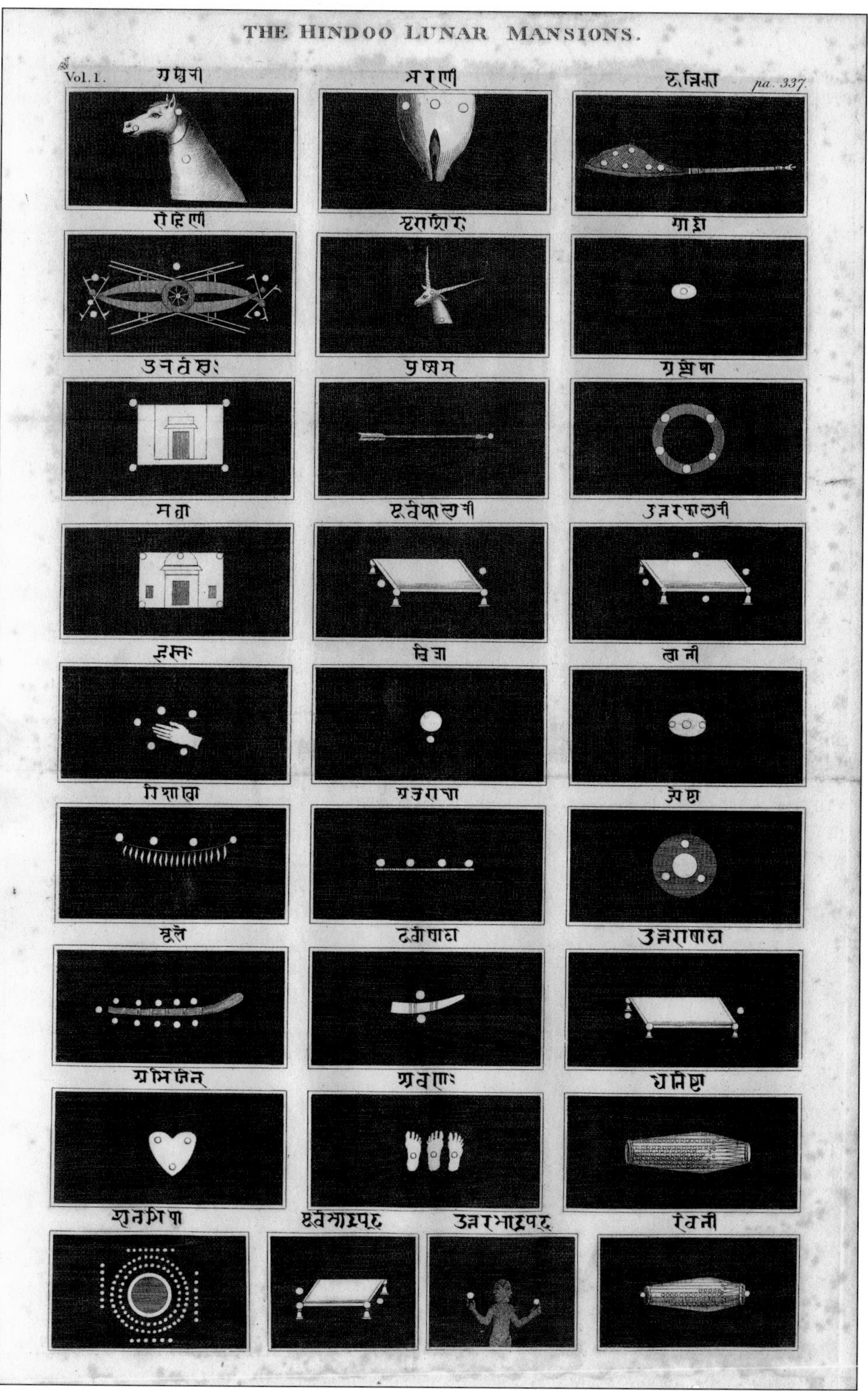

Moor's Hindoo Houses of the Moon. *The early nineteenth-century British traveller Edward Moor recorded these ancient Hindu symbols of the phases of the Moon. Esoteric philosophers have always observed these closely, believing that they bring about changes not only in tides and the forms of plants – but also human consciousness.*

Andrea Mantegna's Minerva chases vices from the garden of virtue. *A Neolithic landscape seen with today's eye would only discern a wilderness with few signs of human life, perhaps a few stones piled up and people wearing little more than animal skins. Seen through the consciousness of the time, it would have looked as Mantegna here depicts it, with gods, goddesses and spirits gorgeously arrayed, playing their parts in the great events that helped give our consciousness the structure it has today. Which version is more true, more* real?

LEFT *After death the human spirit is attacked by demons tearing its sins from it. In the process of initiation the candidate experiences the after-death journey while still alive, which will be of great benefit to him in this life and the next. This process of initiation is what is being depicted here on a panel of the* Isenheim altarpiece *by Matthias Grünewald.*

RIGHT *Detail from a panel of* The Garden of Earthly Delights. *Following the experience of* kama loca *or purgatory, the spirit rises through the heavenly spheres, before descending again into the next incarnation. This descent is what is being depicted here by Hieronymus Bosch, whose paintings are impossible to decipher without esoteric knowledge.*

In the esoteric account of history, great climate catastrophe involves a shift in consciousness. The Flood that came at the end of the Ice Age saw the submersion of the scene of the great events of early human evolution – and the forming of the subconscious. Print from a nineteenth-century Bible.

The esoteric tradition is concerned with nurturing altered states of consciousness – but not with a fuzzy mysticism. In these altered states a supernatural intelligence can be accessed which yields practical results. In the Bible, Joseph's immersion in an underground pit is a coded account of his initiation. His dreams helped the pharaoh to save his people from starvation. Print from a nineteenth-century Bible.

West pinx
SAUL AND THE WITCH OF ENDOR.
1. Samuel, Chap. XXVIII. ver. 11.
London Published by Thomas Kelly Paternoster Row Jan 4 1814

Some modern Christians have a horror of the supernatural, but of course the Bible is full of it. Here a shade is summoned up from the Underworld by the Witch of Endor. Print from a nineteenth-century Bible.

B. Picart del.

The Jesuit, Athanasius Kircher was a great scholar of arcana with links to several of the leading players in this history. His works included these pictures of the Mother Goddess, Cybele, and one of the earliest Western depictions of the Buddha, showing esoteric understanding of the vegetable dimension of the human body.

during the course of the ceremony a series of bells were rung to mark the stages. Yeats's spirit could be seen shining with different degrees of brightness during the different stages, each marked by different patterns of colour.

Initiates who perform these sorts of ceremonies know how to mould the candidate's vegetable body so that when it sinks back into the material body the candidate is able to work to use its organs of perception consciously. At the end of three days the candidate will be 'born again', or initiated, which is marked by the hierophant grasping him by the right hand and pulling him out of the coffin.

In esoteric philosophy the vegetable body is of utmost importance. Not only does it control vital bodily functions, but the chakras are, of course, the organs of the vegetable body. So this body in effect forms the portal between the physical world and the spirit world, and if the chakras are enlivened this may lead to powers of supernatural perception and influence, the ability to communicate with disembodied spirits and also healing powers.

In the temple sleep – which would still be practised by initiates of the Mystery schools two and half thousand years later, and is still practised in some secret societies today – someone who was ill would be allowed to sleep in the temple. This sleep would last for three days, during which time the initiates would work on their vegetative bodies in a way which was not dissimilar to the process of initiation.

Someone undergoing this healing process might have very realistic visions, directed by the initiates. First, he would be plunged in utter blackness. He would seem to himself to be losing all consciousness, to be dying. He would seem to himself to come round again, then be led by an animal-headed being travelling down long passages and through a series of chambers. At different stages he would be challenged and menaced by other animal-headed gods and demons, including monstrous crocodiles who would tear at him.

In the Egyptian *Book of the Dead* the candidate makes his way past these guardians of the thresholds by proclaiming, 'I am the Gnostic, I am the one who knows.' This is a magical formula he uses in the process of initiation and will be able to use again after death.

He approaches the inner sanctum. He sees an extraordinary, bright light shining through the cracks round the edge of the gates. He cries out, 'Let me come! Let me spiritualize myself, let me become pure spirit! I have prepared myself by the writings of Thoth!'

Finally, out of the swirling waves of light a vision emerges of the Mother Goddess suckling her child. This is a healing vision because it takes us back to the paradisaical time we looked at in Chapter 3, before the earth and the sun became separated, when the earth was illumined from within by the Sun god, a time before there was any dissatisfaction, disease or death. And it looks forward, too, to another time when earth and sun will be reunited, when the earth will again be transfigured by the sun.

In all ages and in all places there have been people who have believed that meditating on this image of the Mother Goddess and child brings about miracles of healing.

AFTER HIS STAY IN EGYPT ABRAHAM moved westwards, towards the region we know today as Palestine. He had to arm and train his servants to rescue his brother who had been captured by local bandits. Following a fierce and bloody fight, he was walking through a valley (which today's biblical scholars identify with the Kidron Valley), when he met a strange individual called Melchizedek.

As with Enoch, there is just a brief mention of Melchizedek in the Bible but an accompanying sense of the numinous and of something important left unsaid. Genesis 14: 18–20: 'And Melchizedek king of Salem brought forth bread and wine and he was the priest of the most high God. And he blessed him and said "Blessed be Abram of the most high God, possessor of heaven and earth and blessed be the most high God, which hath delivered thine enemies into thy hand." This sense of the numinous is reinforced by a

Melchizedek features in art and literature quite out of proportion to the brief mention of him in the Bible. For example, he features prominently in France's most esoteric ecclesiastical statuary, for example, here in the North Porch of Chartres Cathedral. He is traditionally shown bearing the chalice or grail.

mysterious passage in the New Testament, Hebrews 6.20–7.17: 'Jesus was made an high priest for ever after the order of Melchizedek. For this Melchizedek, king of Salem, priest of the most high God, who met Abraham returning from the slaughter of the kings, and blessed him; to whom Abraham also gave a tenth part of all, first being by interpretation King of righteousness and after that also King of Salem, which is, King of peace; *without father, without mother, without descent, having neither beginning of days, nor end of life; but made like unto the Son of God; abideth a priest continually ... Who is made, not after the law of a carnal commandment, but after the power of an endless life.* For he testifieth Thou art a priest forever under the order of Melchizedek.'

Clearly something strange is going on. Clearly this mysterious individual, who has the ability to live forever, is no ordinary human being.

In cabalistic tradition Melchizedek's secret identity is Noah, the great Atlantean leader who had taught humankind agriculture, the cultivation of corn and of the vine, who never really died but moved to another dimension. He now reappeared in order to be Abraham's spiritual teacher, to initiate him to a higher level.

In order to understand Melchizedek's initiatic teaching, we must examine a later episode when, according to the ancient tradition, Melchizedek was present, even though this is hidden in the biblical version.

Isaac was twenty two years old when his father took him up a mountain to sacrifice him *on the altar of Melchizedek.*

IT IS VERY IMPORTANT IN CERTAIN FORMS of initiation that at a particular point in the ceremony the candidate believes, perhaps briefly but with total conviction, that he or she is going to die.

He has perhaps understood that he is going to undergo a symbolic death, but it suddenly dawns upon him that there may have been a change of plan. Perhaps he has sworn the most solemn oaths on pain of death that he will mend his ways and live up to high ideals. Now with the blade held against him, he wonders if the initiates who have him in their power know that he has lied to them. He knows, now he comes to think about it, that he has done things he ought not to have done, not done the things he ought to have done, that there is no health in him. He knows in his heart of hearts he does not have enough willpower to keep the oaths he has sworn. He has just condemned himself to death out of his own mouth, and he is utterly unable to help himself.

At this point he realizes he needs supernatural help.

We may catch a faint echo of these emotions of fear and pity if we are moved by a great tragedy, by *Oedipus Rex* or *King Lear*. In initiation the candidate is made to feel the tragedy of his own life, an overwhelming need for catharsis. He begins to judge his own lives as the demons and angels will judge it after death.

AS ABRAHAM'S KNIFE BEGAN TO SLICE open Isaac's throat, an angel substituted a ram whose horns had been caught in a nearby thicket.

What the thorns in the thicket represent is the two-petalled – or two horned – brow chakra, already entangled in matter. Abraham acts as he does because this mode of vision would have to be sacrificed. For the time being at least, perception of the spirit worlds must be put to sleep for the sake of the mission of the ancestors of Abraham – to develop the brain as an organ of thinking.

The Jews will be guided by Jehovah, the great spirit of the moon, the great god of thou-shalt-not who helps humanity evolve away from animal and ecstatic experience, away from the life of tribal or group soul towards the development of individual free will and free thinking.

In the secret history this sacrifice of the brow chakra takes place on the altar of Melchizedek, the great high priest of the Sun Mysteries. What this signifies is that Isaac was initiated to such a level that he understood the necessity for this next, lunar stage of human development. The evolution of individual free will and free thinking will eventually enable humans to play a conscious part in the transforming of the world.

Isaac stayed at the Mystery school of Melchizedek for three and a half years learning of these things.

Because Melchizedek is a priest of the Sun Mysteries, this school should be pictured as containing within its precincts a stone circle. We have reached the great age of these sun temples, examples of which still survive in Lüneberg in Germany, Carnac in France and Stonehenge in England. In the fourth century BC the historian Diodorus of Sicily described a spherical sun temple in the north, dedicated to Apollo. Today scholars believe he was describing Stonehenge or, more likely, Callanish in the far north of Scotland, but in either case the association with Apollo should be understood as a looking forward to the rebirth of the Sun god from the womb of the Mother Goddess.

THE OTHER GREAT CONTRIBUTION TO THE development of thought came, of course, from the Greeks.

The siege of Troy marks the beginning of the rise to greatness of Greek civilization, when the Greeks seized the initiative from Chaldean–Egyptian civilization and forged their own ideals.

We have been tracing a history of the world in which – for the first time – the lives of great cultural heroes from around the world – Adam, Jupiter, Hercules, Osiris, Noah, Zarathustra, Krishna and Gilgamesh – have been woven together into one chronological narrative. For the most part they have left no physical traces, living on only in the collective imagination, preserved only in surviving scraps of story and scattered imagery.

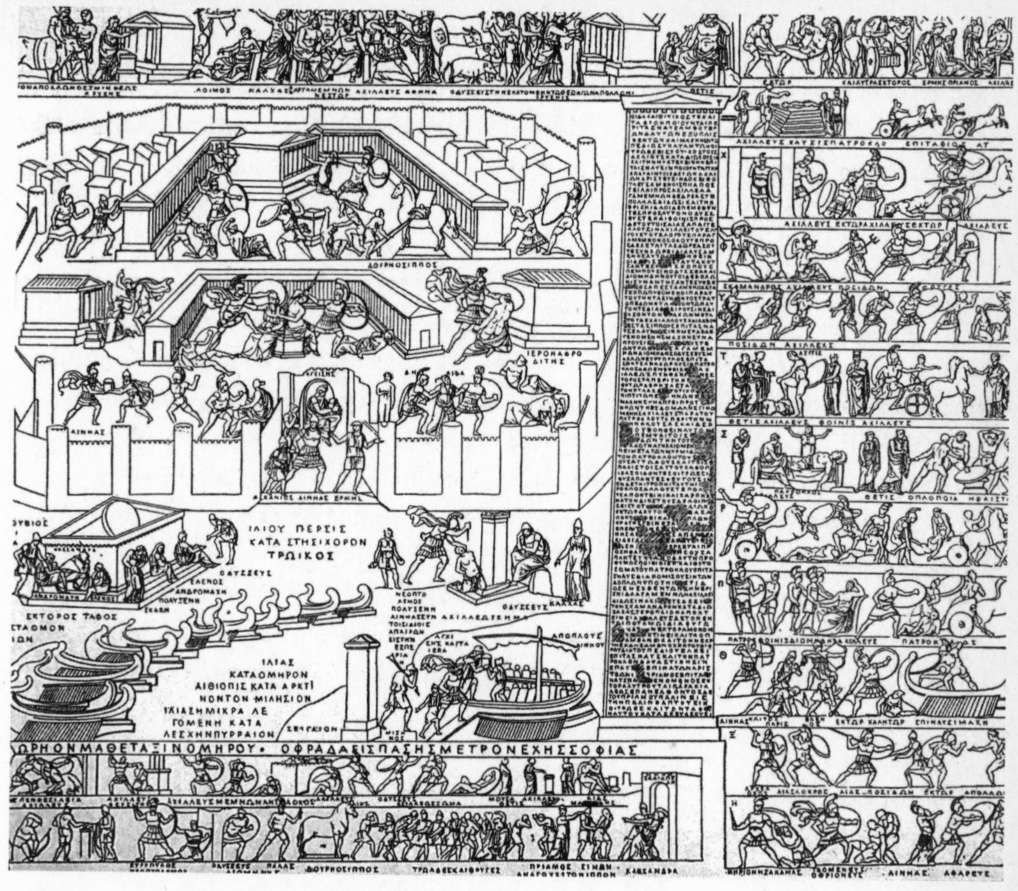

The Trojan horse is depicted in the bottom panel. The story of the siege of Troy has come down to us, for the most part, in the account by 'blind Homer'. In the language of the secret societies 'blind' is not necessarily meant literally. In the case of Homer it may mean he was an initiate, whose gaze was directed at the spiritual rather than the material world. Florence and Kenneth Wood have shown that the Iliad *can be read as an astronomical allegory. But, as we have seen, this does not imply that it is not also a real historical event. As an initiate Homer would have been conscious of the great gods of stars and planets guiding the life below.*

From now on, though, we will see that many legendary figures, presumed by most people to be entirely non-historical, have in fact been shown by recent archaeology to have left physical remains.

The discovery of the ruins of Troy by the German archaeologist Heinrich Schliemann in the 1870s has always been controversial. The archaeological layer he excavated probably dates to 3000 BC, and so is far too old to be Homer's, but today the majority of scholars agree that the layer relating to 1200 BC, in the late Bronze Age, is consistent with Homer's account.

In the ancient world wars were fought for the possession of sacred, initiatic knowledge, partly because of the supernatural powers this conferred. The Greeks fought because they wanted to carry off the statue made by the hand of Athena, called the Palladium. We should see their struggle to possess Helen in the same way.

Today we may see in the face of a beauty 'the promise of happiness', to use Stendhal's phrase. Yes, we may cherish that promise in a crude or trivial sense, but we may also do so in a deeper sense. Great beauty can seem mystical to us, as if it holds the very secret of life. If I could be with that beautiful person, we think, my life would be fulfilled. The presence of exceptional beauty can induce an altered state of consciousness, and male initiates have often been associated with very beautiful women, perhaps partly because their participation intensifies the secret sexual techniques of the schools.

Possession of Helen would enable the Greeks to move forward to the next stage of civilization.

We see the change consciousness that the story of the siege of Troy is all about in the famous saying of Achilles: 'Better to be a slave in the land of the living than the king of the shades.' The heroes of Greece and Troy loved to live in the sun and it was a terrible thing

Odysseus blinding the one-eyed giant Polyphemus, shows the progenitor of the new way of thinking destroying the old Third-Eyed one. The parallel story of David and Goliath, of some two hundred years later, when David slays the giant with a pebble aimed at the middle of the forehead, shows that such stragglers from earlier dispensations were still then a historical reality.

when it was suddenly shut out, and their spirits were sent off to the land of the shades, the Western gloom. This was the 'death-dread' of Gilgamesh intensified to a level that seems almost modern.

Note that Achilles was not doubting the reality of life after death, but his conception of it evidently did not go beyond the dreary, half-life of the sub-lunar sphere. A vision of the heavenly spheres above had been lost to him.

We can see this turning point in consciousness from another angle if we ask ourselves who out of the heroes really won the battle of Troy for the Greeks? It was not the brave, strong hero Achilles, the almost-invincible last of the demi-gods. It was Odysseus 'of the nimble wits', who defeated the Trojans by tricking them into accepting the gift of a wooden horse, which had soldiers hidden inside.

To today's sensibility the story of the Trojan Horse seems almost completely implausible. From the point of view of modern psychology it just seems unrealistic to suppose that anyone could be so gullible.

But at the time of the Trojan war, people were only just beginning to emerge from the collective mind we followed earlier walking through the ancient wood and have just seen Jaynes define. Before the Trojan war everyone shared the same world of thoughts. Others could see what you were thinking. No such lie would have been possible. People interacted with a terrible sincerity. They had a sense that we have lost that in everything they did they were taking part in cosmic events.

... the date of the siege of Troy is also the date of the first trick in history.

12

The Descent into Darkness

Moses and the Cabala • Akhenaten and Satan • Solomon, Sheba and Hiram • King Arthur and the Crown Chakra

EGYPTIAN CIVILIZATION IS PERHAPS THE most successful in recorded history, lasting over three thousand years. Compare this with European-American, Christian civilization, which has so far lasted only about two thousand years. Another notable thing is Egypt's extraordinarily well preserved historical records, which have survived on temple walls, on tablets and in papyri. These have been vital in placing neighbouring civilizations that have left less complete records and remains, in a chronological context.

The Exodus of the Hebrews from Egypt has traditionally been placed in the reign of the pharaoh Ramasees II, one of the greatest and most expansive rulers of Egypt. A great builder at Luxor and Abu Simbel, his monuments also include the gigantic obelisk currently standing in La Place de la Concorde in Paris. In the Romantic poet Shelley's *Ozymandias*, he became the archetype of the earthly ruler who comes to believe his achievements will last forever – 'Look on my works, ye Mighty, and despair!'

A worthy opponent for Moses, you might think. Cecil B. De Mille certainly thought so. But a problem has arisen. Archaeologists discovered that if you look for traces of the Hebrews in the reign of Ramasees II, or if you look, for example, for traces of the fall of Jericho or the Temple of Solomon in the corresponding archaeological layers, you find absolutely nothing.

This led to a consensus among academics that the epic myths of the origins of the Jews were 'just myths', in the sense that they had no basis in historical reality.

Is it worth pausing for a moment to wonder how much these people *wanted* the stories to be untrue, how much their convictions were informed by a sort of adolescent glee at the nursery certainties being overturned?

In the 1990s a group of younger archaeologists, based in Austria and London and led by David Rohl, began to question the conventional chronology of Egypt. More particularly they came to realize that in the period of the Third Intermediate Dynasty, two king lists which had been understood to run one after the other should really be understood as running concurrently.

This had the effect of 'shortening' the chronology of ancient Egypt by approximately four hundred years. Known as the 'New Chronology', it is gradually gaining ground even among the older generation of Egyptologists.

An incidental side effect of the New Chronology – I say 'incidental' because these scholars have no religious axe to grind – was that when field archaeologists began to search for traces of the biblical stories some four hundred years earlier, they made sensational discoveries.

The human condition gives us extraordinary latitude for believing what we want to believe, but for anyone who does not have a strong ulterior motive for believing that the biblical stories are 'just fairy tales', this new evidence is quite compelling.

It shows that Moses did not live in about 1250 BC contemporary with Ramasees II. Instead he was born in about 1540 BC, and the Exodus took place in approximately 1447 BC. Using astronomical retro calculations, Venus observations recorded in Mesopotamian texts that cross-reference both the Bible and also surviving Egyptian records, David Rohl has provided strong evidence to show that Moses was brought up an Egyptian prince in the reign of Neferhotep I in the mid-sixteenth century BC. Rohl has found complementary evidence in an account by Artapanus, a Jewish historian of the third century BC who may well have had access to now lost records from the Egyptian temples. Artapanus related how 'Prince Mousos' became a popular administrator under Khenephres, Neferhotep I's successor. Mousos was then was sent into exile when the pharaoh became jealous of him. Finally Rohl has shown that the pharaoh of the Exodus was Khenephres's successor, Dudimose. Excavations at the Dudimose level have revealed the remains of a foreign settlement of slaves or workers – such as are also referred to in the Brooklyn Papyrus, a royal decree authorizing transfer of just such a group at just this time. This settlement may have been built for and by the Hebrews. There are also death pits and evidence of hasty, mass burials which may be traces of the biblical plagues.

Unearthing stone remains may ground us in historical reality, but in order to understand what was really important in human terms, *what it felt like to be there*, the highest and deepest that human experience had to offer, we must turn again to the secret tradition.

AS AN EGYPTIAN PRINCE MOSES WAS initiated in the Egyptian Mysteries. This is recorded by the Egyptian historian Manetho, who identified Heliopolis as the Mystery school. It is confirmed in Acts 7.22, where the Apostle Stephen says, 'And Moses was instructed in all the wisdom of the Egyptians.'

The teachings of Moses are steeped in Egyptian wisdom. For example, Spell 125 in the *Book of the Dead* describes the judgement of the dead. The spirit is required to declare to Osiris that he has led a good life, then deny having committed a list of specific immoral acts to the forty-two judges of the dead: 'I have not robbed, I have not killed, I have not born false witness' and so on. Of course this *predates* the Ten Commandments.

It is no denigration of Moses to point this out. His teaching could not have done otherwise than grow out of the given historical milieu. What is historically significant about Moses is the way he reframed the ancient wisdom with the aim of leading humankind into the next stage of the evolution of consciousness.

When Moses fled into exile in the desert, he encountered a wise, old teacher. Jethro was an African – Ethiopian – high priest, keeper of a library of stone tablets. When Moses married his daughter, Jethro initiated him to a higher level. This is what is being alluded to in the story of the burning bush. When Moses saw the burning bush not being consumed by the fire, this was a vision of the self that is not destroyed by the purging fire that awaits on the other side of the grave.

A sense of mission arose out of Moses's vision of the burning bush, an impulse to work for the greater good of humanity, to lead us all to a land flowing with milk and honey.

But then, as Moses hesitated before the magnitude of the task in front of him, God stiffened his resolve: 'And thou shalt take this rod in thy hand, wherewith thou shalt do signs.' As Moses journeyed back to Egypt, he intended to ask the pharaoh to 'set my people free'.

As Moses and his brother Aaron stood in the throne room, Aaron suddenly threw his rod down to the ground. It changed, magically, into a snake. The pharaoh ordered his court magicians to match this feat, but as they did so Aaron's snake swallowed theirs.

As the battle of wills between Moses and the pharaoh unfolded, Moses used his own rod – or wand – to direct the course of events: to bring fire and hail down from the sky, to bring on a plague of locusts, to part the Red Sea, to strike a rock to cause water to gush out of it.

What does this mean? I suspect many readers may be well ahead of me already, but the folk legend that this rod was carved out of wood that originally came from the tree in the Garden of Eden points to its deeper meaning. The rod is part of the vegetable dimension of the cosmos. By mastering it and manipulating it as it runs through his own body, Moses, now an adept, was also able to master and manipulate the cosmos around him.

Later, after Moses had given up trying to persuade the pharaoh to set his people free and had led them out into the Sinai desert, he came down from the mountain with the tablets of stone. Moses proved to be a hard taskmaster, in some ways harder than the pharaohs. Again and again his people failed to live up to his demands. At one point they were punished by a plague of fiery and deadly serpents (Numbers 7.19). To save them Moses nailed a bronze serpent across a raised horizontal pole.

John 3:14 comments on his passage in the Old Testament: 'And just as Moses lifted up the serpent in the wilderness, so must the Son of Man be lifted up.'

Clearly John is seeing the bronze serpent as foreshadowing the crucified Jesus Christ. 'Lifted up' carries with it a sense of being transformed or transfigured. The bronze serpent has been smelted, and so looks forward, John suggests, to the transfiguration of the material body of humanity.

The rod that Moses used to smite the Egyptians and to discipline his own people was an image of the Lucifer-serpent of animal consciousness that has been straightened and subdued by willpower and a moral discipline that is very hard to maintain.

The great gift Moses gave his people, then, was guilt. Morality emerges into history with Moses and with it a call to a change of heart.

If we look at the Ten Commandments from the perspective of the esoteric doctrine, what is most significant is the way that the first two commandments banned the use of images in religious practice and called upon the Jews to worship no other gods. Following Abraham, Moses was working towards a new kind of religion that did away with the practices of older religions with their elaborate, overwhelming ceremonies, the loud clashing cymbals, the blinding clouds of smoke and speaking idols. The old religion aimed to diminish consciousness. The worshippers would attain access to the spirit worlds but in an uncontrolled way, in the great, overwhelming and riotous visions of the followers of Osiris. It was this that Moses was concerned to roll back and replace with a thoughtful, more conscious communion with the divine.

By this ban on images, Moses was helping to create the conditions that would make abstract thought possible.

THE TEN COMMANDMENTS AND THE other laws of Exodus and Deuteronomy form Moses's public teaching. They are for all the people. In esoteric tradition he also taught seventy elders the Cabala, the secret, mystical teachings of Judaism, at the same time.

The Cabala is as broad a church as a major world religion, and we will be returning to different aspects of it.

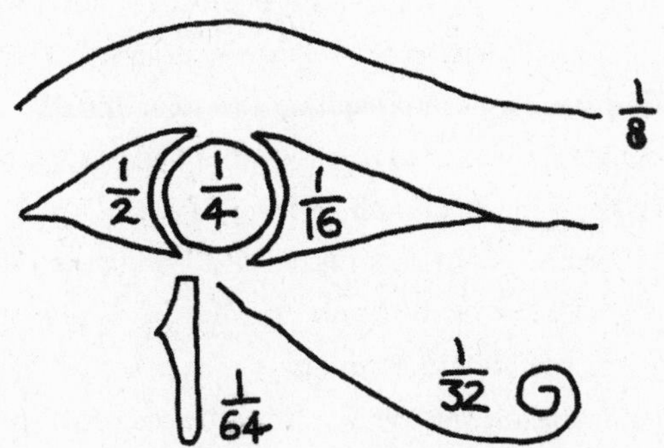

The udja eye as a series of fractions.

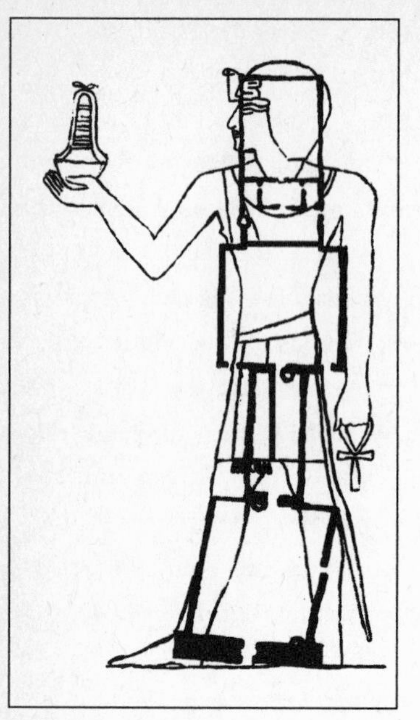

In sacred idealism the human form is a microcosm of the universe. The divine proportions can be found not just in ammonites and nebulae but also in the human body. The renegade Egyptologist R.A. Schwaller de Lubicz spent fifteen years on site tracing the divine-mathematical proportions of the Temple of Luxor. He showed how the ritual laying of the foundation and consecration of the temple was called the ceremony of Giving the House to its Master. Likewise in Hinduism, he wrote, the building of a temple in the form of a human body was a magical process. It was believed that if the overseer of the work of building a temple had made a mistake in the construction of a particular part of a temple, he would suffer an illness or injury in the corresponding part of his own body.

Again, it is no denigration of Moses or the Cabala to point out that it grew out of an older tradition, the mystical number system of the Egyptians.

Reams of mathematical calculations have not come down to us from ancient Egypt, but their understanding of higher mathematics has survived in Egyptian art. For example, the eye of Horus was often represented as the udja eye, which we now know was made up of a number of hieroglyphs representing fractions which add up to a total of 63/64. If you reverse this and divide 64 by 63, you come up with what has been called the greatest secret of the Egyptians, a number called the Comma of Pythagoras.

Highly complex numbers like the Comma of Pythagoras, Pi and Phi (sometimes called the Golden Proportion), are known as irrational numbers. They lie deep in the structure of the physical universe, and were seen by the Egyptians as the principles controlling creation, the principles by which matter is precipitated from the cosmic mind.

Today scientists recognize that the Comma of Pythagoras, Pi and the Golden Proportion as well as the closely related Fibonacci sequence are universal constants that describe complex patterns in astronomy, music and physics. For example, the Fibonacci sequence is a series in which each number is the sum of the two preceding it. Spirals are built up according to this sequence. It is rampant in nature in the spirals of galaxies, the shape of ammonites and the arrangement of leaves on a stem.

To the Egyptians these numbers were also the secret harmonies of the cosmos, and they incorporated them as rhythms and proportions in the construction of their pyramids and temples. A building made in this way would be *ideal.* A hall, a doorway, a window which had the Golden Proportion built into it, would be ineffably pleasing to the human spirit.

The great temples of Egypt are, of course, bursting with vegetable forms, such as the bulrush-shaped pillars of the great hypostyle at Karnak. But it was the vegetable life that gives proportion to human limb, the vegetable life that turns ribs and makes them curve according to a pleasing mathematical formula that the temple-builders were particularly concerned to reproduce.

The point is that Egyptian temples were built in this way because the gods were no longer able to inhabit bodies of flesh and blood. A temple was built to be the body of a god, no less. The god's spirit lived inside the vegetable and material bodies that the temple embodied, just as the human spirit lives inside its vegetable and material bodies.

Hypostyle hall at Karnak.

THE HEBREWS HAVE NOT LEFT A RICH architectural heritage like the Egyptians. Their number mysticism has come down to us encoded in the *language* of the books of Moses.

The great book of the Cabala is *The Zohar*, which is a vast commentary on the first five books of the Old Testament, traditionally ascribed to Moses. If the world is materialized thought then, according to the Cabala, words and letters were the means by which this process happened. God created the world by manipulating and making patterns out of the Hebrew letters of the alphabet. Hebrew letters, therefore, have magical properties and the patterns they make in scripture open up layers, indeed vistas, of hidden meaning.

Exodus chapter fourteen contains three verses – 19, 20 and 21 – which each consist of 72 letters. If you write these verses on top of one another so that the 72 letters appear in columns, then reading a column at a time, you will discover the secret 72 Names of God.

Each Hebrew letter is also a number. Aleph, the Hebrew A, is one, Beth is two and so on. There are complex connections here. The Hebrew word for father has a numerical value of 3 and the word for mother has a value of 41. The Hebrew word for child is 44, the combination of Father and Mother.

It gets more mind-blowing.

The numerical value of the Hebrew phrase for the Garden of Eden is 144. The numerical value of the Tree of Knowledge is 233. If you divide 233 by 144, you get very close – to four decimal points – to the value to the golden ratio phi!

In the last few decades mathematicians have applied themselves to the task of finding messages encoded in the text of the books of Moses. Breakthrough work by Witztum, Rips and Rosenberg aimed at discovering transcription codes using equidistant letter sequences. The published results include some names of post-biblical historical figures from Hebrew history, but as yet no propositions, no sequences of sentences or anything that could be read as a message. Again, it is not my secret to reveal, but one Cambridge-based statistician has shown me the results of applying an extremely complex 'skip code', a code verified as valid by a Cambridge University professor of mathematics. The fragments he showed me were reminiscent of the Psalms.

Imagine if a whole other book – or series of books – were encoded in the text we have! Would each of these texts have different layers of meaning too?

Such an achievement is beyond the capacity of normal human intelligence.

Recent research by an occult group has shown that J.S. Bach composed some of the world's most beautiful melodies – such as the famous *Chaconne* – while at the same time giving each note the value of a letter of the alphabet. Bach's music spells out secret, Psalm-like messages. This again is surely something beyond normal human intelligence?

In esoteric circles language which is imbued by initiates with layers of meaning is sometimes called the Green Language or Language of the Birds. Rabelais and Nostradamus, contemporaries at Montpellier University, as well as Shakespeare, are all said to have written it. Wagner refers to it when he alludes to the tradition that Siegfried learned the Language of the Birds by drinking dragon's blood.

One last possibility while we are still on this topic. Perhaps we all speak the Green Language all the time? Perhaps the only difference between us and great initiates like Shakespeare is that they do it consciously?

SIGMUND FREUD WAS DEEPLY INTERESTED in the Cabala. As we will see, it was a formative influence on his thought. But he got hold of the wrong end of the stick when he argued that the Egyptian pharaoh Akhenaten was the source of Moses's monotheism. We now know Moses came first. Akhenaten's ideas of monotheism were subtly but dangerously different.

At the height of the Egyptian New Kingdom, the reign of Akhentaten's father, Amenhotep III, seemed to signal a new era of even greater peace and prosperity which, even if didn't match the unique achievement of the Great Pyramid, would see the construction of the most magnificent temples of the ancient world.

After the birth of three daughters Queen Tiy gave Amenhotep a son. Perhaps because he had been long awaited, perhaps partly because it was clear his father did not have long to live, the boy who was to become Akhenaten was brought up inside the temple precincts and grew up with a sense of cosmic mission.

Akhenaten had been born with a chromosomal defect that gave him a strange, hermaphroditic, even unearthly appearance: womanly thighs and an elongated face that might be read as ethereal, even spiritual. This defect can also lead to symptoms of mental instability – mania, delusions, paranoia.

Some combination of these factors may have contributed to his actions, which threatened to disrupt the whole progress of human evolution.

Unlike in Babylon, where kings acted independently of the priesthood, leading to extremes of despotic cruelty, the pharaohs of Egypt ruled under the aegis of the initiate priests. This is why the popular view of Akhenaten's revolution that sees it as an act of radical individualism is quite wrong.

The start of Akhenaten's reign coincided with the beginning of a Sothic cycle. This was one of the greatest of the astronomical cycles that shaped history, according to the priestly theology.

The Sothic cycle is 1460 years long. In Egyptian mythology each new beginning of this cycle saw the return of the Bennu bird, the Phoenix heralding the birth of the new age and a new dispensation. When Akhenaten announced the closing of the most magnificent temple in the world at Karnak, and the founding of a new cult centre and capital city approximately halfway between Karnak and Giza, this was not the wilful act of an eccentric individual, but an initiate king acting out cosmic destiny. He was preparing to welcome the return of the Bennu bird in 1321 BC.

His first act was to build a new temple to Aten, the god of the sun disc. In the great courtyard of Akhenaten's new temple was its centrepiece, an obelisk topped by the Benben stone on which the legendary Phoenix was to alight.

His next act, supported by his mother Queen Tiy, was to build his great new capital city and sail the whole machinery of government down to it on barges. He wanted to shift the earth on its axis.

He then declared that all other gods did not really exist and that Aten was the one, true and only God. This was monotheism in something very like the modern sense. The worship of Isis, Osiris, and Amon-Re was forbidden. Their temples were effaced and shut down, and their popular festivals declared superstitions.

There is something appealing to modern sensibility about Akhenaten's reforms. Like today's monotheism, Akhenaten's was materialistic. By definition monotheism does away with other gods – and it tends to do away with other spirits and other forms of disembodied intelligence too. So monotheism tends to be materialistic in the sense that it *tends to deny the experience of spirits* – and that experience, as we have already said, is what spirituality really is.

So it was the *physical* sun that Akhenaten declared divine and the source of all goodness. As a result, the art of Akhenaten's reign did away with the hieratic formalism of traditional Egyptian art with its ranks of deities. Akhenaten's art seems naturalistic in a way we find easy to appreciate. Some of his beautiful hymns to Aten have survived and they seem, remarkably, to anticipate the Psalms of David. 'How manifold is that which you have made. You created the world according to your desire – all men, cattle and wild animals,' declaimed Akhenaten. 'How countless are your works,' sang David, 'you made all of them so wisely. The world is full of your creatures.'

But behind the poetry, behind all the clean intelligence and modernism there lurked a monomaniacal madness. By banning all the other gods and declaring himself the only channel for the wisdom and influence of Aten on earth, he was in effect making the whole priesthood redundant and replacing them with just himself.

But despite making himself the focus of all religious practice, he withdrew deeper and deeper into the maze of courtyards of his palace with his beautiful wife Nefertiti and their beloved children. He played with his young family, composed hymns and refused to hear any bad news regarding unrest among the people or of the rebellions in Egypt's colonies that threatened its supremacy in the region.

Collapse eventually came from within. Fifteen years into his reign the daughter on whom he doted died, despite all his prayers to Aten. Then his mother Tiy, who had always supported him, died too. Nefertiti disappears from court records.

Two years later the priests had Akhenaten killed, and they put on the throne the young boy who was to become known to the world as Tutenkhamun.

Immediately the priests set about restoring Thebes. Akhenaten's capital quickly became a ghost town and every monument to him, every depiction of him, every mention of the name of Akhenaten was ruthlessly and systematically effaced.

Some modern commentators have seen Akhenaten as a prophetic, even saintly figure. It is significant, though, that as we know from Manetho, the Egyptians remembered his reign as a Sethian event. Seth is, of course, Satan, the great spirit of materialism, who always works to destroy true spirituality. If his envoy, Akhenaten, had successfully converted humankind to materialism, then the three thousand years of the gentle, beautiful growth of the human spirit, and many qualities that had evolved since would have been lost forever.

ALTHOUGH IT MAY NOT HAVE SURVIVED in anything like the same state of preservation as some of the Egyptian temples, no temple looms larger in the collective imagination than the Temple of Solomon.

Saul has recently been identified as a historical character who features in the letters of kings subject to Akhenaten. They loyally wrote to him with reports of local events. Saul's name in these letters is 'Labya', the king of the 'Habiru'. Following these identifications in the records of neighbouring cultures, we may now say with confidence that David – 'Tadua' – became the first to unite the tribes of Israel in one kingdom when he became king of Jerusalem in 1004 BC, which is to say in the reign of Tutenkamun. David lay the foundations of a temple at Jersualem, but died before he could build it, and so this task was left to his son, whom we now know was anointed king of Jerusalem in 971 BC.

Before the advances made by David Rohl's New Chronology, it had been believed that Solomon, if he was a real historical character at all, lived in the Iron Age. This was a big problem because archaeology could find in the remains of that period no evidence of the wealth and building projects for which Solomon has always been famous. Relocating Solomon in the late Bronze Age has proved to be a perfect fit. The remains of Phoenician-style architecture that a Hiram might have built have been dug up in the appropriate strata.

The figure of Solomon glows in the popular imagination as the embodiment of all kingly magnificence and wisdom – and in the secret tradition, as the magical controller of demons. In the secret traditions of Freemasonry – as we know from an oration by Chevalier Michael Ramsay in 1736 – Solomon recorded his magical knowledge in a secret book which was later laid in the foundations of the second Temple in Jerusalem.

In Jewish folklore Solomon's reign was so splendid that gold and silver became as common as stones in the street. But because the Jews had no tradition of building temples up to this time, having been a nomadic people, Solomon chose to employ as architect for this project a Phoenician, Hiram Abiff. If the building seems, on the evidence of the measurements given in the Old Testament, no larger than a parish church, it was nevertheless crammed with ornamentation of unparalleled magnificence.

In its middle stood the Holy of Holies, lined with gold plate and encrusted with jewels. It was designed to contain the Ark of the Covenant, containing the tablets of Moses. The Cherubim whose wings stretched protectively over it were, as we have seen, representatives of constellations of the zodiac belt. On the corners of the altar stood four horns, representing the moon, and a golden candlestick with seven lamps – of course, a representation of the sun, the moon and the five major planets on either side. The Pillars of Jakim and Boaz measured the pulse of the cosmos. They were so placed as to mark the furthest points of the sun's risings of the equinoxes, and according to the first-century Jewish historian Josephus, and Clement, the first bishop of Alexandria, they were topped with 'orreries', mechanical representations of the motions of the planets. Decorative, carved pomegranates are mentioned several times in the biblical account. The robes of the priests were decorated with precious stones representing the sun, the moon, the planets and the constellations – emeralds being the only stone named.

The most extraordinary feature of the temple seems to have been a sea – or according to the Koran, a fountain – of molten brass. Again, as with the bronze serpent nailed to a pole by Moses, this image of smelting should alert us to the presence of secret practices dedicated to transforming human physiology.

Hiram, the Master Builder, employed a brotherhood of craftsmen to realize his designs. He classified them according to three grades, the Apprentices, the Companions and the Masters. Here we see ideas of fraternity that will eventually spread beyond the narrowly esoteric to transform the organization of society as a whole, and in the story of the murder of Hiram Abiff we see a warning of how it may all go wrong.

THERE IS AN UNDERCURRENT OF RIVALRY between Solomon and Hiram Abiff in some of the secret traditions. The Queen of Sheba visited Solomon, but she was also curious to meet the man who had designed such a miraculous temple.

And when she felt Hiram Abiff's gaze on her, she experienced a sensation like molten metal inside.

She asked Hiram how he had managed to bring the beauty of the heavens down to earth in the architecture of the Temple. He responded by holding aloft a Tau cross, a cross in the shape of the letter T. Immediately all the many workers swarmed into the temple like ants.

Again the image of the insect. There are traditions preserved in the Talmud and the Koran that the Temple was built with the aid of a mysterious insect able to carve stone

Solomon's Temple in an eighteenth-century print. The Freemasonic scholar Albert Pike called it 'an abridged image of the cosmos'. The twin pillars Jakim and Boaz contain many layers of meaning, including, on a physiological level, the rhythmic motions of red and purple blood and, on a cosmic level, the spirit's rhythmic entry alternately into the spiritual and material worlds.

called the Shameer. As with the image of the beehive, we have here an image of spiritual forces – which Hiram is able to command.

Three of Hiram's workers were jealous of his secret powers. They decided they wanted to know the secrets of the molten sea. They ambushed him at the end of the day as he was leaving the Temple. When he repeatedly refused to disclose his secrets they murdered him, each dealing him a massive, haemorrhage-inducing blow to the head.

It is said that certain secrets died with him and are still lost, that the secrets divulged in the Mystery schools and secret societies ever since have been lesser secrets.

There is a hint of a sexual element in the account of Sheba's burning sensation and the Tau cross, but to begin to understand Hiram's secrets we must ask ourselves, given all the astronomical elements in the design and decoration of the Temple, what was its particular orientation?

Two independent-minded Masonic researchers, Christopher Knight and Robert Lomas, have worked out this orientation, starting from the clue that Hiram came from Phoenicia, where the principal deity was Astarte – or Venus. Of course, this ties in, too, with the decorative details, already mentioned, the pomegranates which are the fruit of Venus and the emeralds which are the precious stones of Venus.

According to Clement of Alexandria, the curtain which sectioned off the Holy of Holies had cut into it the shape of a five-pointed star. The five-pointed star has always been a symbol of Venus, because the pattern that Venus traces around the ecliptic in its eight-year cycle – five appearances in the morning sky and five in the evening sky – forms a five-pointed pattern. It is the only planet to draw a completely regular figure in this way. This figure is seen sometimes as a pentagram, sometimes as a five-pointed star, and sometimes, as we shall see when we come to investigate Rosicrucianism, as a five-petalled flower, the rose.

As well as being a symbol of Venus, the pentagram is highly significant in geometry because, as Leonardo's mathematics teacher Luca Pacioli revealed in his book on divine proportion, it embodies the Golden Proportion in every part of it.

But there is more. This sacred geometry operates in time as well as space.

Five Venus cycles of 584 days take place over *exactly* eight solar years, which means that a Venus cycle is 1.6 of a solar cycle. We have come across this number 1.6 before. It is the beginning of the Golden Proportion, one of the irrational and magical numbers that describe the precipitation of mind into matter.

In the ancient and secret doctrine, the planets and the stars control this precipitation of matter.

The Venus associations multiply, one dimension opening up into another like the bubble universes of modern science. There are many rival etymologies of the name Jerusalem, one being that the original name of the city was Urshalem, 'ur' meaning founded by and 'Shalem' being an ancient name of Astarte – or Venus – in her evening setting. In Masonic tradition its own lodges are modelled on the Jerusalem Temple. The five-pointed star of Venus is represented above the ceremonial chair of the Grand Master, and initiates greet each other in a fraternal five-pointed ceremonial embrace. Lodges contain dormer windows, aligned in such a way that the light of Venus shines through them on certain important days. A Master mason is raised into rebirth facing the light of Venus at an equinox.

Bearing in mind the identification of Venus with Lucifer, these associations might at first seem a bit disconcerting. But in esoteric history Lucifer is always a *necessary* evil. The human capacity for thought was forged out of a balance between Venus and the moon – and the moon, as we have just seen, also features prominently, in the design of the altar of the Temple.

The mission of Solomon was to lead humankind down into a darkening, more material world, keeping the flame of spirituality alive. It was the same mission that Freemasonry would take up in the seventeenth century at the dawn of the modern age of materialism.

THE SOLOMONIC LEGENDS FIND A DISTANT echo in the British Isles. Modern scholarship tends to hold the view that, if the legends of Arthur have any historical basis at all, this lies in the 'Dark Ages' following the withdrawal of the Romans from Britain, when a Christian warlord might have fought glorious but ultimately futile battles to repel pagan invaders. An intriguing case has been made that the historical figure behind the Arthur legends was Owain Ddantgwynne, a Welsh warlord who defeated the pagan Saxons at the Battle of Badon in 470. Arthur would in this case have been a title, meaning 'the bear'.

But the original King Arthur lived at Tintagel a little earlier than Solomon, in about 1100 BC, when the peaceful, rural communities of Bronze Age Britain were overrun by the more militaristic hill-fort people of the Iron Age. His spiritual mentor, Merlin, the wizard of Cellydon Wood, was a survivor from the age of the stone circles. He helped Arthur to keep the Sun Mysteries alive. King Arthur himself was a Sun king, surrounded by the twelve knights of the zodiac and married to Venus, Guinevere being the Celtic form of Venere or Venus. His crown was a crown chakra ablaze to lead his people – as Solomon led his people – down through the darkness.

Herodotus recorded that in Iran the king was believed to emit such an intense unbearable light that he had to remain behind a curtain during audiences with his subjects. A crown was a symbol that a certain grade of initiation had been achieved and that the initiate was crowned with buddhic fire.

13

Reason – and How to Rise Above it

Elijah and Elisha • Isaiah • Esoteric Buddhism • Pythagoras • Lao Tzu

AFTER SOLOMON THE KINGDOM OF ISRAEL began to fall apart again.

An institution grew up called the prophets. Their role was to advise the kings – except that, unlike the relationship between Melchizedek and Abraham or Merlin and Arthur, theirs was adversarial, even subversive. They said uncomfortable and unpopular things no one wanted to hear. They ranted and raved. Sometimes they were thought of as mad.

Elijah was a wild man, strange and solitary, almost like a tramp, with a leather belt and a long cloak. Like Zarathustra he fought fire with fire.

Told by God to hide in the wilderness and to drink from a brook, he was fed by ravens. 'Raven' indicates that Elijah was being initiated in the ways of the wisdom of Zarathustra. 'Raven' was one of the grades of initiation in his mysteries.

The king of Israel, Ahab, married Jezebel and began to erect altars to Baal (the Canaanite name for Saturn/Satan). Elijah fought and won a battle with the prophets of Baal, calling fire down from heaven. On later occasions he called fire down from heaven to kill squads of soldiers sent by Jezebel to capture him.

Elijah was a man of blood and thunder, the prophet who lived closest to the borders of madness. There are stories of repeated, astonishing proofs of his charisma – his clairvoyance, his ability to turn a poisoned well wholesome, to make iron float, to heal a leper. There is a strange story of his bringing a young boy back to life by lying on top of him and infusing him with his spirit. When he had to flee into the wilderness again, he was fleeing for his life – and towards God. He found himself standing on a mountain in the middle of a terrible, raging storm. We may imagine him railing against the storm, a combination of Lear and the Fool.

Eventually he sank down, exhausted, and slept under a juniper tree, where he had a dream of an angel.

Then, while it was still dark, he set off to climb Mount Horeb in search of God as the angel had told him. But a great wind came, shaking the very mountain and sending enormous boulders bouncing down in his direction. Elijah knew that God was not in this wind and he managed to reach the safety of a cave.

Suddenly a sheet of lightning struck the ground right in front of the cave, causing a roaring blaze in the vegetation outside, which trapped him inside. He also knew God was not in this fire.

After a while the storm and the fire died down and as morning approached all was calm. The morning star arose and it was then, in the gentle morning air, that Elijah heard the still small voice of God.

An exuberant, even outrageous figure, he was nevertheless the prophet of a new interiority. This is a development of Moses hearing of the voice in the burning bush, but quieter, subliminal almost. Where people had once had an overwhelming sense of the divine, now they would have to listen very intently, to practise mental discipline and directed attention in order to discern it.

But in order to understand the true meaning of Elijah's mission, it is necessary to understand his death, and in order to do that we will turn first to India.

There are testimonies about Indian adepts able to dematerialize and materialize at will. In Paramahansa Yogananda's marvellous *Autobiography of a Yogi*, first published in 1946, he describes how he was due to meet his spiritual master, Sri Yukteswar, at the local train station, but received a telepathic message not to go there. His master had been delayed. The pupil waited in the hotel. Suddenly a window overlooking the street became brilliant with sunlight and his master clearly materialized in front of him. His master explained that he was not an apparition but flesh and blood, that he had been divinely commanded to give his pupil this very rare experience. Paramahansa Yogananda touched the familiar sandals made of orange canvas and rolled with rope. He also felt the ochre cloth of his master's robe brush against him.

Elijah developed this gift to the next stage. *He learned how to excarnate and incarnate at will.*

You can't take it with you, goes the popular saying, but according to the secret doctrine you can. The great twentieth-century initiate G.I. Gurdjieff said that exactly what is needed truly to become master of oneself in this life is what is needed to survive as a conscious being in the afterlife. Initiation is concerned at least as much with life after death as this life. In the seventh book of *The Republic* Plato said, 'Those who are unable in the present life to apprehend the idea of the good, will descend to Hades after death and fall asleep in its dark abode.'

At the end of his life Elijah was carried up into the heavens in a fiery chariot. So like Enoch and Noah before him, he did not die in the ordinary way. He joined the college of ascended masters, who are for the most part invisible but return to earth at times of great change and crisis.

In cabalistic thought the chariot by means of which Elijah ascends is called the Merkabah. Great initiates are able to work on the vegetable body so that it does not dissolve after death, enabling the ascending spirit to keep aspects of consciousness only usually possible during life on earth. Initiates know of secret techniques by means of which very fine energies may be crystallized in such a way that they are not dispersed.

We will see later that Christian thinkers would call this chariot the Resurrection body.

As Elijah ascended his mantle slipped from him to be taken up by Elisha, whom Elijah had chosen as his successor. By some mysterious process the confering of the mantle gives Elisha an increased portion of Elijah's power. (We will return to look at the way this works when we come to consider the life and work of Shakespeare.)

The succession of Elijah by Elisha was not without ambiguity, though. Once Elijah seemed as if he might want to repudiate Elisha. He hurried off and, when Elisha caught up with him, said, 'Go back. What have I done to you?' Does he see something in Elisha he is not sure of? Later Elisha is mocked for being bald by a large gang of boys and uses his power to call two bears from the woods which attack and kill them. It is as if the prophet is still engaged in a deadly battle with Baal.

Two hundred years later, by the time of the later prophets, a new, transcendent under-

Elijah ascends. Print from a nineteenth-century Bible.

standing of the way the universe works had developed. The concept of Grace put prophets on a much less warlike footing. In 550 BC Isaiah proclaimed, 'The people that walked in darkness have seen a great light ... For unto us a child is born, unto us a son is given: and the government shall be on his shoulder: and his name shall be called Wonderful, Counsellor, the Mighty God, the Everlasting Father, the Prince of Peace.'

The concept of Grace grew out of this prophetic sense of history. The kings of the two kingdoms and their peoples failed to do what was asked of them. They degenerated and the land was laid waste. But then, because of the Grace of God, a living root emerged from the wasteland. The prophets saw Grace operating in this way in their own lifetimes on a military and political level, in the rise and fall and rise again of their own little kingdoms. They also prophesied its repetition in the greater cosmic cycles of history.

For the followers of Baal, on the other hand, life was about the exercise of power. They believed that if they performed the correct religious practices – sacrifices and magical ceremonies – they could compel their gods to do their bidding.

Isaiah repudiated this view. He told his people that Yahweh had shown them Grace by choosing them, by empowering them to obey, by purging them of their sins, by saving them when they had been stiff-necked and disobeyed, and by the promise of restoring them to former glory even though they did not deserve it. Yahweh's gracious love could never be demanded, bought or earned, he said. It is a love given in complete freedom.

Once this kind of divine love had been understood, it would only be a matter of time before this understanding opened a new dimension in the love of one human for another.

Isaiah had a great sense of both the history and the future fortunes of Israel – 'there shall come forth a rod out of the stem of Jesse'. He also has a great vision of the end of history which we will return to later – 'the wolf and the lamb shall feed together, and the leopard shall lie down with the kid'.

The prophetic tradition would die out by about 450 BC. As the Cabalist Rabbi Hayyim Vital would write, at the end of the sixteenth century, after Haggai, Zechariah and Malachi, prophets were only able to see into the lowest levels of the heavens and then only in a heavily shrouded way.

The last words in the Old Testament are the ringing words of Malachi, prophesying Elijah's return, and today this is still looked forward to every year at Passover, when a place is laid for him at dinner, with a cup of wine and the door left open.

BUT IN DIFFERENT PARTS OF THE WORLD other remarkable initiates were opening up other new dimensions in the human condition. A great spirit of enlightenment was weaving through several different minds and several different cultures at the same time.

Prince Siddhartha was born into a time and place characterized by small warring states in Lumbini in modern-day Nepal.

Until the age of twenty-nine he lived in pampered luxury. His every need was met before it began to tug on him and his every vista was a delight. Then one day he left the royal palace and saw something he had never been allowed to see – an old man. He was horrified, but he looked further, discovering that his own people were ill and dying.

He decided to leave the palace – and his wife and child – in order to try to make sense of this suffering. Living among ascetics for seven years, he failed to find what he was looking for in the yoga sutras of Pantanjali and the teachings of the descendants of the Rishis.

Then, finally, when he was thirty-five he went and sat under a Bohdi tree on the banks of the River Neranjara, determined not to move until he understood.

After three days and three nights he realized that life is suffering, that suffering is caused by desire for earthly things, but that you can achieve freedom from all desire. Indeed, you can achieve such freedom, and such affinity for the spirit world, that you need never reincarnate again – and so you may become, as Siddhartha did, a Buddha.

The path to understanding – or enlightenment – was called by the Buddha 'the Eightfold Path', which involved right belief, right conviction, teaching, action, living, intention, thinking, contemplation.

The Eightfold Path may seem impossibly high-minded moralizing to modern Western sensibility. It may also seem a bit abstract, even impractical. But the teachings of the Buddha have an esoteric side, and like all esoteric teachings they have a layer of meaning which is eminently practical. Esoteric philosophy teaches its initiates how to achieve psychological transformation using practical techniques to manipulate human physiology. In the case of the Buddha's Eightfold Path, these eight practices are exercises for enlivening eight of the sixteen petals of the throat chakra.

This represents a historic change in initiatic practice. In the initiation rituals practiced in the Great Pyramid, for example, the candidate had been sent into a deep, death-like trance, then a circle of – five – initiates had raised his vegetable body out of his physical body. They had worked on it, moulding it, coaxing it into forms capable of perceiving higher worlds, so that when the vegetable body sank again into the physical body and the candidate reawoke, he was born into a new, higher form of life. The point is that the candidate was unconscious throughout this process.

Now the followers of Buddha consciously participated in their own initiation, consciously working on their own chakras. Part of this work was living a new, more moral way of life, based on compassion for all living things.

Because people were growing increasingly independent of the spirit worlds, there was a danger that an individual's powers would outstrip his desire to do the right thing and use them wisely. There was also a danger that the evil-minded might gain the supernatural powers that initiation confers.

It has also always been possible for people to gain these powers even though they

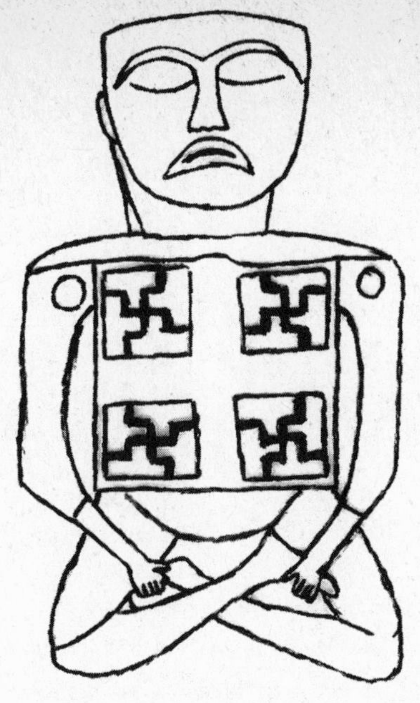

In esoteric Buddhism, the Buddha is the spirit of Mercury. It is no coincidence, then, that the Celts called the planet Mercury 'Budh', meaning 'wise teaching'. That the lotus position characteristic of the Buddha was known to the Celts is proved by this carving on a bucket, found in Oesberg, Norway.

have not been initiated. Sometimes it happens as a result of extreme childhood trauma. This can cause a rent in the psyche through which spirits rush in an uncontrolled way. Some modern mediums have suffered great childhood traumas. Sometimes people acquire powers through the practice of a magic which is either black or at least not attuned to the highest spiritual aims, as it is in the venerable secret schools which keep alive a genuine, ancient tradition. The danger in all this is that a non-initiate, even a well-intentioned one, may have difficulty recognizing the spirits he or she is communicating with.

The aim of the Eightfold Path is initiation as part of a controlled and protecting moral development. If you are able to control the world, you must first be able to exercise control over yourself.

The throat chakra is the organ of the formulation of spiritual wisdom. It connects the heart chakra with the brow chakra. In the physiology of an initiate currents of love stream up from the heart chakra through the throat chakra to light up the brow chakra. When this light streams up on to the brow chakra, it opens up like a flower in the sun.

We may all catch an echo – or foretaste – of this in our own lives. If we look at someone with the eyes of love, we see good qualities not perceptible to others. Just the act of looking at someone lovingly may also bring out these qualities and help them to blossom. If you meet someone with an extremely refined spiritual nature, he or she will probably be happy, smiling, laughing, almost childlike. This is because they look at the whole of humanity with the eye of love.

When the Buddha died he had achieved his aim. He would not be required to reincarnate.

But this is not to say he is no longer a part of this history, as we see when we come to look at the Italian Renaissance.

The Buddhist Emperor Asoka, grandson of the first man to unify India, ruled from 273 BC. *When he lost more than a hundred thousand men in a battle, he renounced war, and from then on tried to rule by the shining example of his Buddhist spirituality. He had some 84,000 stupas, or shrines, erected in India, of which a handful survive. In conventional history he is remembered for his irrigation, roads, hospitals and botanical gardens, his vegetarianism and ban on the killing of animals. In esoteric history he is remembered, too, for having founded the Nine Unknown, a powerful secret society that many in the twentieth century, including D.N. Bose, one of India's leading scientists, believed still operated.*

PYTHAGORAS WAS BORN ON THE PROSPEROUS Greek island of Samos in about 575 BC, as the first blocks of marble were being placed one on top of the other on the Acropolis in Athens.

No individual has had a greater influence on the evolution of Western esoteric thought. Pythagoras was regarded as a demi-god during his lifetime. Like Jesus Christ, nothing he wrote has come down to us, only a few collected sayings and commentaries and stories written by disciples.

It was said that he had the power of being in two places at the same time, that a white eagle had permitted him to stroke it, that he once addressed a river god and a voice called out to him from the water, 'I greet thee Pythagoras!' It is also said that he once told some fishermen who had been having an unproductive day to cast their nets into the sea one last time, whereupon their catch almost burst their nets. He was a great healer, sometimes reciting particular verses from Homer he believed had great power, just as Christian mystics will recite verses from the Psalms and John's Gospel. He used music for healing purposes, too. The early Greek philosopher Empedocles said Pythagoras could heal the sick and rejuvenate the old. Like the Buddha he could remember his past incarnations and it was even said that he could recall the entire history of the world from the beginning.

His wisdom was the result of years of research and multiple initiations into Mystery schools. He spent twenty-two years learning the secrets of the Egyptian initiate priests. He also studied with the Magi in Babylon and the descendants of the Rishis in India, where a memory was preserved of the great wonder-worker they called Yaivancharya.

Pythagoras was seeking to synthesize esoteric thought from all around the world into a comprehensive cosmo-conception – what Leibniz, the seventeenth-century mathematician and Cabalist, would later call the Perennial Philosophy.

At this point in the history of the world according to idealism, we have reached a turning point. The great ideas or thoughts emanating from the cosmic mind are now almost hidden by the matter they have worked together to create. The mission of Pythagoras was to record them as concepts before they disappeared entirely.

Pythagoras's philosophy, therefore, begins the process of translating the primordial vision, the picture consciousness of ancient humanity, into abstract, conceptual terms.

In about 532 Pythagoras fell foul of Polycrates, the despotic ruler of Samos. Forced into exile, he set up a small community – the first of several – in Crotona in southern Italy. Candidates for initiation into his community had to undergo years of training, including a strange diet that included poppy, sesame and cucumber seeds, wild honey, daffodil flowers and the skin of sea onion from which the juice had been completely extracted. There was great emphasis on gymnastics as a way of bringing the three human bodies – material, vegetable and animal – into harmony, and candidates were required to remain silent for years on end.

Pythagoras was able to grant his pupils a great vision of the spirit worlds, which he would then interpret for them. Out of this, the first discursive teaching, would emerge mathematics, geometry, astronomy and music.

In his day Pythagoras was said to be the only human being able to hear the Music of the Spheres, conceived as a scale of different notes each made by the seven planets as they moved through space. This is easy to dismiss as mystical hogwash, but the story of how he measured the first musical scale has an authentic sounding ring to it.

One day Pythagoras was walking through town when he heard metal being pounded on an anvil. He noticed that different sized hammers made different sounds. Returning home, he fixed a plank of wood across a room and hung a series of weights according to the weights of the different hammers in an ascending scale. By a process of trial and error he determined that the musical notes that sound beautiful to the human ear correspond to different weights. He then calculated that they were proportionate to one another in a mathematically precise way. It is from these calculations by Pythagoras that we derive the musical octave we understand and enjoy today.

As Pythagoras and his followers began to describe the rational element in life, they started to formulate a parallel concept. It was a concept which had perhaps never been articulated before, because up till that point it had been a part of everyone's everyday experience. The concept went like this: life can be explained in rational terms only up to a point. *There is a vast irrational element in life, too.*

The teachings of the Mystery schools relating to the rational side would help build cities, develop science and technology, structure and regulate the Outworld. The irrational teaching in its explicit form would be confined to the schools. To talk about it outside was dangerous and might well attract hostility. As Plutarch would put it, 'One who knows the higher truths, finds the "serious" values of society difficult to take seriously. Eternity is a child at play.'

Here, at the birth of rational thought, the Mystery schools nurtured its opposite. It is no accident that individuals like Pythagoras, Newton and Leibniz, those who have done most to help humanity get to grips with the reality of the physical universe, have also been deeply immersed in esoteric thought. This is because it is undoubtedly true, as these great minds have seen, that if you look at life as subjectively as possible, rather than objectively, as you must do in science, some very different patterns emerge. Life viewed objectively may be rational and subject to natural law, but experienced subjectively it is irrational.

By consciously splitting experience in this way, Pythagoras made it possible to think more clearly about both dimensions.

The pupils of Pythagoras were taught to live apart from society, alternating between mystical ecstasy and intellectual analysis. Pythagoras was the first to call himself a lover of wisdom, that is to say 'a philosopher', but like Socrates and Plato who followed him, he was closer to a magus than a modern-day university professor. His pupils were in awe of him. They believed he had the power to make them dream what he willed, and that he could reorient their waking consciousness in an instant, too.

Pythagoras attracted murderous rage from those excluded from his inner circle. He refused to admit a man called Cyron into his Mystery school because of his reckless, imperious behaviour. Cyron stirred up a mob against Pythagoras. They broke into the building where Pythagoras and his followers were meeting and set fire to it. Everyone inside died.

IN THE ERA OF PYTHAGORAS TWO OTHER philosophers on different sides of the world, Heraclitus in Greece and Lao-Tzu in China, briefly come to the surface of history, trying to define rationally, the irrational dimension of life.

We cannot step in the same stream twice, said Heraclitus.

There is a story that Confucius went to see Lao-Tzu and asked to be initiated. Lao-Tzu turned him away, mocking him for his mixture of ingratiating manners and vaulting ambition. It is probably apocryphal, but it points to an important truth which is that Confucianism and Taoism represent exoteric and esoteric thought in China.

Confucius spent years collecting traditional Chinese wisdom and these collections would be adopted as manuals for government by later Chinese leaders.

The sayings of Confucius are eminently reasonable. A thousand mile journey begins with a single step. Value the task more than the prize. If you can't meet your goals, adjust your goals. And so on.

We can compare Confucius with Rudyard Kipling. They were both servants of empire. If scientific materialism described everything there is in life, Kipling's poem 'If' would be the last word on the conduct of life and esoteric philosophy would have nothing to teach us.

> If you can force your heart and nerve and sinew
> To serve your turn long after they are gone
> And so hold on when there is nothing in you
> Except the Will which says to them 'Hold on!'..
>
> If you can fill the unforgiving minute
> With sixty seconds' worth of distance run,
> Yours is the earth and everything that is in it
> And which is more – you'll be a Man, my son!

The problem is that, though there may be times when the best thing to do is to try with all our might and not give up, there are other times, as Orpheus had found to his cost, when it is prudent to give up and go with the flow. Sometimes when you grab at what you want, you just push it further away. Sometimes the only way to keep something is by letting it go. As Lao Tzu says:

> Because the awakened one puts himself behind, he steps ahead.
> Because he gives way, he gains
> Because he is selfless, he fulfils himself
> The still is the lord of the restless.

THIRTY YEARS AFTER THE DEATH OF PYTHAGORAS, an enormous Persian army under Xerxes swept over Greece. Then, in the early years of the fifth century BC, Persian forces were defeated and driven back by the Athenians at Marathon and then by an Athenian–Spartan alliance at Mycale.

Pythagoras had institutionalized the open discussion of options and the making of collective decisions on matters which concerned the whole community – what we today call politics. From this – and in the space created by the Athenian–Spartan alliance – would emerge the unique character of the Greek city-state of Athens.

14

The Mysteries of Greece and Rome

The Eleusian Mysteries • Socrates and his Daemon • Plato as a Magus • The Divine Identity of Alexander the Great • The Caesars and Cicero • The Rise of the Magi

IF WE SEE IN THE ATHENIANS A GIFT FOR free, individual thought, we see in Sparta the development of individual will, competitive edge and admiration, to the point of hero-worship, of strong men. Heroes created the space for the flowering of Greek culture, which in the fifth century BC began to set standards in beauty of form and rigour of intellect that we have aspired to match ever since.

This was the Greece of the great initiates: the philosophers Plato and Aristotle, the poet Pindar and the dramatists Sophocles and Euripides.

The most famous of all the Greek Mystery schools was situated at Eleusis, a hamlet a few miles from Athens. The Roman statesman Cicero, himself an initiate, would say that the Eleusian Mysteries and what flowed from them formed the greatest benefit that Athens gave to the civilized world.

'ELEUSIS' COMES FROM 'ELAUNO', MEANING 'I come', which is to say 'I come into being'. There is almost nothing left of the sanctuary – just a few scattered stones and a couple of panels from inside have survived – but a contemporary description of it talks of an unmarked exterior wall of grey-blue stone. Inside there were painted statues and friezes of goddesses, sheaves of grain and eight-petalled flowers. One account says there was an aperture in the ceiling of the inner sanctum that provided the only light source.

The Lesser Mysteries were celebrated in the spring. They involved rites of purification and also dramatizations of stories of the gods. A statue of a god crowned with myrtle and carrying a torch was led in procession with singing and dancing. The god was sacrificed and died for three days. When the sacrificed god was represented as being raised from the dead, the assembled hierophants and candidates shouted, 'Iachos! Iachos! Iachos!'

There was also an overtly sexual element in these celebrations. Psellus, a Byzantine scholar, wrote that Venus was portrayed as rising out of the sea from in between moving representations of female genitalia, and that afterwards the marriage of Persephone and Hades took place. It was recorded by Clement of Alexandria that the rape of Persephone was enacted, and it was also said by Athenagoras that during this bizarre, violent, almost surreal drama, she was portrayed as having a horn on her forehead, perhaps symbolizing the Third Eye.

There were also accounts of ceremonial pouring of milk from a golden vessel in the shape of a breast. On one level this is obviously connected with the worship of the Mother Goddess, but it should alert us to the fact that on a deeper level these ceremonies were concerned with life after death. We know from Pythagoras that the Milky Way was conceived of as a vast river or troop of spirits. The star-like spirits of the dead ascended through the gate of Capricorn and up through the spheres, before descending back into the material world through the gate of Cancer. Pindar said, 'Happy is he who has seen the Mysteries before being buried beneath the ground, because he knows what happens as life ends.' Sophocles said, 'Thrice happy are those who have seen the Mysteries before they die. They will have life after death. Everyone else will only experience suffering.' Plutarch said that those who die experience for the first time what those who have been initiated have already experienced.

The Greater Mysteries, celebrated on or about the autumn equinox, were

Surviving panel from Eleusis, showing Demeter and a candidate for initiation.

preceded by nine days of fasting, after which candidates for initiation were given a potent drink called the kykeon.

Of course extreme hunger can by itself lead to a visionary state, or at least a propensity for hallucinations. After fasting for so long, the candidate drank this mixture of roasted barley, water and poley oil, which can be narcotic if taken in sufficient quantities.

The Mysteries were known to involve people in the most intense experiences, the wildest fears, blackest horrors and raptures. Plutarch wrote of the terror of those about to be initiated, as if they were about to die, and, of course, in a sense they were.

Imagine if you had seen dramatic presentations of terrifying supernatural events in the Lesser Mysteries and now believed these things were going to happen for real, that you were going to take part in a drama in which you would be killed and in some sense really die! The accounts by Proclus suggest candidates were attacked by 'the rushing forms of troops of earthly demons'. Though it was by this time very difficult for the *higher* spiritual beings, the gods, to squeeze down into a dense, material realm, it was relatively easy for lesser spirits, such as demons and spirits of the dead. The candidate was to be shamed and punished, tortured by demons. Pausanius in his *Description of Greece* describes a demon called Euronomos, with blue-black skin like a fly's, who devoured the flesh of rotting corpses.

Are we to take this as literally true? As mentioned earlier, these initiation ceremonies were part ritual and drama – and part séance. That drugs played a part in conjuring up these demons does not necessarily – from an idealist point of view – mean they were illusory. We should also remember that in rural India perfectly respectable religious ceremonies still take place, the worship of lesser spirits, the Pretas and Bhuts and Pisachas and Gandharvas, ceremonies which we in the West would classify as séances.

The Mystery schools were concerned with granting the candidate an authentic spiritual experience, which in the context of idealistic philosophy means a genuine experience of spirits – first demons and the spirits of the dead, then later the gods.

By the fifth century BC it was, of course, difficult for a god without a material body to affect matter directly, to move a heavy object for example. But the initiate priests could mouth magic words into a cloud of smoke emanating from a sacrificial fire and the face of a god would sometimes appear. Karl von Eckartshausen, the late eighteenth-century theosophist, recorded the most effective fumigations for causing apparitions: hemlock, henbane, saffron, aloe, opium, mandrake, salorum, poppy seed, asafoetida and parsley.

The miraculously lifelike statues for which Greece is famous emerged from the Mystery schools. Their original function was to help bring the gods to earth.

We know from the earlier use of statues in Egypt and Sumeria that it was intended that the gods occupy them, live in them as their physical bodies and make them come alive. If you stood in front of the statue of Artemis in Ephesus, the Mother Earth loomed over you like a great tree. You had a sensation of being absorbed into the vegetable matrix of the cosmos, the great ocean of weaving waves of light, and of being at one with it.

The statues would breath, seem to move. It was said that sometimes they would speak to you.

After various trials the successful candidate was allowed to ascend to the Empyrean realm, a place flooded with light, music and dancing. Dionysus – Bacchus or Iacchos – appeared in a beautiful, radiant vision of light. Aristedes, the orator, recalled: 'I thought I felt the god draw near and I touched him, I was somewhere between waking and sleeping. My spirit was so light – in a way someone who hasn't been initiated wouldn't understand.' By this lightness of spirit, he is referring to an out-of-body experience. It also seems clear that the gods sometimes occupied ethereal, vegetable bodies in the Mysteries and so appeared like luminous spectres or phantoms.

So the process of initiation gave direct, existential, undeniable first-hand knowledge that the spirit could live outside the body, and while in this state the candidate became a spirit among spirits, a god among gods. When the new initiate was 'born again' into the

In the upside-down, other-way-round doctrine of the secret societies, the Greeks created the first statues of perfect human bodies because human bodies only became perfectly formed at this point in time. The Greek cult of the body arose from the fresh experience of the perfect form.

Otherwise known as the Wand of Hermes, the Caduceus was a pole with two snakes entwined. The thyrsus was a representation of the Caduceus, probably made out of a hollow stalk like that of a fennel – in which Prometheus carried fire down to illumine humankind. The thyrsus in which the secret, sacred fire is hidden is the Sushumna Nadi *of Indian occult physiology. On top of the stalk was a pine cone representing the pineal gland.*

everyday material world, when he was crowned as an initiate he retained many god-like powers of perception and abilities to influence events.

The experience of initiation was, therefore, a mystical one. However, as we have seen in the case of Pythagoras, practical and even scientific knowledge was shown to be implicit in this experience, too. After initiation the hierophant would elucidate what the new initiate had just experienced, drawing arcane disclosures from a book made of two stone tablets, called the Book of Interpretation. They taught the way the material world and the material, human body had been formed and the way both were directed by the spirit worlds. To help them in their teaching they also used symbols. These included the thyrsus made of a reed, sometimes with seven knots and topped with a pine cone. There were also the 'toys of Dionysus' – a golden serpent, a phallus, an egg and a spinning top that made the sound 'Om'. Cicero would write that when you come to understand them, the occult mysteries have more to do with natural science than with religion.

There was a prophetic element in this teaching, too. The final initiation at Eleusis involved the candidate being shown a plucked green wheat ear, held up in silence.

Of course on one level the Mysteries were agricultural and looked forward to a good harvest. But there was another level to do with the harvesting of souls.

This wheat was the star Spica, the divine seed held in the left hand of the virgin goddess of the constellation of Virgo. I'm talking, of course, about the goddess the Egyptians called Isis. The grain she holds looks forward to the great cosmic 'seed time'. It will be made into the bread of the Last Supper, symbolizing the vegetable body in Jesus Christ

The importance of Spica in the ancient world is shown by the fact that, apart from Sirius, it is the only star represented on the famous planisphere at Dendera, a section of which is produced here. The great cosmic wheel grinds all the stars except for this single one that is saved, just outside its rim.

and also the vegetative dimension, or altered state of consciousness, we all must work ourselves into, according to esoteric Christianity, if we are to meet him there.

Again we see that the vegetative dimension of the cosmos is the focus of esoteric thought. In Plato's philosophy it is the soul, the mediator between the material body and the animal spirit. If we are to leave behind the material world and enter the spirit worlds, this vegetative dimension must be the subject of our Work.

THERE ARE OTHER WAYS THAT SPIRITS could influence events.

Everyone who contemplates one of the busts of Socrates that have survived may be struck by the lively, satyr-like quality of his physiognomy.

In the secret tradition Socrates was a reincarnation of the great spirit who had previously lived in the body of Silenus.

Gem carvings of Silenus and Socrates.

The death of Aeschylus carved on a gem. Aeschylus was the son of a priest at Eleusis. He was threatened with execution for having betrayed the secrets of the Mysteries by portraying them on stage. He escaped execution by claiming that he had never been initiated, but when an eagle dropped a rock from a great height on to his bald head, killing him, many interpreted this as divine retribution.

Socrates sometimes spoke of his daemon, meaning a good spirit who guided him through life. Today this might seem an alien concept. But the following account of the daemon in modern times is perhaps instructive. It is an incident recalled by a pupil of the Russian esoteric philosopher P.D. Ouspensky, a formative influence on many of the great writers and artists of the twentieth century, including the poet and playwright T.S. Eliot, the architect Frank Lloyd Wright and the artists Kazimir Malevich and Georgia O'Keefe.

This man, a lawyer, had been to hear a lecture by Ouspensky at a house in west London. He was walking away, puzzled by it and full of doubts. But as he did so, a voice inside him said: 'If you lose touch with this, you will be doing something that you will regret for the rest of your life'. He wondered where this voice came from.

Eventually he found an explanation in Ouspensky's teachings. This voice was his higher self. One of the great aims of the process of initiation he found himself undertaking was to so alter his consciousness that *he would be able to hear this voice all the time.*

Socrates was a man guided by his conscience in this way. He carried forward the great project of converting instinctive wisdom of the lower, animal self into concepts, and his philosophy like that of Pythagoras is not merely academic. It is also a philosophy of life. The aim of all philosophy, he said, is to teach one how to die.

There is some dispute, even within the secret schools, as to whether or not Socrates was an initiate.

When accused of corrupting the youth of Athens and of not believing in the gods, Socrates committed suicide by drinking hemlock. He died forgiving his executioners.

The oath against suicide was one of the most terrible taken by initiates.

IT'S BECOME COMMONPLACE TO SAY that religion has had a negative, even destructive effect on human history. Wars of religion, the Inquisition, the suppression of scientific thought and restrictive patriarchal attitudes are routinely cited. It is worth remembering that some of the greater glories of human culture had their origins in the Mystery schools that were a central part of organized religion in the ancient world. Not only sculpture and drama but also philosophy, mathematics and astronomy as well as political and medical ideas arose out of this religious institution.

Above all the Mystery schools influenced the evolution of consciousness.

Conventional history puts little emphasis on the evolution of consciousness, but we can see it in action again if we look at changes in Greek drama. In the plays of Aeschylus and Sophocles, the first dramatists to have their work performed outside the Mystery schools, wrongdoing results in persecution by the winged demons called Erinyes or Furies – for example in the *Oresteia* of Aeschylus of 458 BC. By Euripides's play of 428 BC, *Hippolytus,* this chiding has been internalized and given a name. 'There is only one thing that can survive all life's trials – a quiet conscience.'

In conventional history it is assumed that people have always been pricked by conscience. On this view Euripides was simply the first person to put a name to it. In the upside-down, other-way-round thinking of esoteric tradition the reason that there is no suggestion of conscience in any of the annals of human experience up to that point, is that the Eleusian Mysteries forged this new dimension of human experience.

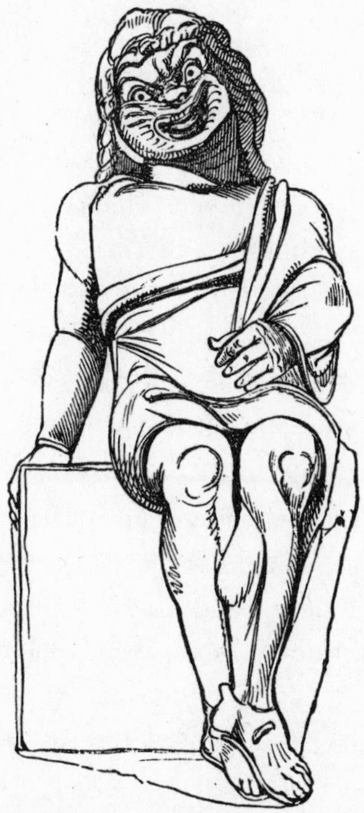

Startling statue of an actor in a mask. Aristophanes satirized the Mysteries in The Frogs. *If tragedy dramatized the machinations of Satan in the world, comedy dramatized the machinations of Lucifer.*

Great dramatic art shows we often don't feel exactly what convention tells us we should feel. It shows us new ways of being – feeling, thinking, willing, perceiving. To borrow a phrase of Saul Bellow's, it opens the human condition a little wider.

When we experience Greek drama we are purged by *catharsis*. The Greek dramatists give their audiences an experience which is an echo of the experience of initiation, and their way of working is based on an understanding of human nature that is essentially initiatic. Our animal body has been corrupted. It has become hardened and carries something like a protective carapace. We become comfortable with this carapace, though. We even grow to rely on it. But our easy, basking lives have been made possible by blood spilled, torture, theft, injustice – and deep down we know it. So deep inside us there is a self-loathing that prevents us from living *wholly* in the moment, from living life to the full. We cannot truly love or be loved until the insect-like carapace is cut open by the agonizing process of initiation. Until we reach that point we don't know what life is meant to be like.

When we see a great production of one of the tragedies inspired by the experience of initiation – *Oedipus Rex*, for example, or *King Lear* – we may catch an echo of this process.

IF SOME OF THE IDEAS OF THE GREEKS ARE hard to understand, hard to accept, others may at first glance look rather obvious, even bland, to the extent you might even think they are hardly worth saying at all. The handful of sayings attributed to Pythagoras that have survived include:

Above all things respect yourself

and

Do not yield to temptation except when you agree to be untrue to yourself.

In order to understand why these were challenging, even astounding things to say, things that shook the world and, as a result have been remembered down the ages, we have to see them in the context of a newly burgeoning sense of self.

Similarly when Socrates said:

An unconsidered life is not worth living,

he was addressing people who up that point had had no faculty for abstract thought with which to contemplate their lives. This was the great gift of Socrates to the world.

WHEN SOCRATES DIED, HIS PUPIL PLATO became the leading figure in Greek philosophy.

Plato was born in 428 into one of the first generations systematically taught to read. He founded the Academy in the garden of the tomb of Academus in Athens.

His *Dialogues* are the greatest expression of the mind-before-matter philosophy called idealism that is at the heart of this book.

In the secret history *everyone* had experienced the world in an idealistic way up to this time. Everyone's form of consciousness was such that he would not have questioned that ideas are a higher form of reality than objects. Everyone believed this unthinkingly, instinctively. It only became necessary for a great initiate to conceptualize the idealistic world-view and write it down in systematic terms at the point when consciousness had evolved to a stage that people could conceive of the opposing point of view. Plato's pupil Aristotle made the philosophical leaps forward that would lead to the materialism that is the dominant philosophy today.

PLATO'S IDEALISM IS EASY FOR US TO misinterpret. It naturally seems to us to follow that if the material world is a precipitate of our mental processes, we should be able to manipulate the world in a very obvious and direct way just by thinking about it. In fact, if the world is nothing more than a sort of giant hologram, then couldn't it just be switched off? In *The Principles of Human Knowledge* Bishop Berkeley, the most influential philosopher of idealism in English, advocated a version of idealism according to which matter has no existence independent of perception – and this is the version of idealism most familiar to students of philosophy in Anglo-American universities.

But as a matter of historical fact it is not the position held by the great majority of people throughout history who have believed in idealism. As I have already suggested, these people experienced the world in an idealistic way. The faculty of imagination was much stronger than the faculty for thinking, which was then only beginning to develop. They believed that the objects of the imagination were more real than the objects of the senses – but this does not necessarily mean that the latter are totally unreal.

Most people in history who have believed in idealism as a philosophy of life, have believed in matter being precipitated out of mind as a historical process that took place gradually and over vast periods of time. They have also believed – and still believe – that the hologram will, as it were, be switched off, but again gradually and over equally vast stretches of time.

Today's university students debating the pros and cons of idealism probably find it difficult to equate Platonic ideas with gods and angels, as we have been doing. This association risks seeming crudely anthropomorphic to modern sensibility.

But again, as a matter of historical fact, people who believed in idealism as a philosophy of life have always tended to believe in spirits, gods and angels.

When considering the great world-weaving cosmic thoughts, the active principles behind the appearances of things, many idealists have asked themselves how far it is appropriate to consider them as being conscious beings like ourselves. Idealists like Cicero and Newton have considered these 'Intelligencers', to use Newton's name for them, neither as crudely impersonal nor crudely personal. Cicero and Newton were neither crudely polytheistic nor crudely monotheistic. They experienced life as meaningful and the cosmos as *meant*. They believed, then, that something like human qualities, indeed something like human consciousness, is built into the structure of the cosmos.

And, crucially, initiates of the secret societies, like initiates of the Mystery schools, encountered these disembodied Intelligencers in altered states of consciousness. It is Goethe perhaps who writes best about what it feels like to be an idealist in modern times. He writes about feeling the real presence of living interconnections with the natural world and living connections with other people, even though such connections may not be measurable or visible. And crucially he writes about the great universal spirits that hold everything together. What Newton called 'the Intelligencers', Goethe calls 'the Mothers':

> 'We all walk in the mysteries. We do not know what is stirring in the atmosphere that surrounds us, nor how it is connected with our own spirit. So much is certain – that we can at times put out the feelers of our soul beyond its bodily limits ... one soul may have a decided influence upon another, merely by means of its silent presence, of which I could relate many instances. It has often happened to me that, when I have been walking with an acquaintance, and have had a living image of something in my mind, he has at once begun to speak of that very thing. I have also known a man who, without saying a word, could suddenly silence a party engaged in conversation by the mere power of his mind.. We all have some electrical and magnetic forces within us; and we put forth, like the magnet itself, some, attractive or repulsive power ... With lovers this magnetic power is particularly strong and acts even at a distance. In my younger days I have experienced cases enough, when, during my solitary walks, I have felt a great desire for the company of a beloved girl, and have thought of her till she has really come to meet me. 'I was so restless in my room,' she has said, 'that I could not help coming here.'

Goethe went on to speak about the living connections that underlie such phenomena ...

> Dwelling in eternal obscurity and loneliness, these Mothers are creative beings; they are the creative and sustaining principle from which proceeds everything that has life and form on the surface of the earth. Whatever ceases to breathe returns to them as a spiritual nature, and they preserve it until there arises occasion for its renewed existence. All souls and forms of what has been, or will be, hover about like cloud in the vast space of their abode ... the magician must enter their dominion, if he would obtain power over the form of a being ...

IN THE FIFTH CENTURY BC ATHENS AND SPARTA had fought for dominance. In the fourth century they were both overtaken by Macedonia, ruled by the robust Philip II. Plutarch noted that Philip's son, Alexander, was born on the very day in 356 BC that the Temple at Ephesus was torched by a lunatic.

Each Mystery school taught a wisdom unique to it, which is why Moses and Pythagoras were initiated into more than one. The hierophants at the Mystery school attached to the temple at Ephesus taught the mysteries of Mother Earth, the powers that shape the natural world. In a sense the spirit of this school entered Alexander at birth. Alexander would spend his whole life trying to identify this divine element within.

One day the handsome, fearless boy with the burning eyes and leonine mane tamed a magnificent but fiery horse called Bucephalus that none of Philip's generals could even mount.

Philip cast about for the greatest mind of the day to be his son's tutor, and chose Plato's greatest pupil, Aristotle. Alexander and the older man recognized each other as kindred spirits.

As soon as Plato gave formal, conceptual expression to idealism, it was inevitable that its opposite would quickly be formulated. Instead of deducing the truth about the world from immaterial, universal principles, Aristotle collected and classified the data of the material world. He worked out physical laws by a process of abstraction. Aristotle was therefore able to invent an entirely new and modern way of describing the hidden powers that shape nature. It is often said that the Roman Empire provided a vehicle for the spread of Christianity, and in the same way Alexander created the largest empire the world had yet seen. This, then, became the vehicle for Aristotle's philosophy.

Philip was assassinated when his son was only twenty, but immediately Alexander established himself as a ruler of genius and an unbeatable military commander. In 334 BC he led an army into Asia, defeating the Persians at the Battle of Issus, even though they were outnumbered by as many as ten to one. Then he swept south through Syria and Phoenicia, before conquering Egypt, where he founded the city of Alexandria. Wherever he went he founded city-states on the Greek model, spreading Greek politics as well as Greek philosophy.

It was part of Alexander's mission to save the newly evolved consciousness, forged by initiates such as Plato and Euripides, from being swamped by the greater wealth, grandeur and military might of Asia. More particularly, he was to save the new rationality from being swept away by ancient ritualistic clairvoyance and picture-consciousness.

In 331 BC Alexander defeated the Persians again, destroying their ancient capital of Persepolis, before pushing further into Afghanistan and finally into India. There he debated with Brahmin philosophers, the descendants of the Rishis. Admitted to watch the sacred, initiatory rites of the Brahmins, Alexander's own priests were astonished to see how similar the ceremonies were to their own.

There is a story that Alexander sent a Greek philosopher to summon a Brahmin teacher into his presence, offering great rewards and threatening decapitation if he refused. The philosopher finally tracked down the Brahmin in the depths of the forest and received the following rather dusty response: 'The Brahmins neither fear death nor desire gold. We sleep deeply and peacefully on forest leaves. Were we to have any material possessions, this would only disturb our slumber. We move freely over the surface of the earth without conflict and all our needs met as by a mother who feeds her baby her milk.'

This was a rare knockback for Alexander. Until the near the end of his life it seemed no one could stand in his way. As has happened only a few times in history, an individual seemed able to bend the whole world to his will.

As I've suggested, Alexander's entire life can be seen as a quest to understand the origins of this divine power. At different times both Perseus and Hercules were claimed as his ancestors, according to variant traditions. Aristotle had given Alexander a copy of Homer's *Iliad*, which he learned off by heart, and he sometimes saw himself as a demi-god like Achilles. In 332 BC he went on an expedition to the temple of Amun at the desert oasis of Siwa, some five hundred miles west of Memphis in Egypt. It was said he nearly died on this expedition, though this may be a reference to a 'mystical death'. What is certain is that he was 'recognized' by the priests and initiated there.

It is sometimes speculated that the priests might have told Alexander he was a son of Amun-Zeus. It is supposed that the ceremonial horns he took to wearing afterwards were a mark of this. In some countries he conquered he was remembered as a horned man. In the Koran he appeared as Dhul-Qarnayn, which means 'the two-horned one'. But according to the secret history, these horns are the horns of a hunter we have already met, and the two fiercely loving friends Gilgamesh and Enkidu, separated by the untimely death of Enkidu, were reunited when they reincarnated as Alexander and Aristotle.

At the age of only thirty-three Alexander ignored warnings by the astrologers of Babylon not to enter their city gates. Two weeks later he died of a fever. It would soon become apparent that Alexander's empire had been held together only by his personal magnetism.

BUDDHISM EMERGED AS THE FIRST PROSELYTIZING, missionary religion in about 200 BC. Before then the religion you believed in was determined by your race or tribe. Now the human condition was changing. For the uninitiated the spirit worlds were a fading vision, leaving faint traces hard to be certain of, difficult to discern. Inspired by Pythagoras, Socrates, Plato and Aristotle, people were developing a capacity for deductive and inductive thought. They were able to weigh up arguments on either side.

By 140 BC Rome was the capital of the world and a vortex of ideas. A citizen might have very different belief systems to choose from: the official cult of the planetary gods, the neo-Egyptian worship of Serapis, Epicurianism, Stoicism, the philosophy of the

Virgil from a painting by the Swiss-born artist Henry Fuseli. Virgil was the great initiate poet of the founding and destiny of Rome. Aeneid *vi 748–51 gives expression to the doctrine of reincarnation, of the spirit's 'desire to return to the body' when a thousand years comes round.*

Peripatetics and the Persian cult of Mithraism. Buddhist monks and Indian Brahmins had certainly reached Alexandria.

For the first time in history choosing one of these belief systems could be a matter of personal choice.

Individuals might choose in proportion to the evidence or they might choose what they *wanted* to believe. With the rise to dominance of the Roman Empire, therefore, we reach the age of inauthentic faith, with a cynicism and conscious cultivation of sensibility that was entirely new.

When we think of Rome we picture sophistication and grandeur but also paranoia. If we compare the Greece of Pericles with the Rome of the Caesars, we see in the latter the same kind of overbearing pomp, elaborate, awesome rituals of smoke, incense and clashing cymbals that had earlier been used to hypnotize the peoples into obedience to Baal. Now it was used to hypnotize people into believing that various strange and egomaniacal members of the ruling elite were in fact gods.

The Caesars forced the Mystery schools to initiate them. In the process they discovered the ancient initiatic teachings regarding the Sun god.

Julius Caesar eradicated the Druids because of their teaching of the Sun Mysteries – that the Sun god was soon to return to earth. Similarly Augustus banned astrology not because he disbelieved in it, but because he was anxious about what astrologers could see written in the sky. If the people could not read the signs of the time, he could perhaps get away with representing *himself* as the Sun god. Because he had been initiated, Caligula knew how to communicate with the spirits of the moon in his dreams. But because he had gained initiation by force and without proper preparation, he could not properly identify them. Caligula would refer to Jupiter, Hercules, Dionysus and Apollo as his brother gods, sometimes appearing in fancy dress to look like them. Nero's reign of madness reached a climax when he realized he was not after all the Sun god. He would rather burn the whole world to the ground than let another, greater, individual live.

THE GOLDEN ASSE OF APULEIUS IS ONE of the great initiatic works of the Roman period. It contains a wonderful story concerning the life of the spirit. *Cupid and Psyche* carries familiar and fairly conventional warnings about the dangers of curiosity, but it also has an esoteric and historical level of meaning.

Psyche is a beautiful, innocent young girl. Cupid falls in love with her and sends messengers asking her to come to him in his hill-top palace at night. She is to make love to a god! But there is one condition. Their love making must take place in total darkness. Psyche must take it on trust that she is enjoying the love of a god.

Her elder sister is envious, though. She taunts her and tells her that it is not a beautiful boy-god she is making love to, but a hideous, giant serpent. One night Psyche can resist no longer, and while Cupid is in a post-coital slumber, she holds an oil lamp over him. She is delighted to discover the gloriously beautiful young god, but at that moment a drop of burning oil falls on him and wakes him. Psyche is banished from his presence forever.

The double meaning in this story is this: the god really is a hideous serpent. This is the history of the Nephilim, of the entry into the human condition of the serpent of animal desire – but told from the human point of view!

THE MYSTERY SCHOOLS WERE FALLING into decay. As we have seen, excavations of the entrance to the Underworld at Baia in southern Italy revealed secret passageways and trap doors used to help convince the candidates that they were having supernatural experiences. In the smoky, druggy darkness priests dressed up as gods would loom out of the darkness over candidates heavily drugged with hallucinogens. Robert Temple has reconstructed the initiation ceremonies of this late, decadent phase. They were largely a matter of scary special effects, even including puppets, like a ghost train today. The difference was that at the end of your initiation, when you re-emerged into daylight, the priests quizzed you, and unless you believed in their illusions without the slightest sliver of doubt, *they killed you.*

The Golden Asse *which contains the story of Cupid and Psyche is a beautiful book, written by an initiate in a larky way that anticipates Rabelais. But it is also a consciously literary production. The colossal and monolithic sincerity of the ancient Mystery schools is no more.*

The sincere men of Rome, the true initiates, withdrew into yet more shadowy schools that operated independently of the official cult. Stoicism became the outward expression of the initiatic impulse of the age, the growing point of intellectual and spiritual evolution. Cicero and Seneca, both deeply involved with Stoicism, tried to temper the egomania of their political masters. They tried to argue that all men were born brothers and that the slaves should be set free.

Cicero was an urbane and sophisticated man and one of the great forces for reform in the Roman Empire. He looked upon his initiation at Eleusis as the great formative experience of his life. It had taught him, he said 'to live joyfully and to die hopefully'.

If Cicero looked askance at the plebs' vain and superstitious beliefs in venal gods, he was also tolerant of them. He held that even the most ridiculous of the myths could be interpreted in an allegorical way. In *The Nature of the Gods* he gives a passionate exposition of the Stoic idea of the moving spirit of the universe, the guiding force that makes plants seek nourishment in the earth, gives animals sense, motion and an instinct to go after what is good for them that is almost akin to reason. This same moving spirit of the cosmos gives people 'reason itself and a higher intelligence to the gods themselves'. These gods should not really be imagined as having bodies like our own 'but are clothed in the most ethereal and beautiful forms'. He writes, too, that 'we can see their higher, inward purpose in the movements of the stars and planets'.

When Rome's political machinations finally caught up with Cicero, he stoically bared his neck to the centurion's sword.

Seneca also believed in this cosmic sympathy of the Stoics – and the ability of adepts to manipulate this sympathy for their own ends. His play *Medea* probably quotes real magical formulae used by the black magicians of the day. Medea is portrayed as being able to direct her power of concentrated hatred so strongly that she can change the positions of the stars.

In this Age of Disenchantment it first became possible to consider that the gods might not exist. Among the intellectual elite, the Epicureans were formulating the first materialistic and atheist philosophies. What remained was belief in the lowest levels of spirits, the spirits of the dead and demons. If you read literature of the time, such as the Gospels of the New Testament, you see they record that the world was experiencing an epidemic of demons.

While the intellectual elite toyed with atheism, the people dabbled in atavistic forms of occultism that made use of the fact that demons and other low forms of spirit life are attracted by the fumes from blood sacrifices.

The high priest of the Jerusalem Temple wore little bells attached to his robes so that the goblins that lived in the shadows could hear him coming and hide their hideous shapes. The Temple needed a vast, complex drainage system to cope with the thousands of gallons of sacrificial blood that flowed through it every day.

All around the world increasingly desperate measures were taken. Plutarch wrote against human sacrifice in a way that implies it was common.

In South America, in a bizarre parody, a black magician was being nailed to a cross.

15

The Sun God Returns

The Two Jesus Children • The Cosmic Mission • Crucifixion in South America • The Mystic Marriage of Mary Magdalene

IN PALESTINE A GREAT TURNING POINT IN the history of the world had been reached. Because the gods were no longer experienced as 'out there' in the material world, it was necessary for the Sun god, the Word, to descend to earth. As we are about to see, *his mission was to plant in the human skull the seeds of an interior life that would become the new arena for spiritual experience.* This planting would give rise to the sense we all have today that we each have inside an 'inner space'.

The cosmic plan had been that human spirits should attain individuality, should be able to think freely, to exercise free will and to choose who to love. To create the conditions for this, matter became denser until each individual spirit was finally isolated inside its own skull. Human thought and will was then no longer wholly controlled by gods, angels and spirits, as it had been a thousand years earlier at the siege of Troy.

However there were dangers in this development. Not only might humanity become altogether cut off from the spirit world, there was a danger, too, that humans would become completely cut off from one another.

This was the great crisis. People no longer felt like spiritual beings, because the human spirit was in danger of being snuffed out altogether. The love that bound tribes and families, an instinctive, psychic blood-love like the one which binds packs of wolves, was weakened in the newly hardened skulls, in the new towns and cities.

Tracing the development towards a sense of individual identity, we have touched on Mosaic law, a rule for communal living strictly enforced, an eye for an eye, a tooth for a tooth. We have touched, too, on the obligation to feel compassion for all living things taught by the Buddha. We saw in both traditions the beginnings of moral obligation as a path of individual discipline and development. Now the Stoics of Rome gave the individual legal and political status in the form of rights and duties.

The irony, then, was that just as individual human identity was formed, the sense that life was worth living was largely lost. The blood baths in the Colosseum showed no notion of the value, let alone the sanctity of individual human life.

Jesus ben Pandira, the leader of the Essenes, might preach purity and universal compassion, but from a point of view of a movement to withdraw from the world altogether. Stoics might teach responsibility, but to them this was a duty without joy. 'Never let the future disturb you', the Stoic emperor Marcus Aurelius would offer as a philosophy of life – 'you will meet it, if you have to, with the same weapons of reason which arm you today against the present'. These words are full of weariness.

Humanity felt itself dragged along by a tide of suffering. We may imagine how people longed to hear someone say, 'Come with me, ye that are heavy-laden, I will give you rest.'

We saw the candidate for initiation being shown the green wheat ear in the inner sanctum at Eleusis and taught to look forward to the 'seed time'. In the inner sanctum of great Egyptian temples, candidates for initiation had been shown Isis suckling the infant Horus. This second Horus, this Horus-to-come, would be a new king of the gods bringing a new dispensation. He was called the Good Shepherd, the Lamb of God, the Book of Life and the Truth and the Life. Isaiah had told his people to make straight the ways of the Lord. He promised their sins would be washed away as he envisioned the coming of the Messiah. In the *Fourth Eclogue* the Roman initiate-poet Virgil predicted the coming of the man-god, the Saviour. 'The Golden Age will return as its first-born descends from on high,' he wrote, '... all the stains of our past wickedness will be washed away.'

In fact the life of Christ Jesus as it has come down to us might look like a patchwork of events in the lives of those who came before him: born to a carpenter and a Virgin, like Krishna: born on December 25, like Mithras; heralded by a star in the East, like Horus; walking on water and feeding the five thousand from a small basket, like Buddha; performing healing miracles, like Pythagoras; raising from the dead, like Elisha; executed on a tree, like Adonis: ascending to heaven, like Hercules, Enoch and Elijah.

It is hard to find *any* act or saying ascribed to the Jesus of the Gospels that had not been foreshadowed in some way. Anyone minded to think corrosively will decide to see this as evidence that his life was a fiction. But in the secret history this is a universal movement of convergence as the whole cosmos strained to give birth to the new Sun god.

Looking at the great imaginative image of the Nativity as it has been depicted in history's greatest art, and decoding it according to the secret doctrine, we can see how the whole secret history of the world had been leading up to this point.

In Mary we should sense the presence of Isis; when the sun arose in the constellation of Pisces, the sign of Jesus, the constellation on the opposite horizon was Virgo. In

Joseph, the patriarch carrying a crooked staff, we see Osiris – his staff symbolizing the Third Eye. The cave in which Jesus Christ is often represented as being born is the bony skull in which a new miracle of consciousness is about to be ignited. The baby in the manger has the luminous vegetative body of Krishna. The ox and the ass represent the two ages that have led to the new Age of Pisces – the Ages of Taurus and Aries. The star that guides the Magi is the spirit of Zarathustra ('the golden star'). One of the Magi is Pythagoras reincarnated, and the Magi have been initiated by the prophet Daniel. The angel who announces the birth to the shepherds is the spirit of the Buddha.

THE SECRET TRADITION SOMETIMES HAS a propensity to see how things are with a, child-like simplicity.

The two Gospels with infancy narratives, Luke and Matthew, give very different, indeed inconsistent, accounts, starting with the different genealogies ascribed to Jesus, the time and place of the births, and the visit by the shepherds in Luke and by the Magi in Matthew. This is a distinction rigidly maintained in the art of the Middle Ages that has since been lost. While it may be glossed over in church, academic theologians accept that where these accounts conflict at least one must be false – perhaps an uncomfortable conclusion for anyone believing that scripture is divinely inspired.

In the secret tradition, on the other hand, there is no problem, because these two narratives describe the infancies of *two* Jesus children. These boys had a mysterious kinship. They were not twins, though they looked almost identical.

In the Gnostic text the *Pistis Sophia*, contemporary with the canonical books of the New Testament – and considered by some scholars to have equal claim to authenticity – there is a strange story concerning these two children.

Mary sees a boy who looks so exactly like him that she naturally takes him to be her son. But then this boy disconcerts her by asking to see her son, Jesus. Fearing that this must be some sort of demon, she ties the boy to the bed, then goes out into the fields looking for Joseph and Jesus. She finds them erecting vine poles. The three of them go back to the house. The boys gaze at each other, amazed, and embrace.

The secret tradition that traces the subtle, complex process by which human form and human consciousness was put together has a parallel in its tracing of the extremely complex process by which the incarnation of the Word was brought about. In this account it was necessary for one of the two Jesus children, who carried the spirit of Krishna, to sacrifice his individual identity in some mysterious way for the sake of the other. The spiritual economy of the cosmos required him to do this so that the boy who survived would in time be ready to receive the Christ-spirit at the Baptism. As the *Pistis Sophia* says, 'ye became one and the same being'.

This tradition of the two Jesus children was maintained by the secret societies

The Leonardo Cartoon *in the National Gallery, London. The esoteric dimension to this work is conveyed by the swirling, star-spangled light that suggests the world between the worlds. It depicts the two Jesus children. Similarly in the London version of the* Virgin of the Rocks *nearby, a later hand than Leonardo's has added the elongated form of the cross that in Christian art is John the Baptist's distinctive insignia.*

and can be seen on the north portal at Chartres, in the apse mosaic of San Miniato outside Florence and in the paintings of many initiates, including Borgonone, Raphael, Leonardo and Veronese.

'IN THE BEGINNING WAS THE WORD, and the Word was with God and the Word was God ... All things were made by him ... And the light shineth in darkness and darkness comprehended it not ... He was in the world, and the world was made by him, and the world knew him not.'

The author of the Gospel of St John is here comparing the creation of the cosmos by the Word with the mission of Jesus Christ, the incarnated Word. John presents this second mission as *a sort of second creation.*

At a time when the material universe had become so dense that it was all but impossible for the gods to manifest themselves on the earth's surface, the Sun god descended.

His mission was to plant a seed. This spiritualizing seed would grow to provide the space that would be the new arena in which the gods could manifest themselves ...

The crucial point here, usually overlooked outside the secret tradition, is this: *Jesus Christ created the interior life.*

We have seen an intimation of the interior life in the still, small voice heard by Elijah. Similarly in Jeremiah the Lord says, 'I will put my hand in the inward parts and in their heart I will write it.' But the planting of the sun seed just over two thousand years ago was the decisive event in the process which has led to each of us experiencing inside of ourselves a cosmos of infinite size and variety.

Romulus and Remus. The story of the two Jesus boys is, in effect, a sanctified version of the story of Romulus and Remus, in which one brother murders the other in order for him to serve as the foundation sacrifice of the Eternal City. Great buildings and cities were founded on sacrifices in ancient times, and this is undoubtedly what the myth of Remus killed and buried in a ditch refers to. In the case of the two Jesus boys, one could be said to sacrifice himself for the sake of the New Jerusalem.

We also have a sense that others have infinity inside them. Over many hundreds of years, the conditions had been coming together which would make possible a sense of individual identity, what we today sometimes call the Ego. But without the intervention of the Sun god, the Ego would have been a small, hard, self-centred point, operating in isolation, intent only on its own immediate gratification, open to no outside interests other than the very lowest. Every human being would have been at war with every other human being. No individual would have any sense at all of any other as an independent centre of consciousness.

When his parents took Jesus to the Temple, at the time of the disappearance of his kindred spirit, he showed himself very wise. What passed into him from the other Jesus was the ability to read minds, to see deep into other people's souls, to see how they related to the spirit worlds and to know what to do or say to make things right for them. He felt other people's pain as his own. He was experiencing something – the gift of empathy – which no one had ever felt before.

Once an individual or small group develops a new faculty, a new mode of consciousness, it often spreads around the world with remarkable speed. Jesus Christ introduced a new kind of love, a *gracious* love based on the gift of empathy. An individual would be free to transcend the bonds of his or her isolated existence to share in what was taking place in another person's innermost nature.

Love BC had been tribal or familial. Now individuals were able to rise above blood ties and to *choose* freely who to love. It is this that Jesus meant when, in Mark 3:32 he appeared to deny the importance of his own mother to him and when, in Matthew 10:37–8 he said: 'He that loveth father and mother more than me is not worthy of me.'

Esoteric teaching is above all about loving in the right way. It says that when you cooperate with the gracious forces that form the cosmos, the force flows through you in such a way that you may become conscious of it. This process is called thaumaturgy, or divine magic.

Whether at this level or at the level of 'little, nameless unremembered acts of kindness and love' or the 'little way' of St Thérèse of Lisieux, the way of self-denial and acts of charity in small things, the new Christian perspective was focused on the inner life. If we compare earlier moral codes, such as the law of Moses or the even older Code of Hammurabi, with the Sermon on the Mount, it is clear that they were only rules to regulate behaviour in the Outworld – do not worship idols, steal, murder, commit adultery etc. The moral teaching in the Gospels, on the other hand, is directed towards inner states. 'Blessed are the poor in spirit ... they that mourn ... the meek ... the pure in heart ...'

When Jesus Christ said, 'But I say unto you, that whosoever looketh on a woman to lust after her hath committed adultery with her already in his heart', he was saying something no one had ever said before, that our innermost thoughts are as real as physical objects. What I think 'privately' has a direct effect on the history of the cosmos.

In an idealist universe, intention is of course much more important than in a materialist universe. In an idealist universe if two people perform exactly the same action in exactly the same circumstances, but one in a good-hearted way and the other not, the consequences are very different. In some mysterious way the state of our soul informs the results of our deeds, just as the elevated state of the soul of a great painter informs his paintings.

In esoteric interpretation of Greek myths, ambrosia, the food of the gods, is human love. Without it, gods fade away and their power to help us is diminished. In esoteric and mystic Christianity angels are attracted to us if we ask for their help, but if we fail to do so they fall into a twilit, vegetative state, and the phantoms and demons that insinuate themselves around our lower beings work on us instead.

We can of course resist the demons and train our baser animal selves in the same way that we train a dog – by a process of repetition. In esoteric teaching it is said that daily repetition of a meditative exercise for twenty-one days is needed to effect a deep-seated change in our habits.

But there is a yet deeper part of our animal selves which lies completely below the threshold of consciousness and is inaccessible to it. We cannot transform this part by the exercise of free will, no matter how persistent, because the corruption of our animal selves has seeped down into our vegetable and mineral selves.

In order to purify and transform these parts of ourselves we need supernatural help.

The mission of the Sun god, then, was to sink right down into deepest matter, introducing his transforming spiritual influence. The Sun god has the ability to reach right down into the most material part of humanity, which is why it was written 'None of his bones shall be broken'.

THE TWELVE-PETALLED LOTUS RADIATES outwards from the region of the heart and envelops those we choose to love. It is also an organ of perception. What I truly love will open itself up to me and reveal its secrets.

Enveloping someone in love in this way is an exercise of the imagination. Of course imagination is not to be confused here with fantasy. It is a true perception of a higher reality – and the organ of this in both East and West is the heart chakra. This is what is being referred to on the road to Emmaus, where disciples who have just recognized who it was they have just encountered say to themselves, 'Did our hearts not burn within us while he talked to us on the road?'

When the heart chakra blossoms and shines, we may perceive the Outworld in a supernatural way. A loving heart can give me conscious experience of the heart of the cosmos, of the loving intelligence that lives beyond the Outworld and controls it. 'Blessed are the pure in heart, for they shall see God.'

Love works on the will as well as powers of perception. When we really love someone, we are willing to do anything for them.

This is why the heart chakra blossoms when love moves me to act according to my conscience. I am not then acting wearily, like Marcus Aurelius. I am not acting in a cold, unenthusiastic or inauthentic way. I am not doing my duty while part of me resents it. I am acting out of love and devotion.

The phrase 'Son of Man' is problematic to exoteric theologians because it seems to refer to both a state of mind and to Jesus Christ himself. In esoteric thought this is resolved because the individual who has evolved to the stage of enlightenment that Jesus Christ made possible, will, as a result, become aware of his or her Higher Self, or divine self. In Christian iconography this evolution is commonly symbolized by a child carried on the shoulder, for example in the story of St Christopher who carried the Christ child on his shoulders. In the Cabala these two same dimensions of meaning are contained in the three-pronged letter shin.

Initiation forges a new form of consciousness. It revives ways of being conscious of the spirit worlds that were common in the earlier stages of human evolution, but now with new elements. The initiations of Pythagoras that set the tone for the ages of the ascendancy of Greece and Rome, for example, had been concerned with achieving an alternative state of consciousness involving free communications with the spirit worlds that had been an everyday occurrence for, say, Gilgamesh or Achilles, but with a crucial difference. Initiates of the school of Pythagoras were able to think about their spiritual experiences in a considered, conceptual way that would have been impossible for Achilles or Gilgamesh.

Four hundred years later the initiations of Jesus Christ introduced a new element, opening up dizzying new dimensions in love.

IN ORDER TO UNDERSTAND THE MOMENTOUS events described in the Gospels better, we must now look at Jesus's involvement with the Mystery schools.

We are trespassing on closely guarded academic territory here. Controversial findings now widely accepted by biblical scholars, but which have not yet filtered down to the wider congregation, show that there are some early Christian texts, rediscovered in Palestine in the 1950s, which contain versions of sayings of Jesus that are likely to be closer to the originals than the versions contained in the four Gospels.

And some of these texts contain sayings which don't appear in the Gospels at all.

And the fact that texts like the Gospel of St Thomas contain 'truer' versions of the biblical sayings is a reason for believing that the entirely non-biblical sayings these texts contain may be authentic.

This is important for our history, because some of them relate to the secret teachings.

The Gospels hint that Jesus gives favoured followers teachings not for public dissemination. When Jesus warns against casting 'pearls before swine' he seems to be talking of holding some sacred truths back from the multitude. More explicitly, Mark 4.11 has Jesus say: 'The secret of the kingdom of God is given to you, but to those who are outside everything comes in parables.'

A more striking and revealing account of Jesus's involvement in secret teaching is to be found in a letter written in the second century by Clement, Bishop of Alexandria. This text was discovered in 1959 in the stacks of the library of the Mar Saba Monastery near Jerusalem by Dr Morton Smith, Professor of Ancient History at Columbia University:

> ... Mark, then, during Peter's stay in Rome, wrote an account of the Lord's doings, not however declaring all of them, nor yet hinting at the secret ones, but selecting those he thought most useful for increasing the faith of those who were being instructed. But when Peter died as a martyr, Mark came over to Alexandria, bringing his own notes and those of Peter, from which he transferred to his

> former book the things suitable to whatever makes for progress towards knowledge, and in this way he composed a more spiritual gospel for use of those who were being perfected ... and dying he left his composition to the church in Alexandria, where it is still carefully guarded.

The Bishop of Alexandria then quotes from this 'more spiritual' version of Mark's Gospel:

> And they came to Bethanay, and a certain woman whose brother had died was there. And coming, she prostrated herself before Jesus and said to him: 'Son of David, have mercy on me.' But the disciples rebuked her.
>
> And Jesus, being angered, went off with her into the garden where the tomb was, and straightaway, going in where the youth was, he stretched forth his hand and, seizing his hand, raised him.
>
> But the youth, looking upon him, loved him and began to beseech him that he might be with him.
>
> And after six days Jesus told him what to do and in the evening the youth came to him, wearing a linen cloth over his naked body. And he remained with him that night, for Jesus taught him the mystery of the kingdom of God. And then, arising, he returned to the other side of the Jordan ...

The Last Supper *by Leonardo da Vinci. It has been suggested that this painting alludes to suppressed, secret doctrines regarding the feminine role in Christianity. We shall see shortly that this is true, though not in the way proposed by* The Da Vinci Code.

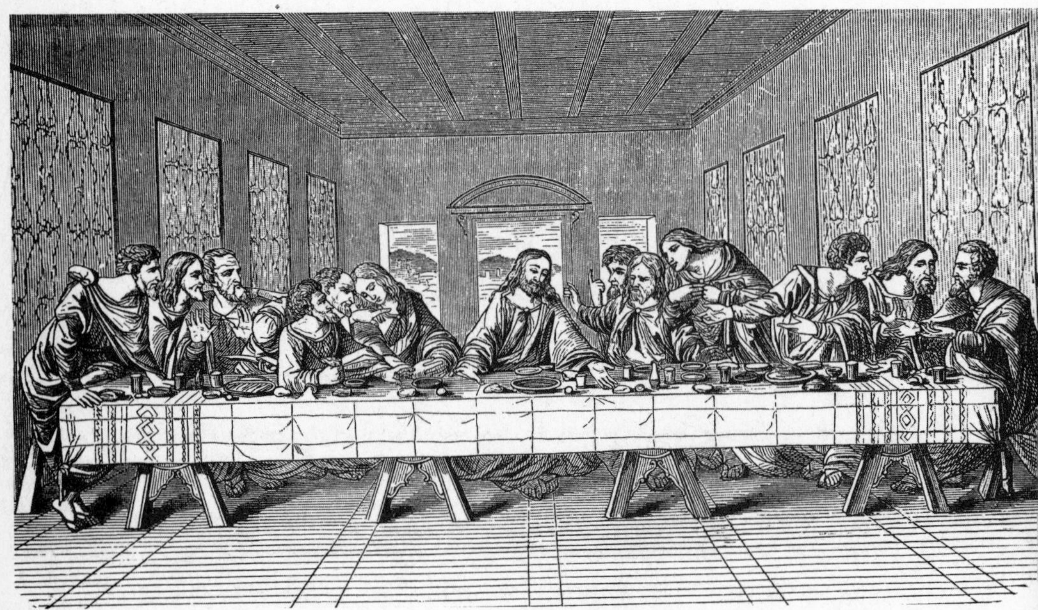

To modern sensibility this story – which appears to be a more detailed version of the story of the raising of Lazarus in John's Gospel – might seem to describe a homosexual liaison, but, as we shall see as we come to examine the nature of initiation ceremonies more clearly, it is certainly a Mystery school initiation that Mark alludes to here.

The raising of Lazarus from the dead has traditionally been seen as an encoded account of initiation. The clues are there. Lazarus 'dies' for thee days and when Jesus Christ raises him, he uses the phrase 'Lazarus, come forth' that the hierophants had used in the Great Pyramid when, after three days, they stretched forth a hand to raise the candidate from the open tomb in the King's Chamber.

What was the initiation of Lazarus like from Lazarus's point of view? What *was* the alternative form of consciousness it conferred? Readers may be surprised to learn that we know the answer to these questions. Because in the secret history the man called Lazarus in the Gospel of John later wrote the Revelation of St John the Divine. According to the secret doctrine, the opening of the seven seals and the great visionary events that follow that are described in Revelation, refer to the revivifying of the seven chakras.

Unpalatable though some may find it, the fact of the matter is that the teachings of Jesus Christ are steeped in the ancient and secret philosophy, and this is equally true of his sayings recorded in the Bible as it is of the newly discovered sayings.

I have led up to this point gently. Those of us brought up as Christians may find it easier to recognize these things in alien cultures, partly, no doubt, because of the greater focus that distance brings, but also because we are less acutely aware of treading on sacred ground. Christianity's most sacred texts are deeply occult:

The meek shall inherit the earth
Faith moves mountains
Ask and it shall be given.

There is deliberate obfuscation by Church leaders when it comes to these and other key tenets of the Christian faith. Modern liberal Christianity has tried to accommodate science by playing down its occult dimensions, but the sayings from the Sermon on the Mount listed above are descriptions of how the supernatural operates in the universe. Not only are they paradoxical and mysterious, not only are they irrational, not only do they describe what is highly unlikely according to the laws of probability, they describe the universe behaving in a way which would be completely impossible if science described everything there is.

For the meek will certainly not inherit the earth and prayers will not be answered by the forces that science describes. Neither virtue nor faith will be rewarded – unless some supernatural agency makes them so.

The New Testament is full of occult and esoteric teaching, some of it explicitly stated. The problem is that we have been educated to be blind to it. But the text quite clearly says

Apollonius of Tyana. Of the many itinerant wonder workers and healers contemporary with Jesus Christ, the one who made the greatest impression on contemporary chroniclers was Apollonius. This Pythagorean from Cappadocia let his hair grow long, wore only linen clothes and shoes of bark. He cast out demons and performed many healing miracles. But perhaps the most interesting parallel to Jesus Christ is his insistence that the day of blood sacrifice was over. 'We should approach God,' he said, 'only with the noblest faculty with which we are blessed – namely intelligence.'

that John the Baptist is Elijah come again – that is, reincarnated. There is magic too. The late Hugh Schonfield, Morton Smith and other academic experts have shown that Jesus's miracles, particularly in the form of words he uses, are based on pre-existing magical papyri in Greek, Egyptian and Aramaic. When in John's Gospel Jesus Christ is described as using spittle to make a paste to apply to the eyes of a blind man, this is not a purely godly action, in the sense of an unmediated influx of spirit, but a manipulation of matter in order to influence or control spirit.

Again, it is no denigration of Jesus Christ to point this out. One must not view these things anachronistically. In terms of the philosophy and theology of the day, this sort of divine magic – or thaumaturgy – was not only respectable, it was the highest activity to which a human being could aspire.

IF YOU POLITELY TURN A BLIND EYE TO the supernatural content of the story of Jesus Christ and the rise of Christianity, you still have to accept that something extraordinary happened which needs explanation. Because whether or not anything miraculous happened in that obscure corner of the Near East in the early years of the first century, its effect on the history of the world is unparalleled in its breadth and depth. It gave rise to the civilization we now enjoy, a civilization of unprecedented freedom, prosperity for all, richness of culture, scientific advance. Before the time of Jesus Christ there was very little sense of the importance of the individual, of the sanctity of individual life, the transcendental power of one individual's freely chosen love for another. Of course some of these ideas were foreshadowed by Krishna, Isaiah, the Buddha, Pythagoras, Lao-Tzu, but what was unique to Christianity, the 'mustard seed' planted by Jesus Christ, was the idea of the interior life. With Jesus Christ not only did the individual began to experience the sense we all have now that, parallel to the limitless, infinitely various cosmos out there, we each have inside us a cosmos which is equally rich and limitless, but Jesus Christ also introduced the sense that each of us now has of a personal narrative history that weaves in and out of the general history. Each of us may fall as humanity as a whole has fallen. Each of us experiences crises of doubt and finds individual, personal redemption – very different from the tribal consciousness of earlier generations of Jews or the city-state consciousness of the Greeks.

THE MINISTRY OF JESUS CHRIST LASTED just three years from the Baptism to Good Friday on 3 April AD 3 when at the place of the skulls, Golgotha, the Sun god was nailed on the cross of matter. Then at the Transfiguration the Sun god began to transform that matter, to spiritualize it.

We have seen how in the Mystery schools from Zarathustra to Lazarus, candidates

The Resurrection, part of the Isenheim Altarpiece *by Matthias Grünewald is a cosmic vision of Jesus Christ as the Sun god. Grünewald depicted what the Church father Tertullian, drawing from the Greek Mystery tradition, called the luminous seed, the 'augoeides'. Planted in the earth, it now arose as a luminous, star-like body, a body of light rays. When the disciples on the road to Emmaus failed to recognize Christ it was because they were encountering his augoeidean body.*

The Cross in the middle of the Four Cherubim who symbolize the Four Elements. As we have seen, the Four Elements, working from the constellations at the four corners of the cosmos work together to hold the material world in place. Jesus Christ is here represented in his cosmic role as Fifth Element, the Sun god who comes to Earth to spiritualize the Four Elements and dissolve matter.

had undergone a three day 'mystical death' and rebirth. The candidate was put into a deep, death-like trance for three days during which his spirit travelled the spirit worlds, bringing back knowledge and power to the material world. The 'death' then was a real event, but on the spiritual plane. *What happened with the crucifixion and resurrection of Jesus Christ was that for the first time this process of initiation occurred as a historical event on the material plane.*

THE SHADOW SIDE OF THIS GREAT EVENT is contained in the story of Christ's journey into Hell. This happened immediately after his death on the cross. It is a story which has fallen into desuetude, part of the process by which we have lost a sense of the spiritual dimension of the cosmos. Initiation is always concerned as much with lighting the way of the journey after death as with this life's journey. In the centuries before Jesus Christ, humanity's sense of the afterlife had shrunk to an anticipation of a dreary half-life of shades in the sub-lunar realm, Sheol. And after death human spirits lost consciousness as they started their ascent through the higher, heavenly spheres. The result was that in their next reincarnation these spirits returned with no intimations of the journey.

By descending into Hell, Jesus Christ was following in the footsteps of Osiris. He was lighting up a way through the Underworld that the dead could follow. The living and dead would have to walk together if the great cosmic mission, the Work, was to be completed.

ACCORDING TO ESOTERIC DOCTRINE, the whole history of the world can be summed up as follows:

There was a Golden Age when earth and sun were united and the sun gave the earth form.

The sun then separated from the earth, causing it to materialize and become colder.

The god of the sun returned to infuse his spirit in the earth, so that the whole cosmos will eventually dematerialize and again become spiritualized.

This is the cosmic vision of the mission of Jesus Christ which inspired the early

The Harrowing of Hell *by Andrea Mantegna. I Peter 6: 18–9: 'He also went to the spirits in prison ... the gospel was also preached to those that are dead.' Following what St Paul termed Jesus Christ's 'descent into the lower parts of the Earth', spirits had Him as their guide to light the way.*

Christians, the Work which helped shape the great churches of the Middle Ages and the art of the Renaissance. It has been lost to modern, exoteric Christianity.

IF THE DEATH OF JESUS CHRIST WAS *meant* to happen on a cosmological level, we should still ask ourselves, what made it happen on a historical level? What were the immediate causes of the crucifixion?

Although Jesus Christ instructed Lazarus in private, his rebirth, and his being called forth to a new life, was a public event. It did not happen, like all previous initiations, within the closely guarded confines of a Mystery school and neither was Jesus Christ a hierophant of one of the state-sponsored Mystery schools. As a result Jesus Christ made deadly enemies of the Sadducees, who controlled the dissemination of initiatic knowledge on behalf of the ruling elite. The act of initiating Lazarus in public was a revolutionary one, signalling that the tie that bound initiates to the ruling elite was being broken. It was the beginning of the end of the Mystery schools and it prepared the way for the secret societies.

Jesus Christ also posed a threat to the Roman elite. The soldiers who draped him in a purple cloak and placed a crown of thorns on his head had no other king, no other god than Caesar. They mocked Jesus Christ by draping on him the purple cloak that was worn as a sign of initiation in the Adonis mysteries. The crown of thorns was a satire on the wreath bestowed when a candidate achieved initiation in the mysteries of Eleusis. The Caesars were the great occult enemy of Jesus Christ.

WHAT IS LESS WELL KNOWN IS THAT ANOTHER enemy was at work on the other side of the world. There an initiate wielded a blacker, more powerful magic than that wrought by the Caesars.

This magician had, according to Rudolf Steiner, worked to build up his supernatural powers over several incarnations, and he now threatened to pervert the whole course of history.

He had achieved this power on the back of multiple human sacrifices. José Ortega y Gasset, the Spanish philosopher, talks of the release of spirits that the spilling of blood brings. Blood is a frightening mystery, he says. It carries life, and when it is spilled and the ground stained, the whole landscape is maddened and excited. Occulists know that humans can be killed in a particular way so that the human spirit is harnessed. We saw how great initiates like Elijah fashion their own vegetable and animal selves in such a way that they can become chariots with which to travel through the spiritual worlds. In occult circles it is also known that black magicians can use the souls and spirits of others, their sacrificial victims, as chariots.

The great enemy, a magician, was therefore able to control people beyond the grave.

In Britain today there is only one piece of 'objective art', which is to say art which expresses the spiritual world perfectly without the distorting influence of a human personality. Many who gaze at The Lohan, *a Chinese statue of a Buddhist monk in the British Museum report strange experiences.*

In Islamic lore the Old Man of the Mountains controlled the whole world without leaving his mountain hideaway. This idea was modernized in the deeply esoteric films of Fritz Laing, in which Dr Mabuse hypnotises the world from his cell in a lunatic asylum.

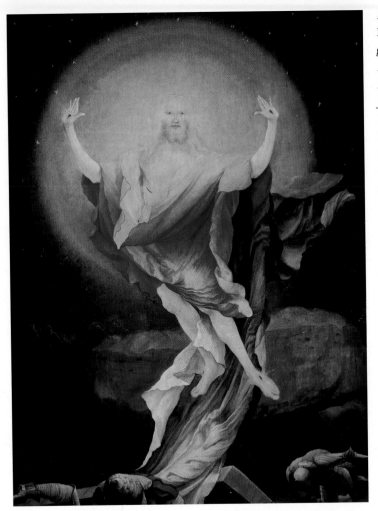

In this detail from the Isenheim Altarpiece, *the great esoteric masterpiece of Northern European art, Matthias Grünewald depicts Jesus Christ as the Sun-god. He has planted a seed of his Sun-nature in the Earth, and now the historic process of the spiritualizing of the whole material universe begins.*

Jesus and the Tempter *by Luca Giordano, a pupil of Caravaggio. Though it is open to misinterpretation, the great esoteric schools give a full account of the evil dimension in the cosmos only as a means to help defeat it.*

ABOVE The Annunciation *from the Church of St Marie Madeleine, Aix-en-Provence. In this late medieval triptych it is possible to discern bats and demons roosting in the arches, an angel with the wings of a short-eared owl and a horned and bearded demon. In local lore it was painted by a Satanist.*

RIGHT *The organs of spiritual perception are depicted in different ways in Christian iconography – in the almond-shaped* vesica piscis *surrounding many depictions of visions, in the horns of Moses as depicted by Michelangelo, and in the blossoming rod of Aaron and other flowerings.*

Leonardo's Mona Lisa *is one of the great icons of art because it catches someone discovering for the first time in history the joy of being free to explore the inner life.*

Albrecht Dürer's Large Clump of Grass. *This is the first time anyone had really* looked at *a clump of grass in a way that we take for granted today.*

ABOVE *In Hieronymus Bosch's* The Table of the Seven Deadly Sins, *Jesus Christ is identified with the Higher Man that evolves when we follow his ascent into the spirit worlds.*

RIGHT The Ecstasy of St Teresa *by Bernini. The Catholic Church's vast, wise esoteric dimension opened up in an extraordinary way in seventeenth-century Spain.*

Eighteenth-century illustration to The Magic Flute *by Mozart. The Egyptian priest Sarastro was widely believed to have been modeled on Cagliostro at the time of the first performance. Goethe said of this opera 'Let the crowd of spectators take pleasure in the spectacle. The higher import will not escape the initiated.'*

The Snake Charmers. *Illustration to the work of James Bruce, the explorer of Sufi thought and devotee of esoteric Freemasonry who rediscovered the* Book of Enoch *in Ethiopia in the late eighteenth century.*

In the art of William Blake, The Bezels of Wisdom, *in which the Sufi mystic Ibn Arabi saw sexual intercourse as the supreme form of contemplation, reaches its apogee. The free flow of thoughts between two spiritually mature lovers, a communication without words, is sometimes called 'true talk'. It is made possible because the vegetable or etheric bodies of the two individuals have become intertwined and grown enmeshed vith each other. Jacob Boehme described his process as the 'weaving of the vedding garment' that spirits will need n heaven.*

he Antichrist as depicted by Leonardo's rother initiate, Luca Signorelli, in Orvieto athedral. By rectifying Western with South merican lore, it is possible to arrive at 2012 s the date for the incarnation of Satan.

LEFT *The Maitreya Buddha, here in a beautiful statue in the Alchi Monastery, Ladahk, India, is to be identified with the Rider of the White Horse in* The Revelation of St John.

BELOW *El Greco's* Opening of the Fifth Seal. *In* The Revelation of St John, *the opening of the seals is a description of what our new powers of perception will reveal when our occult organs of perception are revivified.*

By sacrificing great numbers of victims, he created an army for himself in the spirit worlds.

At the turn of the millennium a Sun hero was sent to earth to oppose him. He was called Uitzilopotchtli, as we know from the *Codex Florentin of Sahagun*, one of the few scraps to survive the Conquistadors. Like earlier Sun heroes, his birth was prophesied. He was born to a virgin mother and after his birth the forces of evil conspired to kill him.

Mary Magdalene. Esoteric thought is essentially reincarnational. It is not primarily concerned with spirits passed on through genes. Jesus Christ came to do away with bloodlines as a way of transmitting clairvoyance and wisdom. Love was to be freely chosen rather than instinctual and tribal. The notion of Jesus marrying Mary Magdalene and having children is therefore irrelevant to his mission. Esoteric literature and the teachings of the schools refer rather to a 'Mystic Marriage' of the sun and the moon, the hieros gamos, *which we will return to in a later chapter.*

But Uitzilopotchli survived the early attempts on his life and after many trials he waged a three-year magical war against the black magician. Finally, he succeeded in crucifying him.

When Jesus Christ was crucified, a huge power to spiritualize the earth was unleashed. When, simultaneously, the great black magician of the South Americas was crucified, a vortex opened up that would draw into itself the great currents of world history, the extremes of both good and evil.

THE GOSPEL OF PHILIP CONTAINS intriguing hints about Jesus Christ's relationship with Mary Magdalene. 'Jesus loved her more than all the disciples and used to kiss her often on ...' Then intrigingly the script fragments. But this seems to be a reference to the *Song of Songs,* 'Let him kiss me with kisses of the mouth' and so, too, to the 'love that is stronger than death'.

The Golden Legend of Jacobus de Voraigne, the most popular collection of saints' stories in the Middle Ages, describes how a particular group of Christians began to be persecuted in Jerusalem. Seven of them were set adrift in the Mediterranean in a small boat. Eventually they were washed ashore in a place east of the town known today as Marseilles.

In the centre of a great cliff rising above the shore it is still possible to see the cave where Mary Magdalene, who stepped out of that boat, spent the last thirty years of her life.

She is usually depicted penitent, naked apart from her long red hair. A painting of her by Fra Bartolomeo in a small garden chapel near Florence shows her with her jar of oil, used to anoint the feet of Jesus Christ. It is resting on a stone inscribed with the following words:

I HAVE FOUND HIM WHOM MY SOUL LOVES

16

The Tyranny of the Fathers

The Gnostics and the Neoplatonists • The Murder of Hypatia • Attila and Shamanism • A Touch of Zen

IN THE SECRET TEACHINGS OF THE SCHOOLS the life and death of the Sun god marked the halfway point of the secret history.

Although it was unnoticed by the official chroniclers of the day, at the end of time this event will come to be seen as the great hinge on which history has turned.

To many people living at the time, the magnitude of this event undoubtedly made it hard to get into perspective. After a long period of spiritual aridity many now began to enjoy vivid, if atavistic, experience of the spirit worlds. Maybe some had an inkling of what the great revolution that had taken place in the spirit worlds actually was, but in the absence of the sort of unified, institutional authority that the hierophants of the Mystery schools had commanded, these new experiences were interpreted in a variety of ways. We see this in a proliferation of sects in the decades following the death of Jesus Christ.

Many of the Gnostic texts are as old as the books of the New Testament, some with clear claims to validity. We have already touched on the Gospel of St Thomas with its more authentic versions of the sayings of Jesus and the *Pistis Sophia*'s account of the two Jesus children. The somewhat fragmentary text of the Acts of St John offers a fascinating glimpse of the inner group practices of Jesus Christ.

A circular dance is described. The disciples first hold hands to form a circle, then whirl in a ring around Jesus Christ. In the liturgy that accompanies this dance, Jesus Christ is the initiator and his interlocutor a candidate for initiation.

Candidate: I would be saved
Christ: And I would save
Candidate: I would be loosed
Christ: And I would loosen
Candidate: I would be pierced

Christ: And I would pierce
Candidate: I would eat
Christ: And I would be eaten

The Acts of John use language in a paradoxical, even absurdist way. It will become easier to understand as we proceed.

Candidate: I have no house and I have houses
I have no place and I have places
I have no temple and I have temples.

Only fragments of the next bit have survived, but they seem to refer to some Osirian/Christian Mystery of death and resurrection. After which Christ says: 'What I am now seen to be, that I am not, but what I am, thou shalt see when thou comest. If thou hadst known how to suffer, thou wouldst have had the power not to suffer. Know then suffering and thou shalt have the power not to suffer'.

A Hindu dance in honour of Krishna is described as 'a circular sunwise dance'. The dancers twist and turn and wheel around the Sun god in imitation of the planets. This should alert us to the fact that the Acts of St John is inspired by a cosmic vision of Jesus Christ as the Sun god returned.

The Gospel of St Philip refers to five rituals, the last and greatest being the ritual of the bridal chamber. Is this a ritual-sexual practice like the ones that took place in the temples of Egypt, Greece and Babylon?

Later the Church would want to emphasize the uniqueness of Christian revelation and distance Jesus Christ and his teachings from what went before. But to the early Christians it was only natural to see Christianity as growing out of what had gone before and as a fulfilment of ancient prophecies. Many early Christians understood Christianity in terms of what they had been taught in the Mystery schools of Egypt, Greece and Rome.

The early Church father Clement of Alexandria may have known people who had known the Apostles. Clement and his pupil Origen believed in reincarnation, for example. They taught more advanced students what they called the *disciplina arcani*, devotional practices which today we would classify as magic.

Early Christian leaders like Origen and Clement were erudite men participating in the intellectual advances of their age. The most exciting of these found representative expression in Neoplatonism.

Plato had pretty comprehensively converted a mind-before-matter experience of the world into concepts. What happened in the second century AD was that what we now call Neoplatonists began to develop Plato's ideas into a living philosophy, a philosophy of life, even a religion with its own spiritual practices. It is important to remember that while we consider Plato in a dryly academic way, for his followers in the centuries after his death his texts had the status of scripture. Neoplatonists saw themselves not as originating ideas but writing commentaries making clear what Plato really meant. Passages which are today considered merely as rather abstruse exercises in abstract logic were used by practising Neoplatonists in their devotions.

They were concerned with describing real spiritual experience. In *On the Delay in Divine Justice*, Plutarch, who was heavily influenced by Neoplatonism, describes what different spirits look like as they can be seen beginning their after-death journey. The deceased are said to be surrounded with a flame-like envelope, but 'some were like the purest full-moon light, emitting one smooth, continuous and even colour. Others were quite mottled – extraordinary sights – dappled with livid spots like adders; and others had faint scratches.'

Plotinus, the greatest Neoplatonist in the Alexandrian school, was a practising mystic. His pupil Porphyry reported seeing his Master in ecstatic raptures, unified with 'the One' several times. Plotinus said of Porphyry, perhaps a bit dismissively, that he had not achieved this once! Neoplatonists who came after them, Iamblichus and Jamblichus, put great emphasis on the importance of theurgic, that is to say godly, magical practices, Iamblichus leaving detailed descriptions of his visions.

Plotinus elaborated an extremely complex metaphysic of emanations of the kind we touched on in chapter one. Neoplatonism influenced other traditions, especially by its systematic approach, particularly the Cabala and Hermeticism.

Hermeticism and the Cabala are viewed by some scholars as, respectively, Egyptian- and Hebrew-flavoured Neoplatonism. But in the secret history the hermetic and cabalistic writings that began to appear at this time are understood as the first written down, systematized expressions of ancient and largely oral traditions.

The *Hermetica* purported to have originated with Hermes Trismegistus, an ancient Egyptian sage, but were written down in Greek and collected at this time in forty two volumes. Yuri Stoyanov, a distinguished researcher at the Warburg Institute, recently confirmed to me that most scholars now accept their genuine, Egyptian origins. The *Hermetica* were genially tolerant of other traditions, no doubt partly because of an underlying assumption that *all* traditions addressed the same planetary gods and opened up the way to the same spirit worlds.

In fact it *is* possible to draw parallels between the numbered emanations of Plotinus, the gods of the *Hermetica* and the spheres of heaven as described in the *Pistis Sophia*.

In the Cabala the emanations from the cosmic mind – the sepiroth – are sometimes thought of as forming a sort of tree as they descend – the sepirothic tree. The allegorical interpretation of scripture that emerged with the Jewish scholar Philo of Alexandria opened up the shared structure of all religions. St Paul hinted at different orders of angels – not only Angels and Archangels, but also Seraphim, Cherubim, Thrones, Dominions,

Mights, Powers, Principalities. He is alluding to a system he evidently expected his readers to understand. This system was set out explicitly by St Paul's pupil Dionysius the Aeropagite. The nine orders he described can be equated with the branches on the sepirothic tree – and with the different orders of gods and spirits in the ancient polytheistic, astronomical religions. For example the 'Powers' of St Paul should be equated with the gods of the solar system of the Greeks and Romans, the Powers of Light being the spirits of the sun and the Powers of Darkness being the gods of the moon and the planets.

The Jewish scholar Rebecca Kenta has even compared the ascent through the gates of wisdom on the cabalistic Tree of Life with Sufi teachings, and made connections between the sepiroth and the chakras of Hindu tradition.

All idealism, the religious systems of all cultures, sees creation in terms of a descending series of emanations from the cosmic mind. But what is distinctly esoteric is this identifying of these emanations with the spirits of the stars and planets on the one hand and occult physiology on the other. It is this that leads to astrology, alchemy, magic and practical techniques for achieving altered states.

It is important to keep bearing in mind that we are not here talking about piled up abstractions, but lived experience. The nine angelic hierarchies were sometimes divided up into three parts, and when St Paul talked of being raised to the Third Heaven, he meant that he had been initiated to such a high level that he had had direct personal experience of the exalted spiritual beings, the Seraphim, Cherubim and Thrones.

The Bride Stripped Bare by her Bachelors, Even *by Marcel Duchamp. Stripped bare, the bachelors reveal their planetary identities.*

CHRISTIANITY WAS FORGED OUT OF INITIATIC experiences and beliefs like these. The greatest of the Church fathers, St Augustine, was an initiate of a late-flowering Persian mystery school called Manichaeism.

Mani was born in 215 in the region that today we call Iraq. At the age of only twelve a being appeared to him. This mysterious being he came to call the Twin revealed to Mani a great hidden mystery – the role of evil in the history of humankind. He learned of the intertwining of the forces of darkness in the creation of the cosmos. He learned, too, that in the great cosmic battle between good and evil, the forces of evil *virtually* triumph.

The cosmic nature of Mani's vision can also be seen in its syncretism, in his account of the great events of history and the exalted parts played by Zarathustra, the Buddha, the Hebrew prophets and Jesus Christ.

The universalism of initiates tends to worry local tyrants. The initiate's heightened awareness of the forces of evil is also always open to misinterpretation. Mani was protected by two successive kings, but their successor persecuted him, torturing and eventually crucifying him.

'I entered my innermost soul and beheld beyond my light and soul, the light.' Augustine's towering intellectual achievement was to give a comprehensive account of Church doctrine in terms of Platonism. What is usually glossed over in conventional Church history is that this account was based on the direct, personal experience of the initiate. Augustine has himself seen with 'the mysterious eye of the soul' a brighter light than the light of the intellect. He is not only concerned with eternal abstractions. His *Confessions* show him tortured by a sense of time passing, in his often quoted phrase 'O Lord make me chaste – but not yet' and also in his poignant cry in another moment of visionary experience: 'O Beauty so old and so new, too late have I loved thee.' St Augustine's sense of time passing carries over into an esoteric sense of history. Later we will see the way in which he understood that the successive stages of the history of the world would unfold when we look at his prophecy of the founding of the City of God.

This was also the age of the great Christian missionaries. Having been captured and sold into slavery, St Patrick later went on a mission to spread the feeling for the sanctity of human life that Jesus Christ had introduced into the stream of world history. He fought to abolish slavery and human sacrifice. But he was also a wizard in the tradition of Zarathustra and Merlin, a terrifying figure casting all the snakes out of Ireland with his wand, casting out demons and raising the dead.

Christianity was readily accepted by the Celts. St Patrick overlaid with historical knowledge of the life and work of Jesus Christ the Celts' cosmic prophecy of the return of the Sun god. Celtic Christianity would happily intertwine Christian and pagan elements. In Celtic art intertwining motifs would also stand for the interweaving waves of light that characterize the first stage of mystical experience in all traditions.

The fiercely independent Celts would continue to insist on the primacy of direct, personal experience of the spirit worlds, and would develop esoteric traditions independent of Rome. Some of the beliefs and practices of these and other early Christians would come to be dubbed heretical by the Roman Church.

When people care deeply about the same things, when they share what the existentialist theologian Paul Tillich called 'ultimate concerns', they are sometimes incredibly sensitive to different shades of opinion. Differences of opinion may lead to murderous hatred, so that my greatest enemy is not the alien conqueror coming over the horizon with bloody tears carved into his cheeks but a brother or sister I rub shoulders with in the congregation.

Sometimes, too, members of a congregation will try to ban beliefs – as had the Emperor Augustus – not because they believe them to be false, but because they believe them to be true.

THE HISTORY OF THE FOUNDING OF THE Roman Church and its dissemination through the good offices of the dying Roman Empire has been written both by the Church and by its enemies. The Emperor Constantine claimed that in the middle of the night, before he went into battle against rebels, he had a dream in which Jesus Christ appeared to him and told him to put the sign of the cross on his battle flag, with the inscription 'In this sign thou shalt conquer'. Constantine obeyed and the rebels were duly defeated.

He declared Christianity the official religion of the Empire, donating the Lateran Palace to the Bishops of Rome. There were undoubted political benefits to this. The new form of consciousness that had been initiated in Jerusalem was spreading with great vigour through the Empire, and Constantine capitalized on this by offering freedom to any slave who converted and twenty pieces of gold to any who were already free.

As we have seen, the Romans made a cult of cruelty. The imposition of power by one man on another, taken to its furthest extremes, was exalted. The Romans were ruthless and ruthlessness was a manly virtue. So the Christian exaltation of meekness and humility turned everything upside down and inside out. The Christians clearly knew of new joys and satisfactions, new ways of being in the world.

Consider how strange meeting a Christian initiate must have seemed to a Roman. Here was a new form of consciousness. Here were people able to live inside their heads. They were lit up inside by an enthusiasm and a certainty about spiritual experience. It must have been as baffling and intriguing as it was, hundreds of years later, for a pygmy in Papua New Guinea to meet for the first time a European explorer. There were whole new worlds behind those eyes.

CONSTANTINE MAY HAVE HOPED THE RIGOROUS new religion would help slow down the decline of the Roman Empire, but he remained anxious about a prophecy in the Sibylline Oracles that Rome would again become the haunt of wolves and foxes.

Exsternsteine in Germany. This ancient carving is a few paces away from an older carving of a Norse god hung on a tree, in a happy acceptance of the fact that Christianity grew out of pagan traditions. Note that esoteric understanding of the different bodies of the individual is alluded to in the fact that while the material body of Jesus Christ is being taken down from the cross, his spirit already rests in the arms of his Father.

He decided to try to thwart this prophecy by transferring the spirit of Rome to another location and founding an alternative capital. So from under a porphyry pillar he dug up the Palladium, the ancient god-carved statue that, as we saw, had been carried from Troy for the founding of Rome. Then he reburied it at the site of the city that would be called Constantinople. It was buried under the same pillar but now topped by a statue of the Sun god, crowned with the nails from the true cross in the form of a sort of nimbus.

This symbolism, incorporating initiatic teaching regarding the Sun god, would have been understood by initiates of all religions, so it is perhaps slightly ironic that under the aegis of Constantine, the Church began to suppress initiatic teachings and to reduce its exoteric teachings to dogma. In 325 the Council of Nicea decided which gospels among the many in circulation were the real thing. Imperial edicts also forbad pagan practices. On the orders of Constantine's sons, women and children were force-fed, their mouths held open by a wooden engine while consecrated bread was stuffed down their throats.

When Constantine's nephew Julian came to power in 361, he reversed the tide of religious intolerance. Having been brought up a pupil of the Neoplatonist philosopher Iamblichus, he well understood the mission of the being he called the 'Seven-rayed god'. He gave equal rights to all subjects regardless of their religious beliefs and gave permission for pagan temples to reopen.

Julian wrote a famous polemic against the narrow, dogmatic Christianity that had grown up during the time of Constantine, which is why later Christian writers came to call him the Apostate, meaning someone who discarded the faith. He believed that Christianity had been seeking to deny the reality of the gods he had encountered through initiation.

Julian led a military campaign into Persia. Just as the Greeks had besieged Troy to control the initiation knowledge hidden within, Julian wished to understand the secret knowledge of the Manichaean Mystery school based in Persia. He knew enough to know that the mission of the Sun god was under threat, and that the inner mysteries of Manichaeism concerned the secrets of the war between the Sun god and Ahriman – or Satan – the spirit of materialism.

But before he could accomplish his mission, Julian was murdered by a follower of Constantine, and a new Saturnine era began, when knowledge of true, initiatic spirituality would finally be driven underground. The Emperor Theodosius began a ruthless policy of suppressing all disagreement with the imperial line on Christian doctrine. He confiscated the property of 'heretics' and took over their temples. Statues of Isis were rededicated to Mary. The Pantheon in Rome has a sublime and cosmic beauty unlike any purpose-built church. This temple to all the gods was converted by Theodosius into a temple of monotheism.

Theodosius closed down the Mystery schools and in 391 besieged the Serapeum in Alexandria. This sacred compound with a vast cloud-capped temple to Serapis was one of the wonders of the ancient world. Inside a statue of the god was suspended from the ceiling by a magnet. There were also libraries that housed the world's greatest collection of books. Fortunately many books were smuggled out before the Serapeum was burned to the ground and its sacred statues dragged through the streets.

Finally Theodosius turned his attention to the Neoplatonic school of philosophy based in Alexandria, foremost preserver of the intellectual legacy of the Mystery schools. The great personality of Neoplatonism at that time was a young woman called Hypatia. Daughter of a leading philosopher and mathematician, she was educated in philosophy, maths, geometry and astronomy. Her father had also developed a series of exercises to make her body a fitting vessel for a brilliant mind. She loved swimming, horse riding and mountain climbing. So she was beautiful as well as clever, and she soon won fame as an inventor of scientific instruments, including one to measure the specific gravity of liquids. Only a few fragments of her writing have survived, but she was known far and wide as one of the most brilliant minds of the time.

She attracted large crowds as a lecturer. Well versed in the wisdom of Plotinus and Iamblichus she explained in her lectures how Christianity had evolved out of the teachings of the Mystery schools, and she argued, like her father, that no single tradition or doctrine could have exclusive claim to the truth.

One afternoon in 414 when Hypatia was leaving a lecture hall, a gang of black-cowelled monks forced her from her chariot, stripped her naked and dragged her through the streets to a nearby church. There they pulled her through the cool, flitting shadows to the altar. In an atmosphere perfumed with incense they swarmed all over her body, her naked form now covered by black cloth, and they tore her limb from limb. Later they scraped the flesh from her bones using oyster shells and burned all her remains.

The church was trying to erase Hypatia from history just as the priests of Amun had tried to erase Akhenaten.

The Pantheon in Rome. Ovid explains that temples represent the whole cosmos in the form of a sphere. The great rotunda of the Pantheon is 143 feet in diameter with an aperture in the roof to admit the sun. The height from the floor to the top, where this hole is, is equal to the diameter, so that it contains a vast sphere of air. The niches around the floor originally held images of the planetary gods.

IT IS TOO EASY TO SEE THE CHURCH AS the evil repressor of free thought and to romanticize outlawed groups and antinomian schools like the Neoplatonists and the Gnostics. From its early history the Church has numbered among its leaders practitioners of black magic and other initiates who have abused their supernatural powers for selfish ends. But it is equally true – and perhaps more important – to say that from the time of St Paul and St Augustine the greatest Church leaders have been initiates of the highest order who have sought to guide humanity according to the divine plan outlined in this book. They knew that it was necessary for any understanding of reincarnation to be suppressed in the West. According to the cosmic plan, the West was to be the cradle for the developing sense of the value of an individual human life.

On the other hand the Neoplatonists, though they had continued the work of Pythagoras and Plato, converting into concepts the direct experiences of the spirit worlds, seemed altogether unaware of the great revolution that had taken place there. In their writings there is no trace of the gospel of universal love that Jesus Christ had introduced. Similarly the Gnostic emphasis on direct, personal experience of the spirit worlds, as distinct from passive acceptance of abstract dogma, was in line with the impulse introduced by Jesus Christ, but many of the Gnostics were also vehement world-haters in a way that ran contrary to the mission of Jesus Christ to transform the material world. Many of the beliefs that the Gnostic sects took from their adventures in the spirit worlds were also quite fantastical. Not only did some Gnostics believe that Jesus Christ had not sunk so low as to inhabit a physical body, that he had lived on the earth only as some kind of phantom, but they also practised bizarre extremes of mortification and debauchery as a way of disrupting their own, despised bodily senses and gaining access to the spirit worlds. Some encouraged snakes to crawl over their naked bodies, some drank menstrual blood, saying 'Here is the blood of Christ', and others believed that their sex magic would lead to the birth of god-like creatures. Others castrated themselves and boasted, 'I am deader than you are.'

ROME WANTED TO STAMP OUT DOCTRINAL differences. Christian conviction and moral purpose were useful for Constantine and Theodosius, unifying the Empire and strengthening it from within at a time when barbarian hoards were threatening it from the East.

A steadily expanding empire in China had caused a domino effect across Central Asia and into Europe. Under pressure from the Far East Goths, Visigoths and Vandals invaded parts of Europe, even reaching as far as Rome before retreating again. Then, in the second quarter of the fifth century, the nomadic Mongolian tribes were united under a great leader, Attila the Hun. He swept through the territories previously invaded by Goths and Vandals and built an empire which stretched from the plains of Central Asia to northern Gaul. He pushed into northern Italy and raided Constantinople.

Attila, the 'scourge of God', has become a byword for barbarity, but an eyewitness account of a visit to Attila's encampment by a Greek historian, Priscus, gives a very different picture. Priscus shows Attila living in a simple wooden house of polished boards, surrounded by a wooden enclosure. Woollen mats served as carpets, and Attila – literally 'little father' – received his visitors wearing simple linen clothes, unadorned by gems or gold. He drank – moderately – from a wooden bowl and ate from a wooden plate. He showed no emotion during the interview except when his youngest son arrived, whom he chucked under the chin and regarded with a look of satisfaction.

It is also said that when Attila conquered the Christian city of Corinth, he was outraged to find a prostitute on every street corner. He gave them the choice of marrying one of his men or exile.

If Attila was not the ravening monster of popular imagination, it is nevertheless true to say that if he had succeeded in overrunning the Roman Empire, this would have been disastrous for the evolution of human consciousness.

The Romans feared Attila more than any of their other enemies. Attila would not allow his people to live in Roman territory or buy Roman goods. When he invaded Roman territories he reversed Romanization, demolishing Roman buildings – and he also took thousands of pounds of gold from Rome in tribute money. When in 452 he finally had Rome itself in his grip, the Emperor sent out Leo, the Bishop of Rome, to meet him.

The future Pope Leo negotiated a deal with Attila by the terms of which Honoria, the daughter of the Emperor, would be his wife together with a dowry of thousands more pounds of gold.

At this point Attila believed he had achieved his ambition to take over the Roman Empire and rule the world.

Attila and his people practised shamanism. In all battles Attila was guided – wisely as it turned out – by his shaman-priests. The great terror-striking uproar of a Hun army going to battle was made up of the howling of dogs, the clanking of weapons, the sounds of horns and bells. All this was intended to summon the battalions of the dead, the ghosts of their ancestors, to fight alongside them. They were also shamanistically calling on the group souls of carnivores, the wolves and the bears, to enter into them and give them supernatural powers.

BECAUSE WE HAVE BEEN CONSIDERING the barbarian invasions from the East, this is perhaps a good place to pause to consider shamanism. The word shaman comes from the Tungus-Mongol noun meaning 'one who knows'.

Shamans, from the time of the barbarian invasions to the present, have used a variety of techniques – Mircea Eliade has called them 'archaic techniques of ecstasy' – to work themselves into a trance state: rhythmic drumming and dancing, hyperventilation, frenzied self-mutilation, sensory deprivation, dehydration, sleep deprivation – and also psychoactive plants, including ayahuasca, peyote cactus, the ergot fungus. Recent studies by Wiliam Emboden, Professor of Biology at California State University, and others have also made it look likely that drugs were used to induce trance states in Mystery centres – for example, the kykeon at Eleusis and the blue water lily taken in conjunction with opium and mandrake roots in ancient Egypt.

Scientists have isolated an enzyme in the brain that induces these trance states. Research seems to suggest that 2 per cent of us have high enough levels of dimethyltryptamine naturally occurring in the brain to give us spontaneous and involuntary trance states. It also seems likely that we all have higher levels until adolescence, when a process of crystallization takes place, cladding the pineal gland and impeding its function. For the rest of us these ancient techniques or similar are necessary.

Anthropologists have noticed that accounts of shamanistic experience across many different cultures show a progression through the same stages.

First, a blacking out of the world of the senses, and a sense of a journey through the darkness. Great pain is often experienced as if the body is being dismembered.

Second, a sea of lights, often with a shifting net of geometric patterns – the matrix.

Third, these patterns morph into shapes, most commonly snakes and half-human, half-animal creatures often with pliable, semi-transparent bodies.

Lastly, when the trance fades the shaman has a sense of enjoying supernatural powers, the ability to heal, information about enemies, mind-to-mind influence on animals and the gift of prophecy.

This may all seem to fit nicely with the accounts of initiations in Mystery schools that we have looked at. Gregg Jacobs at Harvard Medical School has said that 'by the use of shamanistic techniques we can work ourselves into powerful ancestral states of consciousness'.

But in the view of modern esotericists, the example of shamanism will only take us so far when trying to understand the Mystery schools and secret societies. Many of the paintings produced by shamanistic cultures as records of their trances are startlingly beautiful, but they do not give the same magnificent, comprehensive panorama of the spirit worlds found, for example, on the ceilings of the temples of Edfu or Philae. Moreover, the beings encountered by shamans seem to be from the lower levels, rather than the more elevated planetary gods with whom the temple priests communed.

In the view of modern esoteric teachers, then, all shamanism, whether that of the old Hunnic or Mongol hordes or that practised by the *sangoma* in South Africa today, represent a degeneration of a once magnificent primordial vision.

Again we see that in the secret history everything is upside down and the wrong way round. In conventional history religion's early stages were marked by animism and totemism, then developed into the complicated cosmologies of the great ancient civilizations. In the secret history humankind's primordial vision was complicated, sophisticated and magnificent, and only later degenerated into animism, totemism and shamanism.

Attila's tribespeople practised a shamanism that gave them an access to the spirit worlds that many a churchman might envy, but it was access in an atavistic state. It ran contrary to the impulse of the evolution of human consciousness that had been developed by Pythagoras and Plato and had now been given new direction by Jesus Christ and Paul. The aim of this evolution was a beautiful one – that people would be able take joy in their individual intellectual strength and superiority, and that they should be able to choose to move freely, powerfully and lovingly not only through the material world but also through the spirit worlds.

Drug-taking is, of course, a big part of modern shamanistic practice, but it is forbidden by most modern esoteric teachers as a means of reaching the spirit worlds. The aim of these teachers is to achieve experience of the spirit worlds with intelligence and critical faculties as unimpaired as possible, indeed heightened. To enter the spirit worlds on drugs, on the other hand, is to do so without proper preparation, and may open up a portal into a demonic dimension which then refuses to close.

WHEN IN 453 ATTILA PREPARED TO CELEBRATE MARRIAGE to a high-born, soft-skinned young woman – he already had hundreds of wives – he was a man in the prime of life and full of potency, about to oversee the end of the Roman Empire.

The delicate early growth of a new stage of human consciousness was about to be nipped in the bud.

In the morning Attila was found dead. He had suffered a massive nosebleed.

'I BELIEVE BECAUSE IT IS ABSURD.' This famous phrase by the first of the Latin-speaking Church fathers, Tertullian, influenced many thinkers in the late nineteenth and the first half of the twentieth century.

We may imagine how absurd life might have seemed to a citizen of the Roman Empire in the days of its decline. He lived in a disenchanted world, where the great spiritual certainties on which the civilizations of the ancient world had been founded seemed doubtful. They no longer corresponded to his experience. Pan was long dead and the oracles had fallen silent. God and the gods seemed little more than empty, abstract ideas, while the really vigorous thought-life was in the realm of science and technology, in the atomic theories of Lucretius, in amazing engineering projects – aqueducts, drainage systems and roads thousands of miles long – that were springing up all round. Spiritual certainties had been replaced by harsh political and economic realities.

Yet if this citizen had been minded to listen to the inner promptings of his spirit, he might have noticed that this harsh and mechanical grinding of the wheels of necessity, this new way of the world, threw into relief something very like its opposite, something elsewhere called 'the nameless way'. If this citizen had chosen not to shut it out, he might have caught suggestions emanating from underground streams of thought.

At this critical juncture we move from the age of the Mystery schools to the age of the secret societies, from the directing of the course of history by the political elite to something much more subversive coming from below. A new mood was taking over the soul-life of initiates which may be traced in the life of God's joker, Francis of Assisi, in Shakespeare's fools and in the gently undermining work of Rabelais, in *Gulliver's Travels*, *Alice in Wonderland* and in the cuttings and pastings of Kurt Schwitters.

IN ANSWER TO A QUESTION ABOUT THE meaning of Zen, a monk raised a finger. A boy in the class began to ape him, and then afterwards, whenever anyone discussed this monk's teachings, this naughty boy would raise his finger in mockery.

But the next time the boy attended class, the monk grabbed him and cut off his finger. As he ran off crying, the monk called after him. The boy turned round to look at the monk, and the monk looked back at him and raised his own finger.

At that moment the boy was enlightened.

This *conte cruel* is not a historical episode but one of the classic fables of Zen, formulated at the time of Attila's nosebleed.

The capacity for abstract thought had been developing for less than a thousand years, inspired by Pythagoras, Confucius and Socrates. Buddhism had spread from India to China with the visit of the twenty-eighth Buddhist patriarch Bodhidharma. Then in China over the next two hundred years Buddhism and Taoism fused to create a philosophy of spontaneous, intuitive enlightenment called *tch'an* – or Zen as it would later come to be called in Japan.

Tch'an brought a new cautionary sense of the limitations of abstract thought.

The boy and his fellow pupils had been struggling to understand what the monk was saying. We may imagine them frowning with the effort to grasp enlightenment cerebrally.

But the boy is suddenly enabled to see the world from the point of view of an altered state of consciousness. He is suddenly seeing the world from the point of view of the vegetable consciousness that is centred in the solar plexus rather than the skull. It is by means of this vegetable consciousness that we are connected individually to every other living thing in the cosmos. These connections can be visualized as tendrils of a great cosmic tree and every solar plexus as a flower on the tree. In another way of looking at it, this vegetable consciousness is another dimension, the world between the worlds and the gateway to the spirit worlds. It is consciousness, the 'light beyond the light of the intellect', to quote St Augustine, that anyone must slip into who wishes to become enlightened.

The boy is enlightened because from the point of view of this other form of consciousness the monk's finger belongs to him as much as it does the monk. The normal categories of human head-thought are inadequate to cover this.

Laughter erupts when you suddenly see the cosmos upside down, inside out and the other way round. At the beginning of the second half of the fifth century a new sense of absurdity entered the world and from then on the great initiates of the secret societies, in the West as well as in the East, would always have a touch of Zen.

UNDER A STRONG RULER, JUSTINIAN, the Byzantine Empire expanded, even regaining territories from the barbarians. Justinian closed down the remaining schools of Greek philosophy, causing teachers to flee, taking with them texts like the writings of Aristotle, including his now lost alchemical treatise.

Many arrived in Persia where King Khusraw dreamed of founding a great academy like the one that had inspired Greek civilization. In an intellectual ferment that took in elements of Neoplatonism, Gnosticism and Hermeticism, the methodology of Aristotle was applied jointly to the material world *and the spirit worlds*. So began the golden age of Arabian magic.

All our childhoods are lit up by a vision of magic – of genies, magic lamps and abracadabra. These stories began to weave their magical influence on the history of the world in the sixth century. There were rumours of automata and flying machines and caches of self-generating gold, of powerful magic spells that would become collected in forbidden books.

Soon the whole world would be under the spell of Arabia, as books of its spells were published far and wide, books containing the whispers of demons.

17

The Age of Islam

Mohammed and Gabriel • *The Old Man of the Mountains* • *Haroun al Raschid and the* Arabian Nights • *Charlemagne and the Historic Parsifal* • *Chartres Cathedral*

A GRIMLY FORBIDDING FIGURE LOOKED down from the spirit worlds on these developments.

In 570 a child called Mohammed was born in Mecca. When he was six he lost both his parents and was hired out as a shepherd's boy. He grew broad shouldered, with curly black hair and a beard through which shone dazzling white teeth. He became a camel-driver, transporting the spices and perfumes that were the speciality of Mecca to Syria. Then, at the age of twenty-five, he married a wealthy widow of Mecca and became one of the richest and most respected citizens of that city.

Although he had in one way now won back all he had lost at the death of his parents, Mohammed was dissatisfied. The religious centre of Mecca was a large, black, granite stone called the Kaaba, which in some traditions is said to have fallen to earth from the Sirius star system. At that time Arabia was populated by shamanistic tribes, each worshipping their own gods and spirits and at the centre of this whirlwind, next to the Kaaba, stood a sacred tent which housed hundreds of their idols. Mecca had also become corrupted by the sale of holy water – taken from a spring which Ishmael had caused to spring from the sand. To Mohammed's eyes all of this looked lax. He saw a people interested only in money-making, gambling, horsemanship and getting drunk.

While driving camel trains down to places like Syria and Egypt he heard about Judaism and also stories about Jesus Christ. Did the story of the cleansing of the temple strike a chord? Mohammed became convinced that Arabia needed a prophet, someone like Jesus Christ who could purge the people of superstitions and of corruption and could unite them in one cosmic purpose.

Mohammed was sitting in the hills surrounding Mecca, brooding darkly on how all this might be achieved, when an angel appeared before him, saying: 'I am the angel Gabriel.' The apparition then showed Mohammed a golden tablet and told him to read it. Mohammed protested that he was illiterate, but when Gabriel commanded him a second time, Mohammed found that he could indeed read. So began the series of angelic conversations that became the Koran. Later Mohammed went into town and preached what Gabriel had taught him with blazing sincerity and irresistible power. He would summarize his creed in these down-to-earth terms:

> My teachings are simple.
> Allah is the One God
> Mohammed is his prophet
> Give up idolatry
> Do not steal
> Do not lie
> Do not slander
> And never become intoxicated
> If you follow my teachings, then you follow Islam.

When challenged to perform a miracle to prove that his preaching was divinely inspired, he refused. He said that Allah had raised the heavens without recourse to pillars, had made the earth, the rivers, the fig, the date and the olive – and that these *things* were miraculous enough.

We may hear in this ecstatic materialism the first whisperings of the modern age.

DURING THEIR ANGELIC CONVERSATIONS, the Archangel Gabriel asked Mohammed to choose refreshment. Mohammed chose milk, which occultists call moon juice. Alcohol would be forbidden in Islam.

It is highly significant, from an esoteric point of view, that the angel who dictated the Koran to Mohammed was Gabriel, traditionally Archangel of the Moon. Allah is the Muslim name for Jehovah, great god of the moon and thought. Gabriel is here heralding the power of thought to control human passions and quell fantasy, and his god is the great god of thou-shalt-not, represented in Muslim iconography by the crescent moon.

Thought is a death process that feeds on life-giving energies. In the Middle Ages – the great Age of Islam – the sexual impulse would have to be suppressed in order for the human capacity for thought to grow. And in order to quell the outgrowths of Gnostic fantasy, religious leaders imposed their authority on the people.

From the point of view of conventional, Western history, Europe was besieged by the uncivilized Muslims during the latter part of the Dark Ages and on into the Middle Ages.

The caves of the desert fathers in an early nineteenth-century print. The desert fathers, living in isolation, devoted their lives to practising extreme techniques that would gain them access to the spirit worlds, a way of life that would develop into the monastic movement. St Antony the Great, the greatest of the desert fathers, would stay for long periods in tombs in a trance-like state. On one occasion Antony advised a man to cover himself with meat. When this man was shredded by wild dogs, he learned something of what it would be like to be attacked by demons on the other side of the grave. In the episode known as the temptation of St Antony, he himself entered the sphere of the moon, otherwise known as kamaloca, *or purgatory, and was granted a vision of the Devil, a tall black man with his head in the clouds. He also saw angels who were able to guide some human spirits up beyond the devil's reach.*

From the point of view of esoteric history the truth is something pretty nearly the mirror image of this. The impulses seeded at this time that would grow and transform Europe, indeed the whole human race, came from Islam.

MOHAMMED'S PREACHING IN THE MARKETPLACE at Mecca prompted a plot to assassinate him. He escaped to the town of Medina with his disciple Abu Behr in order to marshal his supporters. In 629 he returned to Mecca and in the four years until his death he established control over the rest of Arabia. When Abu Behr became his successor – or 'Caliph' – the will to conquer continued at an astonishing rate.

One of the things that makes a religion successful is if it *works in the world*, that is to say if it brings material benefits. The combination of Mohammed's radical monotheism with the scientific methodology of Aristotle that had earlier pervaded Arabian thought would quickly encircle the globe from Spain to the boundaries of China.

Absorbing new ideas as well as spreading them, the Arabs took in Zoroastrianism, Buddhism, Hinduism and Chinese science, including the manufacture of paper. They made great advances in astronomy, medicine, physics and mathematics, replacing the clumsy Roman numerals with the system we use today.

BY ITS OWN ACCOUNT SUFISM HAD ANCIENT, even primordial roots. Some traditions date its origins to the Saramong Brotherhood – or Brotherhood of the Bee – founded in the Caucasus in Central Asia during the first great post-Atlantean migration. Later, Sufism was undoubtedly influenced by Gnosticism and Neoplatonism.

If there was a tendency in Islam in its triumphant period to become dogmatic and paternalistic, Sufism represented a contrary impulse, a fascination with the sometimes perverse and paradoxical twisting this way and that of the spirit. Esoteric Islam advocated immersing oneself in the gentler, more feminine and feeling side of the spiritual life which would find expression in the great outpouring of Sufi poetry.

The question of what constitutes 'oneself' is also a big issue in Sufism. What we generally imagine to be our own self, it teaches, is really an entity that operates independently of us, made up for the most part of fears, false attachments, dislikes, prejudices, envy, pride, habits, preoccupations and compulsions. A lot of Sufi practice involves breaking down this false self, this false will.

'God is nearer to a man than his jugular vein' according to the verse from the Koran (50:16), yet for the most part, distracted by our false selves, we are not awake to this.

The great Sufi writer Ibn Arabi said that a Sufi master is someone who unveils one to oneself.

Practices under instruction from a Sufi master might involve breathing exercises and music used to attain an altered state. Sufism taught the sometimes painful process of 'waking up', of becoming aware of ourselves and of the cosmic, mystical current that runs through us and becoming more fully alive.

Because they opened themselves totally to this mystic current, Sufis could be wild, unpredictable and disconcerting. We will see later that Sufism has had a vast, though largely unacknowledged, influence on Western culture.

Mohammed's brother-in-law, Ali, was to him as John to Jesus Christ, receiving and transmitting the secret teachings. Sufis obeyed Islamic law but believed it to be the outer shell of esoteric teaching.

Ali and Mohammed's daughter, Fatima, established what became known as the Fatimid

Empire, ruling a large part of North Africa and Cairo, where they established a school for esoteric philosophy called the House of Wisdom. There were seven initiatory grades taught within. Candidates would be initiated into timeless wisdom and gain secret powers. Sir John Woodruffe, the nineteenth-century translator of the key Tantric texts, also uncovered a Sufi tradition with a parallel understanding of occult physiology. In this Sufi tradition centres of power had beautiful and intriguing names such as Cedar Heart and Lily Heart.

One of the initiates to emerge from the House of Wisdom was Hassan-I Sabbah, the famous Old Man of the Mountains.

He founded a small sect which in 1090 captured the castle of Alamut in the mountains south of the Caspian Sea in modern-day Iran. From his mountain fastness he sent his secret agents all over the world to do his bidding, exerting a puppet master's control on distant rulers. His Hashishim – Assassins – infiltrated courts and armies. Anyone who even *thought* of disobeying Hassan was found dead the next morning.

The Western view of Hassan is no doubt distorted by a passage in Marco Polo's account of his travels. He claimed that the Old Man of the Mountains gave his young followers drugs which put them to sleep for three days. When they woke up they found themselves in a beautiful garden they were told was paradise. They were surrounded by beautiful girls who played them music and gave them anything they wanted. After three days the young men were sent back to sleep. When they awoke, they were brought again before Hassan, convinced that the Old Man had the power to send them back to Paradise on a whim. So when Hassan wanted someone killed, his assassins would do it willingly, knowing that Paradise would be their certain reward.

In reality Hassan banned all intoxicants, even executing one of his own sons for being drunk. He banned music, too. Among his own people he was renowned as a holy man and alchemist, an adept who was able to control events all over the world by supernatural means. This was despite the fact that once he arrived and set up his court there, he only ever left his room at Alamut twice.

In the twentieth century the archetype of the man who appears mad, but really controls the whole world from his cell appeared as Dr Mabuse, in the deeply esoteric films of Fritz Lang.

HAROUN AL RASCHID WAS ANOTHER OF the extraordinary, compelling characters of this era. He became Caliph in his early twenties and quickly made Baghdad the most splendid city in the world, building a palace of unparalleled splendour served by hundreds of courtiers and slaves and a harem. It was a place of glittering materiality, where a man might experience every pleasure the world has to offer, grow bored with them all and long for novelty.

The turbaned oriental potentate of all our imaginations and Caliph of the *Tales of the*

Arabian Nights, he drew to his court all the great writers, artists, thinkers and scientists of his day. It was rumoured that, as related in the *Arabian Nights*, he would sometimes slip out of a secret door in the palace in disguise in order to eavesdrop on his people and find out what they really thought.

In one of the most famous tales a fisherman on the Red Sea catches a large iron pot in his nets. When he has hauled it on board he sees that the metal cover is engraved with the interlocked triangles of Solomon's Seal. Naturally curious, the fisherman opens the pot and at once a black vapour rises out of it and spreads itself all over the sky, so that all he can see is darkness. Then the vapour condenses again into the monstrous form of a Jinn, who tells the fisherman he was imprisoned in the pot by Solomon. He says that after two hundred years he swore he would make rich anyone who set him free. After five hundred years he swore he would reward his liberator with power. But after a thousand years of captivity he swore he would kill whoever set him free. So the Jinn tells the fisherman to prepare to die. But the fisherman says he can't believe the Jinn was really inside the pot, and so the spirit, to prove it, turns himself back into vapour and sinks with a slow, spiralling motion back inside – at which point, of course, the fisherman claps the lid back on.

This might seem just a silly story for children, but for occultists it is packed with esoteric lore. But the word 'Jinn' means 'to hide', and a detailed theory and practice of dealing with these entities, said to live in ruined houses, in wells and under bridges, was actively cultivated among Arab peoples. Moreover, the imprisoning of spirits and demons in amulets, rings and stones using magical sigils such as the Seal of Solomon was well known. By the Middle Ages such lore, largely Arabic in origin and concerned particularly with the empowering of talismans by astrological means, would be collected in many famous grimoires. The greatest of these, called the *Picatrix*, would fascinate many of the more influential personalities in this history, including Trithemius, Ficino and Elias Ashmole.

RUMI GREW UP TO BECOME the great poet at court. He was a disconcerting presence even as a small child. At the age of six he began the habit of fasting, and began, too, to see visions. There is a story that one day he was playing with a group of children who were chasing a cat from rooftop to rooftop. Rumi protested that humans should be more ambitious than animals – and then vanished. When the others cried out in fright, he suddenly reappeared behind them. He had a strange look in his eyes, and said spirits in green cloaks had carried him away to other worlds. The green cloaks may have been shadows of El Khidir, the Green One, a powerful being able to materialize and dematerialize at will. The Green One is said by the Sufis to come to the aid of those on a special mission.

At thirty-seven years old, now a young university professor, Rumi was adored by his students. One day he was riding his horse, followed by his students, when he was accosted by a dervish. Shamsi Tabriz had made a name for himself, insulting sheiks and holy men, because he would be guided by nothing but God – which made him unpredictable and sometimes an overwhelming, even shattering presence.

The two men embraced and went to live in a cell together, where they meditated for three months. Each saw what he had been searching for in the eyes of the other.

But Rumi's students grew so jealous that one day they ambushed Shamsi and stabbed him to death.

Devastated, Rumi wept and wailed and grew thin. He was desolate. Then one day he was walking down the street, past a goldsmith's shop, where he heard the rhythmic beat of a hammer upon gold. Rumi began repeating the name of Allah and then suddenly began to whirl in ecstasy.

This is how the Mellevi, or whirling dervish order of Sufis, was born.

The magnificent civilization of the Arabs both fascinated and horrified medieval Europe. Travellers returned with tales of life at court, of hundreds of lions on leashes, of a lake of mercury on which lay a leather bed, inflated with air and fastened by silk bands to four silver columns at the corners. The most common report was of a miraculous mechanical garden made out of precious metals and containing mechanical birds that flew and sang. In the middle of it stood a great golden tree bearing fruit made out of astonishingly large precious stones and representing the planets.

To many these prodigies seemed necromantic. They existed on the border between magic and science. A partial explanation at least may lie in the discovery made in Baghdad in 1936. A German archaeologist called William Koenig was excavating palace drains when he discovered what he identified immediately as a primitive electric battery. It dated back as least as far as the early Middle Ages. When a colleague created a replica, she found she was able to generate an electric current with it that coated a silver figurine with gold in under half an hour.

IN 802 HAROUN AL RASCHID SENT THE Holy Roman Emperor, Charlemagne, a gift of silks, brass candelabras, perfume and ivory chessmen. He sent, too, an elephant and a water clock that marked the hours by dropping bronze balls into a bowl and little mechanical knights that emerged from little doors. It was a gift intended to impress upon Charlemagne the superiority of Arabian science – and the reach of its empire.

If it hadn't been for three generations of Frankish kings, Charles Martel, Pepin and Charlemagne, Islam might have wiped Christianity off the face of the earth.

Born in 742, Charlemagne inherited the spear of Longinus, used to pierce the side of Jesus Christ on the cross. Charlemagne lived and slept with the spear, believing it gave

LEFT *The call to prayer. A great impulse of upside-down, other-way-round thinking entered the world through Sufism. 'The Truth is also seeking the Seeker.'*

RIGHT *P.L. Travers, creator of Mary Poppins, was a disciple of the twentieth-century master G.I. Gurdjieff, who was influenced both by the Sufis and Tibetan Lamas. The character of Poppins – in the books rather than in the more sentimental film – is that of a Sufi adept, disconcerting in the way she is able to turn the world inside out and upside down and bend the laws of nature.*

him powers to foresee the future and forge his own destiny. In the first decade of the ninth century he won victories against the Muslims. He wielded his sacred sword Joyeuse to keep them from invading northern Spain and to protect, too, the route of the pilgrimage to St James of Compostela.

Charlemagne had an imposing physical presence. Some seven foot tall with blazing blue eyes, he was a man of simple, moderate habits, yet he managed to impose his will on the course of history. Not only did his vision of Fortress Europe maintain a Christian sense of identity in the face of Islamic invasion, but he also moved to protect his people against corrupt and tyrannical nobles.

It is from the writings of one of the great magi of the Renaissance, Trithemius, Abbot of Sponheim, that we learn the strange story of the Holy Vehm, or Secret Tribunal of Free Judges, founded by Charlemagne in 770 with secret ciphers and signs to exclude the uninitiated. Sometimes known as the Secret Soldiers of Light, masked men would nail a summons to the gates of a castle whose owner thought he could live above the law. Some nobles disobeyed the summons. They would try to protect themselves with bodyguards, but inevitably they would be found stabbed to death with the characteristic cruciform dagger of the Holy Vehm.

A noble who chose to obey the summons would arrive late at night alone at the designated place, sometimes a lonely crossroads. Masked men would appear and place a hood on his head, before leading him off to be interrogated. At midnight the hood would be removed and the nobleman would find himself perhaps in a vast underground vault, facing the Free Judges, masked and dressed in black. Sentence would be passed.

This secret society is not obviously esoteric or arcane in its philosophy, but the vault motif points to legends of Charlemagne's underground initiation.

The Enchiridion of Pope Leo was a book of spells, including protection against poison, fire, storm and wild beasts, which emerged into exoteric history in the early sixteenth century, but was said to have been worn at all times by Charlemagne, who carried it tied to his person in a little leather bag. One note of authenticity in this story is that the first chapter of St John's Gospel was included in the *Enchiridion* as its most powerful spell. These verses are still used in this way by practising esotericists.

More solid evidence of Charlemagne's initiatic way of thinking can be seen today in the Aachen chapel. Added to Charlemagne's palace, it was the largest building in the world north of the Alps. Its octagonal shape looks forward to the walls that will surround the New Jerusalem, according to the esoteric numerology of the Revelation of St John. Entry is by the Wolf Door – named after the legendary wolf who tricked the Devil out of possession of the chapel. The visitor looks up to the first-floor gallery to see the imposing throne of the Holy Roman Emperor, made from simple slabs of white marble. In the centre of the chapel a solid gold casket contains Charlemagne's bones. Above it 'the Crown of Lights', a gigantic wheel-shaped chandelier, hangs like a crown chakra ablaze.

Charlemagne's achievements include his bringing together of the great scholars of Christendom in an attempt to rival the court of Haroun al Raschid. The greatest scholar was perhaps Alcuin of York.

This British connection is significant in the secret history. The spirit of King Arthur lives and breathes in the history of Charlemagne. He is a defender of the faith who keeps pagans at bay with the help of a weapon that confers invincibility and of a circle of faithful knights, or paladins as they are known in the case of Charlemagne.

We have seen that the original King Arthur lived in the Iron Age, a champion of the Sun god at a time of encroaching darkness. The stories of the Grail which were added to the canon at the time of Charlemagne are based on historical events.

You might assume that the story of Parsifal is an allegory, but in the secret history he was a man of flesh and blood, a reincarnation of Mani, the third-century founder of Manichaeism. Though he did not know it, he was the nephew of one of Charlemagne's paladins, William of Orange, who fought in a battle against the Saracens at Carcassonne in 783. This battle cost the Muslims so dearly that they withdrew from France to Spain.

Raised to be a forester, Parsifal lived with his mother deep in the woods, far away from the glamour of court life and the dangers of chivalry. He did not know his father or his uncle. He was never to be a knight like Roland, famous in his own day, a knight whose deeds were blazed across the sky and celebrated in the official records, but his local deeds, his private battles, would change the course of history.

One day Parsifal was playing by himself in the woods when a troop of knights rode by. The episode is described in a passage by Chrétien de Troyes that lights up the imagination:

> Trees were bursting into leaf, the iris blooming and birds singing when the son of the widow went out into the wild and lonely forest. He was practising hurling spears when he heard a clashing, jangling, thumping sound. Then suddenly he saw five knights ride out from among the trees in full armour, their helmets shining in the sun. The gold, silver, white and blue of their liveries danced before his eyes. He had never seen anything like this before and thought he was being granted a vision of angels.

Parsifal's own imagination was fired. He left his mother, heartbroken, and set off in search of adventure.

For all his ideals Parsifal was a foolish knight and his missions were often fraught with misunderstanding and accident. His was a journey of loneliness and failure.

Then one day, as dusk approached, he was riding by a river and asked two fishermen if they knew where he could find shelter. They directed him to a great castle, set high on a hill. This turned out to be the castle of the Fisher King, Amfortas, who had been wounded and was bleeding from his thighs. It seemed that an evil king, Klingsor, had laid a trap for Amfortas, involving some kind of sexual temptation, and had succeeded in inflicting this wound on him.

While Parsifal was sitting at dinner a wonderful procession appeared, page boys carrying a bleeding spear and a shining bowl. After dinner Parsifal fell into a deep sleep. In some versions of the legend he also faced a series of trials. He was menaced by wild beasts – lions – and was tempted by a beautiful demon. He also had to cross the Bridge Perilous, a giant sword that spanned the moat. As we shall see these variations can be reconciled.

When he awoke he found that the castle was deserted. He rode out to find that the crops had failed and the country become a wasteland.

Parsifal was later accepted at court and received his spurs. But one day an ugly crone, the Loathly Lady, accosted him. She explained that the country was suffering because, when presented with a vision of the Grail, he had failed to ask the question which would have healed the Fisher King and restored his kingdom's fortunes.

On his second visit to the Grail Castle, Parsifal asked Amfortas what ailed him, and he succeeded in the quest for the Grail where all other knights had been denied. Sir Launcelot had failed, for instance, because of his love for Guinevere. He did not have a pure heart.

At the climax of his quest, Parsifal sees first the spear of Longinus – a reminder of the connection with Charlemagne – and then, finally, the Grail itself.

What are we to make of this as history? The visionary element should certainly be understood as an account of an initiation ceremony. Parsifal's trials and visions took place in a deep trance.

But, of course, the fact that events are symbolic or allegorical does not mean that they are not to be understood as literally true, too.

What, then, is the Grail?

LEFT *In chivalry the helmet, the sword and the spurs are symbols of initiation. The ceremony of creating a knight by the tapping of the shoulder with a sword is a memory of the ancient initiation ceremony of tapping the forehead with the thyrsus rod that makes springs of water and of wine flow. In some modern initiation ceremonies this is remembered in the form of quite a fierce blow to the forehead. The blow allows the birth of a higher form of thought, as Athena, goddess of wisdom, was born from the forehead of her father.*

RIGHT *Esoteric heraldic devices featuring many of the creatures and symbols of the secrert history from* A Grammar of British Heraldry, *1854.*

We saw that in the early German version of the story the Grail is a stone. In this version the Grail also seems to have the properties of the philosopher's stone of the alchemists. It shines, it regenerates, makes flesh and bones young again and, in the words of von Eschenbach, 'offers so much of the world's sweetness and delight that it seems like the kingdom of heaven'. Of course, if this stone that fell out of the forehead of Lucifer had been shaped into a bowl, it would also be a stone that had been *worked* on.

In order to understand what the Grail really is, we should recall what its function is, listen carefully to what the well-known story is telling us. It is a chalice or receptacle to hold bodily fluids. More particularly, it was to hold the blood of Christ, used to catch it

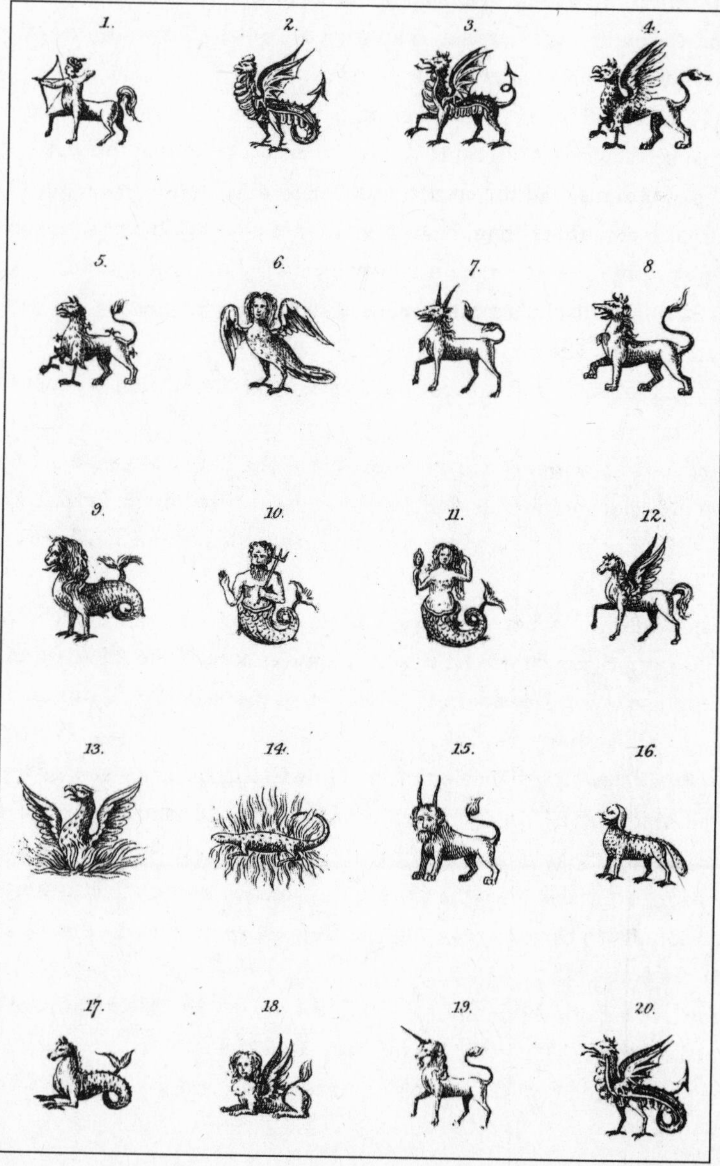

as it spurted from his body on the cross and then later, symbolically, at the Last Supper.

As we have seen, blood is the distinguishing feature of animal consciousness, and in occult physiology the animal part of our nature nestles in or is carried by – as if by a chalice – the vegetable part of our nature.

The secret of the Holy Grail, then, is not that it represents a bloodline. This, I have already suggested, would go against the esoteric doctrine of reincarnation. Rather it alludes to the role of the vegetable part of our nature as a living receptacle for our spirit or consciousness. The quest for the Grail is the quest for a purified receptacle fit to carry a higher form of spirit, and the trials in the course of the quest involve certain esoteric techniques of purification of the vegetable body. Rudolf Steiner, perhaps the greatest teacher of the twentieth century, said that all serious esoteric work begins with work on the etheric, that is to say the vegetable body.

Because of the Fall our animal selves have become so corrupted and we are in thrall to our sexual selves. In fact our animal selves are so corrupt that this has seeped down into our vegetable and material bodies, and it is beyond our power to purify them. We need supernatural help, and esoteric techniques are intended to enlist this help.

If the plant-like dimension of humanity is purified, we will naturally become more plant-like. Saintly individuals can sometimes live on almost nothing but sunlight, after the manner of plants. The twentieth-century German mystic and miracle-worker Therese Neumann lived for some forty years on nothing more than the daily consumption of a consecrated wafer.

But if techniques to transform our vegetable bodies have existed since ancient times, what was new and distinctive about the techniques involved in the Grail initiation?

In his deeply meaningful second encounter with the wounded Fisher King, Parsifal asks the question, What ails thee, brother?

This shows a combination of selfless compassion and – most significantly – shows a free, enquiring spirit which was new in the eighth century. Here, then, is the beginning of a new impulse towards freedom of thought that marked the beginning of the end of the age of Church authority.

When Parsifal achieves a vision of the Holy Grail, this is a vision of the vegetable body or soul which has been so transformed by moral feeling and intellectual questioning that it is fit to carry a higher form of spirit, the Spirit of Jesus Christ.

The historical dimension of the story is contained in the way that Amfortas's wound causes the country to become a wasteland. The private devotions of initiates affect the destinies of nations.

The form of the story is significant, too. The story of Parsifal's attainment of the Grail is presented in terms of Parsifal's inner imaginative vision.

In the temples and Mystery schools of earlier ages wonderful statues were fashioned and gods were called down to inhabit them. In the Middle Ages the great initiates would inspire wonderful imaginative pictures, and it was into these mental images that the gods would descend and breathe life.

On the death of Charlemagne in 814, his empire quickly fell apart, but what has survived to this day is the living idea of a united Europe. Like King Arthur, Charlemagne has never really died but waits to return in time of need.

THE CHURCH GREW IN POWER AND WEALTH. It wanted to be the sole keeper of the keys to the Kingdom. The Church had earlier emphasized that an individual has but one life by suppressing teachings on reincarnation and had emphasized one god by suppressing knowledge of its astronomical roots. Now it emphasized the unity of the disembodied parts of the human being. In 869 at the Eighth Ecumenical Council, the Church effectively closed the door to the spirit worlds by abolishing the ancient distinction between the vegetable dimension of the soul and the animal dimension of the spirit. Soul and spirit were declared to be the same thing, and the result of this was that the spirit worlds, formerly encountered in the Mass, would come to seem an empty abstraction.

Experience of the spirit worlds was replaced by dogma to be accepted on authority.

Meanwhile, a vital Islamic influence, part intellectual, part spiritual, continued to flow into Europe through centres of scholarship like Toledo and Sicily. The study of mathematics, geometry and natural science, inspired in part by the Arabs' translation and preservation of the works of Aristotle, as well as astronomy and astrology, spread northwards, leading to the formation of the first universities in Europe, based on the Islamic model. It led, too, to the arabesques of Gothic architecture, influenced by the intricate vegetal forms of mosque architecture.

IN THE NORTH PORCH OF THE CATHEDRAL at Chartres, founded in 1028, stands Melchizedek bearing the Grail. The astrology that Islam was bringing back to Europe, after it had been driven out several hundred years earlier by Rome, can be seen in the symbolism of the west porch – the fish of Pisces and the twin Templar Knights of Gemini. The pediment also has a fine example of a *vesica piscis*, a Third Eye that sees the spirit worlds coming through into the material world.

Chartres is a fusion in stone of Islamic mysticism, ancient Celtic spirituality and Neoplatonic Christianity. Atop a hill honeycombed with ancient tunnels and caves, it is believed to have been built on a site sacred to the Mother Goddess. A black virgin, resonant of the kinship between Isis, mother of the Sun god, and Mary, mother of Jesus Christ, can still be seen in the crypt.

Set into the floor of the nave is the most famous labyrinth in Europe. Built in 1200 it is some forty feet in diameter. Before it was taken up to help make canons in the French

You must reverse direction seven times but never tread the same path. This spiral represented in two dimensions is depicted here, based on an original drawing by Botticelli.

Revolution, a bronze plaque in the centre depicted Theseus, Ariadne and the Minotaur.

Of course labyrinths and mazes are ancient pagan artefacts, remains of which are found not only at Knossos but at Hawara in Egypt and in the many open-air labyrinths and mazes found cut in the turf in Ireland, Britain and Scandinavia. Many other Christian churches had labyrinths before the eighteenth century, but these were destroyed because of their pagan associations.

One of the burial mounds at Newgrange in Ireland was still called 'the spiral castle' by the locals in the 1950s, because of a spiral carved by the entry portal. The expression 'our king has gone to the spiral castle' was an idiomatic way of saying that he had died.

This is the key to understanding the secret symbolism of the labyrinth and of Chartres Cathedral itself. If you enter the labyrinth and follow its track on foot you find yourself moving in a spiral motion, first to the left then curving back to the right as you move towards the centre. Pilgrims following its route are engaged in a dance like the dance of

Jesus described in the Acts of St John. The aim, as in all initiatory activity, is to enter an altered state in which the spirit journeys up through the spirit worlds, experiencing the after-death journey while still alive.

Ariadne, who intercedes to help save Theseus, is, in the Chartrean context, Mary who gave birth to the Sun king and through whose intercession we may give birth to our own higher selves.

The labyrinth at Chartres can therefore be seen as a sort of mandala or aid to meditation and to achieving an altered state. In the sacred geometry of the cathedral the labyrinth is mirrored by another mandala, the great rose window.

The stained glass of the Middle Ages appeared first in Iran/Iraq in the eleventh century. The extraordinary, luminescent glass of Chartres was manufactured by medieval alchemical adepts who had learned the secrets of the Arabs and whose techniques we cannot now reproduce. Schwaller de Lubicz, the great Egyptologist, explained to his biographer André Vanden Broeck that the brilliant reds and blues of the stained glass at Chartres used no chemical pigmentation but a separation of the volatile spirit of metals that he tested with the famous alchemist Fulcanelli and also found in shards of glass he unearthed in Egypt.

The rose window, which in its outer circle displays the signs of the zodiac, represents the chakra ablaze as it should be when we reach the centre of life's labyrinth, dancing finally to the Music of the Spheres. Not for nothing has Chartres Cathedral been described as an alchemical crucible for the transformation of humanity.

Islam was weaving its way into the fabric of the whole world both esoterically and exoterically. Then, in 1076, Turkish Muslims took control of Jerusalem.

18

The Wise Demon of the Templars

The Prophecies of Joachim • The Loves of Ramón Lull • St Francis and the Buddha • Roger Bacon Mocks Thomas Aquinas • The Templars Worship Baphomet

IN 1076 TURKISH MUSLIMS TOOK control of Jerusalem and began to persecute Christian pilgrims. The Crusaders freed Jerusalem, then lost it again.

In 1119 five knights met under the leadership of Hugo de Payens at the place of the Crucifixion. Like the knights who had ridden in the quest for the Grail, they vowed to make themselves worthy vessels to carry the blood of Christ. In order to protect pilgrims, they set up their headquarters in what was believed to have been the site of the stables attached to the Temple of Solomon.

Founded between the first and second Crusade, they became Christianity's crack troops. The Knights Templar or the Order of the Poor Soldiers of Christ and the Temple of Solomon, to give them their full title, always wore sheepskin breeches beneath their outer clothing as symbol of their chastity, and they were forbidden to cut their beards. They were to own nothing except a sword, holding all property in common. They were never to ask for mercy from the enemy, only retreating if the odds were three to one. And though they might retreat, they would always in the end have to fight to the death.

St Bernard of Clairvaux, the founder of the Cistercian monastic order and the most influential churchman of the day, wrote the 'order', or rule book, of the Templars in 1128, so that they became, formally, a religious order. Bernard wrote of the Templars that they knew no fear, that 'one of them has often put to flight a thousand', that they were gentler than lambs, grimmer than lions, and theirs was 'the mildness of monks and the valour of knights'.

The archaeological evidence seems to confirm that the Templars may have had an ulterior motive for their order – to excavate the site of the Temple. Templar artefacts have been discovered in tunnels deep below it. These tunnels have been cut out of solid rock in a direction that would have taken them directly under the supposed site of the Holy of Holies.

The initiation ceremonies of the Templars clearly brought together different traditions, including Sufism and the Solomonic wisdom of the Temple. A lamb was killed and from its body a cord was made and placed around the candidate's neck. He was led into the initiation chamber by this cord. He had been made to swear that his intentions were completely pure, on pain of death, and now the candidate wondered if the Grand Master could see into his soul by occult means – was he about to die?

Candidates endured frightening ordeals of the type that candidates for initiation by Zarathustra had had to undergo, involving confrontations with dreadful demonic forces, so that they would be prepared to face death or any horrors they might encounter in their later lives.

These confrontations with demons in initiation would come back to haunt the Templars, but for about two hundred years their *esprit de corps* and tight organizational structure made them extraordinarily successful in influencing, if not directing, world affairs.

Because many nobles joined the order, giving over rights to their property, the Templars became extremely rich. They invented letters of credit so that money could be transferred without risk of being stolen by robbers. Their Temple in Paris became the centre of French finances. They were in some ways the forerunners of banks, instrumental in preparing for the rise of the merchant classes. The Templars were also patrons of the first trade guilds to be independent of Church and nobility. Called the Compagnons du Devoir, these guilds were responsible for the Templars' building projects, maintained ethical codes and protected members' widows and orphans.

AT THE END OF THE TWELFTH CENTURY other challenges to the supremacy of the Church were arising.

In 1190–91 Richard the Lionheart, grandson of Guillaume of Poitiers, the first Troubador, was returning from the third Crusade. He stopped off to visit a mountain hermit, who was becoming famous for his gift of prophecy. The report came back with Richard: 'What black tidings lie beneath that cowl!'

Born in a small village in Calabria in about 1135, Joachim had lived as a hermit for many years before joining an abbey and eventually founding his own Abbey of Fiore in the mountains.

He was trying to understand the Revelations of St John, wrestling with it, as he put it – and being defeated. Then one Easter morning he awoke a new man, having been granted a new faculty of understanding. The prophetic commentaries that then poured out of him would influence spiritual thought and mystical groups throughout Europe during the Middle Ages, and then later the Rosicrucians.

There is a cabalistic dimension to Joachim's writings even though the central books of the Cabala had yet to be published, perhaps the result of his friendship with Petrus Alphonsi, a Spanish Jewish convert. Of course, the Old Testament itself has a strong sense of God working through history, but what is specifically cabalistic about Joachim's thought is his interpretation of biblical texts in terms of complex number symbolism and his vision of what he called the Tree of Life. He published a diagram of this tree two hundred years before a similar idea was published by Cabalists, most likely drawing on oral tradition he encountered through his friendship with Alphonsi.

But the aspect of Joachim's teaching that really grabbed the medieval imagination was his theory of three. He argued that if the Old Testament was the Age of the Father, which had called for fear and obedience, and if the New Testament was the Age of the Son, the age of the Church and of faith, then the reality of the Trinity suggests that a third age is coming, an age of the Holy Spirit. Then the Church will no longer be necessary, because this will be an age of freedom and love. Because Joachim was an initiate there was also an astrological dimension to his thought, usually glossed over by Church commentators. The Age of Aries was the Age of the Father, Pisces the Age of the Son, and Aquarius the Age of the Holy Spirit.

Joachim prophesied that there would be a time of transition from the second to the third age, when a new order of spiritual men would educate humanity, when Elijah would reappear, as prophesied in the last verse of the Old Testament in the Book of Malachi. Elijah would be the forerunner of the Messiah, arriving to usher in the great *inovatio*. Joachim also prophesied the Anti-Christ will incarnate before the third age began. As we shall see, Joachim's prophecies still fascinate the secret societies today.

RAMÓN LULL, DOCTOR ILLUMINATUS, was a missionary to the Muslims whose thought was nevertheless saturated with Islamic ideas.

Ramón Lull was born in Palma, the capital of Majorca, in 1235 and brought up as a page in the royal court. He led a carefree life of pleasure. One day, lusting after a Genoese lady and wanting her badly, he rode his horse into the church of Eulalia where she was praying. She turned him away, but one day she responded to verses he had sent her by summoning him to a tryst. When he arrived, without warning she exposed her breast to him – it was being eaten away by a malignant disease.

This shock marked the beginning of the process of Lull's conversion. It helped form his view of the world as a place of oscillating extremes, where appearance might well mask their opposites. In his most famous book, *The Book of the Lover and the Beloved*, he asks, 'When comes the hour in which water that flows downwards shall change its nature

Astrology re-introduced into Europe via Islam, personified here in a sixteenth-century French manuscript.

and mount upwards?' He talks of the Lover falling among thorns, but how they seemed to him like flowers and a bed of love. 'What is misery?' he asks. 'To get one's desires in this world ... If you see a Lover clothed in fine raiment', he says, 'sated with food and sleep, know that in that man thou seeest damnation and torment.' The scent of flowers brings to the Lover's mind the evil stench of riches and meanness, of old age and lasciviousness, of discontent and pride.

Lull wrote of mounting the ladder of humanity to glory in the Divine Nature. This mystical ascent is achieved by working on what he calls the powers of the soul – feeling, imagination, understanding and will. In this way he was helping to forge the deeply personal form of alchemy that, as we will see, would be the great engine of esoteric Europe.

In one of his harsher sayings he said: 'If thou speaketh truth, O fool, thou wilt be beaten by men tormented, reproved and killed'. While preaching to the Muslims in North Africa he was set upon by a crowd, led out of the city and stoned to death.

FRANCIS WAS BORN INTO A WORLD WHERE serfs suffered extreme poverty and where the deformed, the aged, the destitute and lepers were treated with utter contempt. The wealthy clergy made a good living out of the serfs and persecuted anyone who disagreed with them.

In 1206 Francis was a rich young man in his twenties in Assisi in Italy. He was leading a carefree and heartless life, avoiding all contact with hardship, holding his nose if he saw a leper.

It is impossible not to see the parallels with the life of Prince Siddartha.

Then one day he was out riding when his horse suddenly reared up and he found himself looking down at a leper. He dismounted and before he knew it was grasping the leper's bloody hand, and kissing the supurating cheeks and lips. He felt the leper withdraw his hand, and when Francis looked up he saw the leper had vanished.

He knew then that, like St Paul on the road to Damascus, he had had an encounter with the risen Christ.

Francis's life and philosophy were turned upside down and inside out. He began to see with all clarity that the Gospels recommended a life of poverty, devoted to helping others, possessing 'neither gold nor silver nor money in your purse, no wallet for your journey, nor two coats, nor shoes'. Poverty, he was to say, is to have nothing, to wish for nothing, yet to possess all things truly in the spirit of freedom. He came to see that experience itself, not things experienced, were important. The things we possess have a hold on us and threaten to rule our lives. A voice emanating from a painted crucifix in the Church of San Domenico near Assisi told him, 'Go, Francis, and repair my House, which as you can see, is falling into ruin.' Francis felt that this experience was ineffable.

He so transformed his nature in the animal, vegetable and, as we shall see shortly, in the material dimensions, that animals responded to him in an amazing way. A cricket sang when he asked. Birds gathered to hear him preach. When a large, fierce wolf terrorized the mountain town of Gubbio, Francis went out to meet it. The wolf ran towards Francis, but when he ordered it not to hurt anyone, the wolf lay down at his feet. It then began to walk alongside him, completely tamed. A few years ago a wolf's skeleton was found buried underneath the floor of the Church of San Francesco della Pace in Gubbio.

If we compare the mysticism of Ramón Lull with that of St Francis we see that a profound change has taken place in a very short time. Francis's mysticism is the mysticism of simple, natural things, of the open air and the everyday.

In the first biography of St Francis, *The Little Flowers of St Francis*, it is said of him that he discovered the hidden things of nature with his sensitive heart. To Francis all things were alive. His was an ecstatic vision of the cosmos as idealism conceives it, everything created and charged with life by the celestial hierarchies. All creation sings in unison in the Canticle of Brother Sun and Sister Moon:

All praise be yours, my Lord, through all you have made
And first my lord Brother Sun
Who brings the day..

All praise be yours, my Lord, through Sister Moon and Stars
In the heavens you have made them
Bright and precious and fair.

The spirit of Christianity had once helped the evolution of Buddhism. It had introduced a spirit of enthusiasm that helped the Buddha's teaching of universal compassion find fulfilment in the material world. Now, although the Buddha did not incarnate again, his spirit here helped reform Christianity by inspiring a simple devotion and compassion for all living things.

Near the end of his life Francis was meditating on Mount La Verna, praying outside his hermit's cell, when suddenly the whole sky blazed with light, and a six-winged Seraph appeared to him. Francis realized that this great being had the very same face he had seen on the painted crucifix that had set him out on his mission. He understood that Jesus Christ was sending him on a *new* mission.

Shortly after the death of St Francis trouble broke out in the order he had founded, the Franciscans. The Pope asked the order to take on extra responsibilities involving owning property and handling money. Many of the brothers saw this as a violation of St Francis's vision, and they formed breakaway groups called the Spiritual Franciscans, or Fraticelli. Both to themselves and to many outsiders they seemed like the new order of spiritual men whom Joachim had prophesied would oversee the end of the Church.

So it was that followers of St Francis came to be hunted down and killed as heretics.

A famous fresco by Giotto shows St Francis propping up the Church. If Francis saved the Church from complete collapse, can he be said to have succeeded in reforming it as the voice from the crucifix had asked? In esoteric Christianity it is believed that the Seraph who gave Francis the stigmata told him that his new mission was to be fulfilled *after death*. Once a year, on the anniversary of his death – 3 October – he was to lead the spirits of the dead out of the lunar spheres into the higher hierarchies.

Initiation, as we continue to see, is as concerned with life after death as much as this life.

IN THE LIFETIMES OF RAMÓN AND Francis new, different impulses for reform and purification of religious practice were growing up in many parts of Europe, in Yugoslavia, Bulgaria, Switzerland, Germany, Italy and above all in the south of France.

There the Cathars attacked the corruption of the Church. Their Gnostic-like central tenet was that they should keep themselves completely pure from an evil world. Like both the Templars and St Francis they renounced material possessions and kept strict vows of chastity.

The ministry to the dead, carved on a sixteenth-century sarcophagus.

The Cathars had no churches of wood or stone. They rejected a sacramental system that made the Church the only intermediary between God and the people. 'We value virginity above everything,' said one witness. 'We do not sleep with our wives but love them as we would our sisters. We never eat meat. We hold our possessions in common.' They had only one prayer, the Lord's Prayer, and their initiation ritual, the *consolamentum*, was a saying goodbye to an evil world. They welcomed martyrdom.

The Church obliged. In 1208 Pope Innocent III ordered a Crusade against the Cathars. Arriving at the town of Béziers, the Crusaders demanded that it hand over the five hundred or so Cathars inside. When the townspeople refused, all of them, running into many thousands, were slaughtered. When one of the soldiers asked the papal legate Arnaud-Amaury how they might distinguish the Cathars from the others, he is said to have replied with a phrase that has echoed down history: 'Kill them all, God will find his own.' At Bram they stopped off to take a hundred hostages. They cut off their noses and upper lips, then blinded all except one who led a procession to the castle. At Lavaur they captured ninety knights, hanged them, then stabbed them when they took too long to die. An entire army of prisoners was burned alive at Minerve.

In 1244 the last few remaining heretics, who had survived a nine-month siege of the mountain-top castle of Montségur, gave themselves up. Two hundred Cathar monks descended the mountain and walked into the fires awaiting them.

According to legend four monks had escaped the mountain-top refuge a day earlier, taking with them the secret treasure of the Cathars. We do not know whether this treasure was gold, relics or secret doctrine, but perhaps it is too easy to romanticize the Cathars. They taught that the world was evil in a way that suggests that they, like the Gnostics before them, were under the sway of a world-hating, death-loving oriental philosophy. The Church at Rome suppressed the Cathars with maximum force – but the true esoteric thought of the day was closer to it than the jugular vein.

IN THE CLOSING YEARS OF THE THIRTEENTH century a weak and sickly child was born. Shortly after birth he was taken in and looked after by twelve wise men. In Rudolf Steiner's account, they lived in a building that had belonged to the Templars at Monsalvat on the border between France and Spain.

Because the boy was kept completely shut away from the outside world, the locals were unable to see anything of his miraculous nature. He was filled with such a strong, shining spirit that his little body became transparent.

The twelve men initiated him in about 1254, and he died shortly afterwards – having shared his spiritual vision with those who had looked after him. The thirteen had helped prepare for his next incarnation in which he would change the face of Europe.

ALBERTUS WAS BORN IN 1193, APPARENTLY a dull and stupid boy until, inspired by a vision of the Virgin Mary, he began to pursue his studies so zealously that he quickly became the most famous philosopher in Europe. He studied Aristotle's science, physics, medicine, architecture, astrology and alchemy. The short text *The Emerald Tablet of Hermes Trismegistus*, containing the central hermetic axiom 'as above so below', first surfaced into exoteric history as part of his library. He almost certainly explored methods of divining the presence of metals deep in the earth using occult means. It is said he built a strange automaton he called the Android, able to speak, perhaps even think and move about of its own free will. It was made of brass and other metals chosen because of their magical correspondences with heavenly bodies, and Albertus made it come alive by breathing magical incantations into it and with prayers.

The legend that Albertus Magnus was the architect of Cologne Cathedral probably derives from his authorship of *Liber Constructionum Alberti*, containing the secrets of Operative Freemasons, including the laying of the foundations of cathedrals along astronomical lines.

STORIES OF JOURNEYS UNDERGROUND, like those of Albertus Magnus, to discover metals, are often ways of alluding to underground initiations. We know that initiations of this type survived into the Middle Ages because of an account of one that took place in Ireland, which has come down to us from three sources.

A soldier called Owen, who served the English King Stephen, went to the Monastery of St Patrick in Donegal. Owen fasted for nine days, processing around the monastery and taking baths of ritual purification. On the ninth day he was admitted to the underground chamber 'out of which all who enter do not return'. There he was laid down in a grave. The only light was from a single aperture. That night Owen was visited by fifteen men robed all in white, who warned him that he was about to undergo a trial. Then, all of a sudden, a troop of demons appeared. They held him over a fire, before showing him scenes of torment like those described by Virgil.

Finally, two elders came to guide him, and showed Owen a vision of Paradise.

ALBERTUS WAS SPIRITUAL GUIDE TO Thomas Aquinas, nearly thirty-three years his junior. It seems that Thomas smashed his master's Android to pieces, in some accounts because he believed it diabolical – in others because it would never stop talking.

Aquinas had come to the University of Paris to study Aristotle at the feet of the master, but he was to discover that the greatest Aristotelean was in fact a Muslim. Averroës argued that Aristotelean logic showed Christianity to be absurd.

Would logic eat up religion, all true spirituality?

Aquinas's life's work culminated in his massive *Summa Theologica*, perhaps the most influential work of theology ever written. Its aim was to try to show that philosophy and Christianity are not only compatible – they illumine each other. Aquinas applied the sharpest analytical scalpel to thought about the spirit worlds. He was able to categorize the beings of the heavenly hierarchies, the great cosmic forces that create natural forms as well as creating our subjective experiences. The *Summa* contains, for example, the Church's definitive teachings on the Four Elements and this is achieved with a living, penetrating intellect rather than a stultifying reshuffling of dead dogma.

Aquinas is a key figure in the secret history, then, because his great intellectual triumph over Averroës prevented Europe's being overcome by scientific materialism several hundreds years too early.

Again it is important to bear in mind that this triumph was achieved from the standpoint of direct, personal experience of the spirit worlds. There is not a shadow of a doubt that Thomas Aquinas, like Albertus Magnus, was an alchemist, who believed it was possible to harness the power of disembodied spirits to effect changes in the material world. Of the many alchemical texts attributed to him, scholars accept at least one as undoubtedly genuine. In order to understand this better, it's useful to compare him with his contemporary Roger Bacon.

Today alchemy can seem a strange, hole-in-the-wall activity. In fact it is quite familiar to all church-going Christians because it is what is said to take place at the climax of the Mass. Aquinas first formulated the doctrine of the transubstantiation of the bread and

TESTAMENTUM
CREMERI,
ABBATIS WESTMONASTE-
RIENSIS, ANGLI, ORDI-
NIS BENEDICTINI.

TRACTATUS TERTIUS.

FRANCOFURTI,
Apud HERMANNUM à SANDE.
M DC LXXVII.

Title page of Testamentum Cremeri, *showing Thomas Aquinas as a practising alchemist.*

wine. What he described is essentially an alchemical process in which the substance of the bread and wine changes and a parallel transubstantiation takes place in the human body. The Mass brings about not just a new frame of mind, a new determination to do better, but a vital physiological change.

It is no accident that Aquinas formulated his doctrine at the same time that the stories of the Grail began to circulate. They describe the same process albeit using different methods.

Though they were enemies – Bacon mocked Aquinas for only being able to read Aristotle in translation – both Aquinas and Bacon were representatives of the impulse of the age: to strengthen and refine the faculty of intelligence. They found *magic* in thinking. The capacity for prolonged, abstract thought, for juggling with concepts, had existed once before but only briefly and locally in the Athens of Socrates, Plato and Aristotle, before being snuffed out again. A new, living and more long-lasting tradition arose with Aquinas and Bacon. Both put experience before the dead old categories of tradition, and both were deeply religious men who sought to refine their religious beliefs on the basis of experience. 'Without experience,' said Bacon, 'it is impossible to know anything.'

Bacon was the more practical, but when he explored the mind's supernatural capacities, he invoked entities from the same spiritual hierarchies that Aquinas categorized. Both applied rigorous analysis and logic, and their mysticism was quite unlike the unthinking, ecstatic mysticism of the Cathars.

A young scholar at Oxford in the 1250s, Roger Bacon resolved, like Pythagoras before him, to know everything there is to know. He wanted to gather together into his own mind all that the scholars at the court of Haroun al Raschid had known.

Roger Bacon became the image of a wizard. Known as Doctor Mirabilis, he sometimes appeared on the streets of Oxford in Islamic robes. At other times he worked without rest day and night in his rooms in college which would be rocked by explosions from time to time.

Bacon busied himself conducting practical experiments, for example with metals and magnetism, discovering gunpowder independently of the Chinese or scaring his students by shining a light on to a crystal in order to produce a rainbow – something which up until that time people had believed only God could do. He also had a magic looking-glass that enabled him to see fifty miles in any direction, because he, unlike anyone else alive at the time, understood the properties of lenses.

But it is undoubtedly true that Bacon had powers beyond the ability of science to explain today. He sent his complete works to Pope Clement IV in the mind of a twelve-year-old boy called John, whom he had taught to know all his many books off by heart in a few days. Bacon used a method that involved prayers and magic symbols. Similarly, he was able to teach students Hebrew so well that they could read all of scripture in a matter of weeks.

All magic is a power of mind over matter. As we are beginning to see, esoteric philosophy is concerned with methods for developing the faculties of the mind so that natural laws can be manipulated.

In Roger Bacon the faculties of intelligence and imagination were highly developed and each worked one on the other. In 1270 he wrote: 'It is possible to make engines of navigation which have no need of men to navigate them, so that very large sea-going ships may go along with one man to steer and at greater speed than if they were full of men working them. And cars could be made that would move at inestimable speed without animals to draw them. Flying machines can be built so that a man sitting in the middle of the machine may turn an instrument by which wings artificially made will beat there ...' In the Middle Ages this remarkable man had a complete vision of the modern technological world created by experimental science. Bacon was a Franciscan who, like the founder of his order, longed for a better, cleaner, kinder world for the poor and the dispossessed.

There is a telling point in Umberto Eco's *The Name of the Rose* when William of Baskerville, Eco's Sherlock Holmes-like hero, explains that there are two forms of magic, a Devil's magic that seeks to harm others by illicit means, and a holy magic which rediscovers the secrets of nature, a lost science known to the ancients. Like the Arab alchemists who influenced him, Bacon worked on the borderline of magic and science – and this borderline, we will see, is what alchemy essentially is.

Bacon wrote a treatise called *The Mirror of Alchemy* and liked to recall a saying of a great scholar of the Cabala, St Jerome: 'You will find many things quite incredible and beyond the bounds of probability that are true for all that.'

In 1273 Thomas Aquinas, nearing the completion of his massive *Summa Theologica*, was taking Mass at a church in Naples when he had an overwhelming mystical experience. He wrote 'What has been revealed to me now, makes all I've written worth no more to me than a stack of straw.'

WE'VE HAD HINTS OF THE TRAINING OF THE imagination in Lull and Bacon. Of course idealists have a more exalted view of imagination than materialists. For idealists imagination is a faculty for grasping a higher reality.

The discipline of training the imagination is central to esoteric practice, the initiations of the secret societies and, indeed, of magic.

For esotericists and occultists imagination is also important, because imagination is the great creative force in the universe. The universe is the creation of God's imagination – imagination, as we saw in Chapter 1, was the first emanation – and it is our imaginations that allow us to interpret the creation and sometimes to manipulate it.

Human creativity, whether magical or non-magical, is the result of a particular channelling of the powers of the imagination. In alchemical tracts, for example, sperm is described as created by the imagination. This is a way of saying that imagination not only informs desire, it also has the power to transform our very material natures.

Powerful magical transformations in the material world *outside* their bodies can be made by initiates who know how to work on these creative powers of the imagination. An Indian adept is taught from an early age to practise seeing a snake in front of him with such concentrated power, with such a highly trained imagination, that he can eventually make others see it, too.

Of course there is a danger in all this emphasis on the imagination that is perilously close to fantasy. There is always a danger that these workings on the imagination will only end up in delusion. Magic can seem a self-deluder's charter.

The systematic approach of the secret societies was intended to militate against this.

St Bernard of Clairvaux, who wrote the rule book of the Templars, recommended a systematic training of the imagination. By summoning up images of the birth, infancy, ministry and death of Jesus Christ, you could invoke his spirit. If you imagined, say, a domestic scene involving Jesus Christ, imagining the pots and pans, the clothes, his likeness, the lines on his face, the expression in his features, your feelings when he turned to look at you, then if you all of a sudden banished the visual images, what might be left is the very real spirit of Christ.

In thirteenth-century Spain a Cabalist called Abraham Abulafia wrote amplifying the idea of God's creative word. In earlier cabalistic texts the twenty-two letters of the Hebrew alphabet had been described as creative powers. 'In the beginning', then, God had combined these letters in patterns, changed them round and made words out of them, and out of this process unfolded all the different shapes of the universe. Abraham Abulafia proposed that the initiate could participate in the creative process by combining and recombining Hebrew letters in the same way. He recommended retiring to a quiet room, dressing in white robes, adopting ritual poses, pronouncing the divine names of God. In this way a state of ecstatic, visionary trance could be achieved – and with this state, secret powers.

The notion of 'words of power' which give the initiate dominion over the spirit worlds – and so over the material world – is a very ancient one. Solomon was said to have this dominion, and in his Temple the Tetragammaton – the most sacred and powerful name of God – might only be pronounced once a year on the day of the Atonement by the High Priest alone in the Holy of Holies. Outside trumpets and cymbals prevented others from hearing. It was said that someone who knew how to pronounce it could inspire terror in angels. Even earlier, among the Egyptians, it was said that the Sun god, Ra, had created the cosmos using words of power, and it was said that knowledge of these words gave the initiate power not only in this life but in the afterlife.

Abraham Abulafia also recommended using the names of God in diagrammatic form. The practice of working with magical signs and sigils again features largely in Hebrew tradition, but with an admixture of Egyptian and Arab elements it became widespread in the Middle Ages. This was largely because of the spread of grimoires – grammars – of spells such as *The Testament of Solomon* and *The Key of Solomon*. Most of the spells promised the fulfilment of selfish desires, whether sexual, avenging or the finding of treasure. Preparation of materials such as beeswax, the blood of an animal, powdered lodestone, sulphur and perhaps the brain of a raven, might be followed by an act of purification. Then the ceremony itself, perhaps involving sickles, wands, swords, performed at propitious times. The result might be that a ring or perhaps just a scrap of paper was inscribed with the sigil – or signature – so that the carrier of it, wittingly or unwittingly, would be duly affected by the disembodied being for good or for ill. In the mid-fourteenth century, *The Sacred Magic of Abraham the Jew* taught how to excite tempests, raise the dead, walk on water and be beloved of a woman. All of this was to be achieved by using sigils and squares of cabalistic letters.

Today the Church makes a clear distinction between a few strictly regulated ceremonies intended to invoke spiritual powers taking place within a church context – and all other ceremonies intended to invoke or otherwise engage in commerce with disembodied spirits not under its aegis. These latter are labelled 'occult', which in modern Christian parlance usually means black magic.

In the Middle Ages no such distinction would have been practical. Rituals were performed under the aegis of the Church to try to ensure, for example, good crops or success in a duel. Consecrated bread was seen as a cure for the sick and a preservative against the plague, amulets giving protection against lightning and drowning were made out of church candles. Scraps of paper bearing magical formulae were inserted into roofs as protection against fire. Church bells could ward off thunder and demons. Formal curses were pronounced to drive away caterpillars. Holy water was scattered on the fields to ensure a good harvest. Holy relics were wonder-working fetishes. Baptism could restore sight to blind children and overnight vigils at the shrines of saints would bring vivid visionary dreams and cures in the tradition of the 'temple sleep' advocated by Asclepius.

Later Christian apologists tried to distinguish between legitimate Church practice, a matter of petitioning high-level spiritual beings who might choose to agree to a request or not, and magic conceived as a mechanical process involving the manipulating of occult forces. But this involves a misunderstanding. Magic is also an uncertain process of invoking spirits, including some spirits of very high levels.

In the Middle Ages everyone believed in these spiritual hierarchies. Underlying all Church practice and lay spiritual practice was a belief that repeating a formula such as a prayer or performing a ceremony had the power to influence material events for good or ill. By means of these activities people believed that they could communicate with the orders of disembodied beings who controlled the material world.

That prayer was efficacious, that providence rewarded the good and punished the bad was then the universal belief and the universal experience.

If history was seen unquestioningly as a providential process, it was not in a fatalistic way. God had a plan for humankind that different orders of disembodied beings and different orders of incarnated beings were helping to unfold, a plan encoded in the Bible and elucidated by prophets.

But it was a plan that might go wrong at any time.

FRIDAY THE THIRTEENTH IS STILL remembered as an evil day. On Friday 13 October 1307 the kings of the world finally moved to try to eradicate the esoteric influences they feared had been growing further and further from their control.

Just before dawn the seneschals of France, acting on the orders of the French king, Philip the Fair, descended on the temples and lodgings of the Templars, arresting some

15,000 people. In the Paris Temple, France's great centre of finance, they found a secret chamber containing a skull, two thigh bones and a white burial shroud – which is, of course, what you will find if you break into a Freemasonic temple today.

Only a few of the knights – from La Rochelle on the Atlantic coast – managed to escape. They fled to Scotland, where they lived under the protection of the rebel king, Robert the Bruce.

The Inquisition accused the captured knights of making novices spit and trample on the cross of Christ. They were accused, too, of sodomy and worshipping a goat-headed idol called Baphomet. They confessed to seeing this idol with a long beard, sparkling eyes and four feet. Under pressure from Philip the Fair, Pope Clement published a Bill of Abolition, putting an end to the Knights Templar. All their assets were seized by the monarchy.

Appearing before a papal commission the knights said they had been tortured to make them confess. One Bernard de Vardo produced a wooden box in which he kept the charred bones that had fallen from his feet as they were roasted over a fire.

What was the truth behind their confessions?

Shortly before he died I was privileged to work with Hugh Schonfield, the great scholar of the Dead Sea Scrolls. Schonfield did much to explain to Christian scholars Jewish roots of the New Testament that had hitherto been overlooked or misunderstood. Schonfield knew of the ATBASH cipher, in which the first letter of an alphabet is substituted for the last, second for the second last and so on. He also knew that this cipher had been used to encrypt messages in the Book of Jeremiah and in some of the Dead Sea Scrolls. Instinct led him to try it out on the word Baphomet. In this way he found coded in the word Baphomet the word 'wisdom'.

The personification of wisdom that Templars confessed to communing with was, however, the goat-headed god of *worldly* wisdom. Since the time of Zarathustra initiation ceremonies had induced in the candidate altered states in which he underwent terrifying ordeals, was attacked by demons and so prepared to overcome the worst that life – and life after death – had to offer. Now the cunning torturers of the Inquisition were able to cause their victims such pain that they re-entered an altered state of consciousness, and it was then that the demon-king Baphomet appeared to them again, this time in triumph.

They were indeed facing the worst that life and death had to offer.

19

Fools for Love

Dante, the Troubadors and Falling in Love for the First Time • Raphael, Leonardo and the Magi of Renaissance Italy • Joan of Arc • Rabelais and the Way of the Fool

IN 1274 IN FLORENCE A YOUTHFUL DANTE first saw the beautiful Beatrice.

It was love at first sight.

It was also the first time anyone fell in love at first sight.

In the annals of the secret societies this is a great and important historical truth. In conventional history people have been falling in love and been romantically in love since the dawn of time. It's part of our biological make-up, they say. The odes of Pindar and Sappho are expressions of romantic love.

In the secret history, though, these odes from ancient Greece are read as being narrowly sexual. They do not exhibit the moon-calf pain of separation, the ecstatic delight in the beloved's appearance and the interlocked gaze which characterize being in love today.

Dante wrote of *his* first sight: 'She was wearing a beautiful, delicate crimson robe tied with a belt and the moment I saw her I say in all truth that the spirit that loves in the innermost depths of my heart began to tremble in such a way that it overtook my whole being ... the beginning and end of my life's happiness had been revealed to me.' He said he became wholly absorbed in the love in her eyes. Later he wrote of her that when he first saw her he thought by some miracle an angel had materialized on earth. It would be wrong to read this in terms of poetic convention.

In the *Commedia* he described the sensation of being wholly absorbed in her eyes and says that the erotic charge he took from them led him to Paradise. Again, this is no mere poetic fancy. The erotic and the mystical intertwined in a way that was new in the West.

Dante and Beatrice would both marry other people, and she died young. What today we think of as romantic love with its mystical yearnings and sense of destiny – the feeling that this was *meant to be* – all derives from the mystic ferment of Islam. Just as the characteristically Christian understanding of love of your neighbour freely given can be seen to have grown out of the Hebrew prophets' concept of grace, so now the modern world's understanding of the sacred was illumined by the altered states of consciousness achieved by Sufi mystics such as Ibn Arabi. His revolutionary *The Interpretation of Longing* expressed sexual love in terms of divine love. The Sufis expressed a feeling never felt before and so creating the conditions for everyone else to feel it.

For over a thousand years the erotic instinct had been repressed. Sexual energies had been channelled into the development of the human intellect. By the time of Aquinas and Bacon this development was complete. Devised in overnight vigils kneeling at the altar, Aquinas's *Summa Theologica* is more than two million words of densely packed syllogisms, testimony to a capacity for unrelenting intellectual focus that today's greatest philosophers would find it hard to match.

Now, prompted by an impulse spreading up from Arabia, people began to take a new delight in the material world, a sensual pleasure in light, colour, space and the touch of things. The point of evolution of human consciousness moved out of monkish cells and into the pleasure garden. A scintillating sexual sheen was spreading over everything.

The Islamic occupation of Europe lasted longest in Spain. Then, as the brilliant civilization of Mauresque Spain spread northwards, this new way of being spread to the rest of the world, first to the south of France.

In the twelfth century Provence and the Languedoc became the most civilized region in Europe. Provençal poets called Troubadors adapted the Arabic–Andalusian poetic forms, inspired by their erotic éclat. Though she was not an esotericist, Helen Waddell's *The Wandering Scholars* remains the classic account of this period of transition. She relates the story of an abbot riding out with a young monk who is being allowed outside the monastery for the first time, when they pass some women on the road.

'They be demons,' said the abbot.

'I thought,' said the boy monk, 'that they were the fairest things I ever saw.'

The first Troubador to surface in the stream of exoteric history was Guillaume, Count of Poitiers and Duke of Aquitane, who began composing tender, yearning love songs when he returned from the Crusades. But although this early flowering was courtly, it spread through all classes. Among the Troubadors Bernart de Ventadorn was a baker's son and Pierre Vidal was a furrier's son. Perhaps as result of the influence of men like these, poetry now filled with vernacular objects – toads, rabbits, farm machinery, pubs, tumbling pigeons, crackling thorns and a cheek pillowed upon an arm.

The Troubador poet Arnaud Daniel, whom Dante described as *il miglio fabbro*, boasts

The Romance of the Rose *was the most influential work of literature of the age. It describes a castle surrounded by a sevenfold – and therefore planetary – wall covered with emblematic figures. Only those who can explain their meaning are admitted to the beautiful garden of roses.*

of 'hunting hares with an ox, gathering the winds and swimming against the tide'. He is talking in the topsy-turvy way characteristic of esoteric thinkers about the powers initiation has given him.

As well as crossing class barriers, the Troubadors reversed the traditional subjection of women to men. In Troubador poetry men enslave themselves to women. Marriage had worked as an agent of social control, but now the Troubadors encouraged a new form of love that was not arranged but spontaneous, and could flow between individuals of different social status.

Love became subversive like the secret societies themselves.

Being in love in this new way made people feel more fully alive.

It was a new and intense form of consciousness. In the poetry of the Troubadors love, this new way of being, can be reached if you successfully negotiate your way through a number of trials – passing through hell and high water, finding a passage through the labyrinth, combat and the slaying of wild beasts. You must solve riddles and choose the right casket.

Already pale and tortured by doubt the lover is trembling when he is finally allowed into the presence of the beloved. In consummation he achieves an altered state of consciousness, one that confers supernatural powers. All true lovers know that when they gaze deeply into each others' eyes they really are touching each other.

In other words not only was the experience of falling in love introduced into the stream of human consciousness by initiates, but *the experience of being in love was given the deep structure of the process of initiation.*

Troubador literature is full of the symbolism of initiation, too. The most popular symbol of the Troubadors, the rose, was probably derived from Sufism where it was a symbol, among other things, of the entrance to the spirit worlds – and an obvious allusion to the chakras. In the famous story of the *Nightingale and the Rose*, the bird represents the human spirit's longing for the divine. There is also an undeniable sexual level of meaning here, connected with the sensual, fleshy qualities of the rose. The ubiquity of the rose in Troubador love poetry should alert us to the presence here of esoteric, perhaps – as Ezra Pound believed – alchemical techniques of sexual ecstasy. Guillaume of Poitiers wrote, 'I want to retain my lady in order to refresh my heart so well that I cannot age. He will live a hundred years who succeeds in possessing the joy of his love.'

At root the impulse behind the birth of the Renaissance was a sexual one. Let us be clear about the outrageous thing we are saying here – that *the whole of human consciousness was transformed and moved to another level of evolution just because a few people performed the sexual act in a new way.*

They made love for the first time.

When we reach the altered state of consciousness that is orgasm, can we *think*, or is orgasm inimical to thought? We can – and should – ask the same question of a mystical ecstasy.

Secret societies and heretical groups such as the Cathars, Templars and the Troubadors were teaching techniques of mystical ecstasy. Would the hard-won faculty of human thought be strong enough to survive these ecstasies?

IN THE *COMMEDIA* DANTE TOOK THE erotic-spiritual impulse of the Troubadors to another level. He expanded his love for Beatrice to embrace the whole cosmos.

At the beginning of the *Commedia* Dante describes how in middle age Dante found himself lost in a gloomy wood, when he was met by Virgil, one of the great initiates of the ancient world.

Virgil takes Dante through a portal with the words Abandon All Hope Ye Who Enter Here written over it. Virgil then leads him into an underworld like the one described in the *Aeneid* – and containing characters we have already met in our history. They cross the River Acheron and enter the realm of shades. They encounter the judge of the dead, Minos, and Cerberus, the three-headed dog. They enter the minareted city of Dis, encounter the three Furies and the Minotaur. They walk the banks of Lake of Blood in which the violent are immersed, including Attila the Hun. They traverse the Wood of the Harpies and the burning plain of sand. They meet a famous Scottish wizard Michael Scott, Nimrod and finally, in the deepest rung of Hell, Dante sees what he first takes to be a windmill. It is really Lucifer's wings.

It would have been perfectly well understood by Dante's contemporaries that this, the first part of his poem, described a real journey underground – in other words that Dante had undergone an underground initiation. He would perhaps have been led through a series of ordeals and ceremonies like the ones we saw the knight Owen undergo in Donegal.

'Virgil' may well have been the mask for Dante's initiator in real life, a scholar called Brunetto Latini. Journeying as an ambassador to Spain, Latini had there met savants

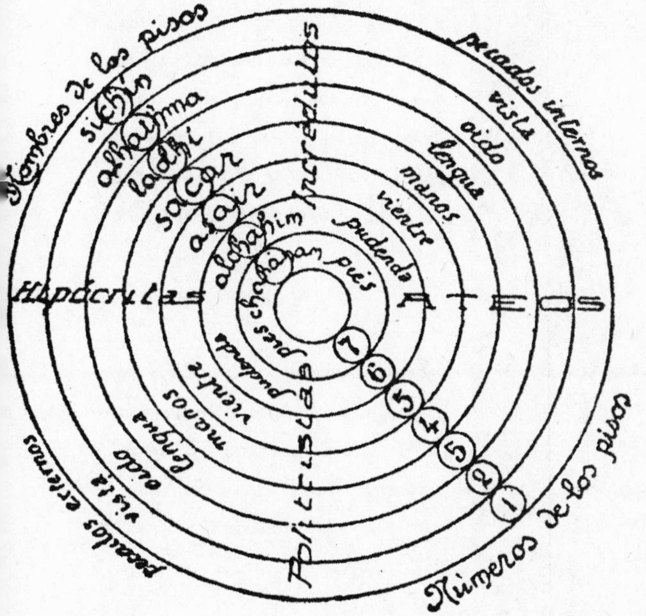

In the ancient world the underworld was conceived of as being seven-layered or seven-walled, as the labyrinth of Minos was depicted on Cretan coins. The same idea is to be found in Origen's account of the Ophites with their invocations to the seven demons who guard the seven gates of the underworld. However, the closest model for Dante's account of the underworld in the Commedia *is now known to be the great Sufi master Ibn Arabi's account of Mohammed's journey into the other worlds in the* Fotuhat. *Illustration from early translation.*

from both the Hebrew and Arab traditions. His great work *The Book of Treasure* included occult teachings on the planetary qualities of precious stones. The uninitiated often fail to appreciate the initiatic quality of Dante's description of the cosmos, that the rungs of hell that spiral downward in the other direction are characterized by planetary qualities. Dante's work is written to read on several different levels – the astrological, the cosmological, the moral, even, some say, the alchemical.

Like the *Fotuhat* and like an earlier model, the Egyptian *Book of the Dead*, the *Commedia* is, on one level, a guide to the afterlife, on another a manual of initiation and on a third level an account of the way that life in the material world – quite as much as the afterlife – is shaped by stars and planets.

The *Commedia* shows how when we behave badly in this life we are already constructing a Purgatory, a Hell, for ourselves in another dimension that intersects with our everyday lives. We are already suffering, tormented by demons. If we do not aspire to move up the spiral of the heavenly hierarchies, if we 'make do' with purely earthly successes and pleasures, we are already in Purgatory.

Oscar Wilde's novel *The Picture of Dorian Gray* has become a part of public consciousness. We all know that, beautiful and vain, Dorian keeps a painting in his attic,

Giordano Bruno executed in the Campo dei Fiori in Rome. It's often assumed that Bruno was burned at the stake by the church for championing the modern, scientific view that the earth revolves around the sun. In fact it was his esoteric views that really frightened the Church. His experiences of the spirit worlds led him to claim that there are an infinity of interlocking universes and dimensions. He invoked the authority of the 'Pythagorean poet', Virgil to back up his belief that the human spirit could travel between these universes, but would eventually 'desire to return to the body' in accordance with the laws of reincarnation.

which decays and becomes monstrous as he plunges into a life of debauchery, while he himself remains perfect and unlined. At the end of the novel the decay in the painting suddenly afflicts Dorian all at once. According to Dante, we're all Dorian Grays, creating monstrous selves and devising monstrous punishments for ourselves. What makes Dante's vision incomparably grander than Wilde's is that not only does he show that we each create a heaven and hell inside us, he also shows what our misdeeds do to the structure and very texture of the world. He turns the world inside out to reveal the hideous effects of our innermost thoughts and the deeds we most want kept secret. According to Dante, everything we do or think materially alters the universe. Umberto Eco has called his poem 'the apotheosis of the virtual world'.

IN 1439 A MYSTERIOUS STRANGER CALLED Gemistos Plethon slipped into the court of Cosimo de Medici, ruler of Florence. Plethon was carrying with him the lost Greek texts of Plato. As fate would have it, he was also carrying various neoplatonic texts, some Orphic hymns and, most intriguingly, some esoteric material which purported to date back to the Egypt of the pyramids.

Plethon came from Byzantium where an esoteric, neoplatonic tradition still thrived dating back to early Church fathers such as Clement and Origen – a tradition that Rome had repressed. Plethon was able to fire Cosimo with the idea of a lineage of universal but secret lore that went back beyond these early Christians to Plato, Orpheus, Hermes and the Chaldean Oracles. He whispered in Cosimo's ear of a perennial philosophy of reincarnation and personal encounters with the gods of the hierarchies which might be achieved by ceremony and the ritual singing of the *Hymns of Orpheus.*

It is this appeal to vivid, personal experience that inspired the Renaissance. Cosimo de Medici employed the scholar Marsilio Ficino to translate Plethon's documents, starting with Plato, but when Cosimo learned about the Egyptian material, he told Ficino to put Plato aside and translate the Egyptian stuff instead.

The spirit that Plethon introduced into Italy by his translations of the hermetica spread quickly among the cultural elite. Appetite for new experience, together with a fresh and vital relationship with the spirit worlds, is captured on the page by the Italian magus Giordano Bruno. He writes of a love that brings 'excessive sweat, shrieks which deafen the stars, laments which reverberate in the caves of Hell, tortures which afflict the living spirit with stupor, sighs which make the gods swoon with compassion, and all this for those eyes, for that whiteness, those lips, that hair, that reserve, that little smile, that wryness, that eclipsed Sun, that disgust, that injury and distortion of nature, a shadow, a phantasm, dream, a Circean enchantment put to the service of generation ...'

This is a new note in literature.

The literature of the Renaissance is lit up by the stars and planets. The great writers

Raphael:
Madonna and Child.

of Renaissance Italy invoked this energy by the active and intelligent use of the imagination. Like Helen Waddell, Frances Yates was not an esotericist – or, if she was, left no hint in her writings – but thanks to her meticulous research and brilliant analysis, and that of the scholars at the Warburg Institute who have followed in her footsteps, we have a detailed understanding of the esoteric discoveries of the Renaissance and of the ways they inspired art and literature. The translations of the hermetic texts by Marsilio Ficino talked of the fashioning of images in esoteric terms: 'Our spirit, if it has been intent upon the work and upon the stars through imagination and emotion, is joined together with the very spirit of the world and with the rays of the stars through which the world-spirit acts.' What Ficino is saying is that if you imagine as fully and vividly as you can the spirits of the planets and the stellar gods, then, as a result of this act of imagination, the power of the spirit may flow through you.

We saw in the last chapter that the Middle Ages was the great age of magic. Then esoteric thinkers and occultists began to construct images in their minds which gods and spirits could inhabit and make come alive, as once the makers of the temples and Mystery centres of the ancient world had manufactured objects such a statues for disembodied beings to use as bodies. In Italy in the Renaissance artists with esoteric beliefs began to recreate the magical images in their minds with paint and stone.

In the Middle Ages, the dissemination of grimoires had been a wholly underground, sub-cultural activity. Now the more widely published hermetic literature of the Renaissance gave instructions on how to construct talismans designed to draw down influences from the spirit worlds which were taken up by the artists of the day. Hermetic literature explained how occult influences could be more effective if they were constructed of metals appropriate to the spirit being invoked – gold for the god of the sun, for example, silver for the god of the moon. Particular colours, shapes, hieroglyphs and other sigils were revealed afresh as sympathetic to particular disembodied beings.

An art critic has talked of Sandro Botticelli's 'predilection for minor tones' and for lighter colours, which suggests an ethereal quality, as if he is depicting beings from another realm not yet fully materialized. We can see Ficino's influence on Botticelli's painting popularly known as the *Primavera*, which illustrates the process of the creation of matter in terms of the successive emanations of the planetary spheres from the cosmic mind. The Primavera herself has shown a remarkable propensity to live and breathe in the minds of those who have seen the painting ever since.

The neoplatonic artists of the Renaissance believed they were rediscovering ancient secrets. Following Plato they believed that all learning is a process of remembering. Our minds are protrusions of the great central cosmic mind into the material world. Everything that has been experienced or thought in history is held in the memory banks of the cosmic mind – or perhaps, more accurately, lives in a sort of eternal now.

If Plato is right, this book is already inside you!

IT IS WITH THE ITALIAN HIGH RENAISSANCE that we come to the idea of the towering genius – not just Botticelli but Leonardo da Vinci, Raphael, Michelangelo. The genius is someone set totally apart from the rest of us by the magnificence and clarity of his or her visions, and it is perhaps appropriate that this flowering took place in Italy because it was a continuation of the tradition of the ecstatic visions of Joachim and St Francis.

Like the saints, the great artists were sometimes mouthpieces for great spiritual beings. According to esoteric tradition the painter Raphael was directly inspired by the Archangel Raphael. The hand that painted the masterpieces was divinely guided.

But there is a stranger and more mysterious tradition – that the individuality who incarnated as Raphael had previously incarnated as John the Baptist. According to Steiner, this explains why there are no major paintings by Raphael of events that took place after the death of John the Baptist. His great masterpieces depicting the Madonna and child with a strange and uniquely compelling quality were in effect painted from memory.

MANY MAGI LIVED IN ITALY IN THE HIGH Renaissance in the time of Leonardo. They often worked within the closed brotherhood of an artist's studio, where artistic and spiritual progress could be guided together and go hand in hand. For example, the mathematician and Hermeticist Luca Pacioli, who was the first to write openly about the secret formulae behind the Venusian pentangle, was one of Leonardo's teachers regarding 'divine proportion'.

Another magus we know had an influence on Leonardo (because Leonardo owned some of his books and mentioned him in his own notebooks) was an architect of an older generation. Leon Battista Alberti was the architect of the Rucellai Palace in Florence, one of the earliest classical buildings in Renaissance Italy, and of the façade of Santa Maria Novella, also in Florence. He was also the author of one of the strangest books in the Italian language: *Hypnerotomachia Poliphili*, the proto-surreal story of Poliphilo (the title may roughly be translated as 'the lover of many things in his struggle for love in a dream').

The hero awakes on the day he is to go on an adventure, but falls into a dream. He pursues his beloved through a strange landscape inhabited by dragons and other monsters, through a labyrinthine course that takes him into many marvellous buildings which are half-stone, half-living organism. The inside of a temple, for example, appears as its viscera. Alberti was obsessed by nature and natural forms and incorporates them in his work in a most unusual way. When we look at, for example, the two versions of the *Virgin of the Rocks*, this same obsession appears in the spiritually epressive forms of the landscape a clear example of Alberti's influence on Leonardo.

Illustration from the Hypnerotomachia. *Here we may catch an echo of the translation from vegetable to animal life, as taught in the secret history.*

The story unfolds with the logic of a dream. On one level the *Hypnerotomachia* is an architectural manifesto. Alberti is proposing that the new architecture of the Renaissance that he was instrumental in creating should have the logic of a dream. Instead of a slavish and inhibited following of precedent, architects should operate in a new, free state of mind where nothing is forbidden, where architects should let themselves be inspired by the combinations of forms that altered states of consciousness may suggest. Alberti is recommending, then, a kind of controlled thought-experiment as a way of facilitating a new way of thinking – and not just in architecture.

That the channelling of *sexual* energies is involved becomes clear at the end of the story when the hero is finally united with his beloved in a series of mystic rites in the Temple of Venus. His beloved is asked by the priestess to stir a cistern with a flaming torch. This causes Poliphilo to fall into a trance state. Then a shell-shaped basin full of whale sperm, musk, camphor oil, almond oil and other substances is set alight, doves are sacrificed, and nymphs dance around an altar. When the beautiful beloved is asked to rub the ground around the base of the altar, the whole building convulses as if in an earthquake and a tree bursts out of the top of the altar. Poliphilo and his beloved taste the fruit of this tree. They are transported into an even higher state of consciousness. The volcanic power of libido has been channelled by the priestess-adept so that all prohibitive rules of behaviour, of morality and creativity, even the laws of nature, have been turned upside down.

Perhaps the most mysterious of all the great masterpieces of the Italian Renaissance is the *Mona Lisa*. Who can explain its power? The great nineteenth-century art critic and esotericist Walter Pater wrote of it: 'Hers is the head upon which all "the ends of the world are come" and the eye lids are a little weary. It is beauty wrought out from within upon the flesh, the deposit, little cell by cell, of strange thoughts and fantastic reveries and exquisite passions ... She is older than the rocks among whom she sits ... she has been dead many times and learned the secrets of the grave and has been a diver in deep seas and keeps their fallen day about her ...'

Pater is perhaps hinting at what he knows. The Mona Lisa is indeed older than the gods.

We saw earlier how the moon separated from the earth in order to reflect sunlight down to the earth and make human reflection possible. We saw, too, how in 13,000 BC Isis withdrew from the earth to the moon to become mistress of this process of reflection. Now at the beginning of the fifteenth century, after the cosmos had spent aeons working to create the conditions to make possible reflection in the sense that we understand it today, it happened at last. Leonardo's masterpiece is an icon in human history because it captured the moment this step in the evolution in consciousness took place. In the face of the Mona Lisa we see for the first time the deep joy of someone exploring her

The Mona Lisa *is perhaps the most reproduced image in the history of painting, here in a nineteenth-century engraving. In his* Treatise on Painting *Leonardo recommends working oneself into a state of receptivity to imaginative imagery in which cracks and stains on old walls can evoke – or invoke – gods and monsters.*

inner life. She is free to detach herself from the world of the senses pressing in on her and roam within. She has what J.R.R. Tolkien in another context called 'an unencumbered, mobile, detached inner eye'.

The Mona Lisa, then, creates a magical space which the spirit of Isis may inhabit. Of course it almost impossible these days to be alone in the Louvre with the Mona Lisa, but like *The Lohan* in the British Museum, it was created so that if you commune with it, it will speak to you.

FAR AWAY FROM THE GLITTER AND GRANDEUR of the courts of the Italian Renaissance, in the unsophisticated north of Europe another spirit was making itself felt. At the age of twelve or thirteen a young girl, living in a simple, rustic cottage in France in the heavily wooded Loire Valley, began to hear voices and see visions. The Archangel Michael appeared to Joan and told her she would have spirit guides. She was reluctant to go along with this, saying she would rather spin by her mother's side. But the voices became increasingly insistent. They told her of her mission. When an invading English army seemed about to take the city of Orleans, they told her to go to the nearby town of Chinon to find the Dauphin, the heir to the throne of France, and from there lead him to be crowned at Rheims Cathedral.

Joan was still little more than a child when she arrived at the court of the Dauphin. He played a trick on her, letting a courtier sit on the throne and pretend to be him, but Joan saw through it and addressed the Dauphin directly. Convinced by Joan, he equipped her with a white horse and a suit of white armour. She wore it in the saddle for six days and nights without respite.

Joan saw a vision of a sword hidden in a church. The sword she described – with three distinctive crosses on it – was discovered hidden behind the altar of the nearby Church of St Catherine de Fierbois.

As sometimes happens in history, when great beings from the spirit worlds bring their powers to bear on a particular individual, she could not be denied. Nothing could stop her even though the odds against her looked overwhelming.

When on 28 April 1429 Joan arrived outside Orleans, now occupied by the enemy, the English troops retreated before the young girl and her small band of supporters. Only five hundred of them defeated an English army of thousands in a way which even her captains described as miraculous.

At Joan's urging the Dauphin was crowned King of France at Rheims. Her mission had been accomplished in less than three months.

It is difficult to think of a clearer example of the influence of the spirit worlds on the course of world history. George Bernard Shaw, who was deeply interested in esoteric philosophy, would write that 'behind events there are evolutionary forces which transcend our ordinary needs and which use individuals for purposes far transcending that of keeping those individuals alive and prosperous and respectable and safe and happy'.

Betrayed by her own people, Joan was sold to the English. She was questioned closely on her voices. She said they were sometimes accompanied by visions and bright lights, that they advised her, warned her and even gave her detailed instructions, often several times a day. Joan was also able to ask their advice and would receive detailed answers to her questions.

Such easy familiarity, such deep and detailed communications with the spirit worlds outside the aegis of the Church was characterized as witchcraft and on 30 May 1430 Joan was burned at the stake in the marketplace in Rouen in northern France. An English soldier turned to another and said, 'We have burnt a saint.'

It was as if the great spiritual powers that had made her inviolable had now deserted her and all of a sudden the forces of opposition rushed on her together in order to overwhelm her.

The English thought of her as the enemy, but according to the perspectives of the secret history it would be England that most benefited from the divinely inspired actions of Joan of Arc. France and England had been locked in conflict for hundreds of years and, though at the time of Joan England had the upper hand militarily, it was dominated culturally, in its language and literature, by the French. Without Joan's severing of France and England, the particularly English contribution to world history – the psychological realism of Shakespeare and the detached and tolerant philosophy of Francis Bacon – would not have been possible.

THE PAINTER ALBRECHT DÜRER WAS returning to Germany following a trip to Italy, where he had been initiated into the esoteric lore of the painter's guilds. Weird visions of the Apocalypse would begin to inspire his woodcuts. He would also paint a portrait of himself as an initiate, holding a flowering thistle, sparkling with dew, the sweat of the stars, as a sign that his organs of spiritual vision were opening up on a new dawn.

On the way he stopped by the wayside to paint a clump of turf. This watercolour was the first still life ever painted. There is nothing leading up to it in the history of art. Before Dürer no one had really looked at a rock and a clump of grass in the way we take for granted today.

Dürer's journey should also be taken as a sign that the impulse for the evolution of human consciousness was moving to the north of Europe. Northerners would find themselves at odds with the more narrowly Catholic countries of the south. New political developments saw the rise of newly powerful northern states which would become vehicles for new forms of consciousness.

In The Zelator *by David Ovason my friend Mark Hedsel is quoted as giving a fascinating analysis of the iconography of the Fool, whose image appears in the frontispiece to the first edition of* Gargantua and Pantagruel *in 1532 and also, of course, in the Tarot. The Fool is following 'the Nameless Way'. The stick across his shoulder represents the vegetable dimension of his being that lies between the spiritual part and the animal part down below, where the dog clawing at his leg represents unredeemed and corrupted animal elements. The unredeemed part of the vegetable body is represented by the burden carried in the sack. His three-pointed hat alludes to the higher bodies he has yet to evolve – the transformed animal, vegetable and mineral bodies – and his upward gaze represents his aspiration towards these. If his beard represents a downward tug, the upward swoop of his hat shows the Third Eye on the point of opening.*

FRANÇOIS RABELAIS, BORN TOWARDS THE end of the fifteenth century, walked the narrow streets of Chinon some fifty or sixty years after Joan's footfalls had died away. His life and work is animated by the spirit of the Troubadors. While Dante, the southerner, had written with a yearning for the spiritual heights, all Rabelais's delight seems, at first glance at least, to be in the material world. His great novel *Gargantua and Pantagruel* tells stories of giants rampaging around the world causing havoc because of their gigantic appetites. The joy in everyday objects that had been characteristic of the Troubadors was given a humorous new twist by Rabelais. *Gargantua* contains a long list of objects you might want to use to wipe your bottom that includes a lady's velvet mask, a page's bonnet, feathered in the Swiss style, a cat, sage, fennel, spinach leaves, sheets, curtains, a chicken, a cormorant and an otter.

The long struggle to wake up to the material world that had begun with Noah is finally completed and the result is sheer delight. Love of light and laughter, food and drink, wrestling and love-making drives the densely packed, punchy prose. In the pages of Rabelais, the world is not the terrible place the Church has made it out to be. The Church's world-denying philosophy is shown to be unhealthy. 'Laugh and face it out boldly whatever it may be,' said Rabelais. Laughter, jolliness and good humour were a cure for both mind and body. Both could be transformed.

Rabelais loves the world and in his writing love of objects and love of words go hand in hand. A profusion of things and the coining of new words come tumbling off the page. But there is a sly initiatic undercurrent for those who wish to look for it. Rabelais is a mystic but not in the otherworldly style of the Middle Ages.

Troubadors had written of the madness of being in love and some of them had written of themselves as fools and madmen. By this they meant that they had found new ways into the spirit worlds, and that when they returned they saw life upside down and inside out.

For the Troubadors, then, everyday reality had looked very different, and Rabelais now turned this new way of seeing into a narrative, creating a subversive style of humour that would become characteristic of initiatic writers such as Jonathan Swift, Voltaire, Lewis Carroll and André Breton. Not only does Rabelais find that he is able to rampage around the spirit worlds with new-found freedom, but when he returns to the material world he is unable to take people's assumptions about it, their conventions, their morality, seriously. In his story his heroes found the Abbey of Thelema, which has the instruction 'Do what thou wilt' inscribed above its gate. Rabelais envisioned a company of initiates whose consciousness is so transformed that they are beyond good and evil.

At the end of *Gargantua and Pantagruel*, after many voyages of exploration over many seas, during which they have seen many wonders, battled with cat-people, armies of sausages and windmill-eating giants, our heroes finally reach a mysterious island. The

Initiatic humour enlivens this startlingly dark image of the Fool by Jacob Jordaens. Like his fellow Dutch artists Rubens and Rembrandt, Jordaens was deeply immersed in the Cabala. The fool's cap mimics the Hebrew letter shin, *which inserted in the Tetragrammaton, or sacred name of God, to yield the name of Jesus. It also symbolizes, in its three prongs, the spiritualizing of the three bodies of man – animinal, vegetable and mineral.*

twentieth-century alchemist Fulcanelli explained that by this arrival Rabelais means to say that his heroes are entering the Matrix.

They are led to an initiation chamber in an underground temple. Stories of going underground should always alert us to the fact that occult physiology is being referred to. The journey underground is a journey inside the body.

In the centre and deepest part of the temple stands a sacred fountain of life. Fulcanelli pointed out that Rabelais allowed his esoteric, alchemical interests to come to the surface in this description of the fountain with its seven columns dedicated to the seven planets. Each planetary god carries the appropriate precious stones, metals and alchemical symbols. A figure of Saturn hangs over one column with a scythe and a crane at his feet. Most tellingly Mercury is described as 'fixed, firm and malleable' – which is to say semi-solidified in the process of alchemical transmutation.

What flows from this fountain and what our pilgrims – which is how we should think of them, we now realize – drink is wine. 'Drinking is the distinguishing character of humanity,' writes Rabelais, 'I mean drinking cool, delicious wine, for you must know, my beloved, that by wine we become divine, for it is in its power to fill the spirit with truth, learning and philosophy.' In some oriental occult physiology wine is used as a symbol of the secretions within the brain that stream into consciousness in ecstatic states. In the twentieth century some Indian scientists went so far as to suggest that 'wine' in Vedic texts referred to what we today call dimethyltryptamine, the enzyme that streams down from the higher regions of the cerebellum that we have already touched on in our discussion of shamanism. Swami Yogananda likewise talked of neuro-physiological secretions he called 'blissful *amrita*', the pulsating nectar of immortality that brings with it moments of heightened consciousness, and enables us to perceive directly the great ideas that weave together the material world.

'Oh Lord,' wrote the Sufi master Sheikh Abdullah Ansari, 'intoxicate me with the wine of Thy love.'

20

The Green One behind the Worlds

Columbus • Don Quixote • *William Shakespeare, Francis Bacon and the Green One*

WHEN IN 1492 CHRISTOPHER COLUMBUS reached the mouth of the Orinoco he believed he had found the Gihon, one of the four rivers that flow out of Eden. He wrote home: 'There are great indications suggesting the proximity of the earthly Paradise, for not only does it correspond in mathematical position with the opinions of the holy and learned theologians, but all other sages concur to make it probable.'

The impulse to discover everything about the world that would inspire the scientific revolution was also inspiring men to voyages of exploration. Never had wonder at the material world been so strong.

Hopes of finding a New World were inextricably connected with expectations of a new Golden Age, but the gold found turned out to be the more earthly kind.

Much has been made of Columbus's connections with the Knights Templar. He was married to a daughter of a former Grand Master of the Knights of Christ, a Portuguese order that had grown up after the Templars had been driven underground. It's been noted as significant that Columbus navigated ships whose sails carried the distinctive red cross 'patte' of the Templars. But the reality is that the Knights of Christ did not pursue the same independent commerce with the spirit worlds that had pushed the Papacy to such desperate measures in the case of the Templars. As with other later crypto-Templar orders such as the Knights of Malta, Rome was here adopting the powerfully glamorous mystique of the original Knights Templar, and using it for its own purposes.

Columbus wrote to Queen Isabella expressing hope that he would find a 'barrel of gold' that would finance the reconquest of Jerusalem, just as she and her husband, Ferdinand, had recently managed the reconquest of Granada, bringing Spain back to the Church. Columbus did not know that that gold would be needed to fund a war against an enemy nearer home and fast growing in strength – an enemy with much greater claims to be called the spiritual heir of the Knights Templar.

The battle lines for control of the world were being drawn, not only geopolitically, but in the spirit worlds, too. It would be a battle for the whole spirit of humanity.

CERVANTES AND SHAKESPEARE WERE pretty nearly exact contemporaries.

Don Quixote, the elderly knight who tilts at windmills, believing them to be giants, and who sees a squat, garlic-chewing peasant girl as a beautiful, aristocratic maiden out of tales of chivalry, called Dulcinea, might at first seem like a character in a rather knock-about comedy. But as the story progresses its tone changes and the reader senses some strange magic at work.

On one level Don Quixote is trying to insist on the old chivalric ideals of the Middle Ages as they pass away. On another he is entering his 'second childhood', harking back to a time when imaginings seemed so much more real. The point is, of course, that in esoteric philosophy imaginings *are* more real. Some Spanish scholars have argued on the basis of a close textual analysis that *Don Quixote* is an allegorical commentary on the cabalistic *Zohar* (or *Book of Splendour*).

At one point in the story Don Quixote and his down-to-earth servant Sancho Panza are tricked by Merlin into believing that the beautiful Dulcinea has been bewitched so that she looks like a squat peasant girl. Apparently the only way she can regain her beautiful form is if Sancho Panza submits to a beating of 3300 lashes. We shall return to examine the significance of the number thirty-three shortly.

An account of an initiation lies at the heart of the novel. It marks the point when simple-minded comedy gives way to something more troubling and ambiguous. This is the strange episode of the Don's descent into the Cave of Montesinos ...

Sancho Panza tied a rope a hundred fathoms long to his master's doublet, then lowered him through the mouth of the cave, Don Quixote hacking his way through brambles, briars and fig trees, dislodging crows and rooks.

At the bottom of the cave the Don could not stop himself falling into a deep, deep sleep. He awoke to found himself in a beautiful meadow. But unlike in a dream he could think reasonably ...

He approached a vast palace of crystal where he was met by a strange old man in a green satin hood, who introduced himself as Montesinos. This man, evidently the genius of the transparent palace, told him he had long been expected. He took the Don to a downstairs chamber and showed him a knight lying on a marble sepulchre. This knight had been bewitched by Merlin, Montesinos told him. Furthermore, he said, Merlin had prophesied that he, Don Quixote, would break the spell, and so would revive knight errantry ...

Don Quixote returned to the surface and asked Sancho Panza how long he had been gone. Told not more than hour, Don Quixote said this could not be, that he had spent three days underground. He said he saw what he saw, touched what he touched.

You're saying the most *foolish* things imaginable, said Sancho Panza.

The whole novel is a play on enchantment, illusion, disillusion – and a deeper level of enchantment. It reads like a series of parables in which the meaning is never explicitly stated and never quite clear. But the deepest level of meaning has to do with the role of imagination in forming the world. Don Quixote is not just a buffoon. He is somebody who has the strongest desire to have his innermost questions answered. He is being shown that material reality is just one of many layers of illusions, and that it is our deepest imaginings that form them. The implication is that if we can locate the secret source of our imaginings, we can control the flow of nature. By the end of the novel the Don has subtlely changed his surroundings.

We saw earlier that when we are in love we choose to see the good qualities in the one we love. We saw how our good-heartedness helps to bring out these qualities and make them stronger. The reverse is also true. Those we despise become despicable.

A similar choice confronts us when we contemplate the cosmos as a whole. Cervantes was writing at a turning point in history when people no longer knew for sure that the world is a spiritual place with goodness and meaning at its heart. What Cervantes is saying is that if, like Don Quixote, we good-heartedly decide to believe in the essential goodness of the world, despite the brickbats of fortune, despite the slapstick tendency in things that seems to contradict such spiritual beliefs and make them look foolish and absurd, then that decision to believe will help transform the world – and in a supernatural way, too.

Don Quixote is reckless in his good-heartedness. He takes an extreme and painful path. He has been called the Spanish Christ, and the effect of his journey on world history has been quite as great as if he had really lived.

CERVANTES DIED ON 23 APRIL 1616, the same date as Shakespeare.

The sparse traces left by William Shakespeare in the written records yield few definite facts. We know he was born in the village of Stratford-upon-Avon in 1564, that he was educated at the village school, became a butcher's apprentice and was caught poaching. He left Stratford for London where he became a bit-part player in a company at one time under the patronage of Francis Bacon, and many successful plays were performed, the published versions of which bear his name. He died leaving his second best bed to his wife in his will.

His contemporary, the playwright Ben Jonson, said sneeringly of William Shakespeare that he knew 'small Latin and less Greek'. How could such a man have created a body of work, saturated in all the erudition of the age?

Many great contemporaries have been pushed forward as the true author of Shakespeare's plays, including his patron, the seventeenth Earl of Oxford, Christopher Marlowe (working on the theory that he wasn't really murdered in 1593, just as the plays of Shakespeare began to appear), and latterly the poet John Donne. An American scholar, Margaret Demorest, has noted the strange links between Donne and Shakespeare, the likeness of their portraits, the similarity in nicknames, 'Johannes factotum' for Shakespeare and 'Johannes Factus' for Donne, odd idiosyncrasies in spelling – both use cherubin for cherubim, for example – and the fact that Donne's publications begin when Shakespeare's cease.

But the most popular candidate is, of course, Francis Bacon.

An infant prodigy, Francis Bacon was born into a family of courtiers in 1561. At the age of twelve a masque he had written, *The Birth of Merlin*, was performed before Queen Elizabeth I, who knew him affectionately as her little Lord Keeper. He was a small, weak, sickly child and his schoolfellows teased him by calling him by a pun on his name, Hamlet, or 'little ham'. He was educated at Oxford and when, despite the Queen's earlier fondness for him, he was blocked again and again in his political ambitions, he conceived an ambition to build himself an 'Empire of learning', conquering every branch of erudition known to man. His intellectual brilliance was such that he became known as the 'wonder of the ages'. He wrote books that dominated the intellectual life of his day, including *The Advancement of Learning*, the *Novum Organon*, in which he proposed a radical new approach to scientific thinking, and *The New Atlantis*, a vision of a new world order. Part inspired by Plato's vision of Atlantis, this would prove very influential on esoteric groups in the modern world. When James I came to the throne Bacon quickly achieved his long-held ambition and became Lord Chancellor, the second most powerful post in the land. One of Bacon's responsibilities was the distribution of land grants in the New World.

Bacon's brilliance was such that it seemed to cover the whole world, and, all other things being equal, he might seem to be a better candidate for the author of the plays of Shakespeare than Shakespeare himself.

Bacon was a member of a secret society called the Order of the Helmet. In *The Advancement of Learning*, he wrote of a tradition of handing down parables in a chain of succession and with them hidden meanings on the 'secrets of the sciences'. He admitted he was fascinated by secret codes and numerological ciphers. In the 1623 edition of *The Advancement of Learning* he explained what he calls the Bilateral Cipher – which would later become the basis of the Morse Code.

It is interesting to note that his favourite code was the ancient 'cabalistic cipher' in terms of which the name 'Bacon' has the numerical value thirty-three. Using this *same* cipher, the phrase 'Fra Rosi Crosse' can be founded encoded on the frontispiece, dedication page and other significant pages in *The Advancement of Learning*.

And using the same cipher, the same Rosicrucian phrase can also be found in the dedication in the Shakespeare Folio, on the first page of *The Tempest* and on the Shakespeare monument in Stratford-upon-Avon. The rolled scroll on the Shakespeare Memorial in Westminster Abbey also has it, together with the number thirty-three, which we have just seen is the number for Bacon.

IN ORDER TO UNDERSTAND THE SOLUTION to this mystery given in the secret history, it is necessary first to take a look at the work.

The plays of Shakespeare play with altered states, with the madness of love. Hamlet and Ophelia are descended from the Troubadours. There are wise fools – like Feste in *Twelfth Night*. In Lear's Fool, the Christ-like jester who tells the truth when no one else dares, the fool of the Troubadors achieves apotheosis.

The characters of Gargantua, Don Quixote and Sancho Panza inhabit the collective imagination. They help form our attitudes to life. But as Harold Bloom, Professor of Humanities at Yale University and author of the key book *Shakespeare: The Invention of the Human*, has shown, no single writer has populated our imagination with archetypes like Shakespeare: Falstaff, Hamlet, Ophelia, Lear, Prospero, Caliban, Bottom, Othello, Iago, Malvolio, Macbeth and his Lady, Romeo and Juliet. In fact, after Jesus Christ no other individual has done so much to develop and expand the human sense of an interior life. If Jesus Christ planted the seed of interior life, Shakespeare helped it to grow, populated it and gave us the sense we all have today that we each contain inside us an inner cosmos as expansive as the outer cosmos.

Great writers are the architects of our consciousness, in Rabelais, Cervantes and Shakespeare, above all in the soliloquies of Hamlet, we also see the seeds of the sense

RIGHT The History of the World, *1614. Sir Walter Raleigh, the famous adventurer, was a member of a secret society called the School of Night. So shadowy was this society that some recent critics have even doubted its existence, but Raleigh undoubtedly shared esoteric ideas with Christopher Marlowe and George Chapman, author of* The Shadow of Night. *One of the secrets they kept was 'atheism'. Raleigh feared the prolonged torture, disembowelling and slow death that had overtaken another friend, Thomas Kyd, for professing atheistic views. But none of them was an atheist in the modern sense of denying the reality of spirit worlds or denying that disembodied beings intervened in the material world in a supernatural way. In* Faust *Marlowe wrote one of the most learned, esoteric works of world literature dealing with the dangers of commerce with the spirit worlds.*

There was a brilliant analysis of this frontispiece of his literary masterpiece by David Fideler in the much-missed Gnosis *magazine. On one level, says Fideler, it was meant to illustrate Raleigh's view of history as the unfolding of Divine Providence according to Cicero's definition: 'History bears witness to the passing of the ages, sheds light upon reality, gives life to recollection and guidance to human existence, and brings tidings of ancient days.' On another level, he points out, this design embodies the cabalistic Tree of Life with planetary correspondences at the nodes. The figure on the left is Bon Fama, the Fama of the Rosicrucian Manifestoes.*

we have today of personal turning points, vital decisions to be made. Before the great writers of the Renaissance, any inkling of such things could only have come from sermons.

There is a shadowy side to this new interior richness, which, again, we see most clearly in the soliloquies of Hamlet. The new sense of detachment that allows someone to withdraw from the senses and roam around his interior world is double-edged, carrying with it the danger of feeling alienated from the world. Hamlet languishes in just such a state of alienation when he is not sure whether it is better 'to be or not to be'. This is a long way from the cry of Achilles, who wanted to live in the light of the sun at all costs.

As an initiate Shakespeare was helping to forge the new form of consciousness. But how do we *know* Shakespeare was an initiate?

In the Anglo-Saxon countries at least Shakespeare has done more than any other writer to form our idea of beings from the spirit worlds and the way they may sometimes break into the material world. We need only think of Ariel, Caliban, Puck, Oberon and Titania. Many thespians still believe that *Macbeth* contains dangerous occult formulae that give it the force of a magical ceremony when performed. Prospero in *The Tempest* is the archetype of the Magus, based on Elizabeth's court astrologer Dr Dee. A spirit spoke

LEFT *Initiatic images of meditating on a skull, often found in the seventeenth, eighteenth and nineteenth centuries from Hamlet through the brooding monks of Zurbarán to the posing of Byron. These are not mere reminders that one day we must die. The skull meditation alludes to arcane techniques of invoking the spirits of dead ancestors – techniques inherited and nurtured by secret societies such as the Rosicrucians and the Jesuits.*

RIGHT *In some religious orders, the novitiate lies in a coffin between four candles, the* Miserere *is sung and he then rises to be given a new name as a sign of rebirth. Painting by Francisco Zurbarán.*

to Dee on 24 March 1583, talking about the future course of nature and reason, saying, 'New Worlds shall spring of these. New manners; strange Men.' Compare this with 'O wonder! How beauteous mankind is. O brave new world, that has such people in it.'

When we enter the Green Wood of *A Midsummer Night's Dream* and the other comedies we are re-entering the ancient wood we walked through in Chapter 2. We are returning to an archaic form of consciousness in which all nature is animated by spirits. In all art and literature twisted vegetation usually signals we are entering the realm of the esoteric, the etheric dimension. Shakespeare's writing is, of course, dense with flower imagery. Critics have often commented on the use of the rose as an occult, Rosicrucian symbol in *The Faerie Queene*, written by Edmund Spenser in 1589, but no writer in English has used the symbol of the rose more often – or more *occultly* – than Shakespeare. There are seven roses on the memorial to Shakespeare in Holy Trinity Church in Stratford-upon-Avon, and, as we shall see shortly, the seven roses are the Rosicrucian symbol of the chakras.

It is here that one of the distinctions created by modern, positivist philosophy may prove useful. According to logical positivism an apparent assertion is really asserting nothing if no evidence would disprove it. This argument is sometimes used to try to disprove the existence of God. If no conceivable turn of events would ever count

against the existence of God, it is argued, then by asserting that God exists we are not really asserting anything.

Looked at in this way the assertion 'the historical personage Shakespeare wrote the plays that bear his name' actually asserts very little. We know so little about the man that it has no bearing at all on our understanding of the plays. Shakespeare is an enigma. Like Jesus Christ he revolutionized human consciousness yet left almost invisible traces on the contemporary historical record.

In order finally to get to grips with this mystery and to understand better the literary Renaissance that overtook England at this time, we must examine the largely overlooked Sufi content in the plays of Shakespeare. Sufism, we saw, was the great source of the rose as a mystical symbol.

The basic plot of *The Taming of the Shrew* comes from the *A Thousand and One Nights*. The Arab title of *A Thousand And One Nights*, ALF LAYLA WA LAYLA, is a coded phrase meaning Mother of Records. This is an allusion to the tradition that there lies hidden underneath the paws of the Sphinx, or in a parallel dimension, a secret library or 'Hall of Records', a storehouse of ancient wisdom from before the Flood. The title *A Thousand and One Nights* means to tell us, therefore, that the secrets of human evolution are encoded within.

Illustration to A Midsummer Night's Dream. *The word 'fairy' entered the English language in the thirteenth century from the old English word to marvel and originally referred to a state of mind –* feyrie *or* fayrie *meaning the state of being enchanted. J.R.R. Tolkein defined faerie as 'beauty that is an enchantment'.*

The main story of *The Taming of the Shrew* comes from *The Sleeper and the Watcher*, a story in which Haroun al Raschid puts a gullible young man into a deep sleep, dresses him in royal clothes and tells his servants to treat him as if he really is the Caliph when he awakes.

This, then, is a story about altered states of consciousness – and both story and play contain descriptions of how a higher state of consciousness may be achieved.

The outer, framing plot of *The Taming of the Shrew* centres on Christopher Sly. In Sufi lore a sly man is an initiate, or member, of a secret brotherhood. Christopher Sly is described in the first folio as a beggar, another Sufi code word, a Sufi being 'a beggar at the door of love'.

Early in the play Sly says: 'the Slys are no rogues. Look at the Chronicles. We came in with Richard the Conqueror.' This is a reference to the Sufi influence that Crusaders brought back from the Crusades.

Sly is also shown as a drunkard. As noted earlier, drunkenness is a common Sufi symbol for a visionary state of consciousness.

Then Sly is woken up by a Lord, which is to say that he is instructed by his spiritual master on how to awaken to higher states of consciousness.

The story that follows, the taming of the shrewish Katharina by Petruchio, is on one level an allegory of the Lord's 'awakening' of his pupil. Petruchio employs sly methods to tame Katharina. She represents what in Buddhist terminology is sometimes called 'monkey mind', the never quiet, never still, always gibbering part of the mind that distracts us from spiritual realities. Petruchio tries to teach her to abandon all preconceptions, all her old habits of thinking. Katharina must learn to think upside down and inside out:

> I'll attend her here –
> And woo her with some spirit when she comes!
> Say that she rail, why then I'll tell her plain
> She sings as sweetly as a nightingale.
> Say that she frown, I'll say she looks as clear
> As morning roses newly washed with dew.
> Say she be mute and will not speak a word,
> Then I'll commend her volubility
> And say she uttered piercing eloquence ...

As we saw in Chapter 17, Sufis trace the origins of their brotherhood further back than Mohammed. Some trace its chain of transmission back to the prophet Elijah or 'the Green One'. The mystical, edgy spirit of the Green One pervades both *A Thousand and One Nights* and *The Taming of the Shrew*.

THERE IS A STORY ABOUT THE GREEN ONE which conveys something of these qualities.

The witness to this strange series of events was standing by the banks of the River Oxus when he saw someone fall in. He then saw a dervish run down to help the drowning man, only to be dragged in himself. All of a sudden, as if from nowhere, another man dressed in a shimmering, luminous green robe appeared, and he too flung himself into the water.

It was at this point that things began to turn really strange. When the green man resurfaced, he had magically transformed into a log. The other two managed to cling on to this log and float to the river bank. The two of them climbed out safely.

But the witness was more interested in what happened to the log, and he followed it as it floated further downstream.

Eventually it bumped up against the river bank. Watching from behind a bush, the witness was astonished to see it change back into the green-robed man, who crawled out, bedraggled, but then – in an instant – dry again.

Coming out from behind the bush, the man who had been watching all this felt compelled to throw himself on the ground in front of this mysterious figure. 'You must be the Green One, Master of Saints. Bless me, for I would attain.' He was afraid to touch the robe, because now he was close enough to see it was made of green fire.

'You have seen too much,' replied the Green One. 'You must understand that I am from another world. Without their knowing it, I protect those who have a service to perform.'

The man raised his eyes from the ground, but the Green One had disappeared, leaving only the sound of rushing wind.

A YOUNGER CONTEMPORARY OF Shakespeare's, Robert Burton, wrote in *The Anatomy of Melancholy* 'that omniscient, only wise fraternity of the Rosie Cross names their head Elias Artifex, their theophrastian master'. Burton then describes him as 'the renewer of all arts and sciences, reformer of the world *and now living*' (my italics).

We have already seen how in the esoteric tradition Elijah is believed to have reincarnated as John the Baptist. His return was prophesied not only in the last words of the Old Testament but by the initiate-prophet Joachim, who profoundly influenced the Rosicrucians' understanding of history. Joachim said Elijah would come to prepare the way for the third age. Did the secret societies of the sixteenth and seventeenth centuries believe that he had reincarnated in their own time and that he was protecting and guiding those with a service to perform?

In Chapter 13 we looked at rather disturbing stories of Elijah and Elisha, his successor. The time has come to consider that in the secret history these passages in the Old Testament are not a description of two separate individuals. Rather, Elijah is such a highly evolved being that not only is he able to incarnate, discarnate and reincarnate at will, he is also able to parcel up bits of his spirit – or mantle – and distribute it among several different people.

Just as a flock of birds turn as one, moved by the same thought, so also several people may be moved simultaneously by the same spirit. Lurking in the darkness behind the surface glitter of Elizabethan England, speaking through the minds of Marlowe, Shakespeare, Bacon, Donne and Cervantes we should be able to make out the stern visage of the Green One, spiritual master of Sufis and architect of the modern age.

We shall look at the aim of Elijah's mission in the last chapter, but for the moment it is as well to recall the role that Arabia played in inspiring not only literature but science. At the court of Haroun al Raschid and later among the Arab peoples, science had made great leaps forward, particularly in mathematics, physics and astronomy. There is a deep mystical connection between the Arab people and the English, because it was the great Arabian spirit of scientific research which lived again in Francis Bacon, the individual most closely associated with Shakespeare in the occult literature. And, as the history of the philosophy of science tell us, it was Bacon who inspired the great scientific revolution that has done so much to form the modern world.

As the inner cosmos was opened up and illumined, so, too, the material cosmos was opened up and illumined. As Shakespeare revealed a world not of character types, which is what had gone before, but a jostling crowd of fully realized individuals, seething with passion and fired by ideas, so Bacon revealed a world bursting with quiddity, a scintillating world of infinitely various, sharply defined objects.

These parallel worlds ballooned and became mirror images of one another. Inner and outer worlds that had previously been darkly and indistinctly intermingled were now clearly separated.

The world of Shakespeare is the world of human values, where, whatever happens, it is human happiness and the shape of human lives that are at stake. The world of Bacon is one where human values have been stripped out.

Human experience is the tricky, paradoxical, mysterious and ultimately unpredictable thing that Shakespeare dramatized. Bacon taught humankind to look at the physical objects that are *the contents of experience* and to note the predictable laws they obey.

He devised new ways of thinking about the contents of experience. He advised the discarding of as many preconceptions as possible while gathering as much data as possible, trying not to impose patterns on it, but waiting patiently for deeper, richer patterns to emerge. This is why in the history of the philosophy of science he is known as the Father of Induction.

In short, Bacon realized that if you can observe objects as objectively as possible very different patterns emerge from the ones that give subjective experience its structure.

This realization would change the face of the planet.

21

The Rosicrucian Age
The German Brotherhoods • Christian Rosenkreuz • Hieronymus Bosch • The Secret Mission of Dr Dee

LITTLE IS KNOWN ABOUT MEISTER ECKHART, the shadowy thirteenth-century German mystic, but, just as his contemporary Dante can be seen as the source of the Renaissance, Eckhart can be seen as the source of the broader but more slowly moving Reformation. In Eckhart we can also see the source of a new form of consciousness which would lead Northern Europe to world domination.

Born in near Gotha in Germany in 1260, he entered a Dominican friary, became a prior and eventually succeeded Thomas Aquinas teaching theology in Paris. His great *Opus Tripartitum,* as ambitious in scope as the *Summa Theologica,* was never finished. He died while on trial for his life, accused of heresy.

A few sermons have come down to us, some of them transcribed by people in Strasbourg. They had never heard anything like these notions before:

I pray to God to rid me of God.

If I myself were not, God would not be either.

If I were not, God would not be God.

God is within, we are without.

The eye through which I see God and the eye through which God sees me is the same eye.

He is He because He is not He. This cannot be understood by the outer man, only the inner man.

Find the one desire behind all desires.

God is at home. It is we who have gone out for a walk.

Through nothing I become what I am.

Only the hand that erases can write the true thing.

These sound exceptionally modern. You would probably even be a bit surprised to hear them coming out of the mouth of your local clergyman today.

Like a Zen Master, Meister Eckhart tries to shock us out of fixed ways of thinking, sometimes with what at first sounds like nonsense.

He also teaches an oriental style of meditation that involves both sustained detachment from the material world and emptiness of the mind. He says that when the powers have all been withdrawn from their bodily form and functions, when man has absconded from the senses, then he 'lapses into the oblivion of things and of himself'.

Like Buddhist 'emptiness' this oblivion is a void containing infinite and inexhaustible possibilities, and so a place of rebirth and creativity. It is also a difficult and dangerous place. Eckhart was showing the way not of consolation for a harsh, repressed life, not rewards deferred, but a strange and testing dimension you enter at your peril, 'the desert of the Godhead where no one is at home'.

Like Mohammed, like Dante, Eckhart had direct personal experience of the spirit worlds. Again and again what he reported back is not what you'd expect:

'When you're frightened of dying and you're holding on, you'll see demons tearing your life away. If you've made your peace, you'll see that the demons are really *angels* freeing you from the earth. The only things that burn us is the part you won't let go, your memories, your attachments.'

Eckhart is sometimes spoken of as one of 'the twelve sublime Masters of Paris', a phrase that reminds us of the ancient traditions of hidden masters and adepts, the Great White Brotherhood, the Thirty-Six Righteous of Cabalistic tradition, the Brotherhood on the Roof of the World, the Inner Circle of Adepts or the Nine Unknown. According to ancient traditions knowledge, the way to gain experience of the spirit words is passed on by an initiatic chain of transmission from master to pupil. In the East this is sometimes called *satsong*. It is not just a matter of information passed on by word, but a sort of magical mind-to-mind process. Plato may be read as referring to something similar when he talks of *mimesis*. In the Allegory of the Cave, Plato is inviting his pupil to create an imaginative image which will work on his mind in a way that operates beyond the narrowly rational. In Plato's opinion, the best writing – he is talking of Hesiod's poetry – casts a hypnotic spell that carries with it the transmission of knowledge.

An initiate I knew told me how, when he was a young man living in New York, his Master had reached over to him, drawn a circle on a table and asked him what he saw.

'A table top,' he replied.

'That is good,' said the Master. 'The eyes of a young man *should* look outward.' Then, without saying any more, he leaned forward and touched my friend on the forehead between the eyes with his outstretched finger.

Immediately the world faded and he was dazzled by a vision of what seemed to him a cold, white goddess of the moon, carrying a skull and a rosary. She had six faces each with three eyes.

The goddess danced and my friend lost track of time. Then, after a while, the vision faded and shrank until it became a dot and disappeared.

My friend knew, though, it was still living inside him somewhere like a burning seed and would do so forever.

His Master said, 'You saw it?'

I was thrilled when I heard this story, because I knew I was very close to the chain of mystic transmission.

THE DIRECT SPIRITUAL EXPERIENCE THAT Meister Eckhart talked about with such conviction in his sermons was experience of a kind organized religion no longer seemed able to provide. The Church seemed pedantically tied to the dead letter of the law both in theology and ritual.

So it was in a climate of spiritual dissatisfaction and restlessness that loose and shadowy associations arose among like-minded people. Groups of lay people questing for spiritual experience, 'wandering stars' as they were sometimes known, were said to meet in secret: the Brethren and Sisters of the Free Spirit, the Brethren and Sisters of the Common Life, the Family of Love and the Friends of God. Stories were rife among all levels of society in Germany, the Netherlands and Switzerland, even among the underprivileged and alienated poor, of people being approached by mysterious strangers who took them to secret meetings or even on journeys into strange, otherworldly dimensions.

One of the more intriguing notions associated with the secret societies is that you can never track them down. Instead they operate some form of occult but benevolent surveillance. When the time is right, when you are ready, a member of the secret schools will come to you and offer himself as your spiritual guide or master.

The same initiate told me how at a gathering of top academics who all shared an interest in the esoteric – he himself was an art historian – it eventually emerged that the great teacher in their presence was none of the doctors or professors but the cleaning lady with mop and pail at the back of the lecture theatre. Such stories may have an apocryphal air about them, but they also have a universal resonance. The spiritual master of the greatest esoteric teacher of the twentieth century, Rudolf Steiner, was a woodcutter and herb-gatherer.

Karl von Eckartshausen, the early theosophist, wrote: 'These sages whose number is small are children of light. Their business is to do as much good to humanity as is in their power and to drink wisdom from the eternal fountain of truth. Some live in Europe, others in Africa, but they are bound together by the harmony of their souls, and they are therefore one. They are joined even though they may be thousands of miles apart from each other. They understand each other, although they speak in different tongues, because the language of the sages is spiritual perception. No evil person could possibly live among them, because he would be recognized immediately.'

People today freely and openly describe meetings with Indian mystics such as Mother Meera, who confer life-changing mystical experiences. On the other hand we tend to be shy of ascribing supernatural powers to remarkable Christians these days. But you really do not need to look very far into the lives of the great Christian mystics to find evidence of psychic powers. Reading von Eckartshausen you might suspect that he had been influenced by ideas about Hindu holy men. That may be true, but this should not stop us from recognizing that the great Christian mystics and Hindu adepts have much in common.

The mystic John Tauler, for example, was a pupil of Meister Eckhart. The older man does not seem to have been Tauler's spiritual master in the sense in which we have just been using that phrase. Tauler was preaching in 1339 when he was approached by a mysterious layman from the Oberland, who told him his teaching lacked true spirituality. Tauler gave up his life and followed this man, who is supposed in some Rosicrucian traditions to have been a reincarnation of Zarathustra.

Tauler disappeared for two years. When he reappeared, he tried to preach again, but could only stand there and cry. On his second attempt he was inspired, and it was said of him that the Holy Spirit played upon him as upon a lute. Tauler himself said of his experience of initiation, 'My prayer is answered. God sent me the man long sought to teach me wisdom the schoolmen never knew.'

Tauler's is the mysticism of everyday life. When a poor man asked if he should stop working to go to church, Tauler replied: 'One can spin, another make shoes and these are the gifts of the Holy Spirit.' In Tauler we may recognize the great sincerity and practical probity of the German people. Martin Luther would say of him, 'Nowhere in either Latin or German have I found more wholesome, powerful teaching, nor any that more fully agrees with the Gospels.'

OF COURSE NOT ALL INITIATES ARE MYSTICS, and neither is everyone who has genuine communication with the spirit worlds. Certain great individuals, such as Melchizedek, have been avatars, embodiments of great spiritual beings who are able to live in constant communication with the spirit worlds. Others, such as Isaiah, were initiates in previous incarnations, carrying the powers of an initiate into their new incarnation. The cosmos prepares people in different ways. Mozart is believed to have undergone a series of short incarnations which had the purpose of interrupting his experience of the spirit worlds only briefly, so that in his incarnation as Mozart he could still hear the Music of the Spheres. Others, such as Joan of Arc, inhabit bodies that have been prepared to be so sensitive, so finely tuned, that spirits of a very high level are able to work through them, even though they are not in any sense incarnations of these spirits. Modern mediums are sometimes people who have suffered a trauma in childhood which has caused a rent in the membrane between the material and spirit worlds.

Anyone who has spent time with mediums or psychics accepts that they often, even routinely, receive information by supernatural means – anyone, that is, whose cast of mind is not such that they are absolutely determined to disbelieve. However, it is equally apparent that most mediums cannot control spirits with whom they converse. Often they cannot even recognize them. These spirits are sometimes mischievous, giving them a lot of reliable information on trivial matters, but then tripping them up on important things.

Unlike mediums, initiates are concerned to communicate their altered states of consciousness, either directly, as happened to my friend in New York, or by teaching techniques to achieve altered states.

THE LIFE OF CHRISTIAN ROSENKREUZ is usually thought of as an allegory – or a fantasy. In the secret tradition the great being who had incarnated briefly in the thirteenth century, as the boy with the luminous skin, was incarnated again in 1378. He was born into a poor German family living on the border of Hesse and Thuringia. Orphaned at the age of five, he was sent to live in a convent, where he learned Greek and Latin not very well.

At the age of sixteen he set out on a pilgrimage. He longed to visit the Holy Sepulchre in Jerusalem. He travelled to Egypt, Libya and Fez. He went, too, to Cyrpus, where a friend who was accompanying him died. Then on to Damascus and Jerusalem and finally to somewhere called Damcar, where he studied for three years and was initiated by a Sufi brotherhood known as the Ikhwan al-Safa, or Brethren of Purity. During this time he translated into Latin *The Liber M*, or *Book of the World*, said to contain the past and future history of the world.

When he returned to Europe, he was determined to pass on what he had learned. He landed first in Spain, where he was laughed at. After several humiliations he returned to Germany to live in seclusion. Five years later he gathered around him three old friends from his day in the convent.

This was the beginning of the Fraternity of the Rosy Cross.

He taught his friends the initiatic sciences he had learned on his travels. Together they wrote a book containing 'all that man could desire, ask and hope for'. They also agreed to submit to six obligations: to heal the sick for free; to adopt the clothing and habits of the countries they visited in order to remain inconspicuous; that every year they would return to the house of Christian Rosencreuz, now known as the House of the Holy Spirit, or otherwise send a letter explaining their absence; before death each brother would choose a successor whom he would initiate. They agreed that their fraternity would remain hidden for a hundred years.

They were joined by four more brothers, before all eight set out to the far corners of the earth in order to reform and transform it.

The extraordinary supernatural gifts attributed to the Rosicrucians made them one of the great romantic legends of European history. They had the gift of great longevity – Rosencrantz died in 1485 at the age of 107. Because they knew 'the secrets of nature' and could command disembodied beings, they could exert their will magically, which they did mostly for the sake of performing healing miracles. They could read minds, understand all languages, even project living images of themselves over great distances and communicate over great distances. They could also make themselves invisible.

The great Cabalist Robert Fludd was, according to esoteric tradition, one of the scholars employed by James I to work on the Authorized Version of the Bible. Often thought to have been a Rosicrucian himself, he was at the least a well-informed and sympathetic fellow traveller. Fludd came to the defence of the Brotherhood in print, repudiating accusations of black magic. He argued that the supernatural gifts of the Rosicrucians were the gifts of the Holy Spirit laid out by St Paul in the Epistle to the Corinthians – prophecy, performing miracles, possession of languages, visions, healings, expelling demons. That the local parish priest could no longer do these things helps to account for Europe's growing fascination with the shadowy Rosicrucians.

By all accounts the priests of antiquity had been able to summon gods to appear in the inner sanctum of the temple, but, following the Church's abolition of the distinction between soul and spirit in 869, the understanding of how to reach the spirit worlds had gradually been lost. By the eleventh century priests were no longer capable of summoning even visions of the spirit worlds during Mass. Now in the fifteenth century the spirit worlds began to flood back via the portal of the Rosicrucians.

But there is something else. Eckhart and Tauler had talked of the material transformation of the body by spiritual practice. Eckhart had left intriguing hints at alchemy – 'Copper', he had said, 'is restless until it becomes Mercury.' But a more systematic account only began to emerge with Rosicrucianism.

NO OTHER ARTIST OF THE FIRST RANK HAS alchemical ideas quite so close to the surface of his work as Hieronymus Bosch.

Little is known about the Dutch magus except that he was married, owned a horse and is said to have contributed altarpieces and designs for stained-glass windows in the cathedral of his native city of Aachen. Bosch died in 1516, so he must have been painting while Christian Rosencrantz was still alive.

In the 1960s Professor William Fraenger published a monumental study of Bosch in terms of the esoteric thought of the times in which the artist lived. Fraenger made sense of paintings which had otherwise just seemed baffling and weird.

Many Bosch paintings have been labelled Heaven, Hell or Apocalypse, sometimes perhaps in a rather perfunctory way, just because they contain strange visionary elements not part of conventional Christian iconography and theology. But in fact Bosch's paintings are really deeply esoteric – and contrary to Church dogma. For example, it was not Bosch's view that unrepentant wrongdoers go to Hell – that's it and serve them right for eternity. He believed that after death the spirit journeys through the sphere of the moon, then ascends through the planetary spheres to the highest heavens – then descends again into the next incarnation. The detail below from a panel of *The Garden of Earthly Delights,* conventionally labelled Hell, in fact shows a spirit about to descend from one sphere to another.

According to Fraenger, Bosch's paintings, for example the famous *Table of Wisdom* also in the Prado in Madrid, shows that he knew of a technique for achieving altered states practised in different esoteric schools around the world. According to Indian esoteric teaching, the golden lord of the cosmic powers – the Purusha – is at work both in the sun and in the pupil of the eye. In the *Upinashads* it is written, 'The Purusha in the mirror, on him I meditate.' By staring at one's reflection mirrored in the right eye, you can expand your consciousness from contemplation of your limited ego-self to contemplation of the sun-like god-self at the heart of everything. This method was also practised by the Dutch mystic Jan van Ruysbroek, who described how self-forgetting and world-forgetting leads at first to sensations of vacuity and chaos. Then the field of vision becomes charged with a cosmic energy. Images which at first appear dream-like and chaotic suddenly move together in a meaningful way.

This eye-to-eye method of meditation can also be practised in a sexual context.

An earlier mystic, Mechthild of Magdeburg, had had visions of a time when the life of sensuality would be fully integrated into the spiritual order of things. This impulse, she believed, would grow and take root in Northern Europe where something very different from the asceticism of Ramón Lull emerged. Esoteric groups like the Brothers and Sisters of the Free Spirit, influential during Bosch's lifetime, were guided by a vision of communities held together not by law but by love. Wisely controlled, love is the way to divine perfection.

Sex, as Fraenger puts it, is the knife blade.

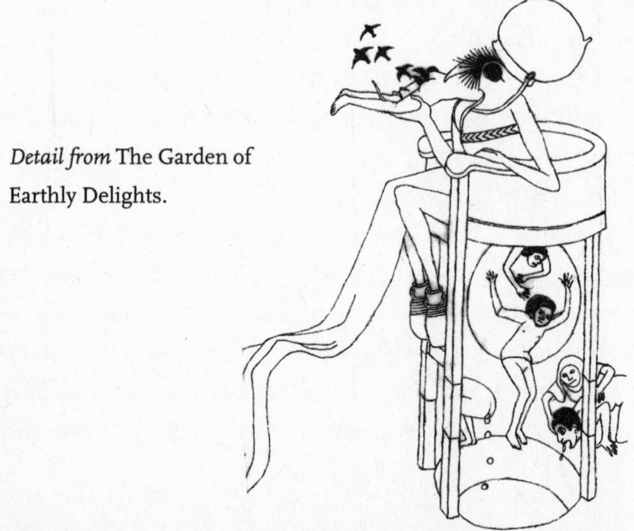

Detail from The Garden of Earthly Delights.

THE AUTHOR MOST CLOSELY ASSOCIATED with the Rosicrucian brotherhood, not least because some of his writings were said to have been buried with its founder, was Paracelsus.

'I am a rough man,' said Paracelsus 'born into a rough country.' More specifically he was born in a village near Zurich in 1493. A strange, aggressive character, he seems never to have grown a beard and to have retained a youthful appearance into old age.

He went to study under Trithemius, Abbot of St Jacob at Würzburg. Trithemius was one of the greatest adepts of the day and teacher, too, of Cornelius Agrippa. Trithemius claimed to know how to send his thoughts on the wings of angels over hundreds of miles. He was asked by the Emperor Maximilian I to summon up the ghost of his dead wife, and when Trithemius obliged, the Emperor was able to be sure that this phantom really was her by the mole on the back of her neck.

Paracelsus's fellow pupil Cornelius Agrippa became an itinerant intellectual vagabond, surrounded by rumours of magic. His great black dog, Monsieur, was said to be demonic, keeping his master informed of events in a hundred-mile radius. *De Occulta Philosophia* was his attempt to write an encyclopaedic account of practical Christianized Cabala, including a massive grimoire of magic spells still used by occultists today.

However, Paracelsus does not seem to have been very impressed by Trithemius. It seems he did not want to study in a library but learn from experience. He went to live among miners in order to learn about minerals for himself. He also travelled widely from Ireland to the crocodile-infested swamps of Africa, learning folk remedies and cures. In one way he can be seen as anticipating the Brothers Grimm, collecting ancient, esoteric knowledge before it disappeared. He knew that consciousness was changing and that, as the intellect developed, humanity would lose the instinctive knowledge of herbs that heal – a knowledge that up till then it had shared with the higher animals. On the cusp of that change, he wrote as systematic an account of these things as he could.

In 1527 he set up as a doctor in Basle in Switzerland and soon became famous for his miraculous cures. Naturally he made enemies of doctors already working in the region. Paracelsus was scornful of the conventional medicine of the day. In a typical piece of bombast he wrote of Galen, author of the standard medical textbooks of the day: 'If only your artists knew that their prince Galen – they call none like him – was sticky in Hell from where he has sent letters to me, they would make the sign of the cross upon themselves with a fox's tail.'

His seemingly miraculous healing abilities attracted rumours of necromancy. He habitually carried a swordstick in the pommel of which it was rumoured he kept his most efficacious, alchemical medicine. He cured a wealthy canon whom the other doctors had failed to cure, but when this man refused to pay, the local magistrates found in the canon's favour, and Paracelsus's friends advised him to flee.

He spent years wandering. Nature, he said, was his teacher. 'I desire neither to live comfortably, nor do I wish to become rich. Happiness is better than riches and happy is he who wanders about, possessing nothing that requires his care. He who wants to study the book of nature must wander with his feet over its leaves.'

You might think that this eminently sane philosophy, combined with a down-to-earth, practical methodology, might lead to something approaching modern medical science. But some of the writings of Paracelsus are wild and strange ...

He wrote, for instance of the Monstra, an invisible being that may arise from the putrefaction of sperm. He also talked about Mangonaria, a magical power of suspension by means of which heavy objects could be lifted into the air. He said he knew of certain localities where large numbers of Elementals live together, adopting human clothing and manners.

Paracelsus also had strange and wonderful ideas about sleep and dreams. He said that during sleep the sidereal body – the animal spirit – becomes free in its movement. It may rise up, he said, to the sphere of its ancestors and converse with the stars. He said that spirits wishing to make use of men often act on them during dreams, that a sleeping person can visit another in his dreams. He talked of incubi and succubae feeding on nocturnal emissions.

Paracelsus was also a prophet and in his later years took to prophesying the return of Elijah, who would come and 'restore all things'.

However, as well as these magical practices, Paracelsus did indeed make the discoveries and advances we will touch on later that have led some to call him 'the father of modern experimental medicine'.

In this paradox lies the key to understanding the secret of our age.

SOMETIMES ALSO SAID TO BE A Rosicrucian, though he nowhere made the claim himself, the great English magus Dr Dee was motivated by an overwhelming desire to experience the spirit worlds directly.

Dr Dee is perhaps the greatest archetype of the magus since Zarathustra. The image of Dee has entered popular mainstream culture. Here is the black-gowned, skull-cap-wearing wizard with a long white beard working in a laboratory surrounded by alchemical instruments. Amid flashes of lightning, he summons disembodied spirits by means of pentacles and other devices drawn on the ground with chalk.

John Dee was born into a Welsh family living in London. A brilliant young scholar he was teaching Euclid in Paris in his twenties and became a friend of Tycho Brahe. In the late 1570s he formed a circle called the Dionisii Areopagites with Sir Philip Sidney and Edmund Spenser, whose poem *The Faerie Queene* is famously replete with Rosicrucian and other esoteric imagery. A memoir of Sidney talks of him as 'seeking out the mysteries of chemistry led by Dee'.

Dee had built up a magnificent library, said to be second only to that of the celebrated

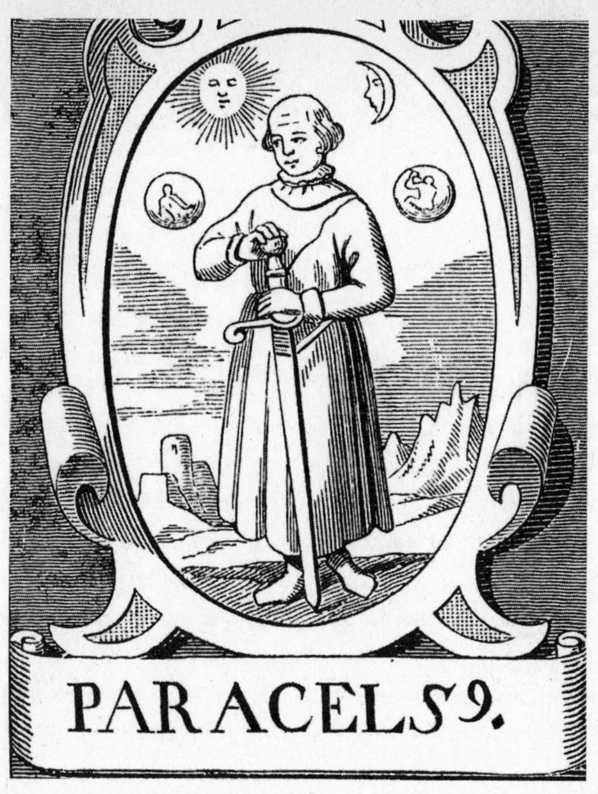

Paracelsus and his swordstick. One of the popular legends about Paracelsus was that he carried in the pommel of his swordstick a portion of the 'azoth'. A small thing missed in The Devil's Doctor, *the excellent, recent biography of Paracelsus by Philip Ball is that there is a sly joke in all of this. The azoth was the name given to the secret fire of the alchemists, a fire that would liberate the soul from the body. It is contained in a seed. We may be reminded that in Indian alchemy Mercury is sometimes called the semen of Shiva. The sword of Paracelsus, then, is one that has been forged in the heat of sexual desire. It is a fleshly sword and the azoth that issues from the top of it is the philosophical Mercury. In the natural course of things there is a quality in semen that is like a net in which a spirit may land and then be incarnated. Paracelsus also knew of some unnatural practices, secret sexual techniques performed before going to sleep, that could loosen the vegetable body from the material body and could also help other kinds of spirits to come to earth and appear to him in dreams.*

French historian de Thou. The Cabala was central to all his studies. He believed in the mathematical foundation of all things, a set of unifying principles he believed he could discern in the teachings of the ancients. He embodied these principles in his highly complex glyph, the *Monas Hieroglyphica*.

Dee's reputation was such that the young princess invited him to choose a date for her coronation as Elizabeth I by means of his astrological calculations. Dee also helped direct

The Monas Hieroglyphica. *My friend, the esoteric scholar Fred Gettings, has deconstructed this glyph, revealing a layer of meaning to do with the evolution of the two parallel universes – we might call them the Baconian and the Shakespearean – we discussed in the previous chapter.*

Elizabethan foreign policy, both in Europe and as regards the settling of America. It is a little known fact, but documented, that at the height of his fortunes Dr Dee owned a charter granting him ownership of the vast landmass called Canada, and his vision of a British Empire – a phrase he coined – helped inspire and guide the nation's voyages of discovery.

In 1580, evidently craving more direct, spiritual experience, he decided to hook up with a medium.

Dee's dreams had been disturbed. There had been strange knocking sounds in his house. He had employed a medium called Barnabus Saul, who said he could see angels in his magic crystal, but Dee had dismissed him after six months. Then in 1582 he met Edward Kelley, a strange man who apparently wore a skull cap to hide the fact that his ears had been cut off as a punishment for coining. Kelley claimed to be able to see the Archangel Uriel in Dee's shewstone, and so began hundreds of séances. These enabled Dee to learn how to decipher the speech of the angels which he called the Enochian language.

The great magus's decline can be traced from this association with Kelley. The man whose dreams of empire would help shape the globe was beginning to explore the more discreditable byways of esoteric speculation and practice.

On a trip to Prague, Dee told the Holy Roman Emperor Rudolf II that he had tried for forty years to find what he wanted and no book had been able to tell him. He had therefore decided to call upon angels to intercede for him with God, in order to ask the secrets of creation. He told Rudolf he used a stone for this and always made sure the spirits he dealt with were good and not demonic.

Was Kelley always so scrupulous? On the same trip the pair boasted to Rudolf that they could transform base metals into gold. They were forced to flee when they were unable to do so. It seems Kelley was abusing the older man by this time, forcing him into a humiliating wife-swapping. Many suspected Kelley of being a fraud, of only pretending to receive responses to the Enochian invocations.

Then in 1590 Kelley seems to have received a message in the Enochian language that so terrified him that he ceased operating the system and cut off relations with Dee altogether. Translated from the Angelic language into English it reads as follows:

'The Lion knoweth not where I walk, neither do the beasts of the field understand me. I am deflowered, yet a virgin; I sanctify and am not sanctified. Happy is he that embraceth me: for in the night season I am sweet ... my lips are sweeter than health itself, I am a harlot for such as ravish me, and a virgin with such as know me not. Purge your streets, O ye sons of men, and wash your houses clean ...' Did Kelley see in this the Scarlet Harlot of Revelation and a vision of the imminent end of the world?

Dee was left back in England in Lear-like penury, unable to support his family, ranting and raving, grandly paranoid, seeing everywhere conspiracy and counter-conspiracy. After his death a cult of Dr Dee emerged and many, including the diarist John Aubrey and the eminent Freemason Elias Ashmole, supposed him to have been a Rosicrucian.

That, anyway is the 'pop' story of Dee. A deeper layer of meaning – and Dee's real motivation in all of this – concerns the history of humanity's relations with the spirit worlds.

As we have seen Christians were experiencing a withdrawal of the spirit worlds. The Church seemed unable to provide direct spiritual experience or personal contact with spiritual realities. The people demanded wonders and only the secret societies knew how to provide them.

Dr Dee had also told the Holy Roman Emperor that if his occult techniques of ceremonial magic were introduced, every church in Christendom could enjoy apparitions every day of the week. It would be a return to the spiritual fervour of the early Church, the Church of Clement and Origen where cabalistic and hermetic elements were not excluded. The world Church would again become a magic Church.

This was Dr Dee's great evangelical vision.

It might seem outrageous to modern sensibility, but it's important to see it in the context of Church practice at the time. As we have seen, it was impossible to draw a clear line between priestcraft and witchcraft. Yet to Dr Dee the magical, spirit-invoking practices of the parish priests seemed mere superstitious folklore, lacking in intellectual rigour, sophistication and a systematic approach.

The neoplatonic drive to think systematically about spiritual experience and the spirit worlds had been spreading up from Southern Europe, influencing scholars like Trithemius, Agrippa and Dee. The German Johannes Reuchlin formulated a Christianized Cabala. He proved the divinity of Jesus Christ using cabalistic arguments, showing that the name of Jesus was encoded in the Tetragrammaton, or sacred name of God.

Dee was undoubtedly interested in all these theories, but, as we have seen, he craved *experience*. His approach was experimental as well as systematic. Dee was proposing reasoned application of techniques to produce spiritual phenomena on a controlled, regular, predictable basis. In Dee as in Bacon we see early stirrings of the scientific spirit. The development of the mental faculties that would be needed to devise modern science evolved partly in an occult context.

What Dee was whispering into the Holy Roman Emperor's ear was that if he fasted for a set length of time, performed this breathing exercise for a prescribed number of times and at prescribed intervals, that if he engaged in this sexual practice and pronounced this formula at this astrologically pre-determined time, he would enter an altered state of consciousness in which he could communicate in a free and reasoned way with denizens of the spirit worlds. All this had been established by repeatable experiment and the precedent of thousands of years of practice and led to predictable results.

Dee's mission, then, was to introduce something entirely new into the stream of history. It is always the aim of initiatic brotherhoods like the Rosicrucians to help spread newly evolving forms of consciousness, appropriate for the changing times. Michael Maier, a contemporary commentator writing with apparent insider knowledge of the Rosicrucians, said 'the activities of the Rose Cross are determined by the knowledge of history and by knowledge of the laws of evolution of the human race'.

These 'laws of evolution' operated both in history and in individual human lives. They are the laws that describe the paradoxical nature of life that we earlier called the deeper laws. They are described in the *Autobiography of a Yogi* by Paramahansa Yogananda as 'subtler laws that rule the hidden spiritual planes and the inner realm of consciousness ... knowable through the science of yoga'. Formulations of these laws can be found scattered throughout Rosicrucian literature:

Heaven is never where we believe it to be.

If you cease to limit a thing within yourself, that's to say by wanting it, and if you withdraw from it, it will come to you.

That which kills produces life. That which causes death leads to resurrection.

Rosicrucian conceptions of these laws would shortly surface in the mainstream of history and transform the culture of the West.

PERHAPS WHAT IS MOST EXTRAORDINARY about Dee's career is how close it runs to the surface of exoteric history. Not only was he openly installed at the court of Elizabeth I as her resident Merlin, not only did he attempt to introduce ceremonial magic into the Church under the aegis of the Holy Roman Emperor, but he was so well known that playwrights could portray him and expect their audience to recognize him – in Ben Jonson's *The Alchemist* and William Shakespeare's *The Tempest*.

As we shall see, Dee was only the first of several strange and tragic personalities who tried to introduce esoteric doctrines into public life.

22

Occult Catholicism

Jacob Boehme • The Conquistadors and the Counter-Reformation • Teresa, John of the Cross and Ignatius • The Rosicrucian Manifestoes • The Battle of White Mountain

IN 1517 THE POPE DECIDED TO REVIVE the selling of indulgences in order to pay for a new basilica of St Peter in Rome. It was to be the most splendid, lavish building in the world. Martin Luther, a teacher at Wittenberg, nailed his arguments against this selling of indulgences to the door of the local church that acted as a notice board to the community.

When this drew a papal bull excommunicating Luther, he burned this document in front of an admiring crowd. 'Here I stand,' he proclaimed. In Northern Europe, Germany in particular, a groundswell of restlessness had been rising, a resenting of the demand for unthinking obedience, a yearning for spiritual freedom. The hero of the hour, Luther escaped burning at the stake, protected by a local lord, and as more German leaders began to join in his protests against the excesses of the Papacy, Protestantism was born.

Some saw Luther as the reincarnation of Elijah whom Malachi and then Joachim had prophesied would come again to herald the new age.

Luther was steeped in mystical thought, the teachings of both Eckhart and Tauler. His closest friend and literary collaborator was the occultist Philip Melanchthon, nephew of the celebrated Cabalist Reuchlin. Melanchthon was an advocate of astrology, who wrote a biography of Faust. Luther himself communicated with the spirit worlds on familiar terms, heard voices guiding him and on one famous occasion hurled an inkpot at a demon who had mocked him.

But was he an initiate of the secret societies? There are intriguing hints. He once referred to himself as a 'passed master', a phrase that a Freemasonic initiate of a certain level might use to describe himself. He spoke approvingly of alchemy, praising it for its 'allegory and secret meaning' and recognizing, too, that it had a role in the resurrection of humanity.

The interest of some commentators has also been piqued by the fact that Luther adopted the rose as his symbol.

However, Luther's white five-petalled rose containing a small cross is not the mystic red rose of the Rosicrucians pinned to the great cross of matter in order to transform it. Nor is there any reason to suppose that Luther saw his rose having a layer of meaning concerned with occult physiology.

Although Paracelsus had been an early supporter of Luther, the Swiss magus grew disillusioned when Luther promulgated his doctrine of predestination, which seemed to Paracelsus the old Roman elitism under a new name. Moreover, Paracelsus was a pacifist, and, while Luther was not directly responsible for the massacres of Catholics that took place once he had achieved political power, he could have stopped them. Although Luther had been swept to power on a tide of enthusiasm and mystical fervour, once there he began to fear these things as threats to his authority and all he had achieved. Morbid and paranoid, he seemed unwilling to stop the persecutions carried out in his name.

The Rosicrucians should be seen as the extreme radical left wing of the Reformation, and the way that the Lutheran Church turned on it can be seen in the story of Jacob Boehme.

Boehme's *Mysterium Magnum*, a commentary on Genesis, opened up great and dizzying vistas of secret, cabalistic meaning. It lit up the popular imagination in the great age of Protestantism, not least because of its influence on John Milton's *Paradise Lost*. His detailed descriptions of the occult physiology of the human body are the clearest evidence for an independent Western tradition of the chakras before the influx of oriental teachings in the eighteenth century. He also gives a near comprehensive account of the correspondences between the heavenly bodies and minerals and plants that had been suggested earlier but in more sketchy form by Agrippa and Paracelsus.

All this is all the more astonishing because Boehme was almost completely uneducated. In some ways he is anticipated by Fludd in his interpretation of the Bible, which sees the story of the creation as a series of alchemical separations, but there is no evidence to suggest he ever read Fludd.

Born in 1575 to illiterate parents, Jacob Boehme was apprenticed to a cobbler. One day a stranger came into the shop, bought a pair of boots, then, as he was leaving, called Jacob by name, asking him to follow him into the street. Jacob was surprised this stranger knew his name, but more surprised when he fixed him with a penetrating stare and said: 'Jacob, thou art yet but little, but the time will come when thou shalt be great and the world shall be moved at thee. Read the Holy Scriptures where thou wilt find comfort and instruction, for thou must endure much misery and poverty and suffer persecution. But be courageous and persevere, for God loves thee.' The stranger turned and disappeared, and Boehme never saw him again. But the meeting had made a deep impression upon him.

He became much more serious in a way that some found disconcerting. When his master threw him out, he became a journeyman tradesman, working hard, and eventually he set up his own shop.

One day he was sitting in his kitchen when the sun shining on a pewter plate blinded him. For a while everything grew dim. Then gradually the table, his hands, the walls, everything became transparent. He realized that, although we usually think of the air as being transparent, it is actually quite cloudy. Because now he saw it become truly transparent, like a cloud clearing, and suddenly he saw whole new spirit worlds opening up before him in every direction. He saw that his whole body was transparent and realized that he was looking down on himself, that his centre of consciousness had floated free of his body and was able to move freely into the spirit worlds.

So it was that Jacob Boehme first journeyed through the spiritual hierarchies while still alive, as St Paul, Mohammed and Dante had done before him.

Boehme was generally physically unimpressive, short with a low forehead, but his remarkable blue eyes now began to shine with a special luminosity. People who met him were impressed by his ability to see into their past and their future. He was sometimes able to speak different languages from different parts of the world and different periods.

His second illumination took place while he was walking through fields. He suddenly felt he could experience directly the mystery of creation. Afterwards he wrote: 'In one quarter of an hour I saw and knew more than if I had been at university for many years.' What Boehme had experienced did not contradict his Lutheran, Bible-based beliefs, but it clarified and illumined them, opening up new dimensions of meaning.

What distinguishes Boehme's writings, though, are his descriptions of these teachings in terms of urgent, personal experiences. He originally wrote his first work, *Aurora*, as an *aide-mémoire* to one of his mystical experiences, but when a local nobleman saw it, he had several copies made. One of these fell into the hands of the local pastor of Goelitz. Perhaps jealous of someone who obviously knew so much more than he did of the spirit worlds, the pastor began to persecute the cobbler. He accused him of heresy, threatening prison and finally driving him out of town under threat of being burned alive.

Shortly after his expulsion Boehme called his son, Tobias, to his bedside, asking if he could hear the beautiful music, and asking, too, if he would open the window so they could hear it better.

After a while he said 'Now I go hence to Paradise', gave a deep sigh and died.

In response to the question, Where does the spirit go after death?, Boehme had once answered in a way that has something of the Teutonic Zen of Eckhart: 'It has no need to go anywhere. The spirit has heaven and hell within itself. Heaven and hell are within one another and are to one another as nothing.'

BOEHME AND THE PASTOR OF GOELITZ had looked at each other across the village green with mutual incomprehension. These were two very different forms of consciousness. On the other side of the world the disgust and intolerance that arises when two very different forms of consciousness encounter each other worked itself out on a much greater and more tragic scale.

Less idealistic men had followed in the wake of Christopher Columbus. In 1519 Hernando Cortés had been sailing along the Yucatan Gulf coast when he established a base he called Veracruz. He and his fellow Spaniards had heard rumours of the fabulous wealth of the Aztecs, but they were astonished when an ambassador from their ruler, Moctezuma, approached the base bearing gifts.

The gifts included a gold image of the sun as big as a cartwheel and an even larger silver representation of the moon. There was also a helmet overflowing with grains of gold and a great headdress made of feathers of the 'quetzal' bird.

The Aztec ambassador explained that these were the gifts his lord, Moctezuma, was giving to the great god Quetzal Coatl. This god, the ambassador further explained, had a long time previously quitted the earth to make the moon his home.

The Conquistadors then realized that Cortés, bearded, helmeted and fair-skinned, must resemble the prophetic depictions of Quetzal Coatl. By coincidence, as they saw it, they had arrived at precisely the time that the Aztec astrologers prophesied that this god would return.

Some of the wonderfully intricate and delicate Aztec objects would be shipped back to Europe, where Albrecht Dürer saw them. He said that they were so subtle, so ingenious, they made his heart sing. But the followers of Cortés entertained other, less elevated thoughts. When they arrived at the Aztec capital Tenochtitlan (now Mexico City) they discovered it lay in the middle of a great lake, accessible only by narrow artificial bridges that could easily be defended. But Moctezuma came out to greet them, bowed before the godly Cortés and invited them to enter. Cortés's plan had been to kidnap Moctezuma and make off with the ransom, but when his men saw all the gold that lay about the palace, they impatiently killed the king. Because of this stupidity they were able to escape only after a long battle. This was the beginning of one of the bloodiest episodes in history.

The Conquistadors heard rumours of a secret source of all the gold and of a gilded king, El Dorado, who bathed in liquid gold every morning. Walter Raleigh, who would join in the quest for this fabled king's city was writing of 'Imperial El Dorado, roofed with gold'.

Cortés's rival, Francisco Pizarro, sailed to Peru, intending to rob an entire country protected by tens of thousands, and to do it with an army of only two hundred.

Like Cortés he kidnapped the king, after offering to meet him unarmed. As a ransom he demanded that a room be filled to the ceiling with gold. For weeks a procession of natives brought plates, goblets and other finely wrought artefacts, but when the room was nearly full the Spaniards claimed that the deal had been to fill the room with gold ingots. They began melting down the artefacts to create more space to fill.

Eventually, as had happened with Cortés, Pizarro's men grew impatient and killed the king. Open hostilities broke out. When Pizarro's small army pushed its way into the capital they found palaces with golden walls, golden furniture, statues of gods and animals and golden armour. There was even an artificial garden in which the trees, flowers and animals were made of gold and a field three hundred by six hundred feet in which every stalk of maize was made of silver and its ears of gold.

It is estimated that some 100,000 Aztecs were killed at the battle for Tenochtitlan, with a loss of only a handful of Conquistadors. It has also been estimated that in the course of the Conquest some two million natives died.

The natives would not always be such easy meat. After a while they learned to adopt the treacherous fighting mentality of the Europeans, and so the Conquistadors began to take heavier casualties.

The Conquistadors never did find El Dorado or mines or any source of the gold that lay around the capitals in such abundance, but the gold from South America was sufficient to fund the Counter-Reformation. With its powerhouse in Spain, and enforced in large measure by the Spanish Inquisition, the Counter-Reformation made attendance at Mass compulsory. There were occult forces and initiatic brotherhoods at work in the service of the Counter-Reformation, too.

The world's greatest library of occult literature is to be found in the Vatican. The Church has never believed that the occult sciences do not work. It has only sought to keep exclusive control of them. Sociologists have attributed religion's power over the people to its ability to explain life's unknown, numinous dimensions and so keep dread

In seventeenth-century Catholicism esoteric teachings rose very near the surface. The visions of Marie des Vallées and Mary Alacoque led to popular Church teachings on the mysteries of the sacred heart. In the twentieth century, in London where I work, the most occult bookshop – by occult, I mean an emphasis on supernatural happenings such as levitations, apparitions, bodily transmogrifications – is not one of the obvious ones which advertise themselves as such but the Padre Pio Bookshop in the shadow of Westminster Cathedral.

at bay. Religion must seem to be able to manage the dark volcanic power of the spirits which sometimes erupts into the material world.

In Northern Europe many had made spiritual quests outside Roman Catholicism. Spain was galvanized by a mysticism equally dark and dangerous, but operating within the Church.

Teresa was born at Avila near Madrid in 1515, probably to a family of Jewish converts. She ran away from home to join a nunnery. There, while ill, she drifted out of everyday consciousness and into a mystical state. When the states kept returning she used the manuals of medieval mystics and texts by Ramón Lull as guides to achieving a working knowledge of mystical experience.

Teresa's mystical ecstasy upon encountering a Seraph was, of course, sculpted by Bernini, the great initiate-artist of the Counter-Reformation. 'He was not tall but short, marvellously beautiful. In his hands was a long golden spear and at the point of the iron there seemed to be a little fire ... that he thrust several times into my heart ... he drew out the spear, leaving me all on fire with a wondering love of God ... so exciting sweet is this greatest of pains.' There is an irrepressible suggestion of sexual ecstasy about this that invites comparison with the sex-magical practices of mystical societies of the same period. These practices are among the most closely guarded secrets of esoteric lore, and we will examine them in Chapter 25.

Teresa's spiritual journals also describe an ascent of the soul that ties in with cabalistic accounts of the ascent of the sephirothic Tree. She describes, too, out-of-body experiences and the soul's organs of spiritual vision – the chakras, which she calls 'the eyes of the soul'. But though her writing might be informed by a knowledge of the Cabala, what comes through most strongly is an immediate account of direct personal experience, an understanding of the way the spirit worlds work which is rare outside of India. There is no element of inauthenticity or literary artifice.

Ecstasy of St Teresa *in the Cornaro Chapel in Rome.*

Other levitating saints include Thomas Aquinas, Catherine of Siena, Francis of Assisi, Joseph of Cupertino and, in the twentieth century, Padre Pio and Gemma Galgani.

St Teresa's extreme spiritual states sometimes induced supernatural phenomena, including frequent levitations. These were witnessed by many. Nuns would struggle to hold her down.

It would be a mistake to assume that the experience of bodily levitation is necessarily a blissful one. Teresa talks of being 'suspended between heaven and earth and receiving no comfort from either'. There is in this some of the sense of loneliness, of spiritual aridity, which had been predicted by Eckhart, and which would be given its finest, defining expression by Teresa's pupil, St John of the Cross.

Because we live in an age when experiences of the spirit worlds are rare, there is a danger that we read St Teresa or her pupil, St John of the Cross, as mere allegory, an idealized account of finer feelings or even as a description of relatively trivial mood changes described in an aspirational or wishful-thinking way. But St John of the Cross's account of his dark night of the soul, written after a period in prison in solitary confinement is an account, not of altered moods, but of *an altered state of consciousness*, an alteration of mental faculties as radical as that achieved by taking hallucinogenic drugs.

The Spanish throw themselves at death. The work of their mystics, writers and artists shows they keep the immanence of death in mind, not in a theoretical way, but a pressing

Bernini's famous Obelisk of Santa Maria sopra Minerva *is derived from Alberti's* Hypnerotomachia *– as we have seen, also a key occult influence on Leonardo.*

existential way. They see it weaving around them and through them. They are ready to wrestle with it. They risk defeat by it in order to snatch what is most valuable in life from its jaws. This Spanish spirit finds electrifying expression in *The Dark Night of the Soul.* We have touched on the Mystic Death, the stage in the process of initiation the candidate must pass through. After the first comforting, illumining manifestations of the spirit, the candidate is pitched into a state of profound misery. Not only does he have no doubt that he is about to die, he has no doubt God has abandoned him, that the whole cosmos finds him despicable. He does not now even want anything more than the shady half-existence he is being shown.

If John is describing this experience in terms which are recognizable to us today, this is partly because he helped formulate the very language we use to describe the beginnings of the spirit's journey through Purgatory, the sphere of the moon.

In John's account there is also a prophetic level of meaning. He was anticipating an era of history in which incarnated humanity as a whole would have to go through its own Dark Night of the Soul.

But perhaps the most characteristic form of occultism in what would become known as the Counter-Reformation was the Jesuits.

Ignatius Loyola was a professional soldier. When his right leg was shattered during a siege at Pamplona, he was invalided out of the Spanish army. During a period of convalescence he was reading a book on the lives of the saints when he realized his religious vocation. So in 1534, while studying in Paris, he gathered around him seven fellow students to form a brotherhood. They were to be the highly disciplined soldiers of the Church. In 1540 the Pope recognized this order as the Society of Jesus. The Jesuits were to be the Church's intellectual elite, its military intelligence, servants unto death, searching out heresy and unlawful entry into the spirit worlds. The Jesuits also became the Pope's educators and missionaries, instituting a rigorous system that would orient the young towards Rome and instil obedience. They also had remarkable successes as missionaries in Central and South America and in India.

Ignatius Loyola devised trials and techniques for achieving altered states that included breathing exercises, sleep deprivation, meditation on skulls, training in lucid dreaming and in active imagination. This latter involved constructing an elaborate, sensual mental image which a disembodied spirit might inhabit, a process known to the Rosicrucians as 'building a hut by the palace of wisdom'.

However, in Loyola's exercises there is a subtle but important difference. While the Rosicrucian techniques were designed to help achieve a free-willed, free-thinking exchange with beings from higher hierarchies, the spiritual exercises of Ignatius Loyola are intended to still the will and induce a state of unquestioning obedience like a soldier's. 'Take, Lord, and receive all my memory, my understanding and my whole will, everything I have.'

In the West esoteric bookshops are dominated by Hindu, Buddhist and other oriental esoteric literature, but the *Spiritual Exercises of Ignatius Loyola* remain the most readily available and widely published esoteric techniques from the Western tradition.

El Greco's stretched figures have eyes that are half-closed as they contemplate some inner mystery. They stand in convulsive landscapes and stormy skyscapes. Not only does El Greco portray people in altered and mystical states, but he conveys a sense of what it is like to be in that state. René Huyghe, the French art critic, analysed the light in El Greco's panoramic view of Toledo. In reality Toledo is bathed in a fierce, clear Mediterranean light, whilst in El Greco's vision the ordinary light of day has been swallowed up by a fantastic, supernatural light. As an initiate, El Greco painted what St John of the Cross described when he wrote of 'the dark night of the fire of love ... without a guiding light other than that which was burning in my heart'.

Mary as Isis the Moon goddess by Murillo.

IN 1985 A BOOK WAS PUBLISHED anonymously called *Meditations on the Tarot.* It created a big stir in esoteric circles because it shows in an extremely erudite fashion that the symbolism in the tarot cards points to a unified set of beliefs underlying Hermeticism, the Cabala, oriental philosophies *and Catholic Christianity.* This book is a wonderful treasure chest of esoteric lore and wisdom.

It later emerged that the author was Valentine Tomberg, who had been initiated by Rudolf Steiner, but then left Steiner's Anthroposophy to become a Catholic convert. The underlying purpose of *Meditations on the Tarot* – to try to draw those interested in esoterica back into the Church – becomes apparent when you know this. Was there any intellectual dishonesty involved? Tomberg, like Loyola before him, was working to ensure that the initiative in esoteric matters should not entirely be taken away from Rome.

WE LOOKED AT THE LIVES OF SOME individuals working in Northern Europe, it seems, more or less in isolation – Eckhart, Paracelsus, Dee, Boehme.

What is the evidence of a network, of anything like the rumoured secret society of Rosicrucians? Is there any documentary evidence to support the rumours about secret brotherhoods?

In 1596 a man called Beaumont was convicted of magical practices by a court at

Angoulême in France. As the famous French historian de Thou recorded, Beaumont confessed that he 'held commerce with Aerial and Heavenly Spirites – that Schools and Professors of this noble Art had been frequent in all Parts of the World, and still were so in Spain at Toledo, Cordova, Grenada and other Places that they had also been formerly celebrated in Germany, but for the most part had failed since Luther had sown the seeds of his Heresy, and began to have so many Followers: that in France and in England it was still secretly preserved, as it were by Tradition, in the families of certain Gentlemen; but that only the initiated were admitted into the Sacred Rites; to the exclusion of profane Persons.'

Then, less than thirty years later, a series of short pamphlets began to appear which purported to give the inside story.

Published anonymously in Kessel in Germany in between 1614 and 1616, the first was called the *Fama Fraternitatis* (or 'Rumour of the Brotherhood') and it called for a spiritual revolution.

The second, the *Confessio Fraternitatis*, told the story of CRC (Christian Rosenkreuz), the founder of the brotherhood, gave an account of the rules he instituted and also revealed that his tomb had been discovered in 1604.

A door had been uncovered underneath an altar leading down to a crypt. The door carried an inscription: *After one hundred and twenty years I shall be opened.* Down below was a seven-sided mausoleum, each side being eight feet high with an artificial sun suspended in the middle above a circular table. Underneath this table lay the uncorrupted body of CRC, surrounded by books, including the Bible and a text by Paracelsus, and the body was clutching a rolled scroll, which bore the words: 'Out of God we are born, We die in Jesus, We will be reborn through the Holy Spirit.'

An observant literary detective might have noticed that the title page of the first folio of this second pamphlet featured the unique and unmistakable shape of Dr Dee's occult emblem of evolved consciousness, the *Monas Hieroglyphica*.

The third pamphlet, *The Chemical Wedding of Christian Rosenkreuz*, was an allegorical account of initiation, a sex-magical Chemical Marriage in the tradition of the *Hypnerotomachia*.

These publications caused a sensation across Europe.

Who were the Rosicrucian brothers and who was the author?

Then it gradually emerged that the author was a young Lutheran pastor called John Valentine Andrae. His spiritual mentor had been a famous mystic, Jean Arndt, the disciple of John Tauler, disciple in his turn of Meister Eckhart.

ANYONE WHO CONSIDERS THE CLAIMS of esoteric history is frustrated by the sparse nature of the evidence. Almost by definition the operations of secret societies leave scant traces. If they are successful, they leave little to go on. Yet the claims are very grand indeed:

that these societies are representatives of an ancient and universal philosophy, that this is a coherent, consistent philosophy that explains the universe more adequately than any other, and that many if not most of the great men and women of history are guided by it.

Anyone considering this dichotomy naturally asks, Can these societies really involve a secret coalition of the greatest geniuses – or it is really just the fantasy of a few, isolated and marginal people who are really a bit dim?

This is perhaps a good juncture to confront this question because for the past few pages we have been following two traditions running very closely parallel, the largely exoteric tradition of great mystics, passing from one generation to another and a largely esoteric tradition, an apparently loose association of magicians and occultists, the mystical force behind the Reformation, a chain of initiates that connects Eckhart, Tauler and Arndt with the network of magi that includes Rosencrantz, Paracelsus and Dee.

We have just seen how in 1614 these two traditions finally become inextricably intertwined in the person of Valentine Andrae.

THE HIDDEN HAND OF THE SECRET SOCIETIES does not often show itself, and as we saw in the case of Dr Dee's Lear-like disgrace, when it does, it puts itself in danger. It changes its very nature, risking losing its power as soon as it emerges into the light of day.

In the years following the publication of the *Fama*, the Rosicrucians would come out of the shadows to the sound of canons and muskets. They would fight a bloody and hopeless battle against the Jesuits for the spirit of Europe.

In conventional histories, sceptical of the Rosicrucian Manifestoes and suspecting them to be just a fantasy, their publication marked the beginning of the Rosicrucian phenomenon. In this secret history the manifestoes marked the end of true Rosicrucians – or at least the beginning of the end.

The publication of these manifestoes at the beginning of the seventeenth century also marked the founding of another secret society that would dominate world affairs up until the present day.

The institution of the Holy Roman Emperor, founded by Charlemagne in 800, was built on the ideal of a world leader who with the Pope's blessing held Christendom together and defended the faith. This ideal was shining less brightly by the beginning of the seventeenth century. No Holy Roman Emperor had been crowned between 1530 and Rudolf II's coronation in 1576, and many of the small kingdoms and princedoms of Germany had become Protestant, which naturally undermined any notion of a Europe united under a Roman Emperor.

Following the death of Rudolf, the tolerant, intellectually curious and occult-minded Emperor whom Dr Dee had failed to impress, a dispute over his succession drew the Rosicrucian brotherhood into a plot. If Frederick V, a Rhineland prince and Rosicrucian fellow traveller, could be placed on the Bohemian throne, then Europe might be seized for Protestantism.

The Rosicrucians had been cultivating James I of England. Michael Maier, whose alchemical prints are among the most explicit ever printed, sent him a Rosicrucian greeting card. In 1617 Robert Fludd dedicated his work of esoteric cosmology *Utriusque cosmi historia* to James, saluting him with an epithet sacred to Hermes Trismegistus. In 1612 James's daughter, Elizabeth, married Frederick. *The Tempest* was given a special performance at court to celebrate the wedding day, with the masque scene newly inserted. We may say with a small degree of literary artifice that Dee was there in spirit.

The plan was that when in 1619 Frederick travelled from Heidelberg to Prague to be crowned, James would move to defend his romantic teenage son-in-law and his young bride from Catholic attack.

In the event James did nothing when Frederick's forces were decisively defeated at the Battle of White Mountain. Frederick and Elizabeth had to flee Prague, and because they had reigned for such a laughably short time, they were known forever after as the Winter King and Queen.

The Thirty Years War was waged by Ferdinand of the great Catholic dynasty of the Hapsburgs, whose intellectual outriders were the Jesuits. The aim of the Hapsburgs was to re-establish Catholic supremacy in Europe. During this time five out of six German towns and villages were destroyed and the population reduced from some nine million to four million. The Rosicrucian dream was destroyed in a carnival of bigotry, torture and mass slaughter. Central Europe was a desert.

Yet the Church's victory was a phyrric one. If the Church really saw itself as engaged in warfare with the secret societies, fighting black magic, then perhaps it was making the mistake of believing its own propaganda.

The real enemy was the oldest enemy of all in a new disguise.

23

The Occult Roots of Science

Isaac Newton • The Secret Mission of Freemasonry • Elias Ashmole and the Chain of Transmission • What Really Happens in Alchemy

IN 1543 NICHOLAS COPERNICUS published *On the Revolution of the Celestial Bodies.* His thesis was that the earth goes round the sun.

In 1590 Galileo Galilei performed experiments to show that the speed of falling objects is proportional to their density not their weight.

In 1609 Johannes Kepler, using the star maps of Tycho Brahe, calculated the three laws of the motions of planets.

In the 1670s Isaac Newton devised a unifying theory which tied all these discoveries together to describe the behaviour of the mechanical universe in three simple formulae.

Of course, it is too easy to see this as humanity's triumphant rush into the modern world, emerging out of millennia of dark superstition and ignorance into the clear light of reason. But the initiate-priests of the Egyptian temples who knew that Sirius was a three-star system were well aware, thousands of years earlier, that the earth rotates around the Sun.

Moreover, as we are about to see, there is evidence to show that the heroes of modern science – the people of whom we would least expect it – were deeply immersed in the ancient wisdom.

Copernicus acknowledged that his ideas came from reading texts from the ancient world, and, when Kepler formulated his theories, he was conscious of the ancient wisdom working through him. In the foreword to the fifth volume of *Harmonices Mundi* (1619) he wrote, 'Yes, I have stolen the golden vessels of the Egyptians to build a shrine to my God ...'

Kepler was a life-long friend of Richard Beshold, who worked closely with Valentine Andrae and is often thought to have been his collaborator on the Rosicrucian Manifestoes.

Isaac Newton, born in Woolthorpe, Lincolnshire, never grew above five feet. He was strange, eccentric, sexually confused and lonely. Then in his schooldays he lodged with an apothecary who turned out to be an alchemical adept – and Newton's path lay clear before him. Newton, no less than Cornelius Agrippa, tried to discover the complete system of the world.

Newton came to believe that the secrets of life are encoded in numerical form in the fabric of nature. He believed, too, that the clues for deciphering these codes are hidden in both numerical and linguistic codes in ancient books of wisdom, and in ancient buildings like the Great Pyramid and the Temple of Solomon. It was as if God had set humanity a test. Only when humanity had developed sufficient intelligence would it be able to recognize the presence of these codes and decode them. That time, thought Newton, had arrived.

In Newton's view every part of the universe is intelligent. Even a stone is intelligent, and not just in the sense that it shows evidence of design. According to the ancient way of thinking that Newton subscribed to, it is not the case that animal, vegetable and mineral are totally distinct categories. They naturally overlap, intermingle and in special circumstances may morph one into the other. As Newton's cabalistic contemporary Lady Conway

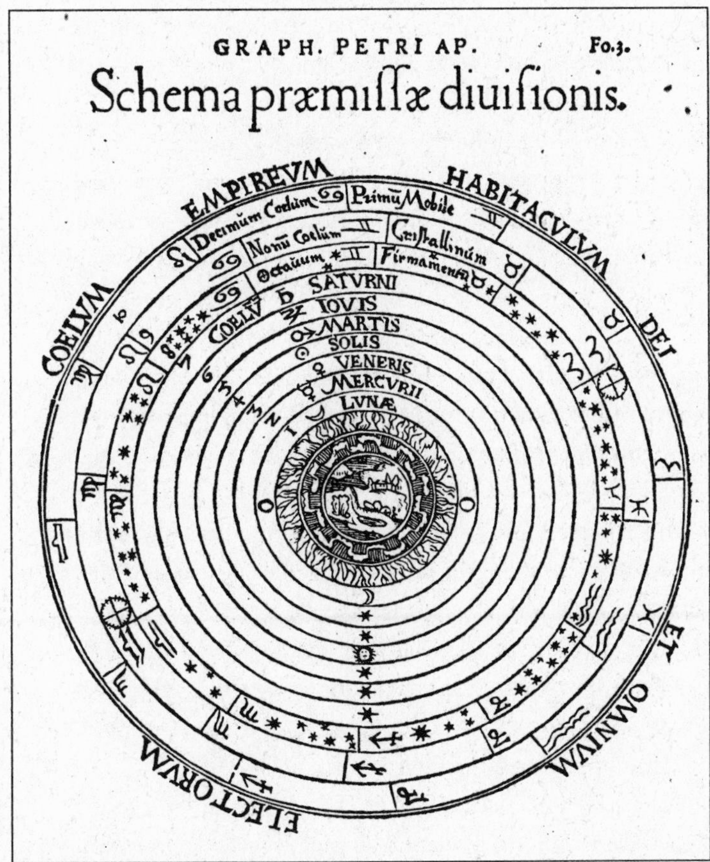

Ptolemy's map of the spheres is conventionally presented as having been superseded by the ideas of Copernicus, Galileo et al. but in fact it was and remains an accurate map of the spiritual dimension of the cosmos, a dimension which seemed more real to the ancients than the material cosmos.

put it, 'There are transformations from one species to another, as from stone to earth, from earth to grass, from grass to sheep from sheep to human flesh, from human flesh to the lowest species of man, and from these to noblest spirits.' In Newton's view, then, everything in the universe strains towards intelligence. Inanimate matter strains towards vegetable life, which aspires to animal life by means of a rudimentary sensitivity. The higher animals have an instinct that is almost reasonable like the faculty in human beings, who wait to evolve into super-intelligent beings.

And this universal aspiration to the super-intelligent looks to the heavens as the stoics had intimated. Isaac Luria, the sixteenth-century Cabalist put it like this: 'There is nothing in the world, not even among silent things such as dust and stones that does not possess a certain life, spiritual nature, a particular planet and its perfect form in the heavens.' Luria was talking about the intelligence in a seed that responds to the intelligent intention in the sun's light. The ancient esoteric tradition did not suppose that all the information needed for a seed's growth into a plant is contained in the seed. Growth is a process resulting from the intelligence in the seed interacting with the intelligence in the greater cosmos surrounding it.

We know from John Maynard Keynes's investigation into the occult dimensions of Newton's world-view that these schools of thought fascinated him. Newton asked himself whether it was possible to discern different intelligences, perhaps even distinct principles with distinct centres of consciousness behind the material surface of things. This is not to say that he ever saw these principles as angels sitting on clouds or visualized them in any naively anthropomorphic way – but neither did he see them as being completely impersonal, let alone as pure abstractions. He called them 'Intelligencers' to imply volition.

AS WE HAVE SEEN, ALL ESOTERICISTS are especially interested in the interface between the animal and vegetable on the one hand and in the interface between the vegetable and the mineral on the other. In the esoteric view this is the key to understanding the secrets of nature and manipulating them. The vegetable is the intermediary between thought and matter. It may be called *the gateway between the worlds.*

To help us understand why anyone might believe this, we should perhaps remind ourselves of the mind-before-matter account of the creation given in the early chapters of this book. If you believe that the world is formed by intelligence, by mind, you have to explain how the immaterial forms the material. This has traditionally – in all the world's ancient cultures – been seen in terms of a series of emanations of mind, initially too ethereal for any form of sensory perception – finer even than light. It was from these ethereal emanations that matter was eventually precipitated.

This ethereal dimension, then, lay and continues to lie between mind – the animal dimension – and matter. Hence the traditional gradation: animal, vegetable, mineral.

Mind could not – and cannot – create or order matter directly, but only through the medium of the vegetative dimension. The mineral dimension of the cosmos, as it were, grows out of this vegetative dimension. Something crucial for practical occultists flows out of this. What Paracelsus called the *ens vegetalis* is malleable by mind, and *because the mineral dimension grows out of this vegetative dimension, it is possible to exercise a power of mind over matter via this medium.*

Newton's name for this subtle medium, which may be used by mind to reorganize the cosmos, is the *sal nitrum*. In his accounts of his experiments he describes how he has conducted tests in order to see how the *sal nitrum* may be used to make metals come alive. These notes are an account of a real alchemist at work. Newton saw the *sal nitrum* circulating from the stars to the depths of the earth, investing it with life, routinely with plant life but in certain special circumstances giving life to metals. It is with growing excitement that he describes metal compounds coming to life in nitrate solutions and growing like plants. This 'vegetation of metals' confirmed him in his conviction that the universe is alive, and in his private papers he used the notion of the *sal nitrum* to help explain the effects of gravity.

WHEN WE PEER INTO THE HIDDEN LIVES of the heroes of science, the people who forged the mechanical world-view and made the great leaps forward in technology that have made our lives so much safer, easier and more pleasant, we often find they are deeply immersed in esoteric thought – particularly alchemy.

We might also consider the lesser but related paradox that many of the world's most notorious occultists and outlandish visionaries were also in their own way practically minded men, often responsible for smaller but nevertheless significant inventions.

Looking at both groups together, it is difficult to see a clear distinction between scientists and occultists, even as we move into modern times. Rather there is a spectrum in which the individual is a bit of both, albeit to varying degrees.

Paracelsus, perhaps the most revered of occultists, revolutionized medicine by introducing the experimental method. He was also the first to isolate and name zinc, made great breakthroughs in the importance to medicine of hygiene and also was the first to formulate principles which would come to underlie homeopathy.

Giordano Bruno is a great hero of science because he was burned at the stake in 1600 for insisting that the solar system is heliocentric. But as we have already seen, this was because he believed fervently in the ancient wisdom of the Egyptians. He believed that the earth goes round the sun because, in the first instance, so too did the initiate priests of the ancient world.

Robert Fludd, the occult author and defender of the Rosicrucians, also invented the barometer.

Jan Baptiste van Helmont, the Flemish alchemist, was important in the secret societies for reintroducing into Western esotericism ideas of reincarnation – which he called 'the revolution of humane souls'. He also separated gases in the course of his alchemical experiments, coined the word 'gas', and in the course of experiments on the healing powers of magnets, coined the word 'electricity'.

Gottfried Wilhelm Leibniz, the German mathematician, was Newton's rival in the devising of the calculus. In Leibniz's case his discoveries arose out of fascination with cabalistic number mysticism which he shared with his close friend, the Jesuit scholar of the occult Athanasius Kircher. In 1687 Kircher, an alchemical student of the properties of the vegetable dimension, resurrected a rose from its ashes in front of the Queen of Sweden. Leibniz himself has also provided us with the most detailed and credible account of the alchemical transformation of base metals into gold.

The Royal Society was the great intellectual engine of modern science and technological invention. Among Newton's contemporaries, Sir Robert Moray published the world's first ever scientific journal, *Philosophical Transactions* – and was a fervent researcher into Rosicrucian teaching. The strange monk-like figure of Robert Boyle, whose law of thermodynamics paved the way for the internal combustion engine, was a practising alchemist. In his youth he wrote of having been initiated into an 'invisible college'. Also practising alchemists were Robert Hooke, inventor of the microscope, and William Harvey, discoverer of the circulation of the blood.

Descartes, who fathered rationalism in the mid-seventeenth century, spent a

Frontispiece, designed by John Evelyn, to the official history of the Royal Society, published in 1667. Francis Bacon is depicted as the founding father. He sits under the wing of an angel in a way that echoes the closing phrase of the Fama Fraternitatis *of the Rosicrucians.*

considerable amount of time trying to track down the Rosicrucians and in researching their philosophy. He rediscovered the ancient, esoteric idea of the pineal gland as the gateway to consciousness, the inner eye, and his philosophical breakthrough came to him all of a piece while in a visionary state. His most famous dictum may be seen as a recasting of the Rosicrucian teaching intended to help foster the evolution of an independent, intellectual faculty: *I must think in order to be.*

Blaise Pascal, one of the great mathematicians of his day and an eminent philosopher, was discovered after his death to have sewn into his cloak a piece of paper on which was written: 'The year of grace 1654, Monday 23 November, day of St Clement, Pope and Martyr. From about half-past ten in the evening until about half-past twelve at night, FIRE.' Pascal achieved the illumination that the monks of Mount Athos sought.

In 1726 Jonathan Swift in *Gulliver's Travels* predicted the existence and orbital periods of the two moons of Mars, which were not discovered by astronomers using telescopes until 1877. The astronomer, who then saw how accurate Swift had been, named the moons Phobos and Deimos – fear and terror – so awestruck was he by Swift's evident supernatural powers.

Emmanuel Swedenborg, the great eighteenth-century Swedish visionary, wrote detailed accounts of his journeys into the spirit worlds. His reports of what the disembodied beings he met there told him inspired the esoteric Freemasonry of the late eighteenth and nineteenth centuries. He was also the first to discover the cerebral cortex and the ductless glands, and also engineered what is still the largest dry dock in the world.

As we have already seen, Charles Darwin attended séances. He may have had the opportunity to learn the esoteric doctrine of the evolution from fish to amphibian to land animal to human from his close association with Max Müller, early translator of sacred Sanskrit texts.

Nicholas Tesla, recently described by a historian of science as 'the ultimate visionary crank', was a Serbian Croat who became a naturalized American. There he patented some seven hundred inventions including fluorescent lights and the Tesla coil that generates an alternating current. Like Newton's most important breakthroughs, this last arose out of his belief in an etheric dimension between the mental and physical planes.

In the late nineteenth and early twentieth centuries many leading scientists thought it worthwhile to pursue a scientific approach to occult phenomena, believing that it would ultimately be possible to measure and predict occult forces such as etheric currents that seemed only a shade more elusive than electromagnetism, sound waves or x-rays. Thomas Edison, inventor of the phonograph and therefore the godfather of all recorded sound, and Alexander Graham Bell, inventor of the telephone, both supposed that psychic phenomena were perfectly respectable areas of research for science, involving themselves in esoteric Freemasonry and theosophy. Edison tried to make a radio that would tune into the spirit worlds. Their great scientific discoveries arose out of this research into the supernatural. Even the television was invented as a result of trying to capture psychic influences on gases fluctuating in front of a cathode ray tube.

LOOKING FOR CLUES ON HOW BEST TO understand this strange vision of the occult and the scientific joined at the hip, we will return to the great genius behind the scientific revolution, Francis Bacon.

As we saw, Francis Bacon's great discovery was that if you view the objects of sense experience as objectively as possible, stripping out all preconceptions and notions that all of it was meant to be, then new patterns emerge beyond the ones traced by priests and other spiritual leaders. You can use these new patterns to predict and manipulate events.

Historians of the philosophy of science see this as the great beginning, the moment when inductive reasoning became a part of humanity's approach to the world. From this moment flowed the scientific revolution and the whole industrial and technological transformation of the world.

However, if you look more deeply into Bacon's account of the process of scientific discovery, it appears less straightforward and, initially at least, rather mysterious.

'Nature is a labyrinth,' he said, 'in which the very haste you move with will make you lose your way.' Bacon was writing as if the scientist plays a game of chess with nature. In order to get answers, he must first put nature in check. It's as if nature needs to be tricked into giving away her secrets, because nature is inherently tricky herself. As if she means to deceive.

Today's historians of science try to present Bacon as a thorough-going materialist, but this is wishful thinking. Although he believed that interesting new results would emerge if you looked at sense data *as if* they were not infused with meaning, this is not what he believed to be the case. We know, for example, that he believed in what he called 'astrologica sana', which is to say receiving the magical celestial influences into the spirit in the way that the Renaissance magus Pico della Mirandola had recommended. Bacon also believed in the same ethereal intermediary between spirit and matter as Newton, and that this same intermediary existed in humans who are 'inclosed in a thicker body, as Ayrein Snow or Froath' – what he called the 'Aetheric body'.

Bacon said: 'It is no less true in this human kingdom of knowledge, than in God's kingdom of heaven that no man shall enter into it "except he become first as a little child".' This seems to be saying that a different and child-like state of mind needs to be reached first in order for higher knowledge to be reached. Paracelsus had said something similar, writing of the process of experimentation also using biblical phrasing: 'Only he who desires with his whole heart will find and to him only who knocks vehemently shall the door be opened.'

The implication is that higher knowledge of the world comes from altered states of

Rosslyn Chapel, near Edinburgh. The Scottish roots of Freemasonry were deliberately covered up in the eighteenth century because they had become entangled with the Stuart dynasty, supporting its claims to the throne. Rosslyn Chapel, built in the fifteenth century by William Sinclair, the first Earl of Caithness, incorporated replicas of the twin pillars of Solomon's Temple – Jakim and Boaz – in a way that anticipated every Masonic lodge in the world. A carving on the lower frame of the window in the south-west corner of the chapel seems to be of a Freemasonic First Degree. Scottish lodges of some description undoubtedly existed at least a hundred years before the recorded English ones.

consciousness. Working in the same circles as Bacon and Newton, Jan Baptiste van Helmont wrote: 'There is a book inside us, written by the finger of God, through which we may read all things.' Michael Maier, who wrote about the Rosicrucians as if from the inside and published some of the most beautiful alchemical literature, said: 'To drink the interior life in a long draft is to see the higher life. He who discovers the interior, discovers what is in space.' In all these sayings there is a clear implication that the key to scientific discovery somehow lies within.

We've seen that throughout history small groups have worked themselves into altered states. Is the suggestion by Bacon and his followers that the scientist needs somehow to tune himself to the etheric or vegetable dimension? That if you can somehow work yourself into the dimension of interweaving forms, you are on your way to understanding the secrets of nature?

We have seen that great scientific geniuses, the founders of the modern age, have tended to be fascinated by ideas of ancient wisdom and altered states. Could it be that it is not so much that genius is next to madness but that *genius is next to the altered states brought on by esoteric training*?

IF THE HEROES OF THE ROSICRUCIANS – Dee and Paracelsus – were wild and strange, the magi of the next epoch came on like respectable businessmen.

Freemasonry has always presented a straight face to the world. The Anglo-Saxon lodges in particular have been coy about their esoteric origins. The notion that Freemasons at sufficiently high levels of initiation are taught the secret doctrine and history of the world outlined in this book might seem implausible, even to many Freemasons.

In Freemasonic lore the society's roots may be traced back to the building of Solomon's Temple by Hiram Abiff, the suppression of the Knights Templar, and to secretive guilds of craftsmen such as the Compagnons Du Devoir, the Children of Father Soubise and the Children of Father Jacques.

An often overlooked influence on the formation of secret societies, especially Freemasonry, is the Co-fraternities. Founded in the fifteenth century, they were originally lay brotherhoods affiliated to monasteries. The brothers pursued the spiritual life while also working in the community, organizing charities, commissioning art and leading processions on holy days. Their secrecy was originally designed to ensure that charitable works remained anonymous, but it gave rise to rumours of robes, secret rituals and initiates. In France in the fifteenth century these Co-fraternities, which had been absorbing ideas from Joachim and the Cathars, were eventually driven underground.

But modern 'speculative' Freemasonry is dated by its official historians to the seventeenth century.

It's sometimes claimed that the first recorded case of initiation into Freemasonry was that in 1646 of the celebrated antiquary and collector, and founder member of the Royal Society, Elias Ashmole. He was certainly one of the earlier English Freemasons and very influential.

Born in 1617, the son of a sadler, Elias Ashmole qualified as a lawyer, and became a soldier and a civil servant. He was restless collector of curios. The Ashmolean Museum in Oxford, built around his collection, was the first public museum. He was also a man of boundless intellectual curiosity. In 1651 he met an older man, William Backhouse, owner of a manor house called Swallowfield. This turned out to have an extraordinary long gallery, a treasure house of 'Inventions and Rarities', including rare alchemical manuscripts. Backhouse was evidently a man much after Ashmole's heart, and Ashmole's diaries reveal how Backhouse invited him to become his son.

By this, we learn, Backhouse meant that he intended to adopt him as his successor

Illustration to Theatrum Chemicum Britannicum, *an anthology collected by Elias Ashmole.*

and heir. Before he died, he promised, he would pass on to Ashmole the ultimate secret of alchemy, the true matter of the Philosopher's Stone, so that Ashmole could carry forward a secret tradition that dated back to the time of Hermes Trismegistus. Over the next two years Backhouse's teaching of the eager Ashmole was slow and apparently hesitant. But then in May 1653 the younger man recorded 'my father Backhouse lying sick in Fleet streete over against St Dunstans Church, and not knowing whether he should live or dye, about eleven o clock, told me in S.lables the true Matter of the Philosophers Stone which he bequeathed to me as a Legacy'.

Ashmole's is an unusually clear and unambiguous account of the passing down of secret knowledge, but there is other evidence, too, hints and allusions of occult activity among the intellectual elite. The second grand master of the London Lodge was John Théophile Desaguliers, a follower of Isaac Newton who likewise spent many years poring over alchemical manuscripts.

The symbolism of Freemasonry as it was formulated in this period is shot through with alchemical motifs from the central notion of the Work to the ubiquitous cornerstone and philosopher's stone – ASHLAR – to the compasses and l'equerre.

Depiction of the English king, Charles I in 1649 awaiting execution. This event was predicted with astonishing accuracy by the French prophet and astrologer Michel de Nostradamus in 1555. As David Ovason, the most learned of the Nostradamus scholars, has pointed out, his line 'CHera pAR LorS, Le ROY' is cabalistic code for 'Charls Le Roy', so that the apparently bland line 'It will come about that the King' actually contains a prediction of the name of the man who, as parts of the quatrain make clear, was to be 'kept in a fortress by the Thames' and be 'seen in his shirt'. Charles made a point of wearing two shirts, as he stepped outside on to the executioner's platform, so that he would not shiver from the cold and appear fearful.

THE TIME HAS FINALLY COME TO ASK

What exactly is alchemy?

Alchemy is very old. Ancient Egyptian texts talk of techniques of distillation and metallurgy as mystical processes. Greek myths such as the quest for the Golden Fleece can be seen to have an alchemical layer of meaning, and Fludd, Boehme and others have interpreted Genesis in the same alchemical terms.

A quick survey of alchemical texts ancient and modern shows that alchemy, like the Cabala, is a very broad church. If there is one great mysterious 'Work', it is approached via a remarkable variety of codes and symbols. In some cases the Work involves Sulphur, Mercury and Salt, in others roses, stars, the philosopher's stone, salamanders, toads, crows, nets, the marriage bed, and astrological symbols such as the fish and the lion.

There are obvious geographical variations. Chinese alchemy seems less about the

Illustration to Milton's Paradise Lost. *Milton often wrote about the way his muse dictated poetry to him. It is tempting to modern sensibility to see this as mere metaphor. But Milton's journals also show how much he was influenced by Boehme in his descriptions of Paradise and by Fludd in his cosmology. Milton's writings also make it clear that he was used to encounters with disembodied beings: 'If answerable style I can obtain Of my Celestial Patroness, who deigns Her nightly visitation unexplored; or inspires Easy my unpremeditated verse'.*

quest for gold and more about a quest for the elixir of life, for longevity, even immortality. Alchemy also seems to change through the ages. In the third century the alchemist Zozimos wrote that 'the symbol of the chymic art – gold – comes forth from creation for those who rescue and purify the divine soul chained in the elements'. In early Arab texts the Work involves manipulations of these same Four Elements, but in European alchemy, rooted in the Middle Ages and flowering in the seventeenth century, a mysterious fifth element, the Quintessence, comes to the fore.

If we begin to look for unifying principles, we can see immediately that there are prescribed lengths of time or numbers of repetitions for the various operations, the distilling, the applying of gentle heat and so on.

There are obvious parallels, then, with meditative practice and this suggests immediately that these alchemical terms may be descriptions of subjective states of consciousness rather than the sort of chemical operations that might be performed in a laboratory.

Tying in with this we have also seen repeated suggestions, particularly from Rosicrucian sources, that these operations are often intended to have an effect during sleep and on the border between sleeping and waking. Could they be to do with visionary dreams or lucid dreaming? Or are they to do with the carrying over of elements of dream consciousness in waking consciousness?

There are many hints of a sexual element, too, from the recurring image of the Chemical Wedding to Paracelsus's teasing references to the azoth. The *Codex Veritatis* in a commentary on the Song of Solomon advises, 'Place the red man with his white woman in a red chamber, warmed to a constant temperature.' Equally, Tantric texts equate alchemical Mercury with sperm.

There is a school of thought that interprets alchemical texts as manuals giving techniques to make the kundalini serpent rise up from the base of the spine through the chakras to light up the Third Eye.

Yet another school, inspired by Jung, sees alchemy as a kind of precursor of psychology. Jung wrote a study of the alchemist Gerard Dorn, making this case, and Dorn certainly lends himself to this interpretation as he is an overtly psychological kind of alchemist. 'First transmute the earth of your body into water,' he says. 'This means your heart that is as hard as stone, material and lazy, must become subtle and vigilant.' In Dorn we see both the practice of working on individual human faculties that we noted in Ramón Lull, and the combining of esoteric training with moral development that we saw earlier in esoteric Buddhism and the Cabala.

Alchemical-sexual practices certainly exist – we will look at these in Chapter 25. And there may well be alchemical texts which deal with the kundalini rising, but in my view this is not central to the golden age of alchemy that reached its peak with the Rosicrucians and the Freemasons.

Jung's purely psychological alchemy is interesting in its way but it is totally *uninteresting* from an esoteric perspective, because it disregards notions of journeys into the spirit worlds and communication with disembodied beings.

The key to understanding alchemy surely lies in the surprising phenomena we have been following in this chapter. Bacon, Newton and the other Rosicrucian and Freemasonic adepts were interested in *both* direct personal experience and in scientific experiment. As idealists they were fascinated by what connects matter to mind, and like all esotericists they conceived of this subtle connection in terms of what Paracelsus called the *ens vegetalis,* or vegetable dimension.

Did it perhaps provoke them that the vegetable dimension seemed immeasurable, even undetectable by any scientific instrument? Maybe, but then perhaps what sustained them, what prompted them to explore further, was the belief that this vegetable dimension had apparently been experienced in all times and all places, and that there was an ancient authentic tradition of manipulating it to which many of the great geniuses of history had subscribed.

Roger Bacon, Francis Bacon, Isaac Newton and others had developed scientific, experimental procedure. They had tried to find universal laws to make sense of the world viewed as objectively as possible. Now they applied the same methodology to life viewed as subjectively as possible. The result was a science of spiritual experience, and this is what alchemy really is. The gold they experienced at the end of their experiments was a spiritual gold, an evolved form of consciousness that meant a mere metal bringing worldly wealth no longer interested them.

In the golden age of alchemy, Sulphur represents the animal dimension, Mercury is the vegetable dimension and Salt the material dimension. These dimensions are centred in different parts of the body, the animal down below in the sex organs, the vegetable in the solar plexus, and Salt in the head. Will and sexuality are seen as deeply intertwined in the esoteric philosophy. This is the Sulphurous part. Mercury, the vegetable part, is the realm of feeling. Salt is the precipitate of thinking.

In all alchemical texts Mercury is the mediator between Sulphur and Salt.

In the first stage of the process the vegetable dimension must be worked on to achieve the first stage of mystical experience, the entering of the Matrix, the sea of light that is the world between the worlds.

The second stage is what is sometimes called the Chemical Wedding, when soft, female Mercury makes love to hard, rigid, red Sulphur.

By meditating on images which inspire a loving feeling repeatedly and over long periods – it takes twenty-one days for any exercise to make a material change in human physiology – the candidate brings about a process of change which sinks down into the obstinate Will.

The Alchemist *by William Hogarth.*

If we succeed in making our selfish, sexual desires into living, spiritual desires, then the bird of resurrection, the Phoenix, rises. If our heart is overtaken by these transformed energies then it becomes a centre of power. Anyone who has met a truly holy person will have felt the great power that a transformed heart radiates.

Love fascinated the alchemists of the golden age. They knew that the heart is an organ of perception. When we look at someone we love, we see things other people cannot see, and the initiate who has undergone alchemical transformation has made a conscious, willed decision to see the whole world in this way. An adept sees how the world really works in a way that is denied to the rest of us.

So if we persist with our own alchemical spiritual exercises, if we succeed in purifying the fragmentary material barrier between ourselves and the spirit worlds, as the French mystic St Martin urges, then our own powers of perception will improve. In the first instance, the spirit worlds will begin to shine through into our dreams, less chaotically than they routinely do and more meaningfully. The promptings of the spirits, first in the form of hunches or intuition, will also begin to invade our waking life. We will begin to detect the flow and operation of the deeper laws beneath the everyday surface of things.

In the specifically Christian alchemy of Ramón Lull and St Martin, for example, the Sun-spirit that transforms the human body into a radiant body of light is identified with the historical personage of Jesus Christ. In other traditions, though this historical identification may not be made, *the same process is described*. The Indian sage Ramalinga

Swamigal wrote: 'O God! You have shown me eternal love by bestowing on me the golden body. By merging with my heart, you have alchemized my body.'

These phenomena, reported in different cultures, show that the Third Eye is beginning to open.

It would be all too easy to interpret all this as some kind of fuzzy mysticism. But the stories about scientists like Pythagoras and Newton suggest that by means of these peculiar kinds of altered states they were able to discover new things about the world, to see its inner workings and understand patterns that are perhaps too complex or too large for the human mind to grasp with its everyday, commonsensical state of consciousness. *Alchemy confers on its practitioners a supernatural intelligence.*

A common word in alchemical texts is VITRIOL. This is an acronym for *Visita Interiora Terrae Rectificando Invenies Occultum Lapidem.* Visit the interior of the earth to find the secret stone.

When alchemical texts recommend visiting the interior of the earth, this is a way of talking about sinking down into one's own body. Alchemy, then, is concerned with occult physiology. By acquiring a working knowledge of his own body's physiology, the alchemist was able to gain a degree of control over it. Great alchemists like St Germain were said to be able to live as long as they wanted.

But on a more down-to-earth level alchemists were also able to advance science in practical ways. We have seen alchemists who have made contributions to the growth of modern medicine. In altered states of consciousness men like Paracelsus and van Helmont were able to solve medical problems and devise treatments that were beyond the understanding of the medical profession of the day. By going *inside themselves,* these initiates saw the Outworld with supernatural clarity. To put it in cabalistic terms, man is the synthesis of all the Holy Names. All knowledge is therefore contained inside ourselves if we learn how to read it. The *Yoga Sutras of Pantanjali* allude to travelling the heavens and shrinking to the size of the smallest particle as being among the powers that reward those who practise its arcane techniques. Indian adepts still talk of being able to travel to the far reaches of the cosmos and also to so concentrate their powers of perception that they see right down to the atomic level.

These are great *siddhis,* or 'excellencies'. It was surely excellencies that enabled the initiate priests of antiquity to perceive the third star in the Sirius system, to understand the evolution of the species and to understand, too, the form and function of the pineal gland.

BUT IS IT POSSIBLE FOR US TO BELIEVE in the efficacy of such altered states today? Aren't we more likely to see them as diminishing intelligence, making us less conscious, more likely to be deluded?

I offer one counter-example to the common-sense view, which was first pointed out to me by Graham Hancock while he was working on his breakthrough book on shamanism, *Supernatural.*

Each human cell has coiled inside it double-stranded ribbon only ten molecules wide but some six feet long which contains all the genetic information necessary for the construction of that person. Every living cell on the planet has a version of this ribbon, but the ones in human cells are the most complex, carrying a coded message of some three billion characters. These characters contain inherited instructions which enable the cells to organize themselves in the patterns that create each individual human being.

Scientists noticed that these billions of characters seem to have very complex patterns of relationships, a deep structure suggestive of a human language. This hunch was confirmed by statistical analysis. But it was the brilliant Cambridge biologist Francis Crick who cracked the code, discovering the double helix structure that won him and his colleague James Watson the Nobel Prize and launched modern, genetic medicine.

What is pertinent to the secret history is that, although in so far as I know Crick had no connections with the secret societies, he achieved his moment of inspiration and unlocked the structure of DNA while in an altered state brought about by taking LSD. As we have seen, hallucinogens have been used as part of techniques for achieving higher states of consciousness and grasping higher realities since the Mystery schools.

What is even more intriguing still is that later in life Crick published a book called *Life Itself: Its Origin and Nature*, in which he argued that the complex structure of DNA could not have come about by chance. Like an earlier Cambridge man, Isaac Newton, he believed that the cosmos had encoded deep within it messages about our – and its – origins that had been put there, so that we would be able to decode them when we had evolved sufficient intelligence.

WHAT IS THE MORAL OF THIS? AS THE Duchess in *Alice in Wonderland* will always ask.

What lies outside the collective is the realm of the demonic – but this realm is also the realm of the innovative, the evolutionary and that which addresses our deep and unquenchable need for the infinite. *History shows that the people who have worked on the very boundaries of human intelligence have reached this place in altered states.*

24

The Age of Freemasonry

Christopher Wren • John Evelyn and the Alphabet of Desire • The Triumph of Materialism • George Washington and the Secret Plan for the New Atlantis

IF ALCHEMY WAS THE CORE PRACTICE connecting the Rosicrucians and early Freemasons, the outward forms of these societies were quite different.

There were only eight Rosicrucian brothers in the original brotherhood, and their 'House of the Holy Spirit' was supposed by many to exist on another plane. Later generations were still elusive enough to suggest that there were only ever a few of them.

By contrast Freemasonry spread around the world quickly recruiting thousands, then hundreds of thousands. Today, even if it doesn't advertise its existence, there is a substantial Freemasonic Lodge in most large towns. Outsiders know where it is, even if they don't know what goes on inside.

Following the Rosicrucians' catastrophic attempt at direct political action, ending in the Battle of White Mountain, Freemasons would now operate behind the scenes. Rather than seeking to impose reforms from above, they reverted to the original aims of the secret societies, influencing from below.

In the case of Freemasonry the aim was partly to help foster the social conditions which would bring people to a stage in their development when they would be ready for initiation. Freemasons worked to create a tolerant and prosperous society with a degree of social and economic freedom that would give people the chance to explore better both the outer and inner cosmos. The evolution of free will would bring about many of the great changes foreseen in Francis Bacon's *New Atlantis*, his vision of the perfect Rosicrucian state.

Prompted by Francis Bacon, people had begun to see the inner cosmos and outer cosmos as distinct. There arose out of this an understanding of the material world and

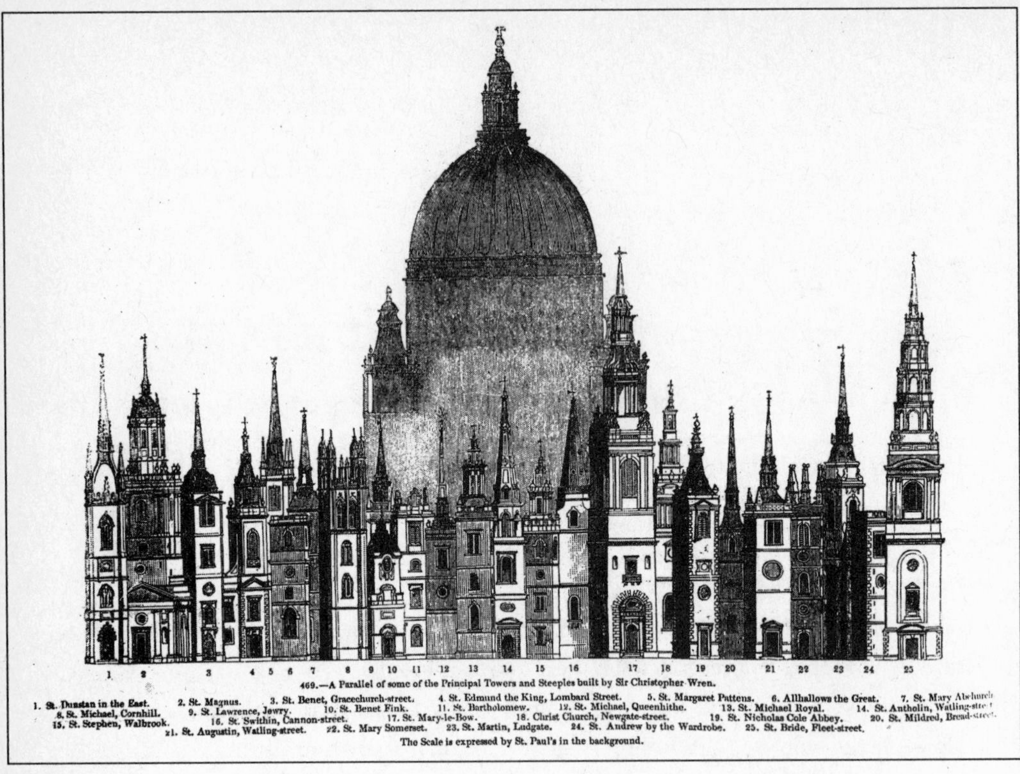

1 2 3 4 5 6 7 8 9 10 11 12 13 14 15 16 17 18 19 20 21 22 23 24 25
469.—A Parallel of some of the Principal Towers and Steeples built by Sir Christopher Wren.
1. St. Dunstan in the East. 2. St. Magnus. 3. St. Benet, Gracechurch-street. 4. St. Edmund the King, Lombard Street. 5. St. Margaret Pattens. 6. Allhallows the Great. 7. St. Mary Abchurch
8. St. Michael, Cornhill. 9. St. Lawrence, Jewry. 10. St. Benet Fink. 11. St. Bartholomew. 12. St. Michael, Queenhithe. 13. St. Michael Royal. 14. St. Antholin, Watling-street
15. St. Stephen, Walbrook. 16. St. Swithin, Cannon-street. 17. St. Mary-le-Bow. 18. Christ Church, Newgate-street. 19. St. Nicholas Cole Abbey. 20. St. Mildred, Bread-street.
21. St. Augustin, Watling-street. 22. St. Mary Somerset. 23. St. Martin, Ludgate. 24. St. Andrew by the Wardrobe. 25. St. Bride, Fleet-street.
The Scale is expressed by St. Paul's in the background.

St Paul's Cathedral, London. The famous diarist John Evelyn helped his fellow Freemason Christopher Wren with plans for St Paul's and the reconstruction of London after the Great Fire of 1666. Evelyn and Wren submitted to Charles II a new street plan for London, doing away with the old higgledy-piggledy streets. Instead the streets were to be mapped according to the pattern of the cabalistic Tree of Life. In this plan St Paul's is situated at Tiferet, *the 'heart' of the Tree, associated with Jesus Christ in Christianized Cabala.*

the way it worked which would not otherwise have been possible, and in a few short decades this understanding had thrown a metallic embrace around the world, as railways and machines of mass manufacture transformed the landscape.

The great thing about science was that it *worked.* It produced testable, reliable results and tangible, life-changing benefits.

The contrast with religion could not have been more pointed. The Church was no longer a reliable source of spiritual experience. The Scottish philosopher David Hume asked, sarcastically, why was it that miracles always happen only in remote times and places?

The result of all this was that physical objects became the yardstick of what is real.

The inner world began to seem like just a shadowy reflection or shadow of the outer one. In philosophy's central debate, the one between idealism and materialism, idealism had been dominant since philosophy's beginnings. As we have suggested, this was perhaps not because the majority of people had weighed up the arguments on both sides and come down in favour of idealism, but because they had experienced the world with an idealistic form of consciousness.

Now a decisive shift took place in favour of materialism.

Blake's pictures sometimes feature naked bodies in the forms of letters of the Hebrew alphabet. William Blake was a Freemason, like the more respectable Christopher Wren and John Evelyn. These respectable Freemasons, members of the Royal Society famous for their good and public works, knew to keep their esoteric interests secret. What John Evelyn kept out of diaries written with an eye to publication, however, was that he had a 'seraphic' or cabalistic girlfriend thirty years his junior whom he taught secret techniques of meditation. John Evelyn initiated Margaret Blagge into cabalistic exercises based on Abraham Abulafia's imaginative manipulations of the Hebrew alphabet. The difference was that these exercises involved imagining naked bodies erotically contorted into the shapes of the Hebrew letters. Margaret began to experience ecstatic trance states. In a way Evelyn anticipated the twentieth-century artist Austin Osman Spare, whose 'Alphabet of Desire' was based on correspondences between inner movements of sexual impulses and their outer form, manifested in erotic, magically-charged sigils or fetishes.

We may see Dr Johnson, author of the first English dictionary, as a transitional figure. He was a church-going Christian who countenanced the existence of ghosts and on one occasion heard his mother crying out to him over a distance of more than a hundred miles, yet he was one of the apostles of the common-sense view of life that is the ruling philosophy today. Once, walking down a London street, he was challenged to refute the idealism of the philosopher Bishop Berkeley. He kicked a stone by the side of the road and said, 'I refute it thus!'

This new way of looking at things was very bad for religion. If nature obeyed certain

A magus sees a cabalistic vision in his study. Rembrandt created few pictures with explicit esoteric content, but his greatest contribution to the evolution of consciousness was his series of self-portraits. These show more clearly than any other medium the human spirit conscious of its being trapped in an ageing body of flesh.

universal laws that ran along certain straight, predictable tracks, then it was indifferent to the fate of human beings. Life, as Thomas Hobbes put it, is a war of all against all.

THE WASTELAND OF CENTRAL EUROPE following the Thirty Years War became the spiritual wasteland of the Western world. It's possible, if you are so minded, to see the decline of religion with sardonic glee, but for most people the gradual withdrawal of the spirit worlds has been experienced with an increasing sense of alienation. Without the living presence of beings from the higher hierarchies of gods and angels to help them, people were left alone to confront, as we say, their own demons – and demons.

Humanity was entering a new Dark Age. Neo-Solomonic temples sprang up all around the world. The esoteric aim of Freemasonry would be precisely this: to help lead humanity through the age of materialism while keeping the flame of true spirituality alive.

Of course Freemasonry is often thought of as atheistic, particularly by its enemies in the Church, but a Freemason has traditionally sworn an oath to 'study the hidden secrets of Nature and Science in Order the better to know his Maker'.

From the start Freemasons had wanted to discard unthinking religion, false piety and the accretions of centuries of Church practice and dogma, particularly the crude idea of a vindictive father figure. But the higher orders have always sought direct personal experience of the spirit worlds. As philosophers they have always been interested in attempting to define what we can reasonably say about life's spiritual dimension.

As we are about to see, many famous Freemasons of the eighteenth century who are usually thought of as sceptical, if not downright atheistic, were practising alchemists – and some even participated in ceremonial magic. Moreover, some great Freemasons from this period were reincarnations of great personages from the distant past. They were returning to fight in the greatest battle with the forces of evil since the first War in Heaven.

IF SCOTTISH AND ENGLISH FREEMASONS supported a constitutional monarchy working with a democratic parliament, the situation was very different for the American colonies.

George Washington was initiated in 1752.

On 16 December 1773 a group of men, apparently native Indians, played a large part in inspiring the American Revolution. After they had dumped British tea into Boston harbour they hurried back inside St Andrews Masonic Lodge ...

In 1774 Benjamin Franklin met Thomas Paine in a Lodge in London and urged him to emigrate to America. Fond of quoting the words of Isaiah, Paine became the great prophet of Revolution, proposing a federation of states, coining the phrase, 'The United States of America'. He argued for the abolition of slavery and state funding for the education of the poor.

In 1775 members of the Colonial Congress were staying as guests in a house in

Cambridge, Massachusetts. Their aim was to design the American flag. George Washington and Benjamin Franklin were present and so was an old professor, who seemed to be staying there by coincidence. Somewhat to the surprise of the others, Washington and Franklin deferred to the professor. They seemed to recognize him as their superior, immediately and unreservedly, and all of his suggestions for the design of the flag were promptly adopted. Then he vanished and was never seen or heard of again. Was this stranger one of the Hidden Masters who direct the history of the world?

In their individual shape and in the pattern of their arrangement, the five pointed stars on the flag echo the symbols on the ceiling of a chamber in the Egyptian pyramid of Unas. In Egypt they were a symbol of the spirit powers raying down their sustaining and guiding influence on human history.

If we insist, against all the evidence, on seeing Freemasonry as an atheistic organization, spiritual only in an empty, modern sense, we will fail to understand how its leaders felt themselves both prompted by mysterious powers, some incarnated like the old professor, others the disembodied spirits of the stars.

The architecture of Freemasonry grows out of an occult, magical tradition of invoking disembodied spirits that goes back to ancient Egypt. 'When the materials are all prepared and ready,' it is said, 'the architect shall appear.'

On the doors of the Capitol building in Washington, DC, there is a depiction of a Masonic ceremony that took place in 1793, when George Washington laid its cornerstone. If we contemplate Washington's designs for the capital that would bear his name, with this building at its heart, we can begin to understand Freemasonry's secret plans for the age. The key to this understanding – perhaps shockingly for those who would like to see Washington as a model of Christian piety – is astrology.

Freemasonry's interest in astrology had good strong roots in the Royal Society. When Newton was challenged on the subject, he said, 'Sir, I have studied the subject. You have not.' Elias Ashmole had cast a horoscope for the founding of the Royal Exchange in London, soon to become the centre of world finance, as well as for St Paul's Cathedral. When George Washington had a horoscope cast for the founding of the Capitol building he was acting in accordance with a solemn Freemasonic tradition which charted the history of humankind according to the movements of the stars and planets.

For esoteric Freemasons like Wren and Washington, the act of consecrating a cornerstone at an astrologically propitious moment meant inviting the hierarchies of heavenly beings to participate in the ceremony.

It is significant that at the very moment George Washington laid the foundation stone of the Capitol building, Jupiter was rising in the East. The phrase 'Annuit Coeptis' which hovers above the pyramid on the dollar bill is adapted from a line in Virgil's *Aeneid* – 'Jupiter, favour us in our undertaking.'

The phrase 'Novus Ordo Seclorum', also to be found on the dollar bill and which worries conspiracy theorists so much, is also adapted from Virgil. In the *Eclogues* he looks forward to a new age, when the people will be reunited with the gods so there will be no need for religion. The dollar bill, therefore, looks forward to the end of the Catholic Church's world domination and the beginning of a new spiritual era. Replete with esoteric symbolism, it was designed under the aegis of President Roosevelt, a 33rd degree Freemason, who was advised on occult symbolism by his Vice President, Henry Wallace, a fellow Freemason and disciple of the theosophist and artist Nicholas Roerich.

After years of research and having been granted access to the Masonic archives, my old friend David Ovason wrote a magisterial book revealing in all but completely plain terms the esoteric plans that have motivated America's leaders.

David Ovason has shown how the astrological orientation of Washington, DC, marks a complex pattern involving Jupiter, the sun, the moon, Sirius and the constellation of Virgo. He shows that a great triangle of streets with Pennsylvania Avenue as the hypotenuse was intended by Washington and Latrobe to mirror the constellation of Virgo. He shows, further, that in a spectacular light display to rival the greatest achievements of the Egyptians, Washington, DC, is laid out so that on 3 August every year the sun streams down Pennsylvania Avenue and strikes the pyramidion on the top of the Post Office tower.

It requires a whole book – David's book – to give a full account. What is important to this history, and helps us to begin to pull its main themes together, is that Washington, DC was laid out to welcome Isis, the goddess associated with Virgo.

Washington, then, built his city under the sign of Virgo, inviting the Mother Goddess to participate in the destiny of the United States.

We've seen that secret techniques for achieving altered states are taught inside secret societies. Different grades of initiation that lead to different levels of altered state. Higher levels may grant the gift of prophecy. Great initiates have such an all-embracing knowledge of the higher spirits and their plans for humanity that they are able to work consciously towards helping the fulfilment of those plans.

Initiates from different esoteric traditions and different parts of the world had been predicting the dawn of a new age. Joachim, Dee and Paracelsus prophesied the return of Elijah, working behind the scenes of history to help humankind become strong enough to face the trials that it would have to face. By inviting the Mother Goddess to participate in the destiny of the United States, Washington was also looking forward to a new age, a new dispensation. The United States would dominate the world – if Washington's great prayers in stone were answered and the ancient prophecies came true.

Abbot Trithemius, influenced by Joachim and influencing in his turn both Cornelius Agrippa and Paracelsus, had predicted that the epoch of Gabriel, the Archangel of the

Cleopatra's Needle shortly before its transportation to London.

Moon, would be succeeded by the epoch of Michael, Archangel of the Sun. He predicted that this great event would take place in 1881.

We saw in Chapter 3 how St Michael had fought the good fight against the forces of evil, leading the hosts of the good angels. The Freemasons of the eighteenth and nineteenth centuries foresaw that St Michael, Archangel of the Sun, would come again.

Michael was coming to fight the forces of corrupted angels and demons that were predicted to assault the earth in the late nineteenth and early twentieth centuries.

Michael's defeat of these forces – with human help – was to lead to the end of the Kali Yuga, the Dark Age of the Hindus, which had begun in 3102 BC with the murder of Krishna. The Yugas are astronomically determined, there being eight divisions of the Great Year.

In fact the initiate astrologers of the Freemasons realized that Trithemius had made a small mistake in his astronomical/astrological calculations and that the Michaelic age was due to begin in 1878. All around the world, as this year approached, Freemasons were planning to erect monuments. Above all they planned to erect obelisks.

The Egyptians saw the obelisk as a sacred structure on which the Phoenix would alight to mark the end of one civilization and the beginning of another. An obelisk is a symbol of the birth of a new age. Like a gigantic lightning conductor, it draws down the spiritual influence of the sun.

Constantine the Great had converted a temple in Alexandria into a church, reconsecrating the obelisks sacred to Thoth or Hermes that stood outside it to the Archangel Michael. In 1877 Freemasons on both sides of the Atlantic worked to transport these two obelisks by sea, one to London where it was to be raised on the Victoria Embankment overlooking the Thames – and popularly known as Cleopatra's Needle. There it was to

Drawing of a bust of Albert Pike, Grand Master and initiate. The Masonic star with thirty-three rays is prominently displayed on public monuments at the centre of cities all round the world. We have found the number thirty-three encoded in the works of Bacon, Shakespeare and in the Rosicrucian Manifestoes. It is encoded on the tombs of Shakespeare and Fludd, translator of the Authorized Version of the Bible. Jesus Christ lived thirty-three years. The significance of this number is one of the oldest and most closely guarded secrets of esoteric philosophy. Thirty-three is the rhythm of the vegetative realm of the cosmos, the dimension that controls the interactions between the spirit worlds and the material world. The closest to an explicit reference to it perhaps comes in Ovid's Metamorphoses, *where the murdered Caesar's spirit is described exiting by his thirty-three wounds. The secret of thirty-three refers to the number of gateways by which the human spirit may travel between the material world and the spirit worlds. Practical knowledge of these pathways is known only to initiates of the highest level, because it enables them to slip unobtrusively in and out of the material realm.*

be raised on 13 September 1878 when the sun was at its zenith. Its twin obelisk was raised in New York's Central Park, organized by a group of Freemasons led by members of the Vanderbilt family.

Michael was, as we have seen, the leader of the heavenly hosts, and the transition from one order to another is always marked by battles. And because what happens on earth is always an echo of what has happened earlier in the spirit worlds, a great war would be fought in the heavens before being fought down here on the earthly plane. As Freemasons erected an obelisk in Central Park, New York, they were invoking St Michael and all his angels, asking for their help as they sought to establish the leadership of the United States among the nations in the war-torn age that would soon be dawning.

IT MAY ALREADY HAVE OCCURRED TO some readers that obelisks are placed with similar prominence in ecclesiastical contexts, for example the obelisk erected by the initiate artist Gianlorenzo Bernini in the square in front of St Peter's in Rome.

The upper echelons of the Church hierarchy wish to keep its flock from *conscious* knowledge of the astral roots of their religion.

But these monuments work on different levels. They attract the disembodied beings of spiritual hierarchies. They work on people at levels below the conscious one, levels where the great disembodied beings weave in and out of their mental space. Initiates inside and outside the Church create great works of art and architecture to help condition humanity for its future evolution.

They also carry enough clues for those who are so minded as to be able to decode them.

25

The Mystical-Sexual Revolution

Cardinal Richelieu • Cagliostro • The Secret Identity of the Comte de St Germain • Swedenborg, Blake and the Sexual Roots of Romanticism

... HOWEVER, IN THE MIDDLE OF THE eighteenth century the rise to supremacy of the United States was only a mystical vision. In the late seventeenth and eighteenth centuries France became the most powerful and influential nation. Extremes of good and evil, rapier and sharp tongue, decided the fate of the world in the corridors of the Louvre, then Versailles.

It is perhaps significant that, though Descartes spent many years researching the Rosicrucians, even journeying to Germany to try to track them down, he never succeeded. A prey to visions, he was evidently not, like Newton, adept at alchemical techniques that might give repeated, perhaps even controlled, access to the spirit worlds.

In collaboration with the mathematician and theologian Marin Mersenne, whose patron was Richelieu, Descartes developed a rationalist philosophy, a closed system of reasoning without the necessity of reference to the realm of the senses.

The philosophy of Descartes and Mersenne helped evolve a new form of cynicism. It enabled a succession of French diplomats and politicians to run rings round their opposite numbers. They might wear similar, though rather more fashionable clothes than the ones worn by their contemporaries in Germany, Italy, Holland, Spain or England, but the difference in consciousness was as drastic as that between the Conquistadors and the Aztecs.

The French court was the most magnificent in human history, not only in material terms, but in the sophistication of its culture. Beautiful and heartless, it wittily interpreted all human actions as motivated by vanity, according to the maxims of La Rochefoucauld. 'When we dwell on the good qualities of others, we are expressing esteem for our own finer feelings' is one of his sly, devastating critiques of human nature. 'No matter

Et in Arcadia Ego *by Nicholas Poussin. Poussin's connection with the Rennes-le-Château mystery has led to much speculation on his esoteric interests. But to look for Rosicrucian interests, as some have done, is to bark up the wrong tree. Poussin's spiritual mentor was the Jesuit Athanasius Kircher, perhaps the greatest scholar of esoterica in the seventeenth century. As the most learned Egyptologist of the day, Kircher was concerned to verify the perennial philosophy and universal secret history encoded in Egyptian texts, the Bible and the classical tradition, represented here by an allusion to an episode in Virgil. What the crouching shepherd is pointing to – on a tomb which existed in Poussin's time, though it has recently been destroyed – is an inscription that confirms the secret history in this book.* Even I was in Arcadia *refers to the turning point in history described in Chapter 5, when the idyllic vegetative life of humanity was invaded by animal desire and death. This was the Fall of the Mother Goddess. In esoteric Christianity Mary Magdalene was the incarnation of the goddess, redeemed by her Beloved. As we saw, Mary Magdalene spent the last years of her life in the south of France, according to Church tradition. What Poussin was literally pointing to here, therefore, was* the tomb of Mary Magdalene.

how well we are spoken of,' he said, 'we learn nothing we do not already know.' In the gap left by the departure of sincerity arose a tyranny of taste and style.

As spirituality was severed from sexuality, libertines like Choderlos de Laclos, author of *Les Liaisons Dangereuses*, said to be a spider at the centre of a vast web of sexual and political intrigue, Crebillon fils, author of the best of the libertine novels, *Les Egarements du Coeur et de l'Esprit*, Casanova and de Sade became representative men, admired for the complexity and cleverness of their power plays.

In all sex there is an element of striving. Now this striving became an end itself. Even among the most sensitive and intelligent, sex could be reduced to an exercise of power.

Following Cardinal Richelieu's unprincipled machinations to promote national interests in the reign of Louis XIII, Louis XIV aggregated to himself the title of Sun King – but of course there was a dark side. While *haute cuisine* was devised to keep nobles contented at court, peasants were taxed to the point of starvation and Richelieu massacred religious dissenters. Later Marie Antoinette would be shielded from sight of the sick, old or poor, and Louis XVI obsessively read and reread an account of the beheading of Charles I, drawing to himself the thing he feared most.

Rumours of powerful, esoteric secrets echoed round the court. Cardinal Richelieu carried a wand of gold and ivory and enemies feared its magic powers. His mentor Père Joseph, the original *eminence grise*, taught him spiritual exercises that developed psychic powers. He employed a cabalist called Gaffarel to teach him the secrets of the occult. A man called Du-boy, or Duboys, rumoured to be a descendant of Nicholas Flamel, went to see him carrying an obscurely phrased magical primer. But Du-boy was unable to interpret it for the Cardinal and get him results, and so Du-boy was hanged. It seems Richelieu became desperate to achieve the breakthrough to the other side that he craved, because he employed increasingly extreme methods. Urban Grandier, an alleged devil-worshipper, was being slowly tortured to death at Richelieu's behest, when he is reported to have warned: 'You are an able man, do not destroy yourself.'

Louis XIV's mistress, Madame de Montespan, caused her young rival to die by means of a Black Mass.

One of Louis XIV's doctors, called Lesebren, gave a strange account of what happened to a friend of his who had concocted what he believed to be the elixir of life. He had started to take a few drops every morning at sunrise with a glass of wine. After fourteen days his hair and nails began to fall out, and he lost his nerve. He started giving the potion to an elderly female servant, but she too became frightened and refused to continue. So finally he started an old hen on a course of this medicine, by soaking corn with it. After six days its feathers began to fall out until it became completely naked. Then two weeks later new feathers began to grow brighter and more beautifully coloured than the feathers she had had in her youth, and she began to lay eggs again.

Amid extremes of cynicism and gullibility, where quacks and frauds were common, genuine initiates developed ways of presenting themselves to the outside world. Esoteric teachers had always known their wisdom looked foolish to the uninitiated. They had always focused on the tricky paradoxical nature of the cosmos. Now initiates began to present themselves in the guise of tricksters and scoundrels.

A poor boy from the backstreets of Sicily reinvented himself as Count Cagliostro. By a mixture of mesmeric charm, his habit of using as bait Seraphita, his beautiful young wife, and above all his rumoured possession of the philosopher's stone, he rose to the top of European society.

To those at the bottom of society he seemed some kind of saint. Healing miracles performed among the poor of Paris, unable to afford a doctor, made him a popular hero, and when, after a short imprisonment, he was released from the Bastille, some eight thousand people came to cheer. When Cagliostro was challenged to a debate in front of his intellectual peers, his opponent Court de Gébelin, a friend of Benjamin Franklin's and a renowned expert on esoteric philosophy, soon admitted he was up against a man whose erudition far surpassed his own.

Cagliostro also seems to have had remarkable powers of prophecy. In a famous letter of 20 June 1786 he prophesied that the Bastille would be completely destroyed, and it is said that he even predicted the exact date of this event – 14 July – in graffiti found inscribed on the wall of the prison cell in which he died.

Anyone with supernatural power is bound to suffer temptation. Perhaps the most charismatic and disconcerting initiate of the twentieth century was G.I. Gurdjieff. He deliberately presented his ideas in an absurd way. He wrote of an organ at the base of the spine that could enable everyone to see everything upside down and inside out, calling it the 'Kunderbuffer'. In this way he deliberately gave the power of the kundalini serpent, the reserve of unredeemed energy that lies coiled at the base of the spine, and which is central to Tantric practice, a laughable name. Similarly he wrote of gods in giant spaceships and that the surface of the sun is cool. Anyone who dismissed it showed himself unworthy. Anyone who persisted and was able to tune in found that Gurdjieff's spiritual disciplines worked.

Since his death it has emerged that he sometimes used his undoubted powers of mind control to prey on vulnerable young women.

A friend of mine journeyed to India, to visit the renowned teacher, adept and miracle-worker Sai Baba. My friend was travelling with his beautiful young girlfriend. After an exquisite dinner the servants withdrew and Sai Baba took his guests into the library. My friend was perusing a book while his girlfriend talked to Sai Baba. He noticed that he was standing unusually close to her and became anxious when Sai Baba turned the conversation to the subject of the sexual dimension in Hindu myths. Suddenly Sai Baba reached to ring a copper bell engraved with sigils and simultaneously seemed to grab something out of mid-air. He turned his hand palm up to reveal a golden chain with a crucifix on it. He told the girl that this was real magic and held his palm out to her, offering her the object, which seemed to my friend to glow with a dark aura.

He also noticed that the sigils on the bell were Tantric, and realized that the intention was probably to bewitch his girlfriend with a view to seducing her. He asked where the chain came from.

'It appeared before your very eyes,' said Sai Baba.

My friend took the chain from him, to prevent his girlfriend from touching it. Holding it over his palm, he used the art of psychometry to determine its origins. He had a disturbing vision of grave robbers, and realized that this crucifix and chain had been dug up from the grave of a Jesuit missionary.

He confronted Sai Baba with this and so, by demonstrating his own magical powers, he was able to make him back down.

Telling me about this many years later, my friend said that since Prospero had broken his wand at the end of *The Tempest*, initiates had been forbidden to exercise their magical powers, unless in exceptional circumstances like these. There is a law that if a white magician uses his occult power, an equal amount of power is made available to a black magician.

Is there any other evidence to suggest that magic is still practised today? In a second-hand bookshop in Tunbridge Wells I recently came across a small cache of letters in which an occultist gave out advice on how to use magic spells to achieve their goals. One included introducing menstrual blood secretly into food as a way of awakening a man's sexual desires. This might seem outlandish, but in 2006 the British government announced its plans to give large grants for the development of 'biodynamic' farming. This method, devised by Rudolf Steiner, depends on the correspondences between plants and the spirits of the stars described by Paracelsus and Boehme. Steiner recommends that an infestation of field mice should be dealt with by burying in the field the ashes of a field mouse prepared when Venus is in the sign of Scorpio.

IF CAGLIOSTRO REMAINS AN ENIGMA, the man he looked up to is an even greater mystery.

Cagliostro's own account of meeting the Comte de St Germain at a castle in Germany in 1785 records that he and his wife arrived at 2 a.m, the appointed time. The drawbridge lowered and they crossed to find themselves in a small, darkened room. Suddenly, as if by magic, great doors opened to reveal a vast temple made dazzling by the lights of thousands of candles. In the middle of the temple sat the Comte de St Germain. He was wearing many fabulous diamond rings and on his chest there rested a bejewelled device that seemed to reflect the light of all the candles and beam it on Cagliostro and Seraphita. Sitting either side of St Germain two acolytes held up bowls from which incense arose, and, as Cagliostro entered, a disembodied voice he took to be count's – though his lips did not seem to move – resonated around the temple.

'Who are you? Where did you come from? What do you want?'

Of course in at least one sense St Germain knew exactly who Cagliostro was – the visit had been pre-arranged, after all – but here he was asking about his previous incarnations, his daemon, his deeper motives.

Cagliostro threw himself on the ground in front of St Germain, and after a while said, 'I come to invoke the God of the Faithful, the Son of Nature, the Father of Truth. I come to ask one of the fourteen thousand and seven secrets he bears in his bosom. I come to give myself up as his slave, his apostle, his martyr.'

Clearly Cagliostro thought he recognized St Germain, but *who was he*?

There was a clue in the fact that St Germain then initiated Cagliostro into *Templar* mysteries, taking him on an out of body journey, flying him above a molten sea of bronze to explore the heavenly hierarchies.

St Germain had appeared in European society quite suddenly in 1710, apparently from Hungary and seemingly about fifty years old. Small and dark skinned, he always wore black clothes and extraordinary diamonds. His most arresting features were his hypnotic eyes. By all accounts he quickly commanded attention in society because of his accomplishments, speaking many languages, playing the violin and painting. And he also seemed to have an extraordinary ability to read minds.

He was believed to practise secret breathing techniques taught by the Hindu fakirs and, in order to meditate better, he adopted yoga positions unknown in the West at that time. Though he attended banquets, he was never seen eating in front of others and drank only a strange herbal tea he concocted himself.

But the greatest mystery surrounding the Comte de St Germain was his longevity. Having appeared in public life in 1710, apparently in late middle age, when he met the composer Rameau in Venice, he remained in public life at least as late as 1782 *without appearing to age at all*. Sightings of him by the great and the good continued as late as 1822.

It would be tempting to dismiss all this as a romance in the style of Alexander Dumas were it not for the fact that witnesses who left accounts of meeting him over such a long period were of such high standing. As well as Rameau, they included Voltaire, Horace Walpole, Clive of India and Casanova. He was a prominent figure at the court of Louis XV, an intimate of both Madame de Pompadour and the king himself, for whom he took diplomatic missions in Moscow, Constantinople and London. There in 1761 he negotiated an agreement called the Family Compact, which paved the way for the Treaty of Paris, putting an end to the colonial wars between France and Britain. St Germain's efforts always seemed to be in the cause of peace, and, though he is often lumped in with Cagliostro, he was never caught out in any act of dishonesty. Although nobody knew where his money came from – some said alchemy – he was evidently independently wealthy and by no means a desperate adventurer.

So who was the Comte de St Germain? A key to his secret identity lies in Freemasonic history. It is said that it was he who coined the Freemasonic mantra Liberty, Equality, Fraternity, and whether or not this is accurate, he may be seen as the living spirit of esoteric Freemasonry.

More particularly, St Germain should be identified with another personality beset by rumour, counter-rumour and uncertainty about whether he really lived at all. *In the secret history St Germain is Christian Rosenkreuz reincarnated* in the age of enlightenment, of imperial expansion and international diplomacy.

To borrow a phrase from the eminent science fiction writer and esotericist Philip K. Dick, he had learned how to reconstitute his body after death.

This should alert us to an even deeper mystery. In an earlier incarnation Rosenkreuz/Germain had been Hiram Abiff, the Master Builder of Solomon's Temple. The

La Très Sainte Trinsophie *is a booklet often attributed to St Germain and which certainly comes from the same school of occult Freemasonry. It is an avowed account of initiation, in which the candidate descends into the volcanic bowels of the earth, and passes the night there. At dawn he climbs out of his underground chamber, following a star. He is freed of his material body and flies up to the planets where he meets 'the old man of the palace'. In the palace he sleeps for seven days and, when he awakes, his robe is changed to beautiful, scintillating green. Then there is a strange passage in which he sees a bird with butterfly wings and knows he must catch it. He drives a steel nail through its wings, so that it is pinned down, but its eyes grow bright. Finally, in a hall with a beautiful, naked woman, he stabs the sun with his sword. The sun shatters into dust and each atom of dust becomes a sun in itself. The Work is completed. This depiction of a portal is by Paolo Veronese, believed by Theosophists to be an incarnation of one of the Hidden Masters.*

murder of Hiram Abiff had led to the Word's being lost. On one level the lost Word was a power of supernatural procreation which humankind had wielded before the Fall into matter. Part of the mission of St Germain, through esoteric Freemasonry, was the reintroduction of knowledge of the Word into the stream of history.

The deepest mystery of this individuality, though, concerns an even earlier incarnation from the time when human bodies were on the borderline of becoming solid flesh. Enoch was the earliest prophet of the Sun god, a man whose face shone with a sun-like radiance.

When St Germain took Cagliostro on a tour of the heavens they were going on the tour described in the *Book of Enoch*. In the phrase Liberty, Equality, Fraternity, St Germain looked forward to a time when humanity would reach out to the Sun god with freedom of thought and will, as they had failed to do the first time He came.

The secret history of the world from the late sixteenth century to the nineteenth century is dominated by the work behind the scenes of the great ascended masters of Western tradition, Enoch and Elijah, and by preparations for the descent from the skies of the Archangel of the Sun – and, beyond this, for the descent of an even greater being.

These men were preparing the way for the Second Coming.

AS THE EIGHTEENTH CENTURY PROGRESSED, sightings of the mysterious count become rarer, but a mood of optimism and expectation filled the lodges of the secret societies. In France 'the Unknown Philosopher', St Martin, was teaching that 'every man is a king'. Chevalier Ramsay, the Scottish laird who had founded a Grand Lodge in Paris in 1730, made a speech to new initiates in Paris in 1737: 'The whole world is nothing but a great republic. We strive for the reunion of all people of an enlightened mind ... not only through the love of the fine arts, but even more through the elevated principles of virtue, science and religion, in which the interests of the brotherhood and that of the entire family of humankind can meet each other ... and from which the subjects of all kingdoms can learn to love each other.'

Freemasonry provided a protected space for the tolerant discussion of ideas, for free scientific enquiry and for investigation into the spirit worlds.

Following the establishment of mother lodges in Scotland, London and Paris, the great event of Freemasonry in the eighteenth century took place in the 1760s. This was the founding of the Order of Elus Coens (or 'chosen priests') by the Portuguese magus Martines de Pasqually. The rituals of the Elus Coens, devised by de Pasqually, were sometimes up to six hours long and involved an incense that blended hallucinogens and fly agaric mushroom spores. In the later rituals of Stanislas de Guaita, much influenced by de Pasqually, a blindfold was removed and the candidate might find himself facing men wearing Egyptian masks and headdresses who silently pointed swords at his chest.

In the way that Dr Dee had worked to bring back real spiritual experience into the

Church by the practice of ceremonial magic, men like de Pasqually and Cagliostro did the same in Freemasonry. In 1782 Cagliostro founded Egyptian Right Freemasonry, which would be highly influential in both France and America.

De Pasqually's pupil and successor, St Martin, placed less emphasis on ceremony and more on internal, esoteric disciplines. Influenced in this by his reading of Boehme, his version of Martinist philosophy has remained highly influential in French Freemasonry to this day. Living in Paris at the time of the Terror, St Martin allowed men and women to come to his apartment, initiating them by a mystical laying on of hands. They were in such peril that they continued to wear their masks even during their meetings in order to hide their identities even from one another.

Famous for his genially excoriating attacks on religion, Voltaire is often thought of as a God-hater. In reality, it was organized religion he was against. When he was initiated by Benjamin Franklin, he was given the apron belonging to Helvetius to kiss. Helvetius was the famous Swiss scientist whose account of alchemical transmutation remains the second most highly authenticated account after that of Leibniz.

The historian of Freemasonry and mystical experience A.E. Waite wrote of Masonry's 'dreams of antique science, proclaiming that the reality behind dreams must be sought in the spirit of dreams'. He talked of Voltaire as the man 'who held the keys – who had forged the key – which opened up the door to this reality and unfolded amazing vistas of possibility ... Condemned practices, forbidden arts might lead through some clouds of mystery into the light of knowledge.' We will see more clearly what this means in the next chapter, but for the moment it is enough to say that the initiates of the secret societies were amazed by these new vistas.

Their breasts were full of such faith and optimism that they would undoubtedly have agreed with Wordsworth that bliss was it that dawn to be alive.

Among the artists, writers and composers of the secret societies this great wealth of enthusiasm and these expectations of the dawn of a new age gave rise to the Romantic movement. Whenever there is a great flowering of imaginative art and literature, as, for example, in the Renaissance and Romanticism, we should suspect the presence somewhere in the shadows of sacred idealism as a philosophy of life and of the secret societies which cultivate that philosophy.

THIS HAS BEEN A HISTORY OF THE WORLD according to idealism – if we take idealism in its philosophical sense of proposing that ideas are more real than objects. Idealism in the more common, colloquial sense – meaning living according to high ideals – was, as George Steiner has pointed out, an invention of the nineteenth century.

In the previous century the lodges of England, America and France had worked to create societies that were less cruel, superstitious and ignorant, less repressive and prejudiced and more tolerant. The world had become all of these things – and also more insincere and frivolous.

Even before the Terror there was disquiet, an anxiety that, although society might be made to run along straight lines, this enterprise was adequate neither to human nature nor to other, darker forces operating outside the laws of nature. Romanticism was partly an attempt to come to terms with a galvanic feeling of intensity rising up from below and what today we would call the unconscious. It would give rise to intense music and poetry. It would be impatient of convention, encouraging spontaneity and self-abandon.

In the land of Eckhart various writers saw France in particular as a land of 'soulless little dancing masters who did not understand the inner life of man'. In Lessing, Schlegel and Schiller philosophical idealism became a philosophy of life once more. Above all, this idealism would exalt the imagination, holding the mystical and esoteric belief that the imagination is a higher mode of perception than that offered by the senses. Imagination can be trained to grasp higher realities than the materialism being peddled by the apostles of common sense.

In conventional history Romanticism was a reaction to the polite, ordered eighteenth century. In the secret history it was demonic forces, rather than merely subconscious forces, that caused this reaction.

The roots of this reaction were sexual.

IN JULY 1744 JOHN PAUL BROCKMER, a London watchmaker, worried what on earth was wrong with his lodger. Emmanuel Swedenborg, a Swedish engineer, had seemed a quiet, respectable character, attending the local Moravian chapel every Sunday.

Now his hair stood on end. He foamed at the mouth and chased Brockmer down the street, gibbering and apparently claiming to be the Messiah. Brockmer tried to persuade him to see a doctor but instead Swedenborg went to the Swedish embassy. When they wouldn't let him in, he ran to a nearby drainage ditch, undressed himself and rolled around in the mud, throwing money at the crowd.

In a recent breakthrough book, the fruit of years of meticulous research, Marsha Keith Suchard reveals that Swedenborg had been experimenting with certain sexual techniques for achieving extreme altered states of consciousness that were taught at the outwardly respectable Moravian chapel. Marsha Keith Suchard also shows that William Blake was brought up in this church and that these sexual practices inspired his poetry.

We have touched on various techniques for inducing altered states, including breathing exercises, dancing and meditation. But these sexual techniques are the hard stuff, the most closely guarded secrets of the secret societies. It's instructive, then, to follow with Marsha Keith Suchard the different stages of development of Swedenborg's practice, as recorded in his journals and alluded to in his publications.

Even as a boy Swedenborg had experimented with breath control. He noticed that if he held his breath for long periods, he went into a sort of trance. He discovered, too, that by synchronizing his breath to his pulse he could deepen the trance. 'Sometimes I was reduced into a state of insensibility as to the body senses, thus almost unto the state of dying persons, retaining however my interior life unimpaired, attended with the power of thinking and with sufficient breathing for life.' Persistence in these techniques could bring practitioners great rewards ... 'there is a certain cheering light and joyful, confirmatory brightness that plays around the sphere of the mind, and a kind of mysterious radiation ... that darts through some temple in the brain ... the soul is called into a more inward communion, and has returned at that moment into the golden age of its intellectual perfections. The mind ... in the kindling flame of its love despises all in comparison ... all merely corporeal pleasures.' Swedenborg seems to be describing different stages of altered states of the kind we have seen involved in the process of initiation. As Marsha Keith has pointed out, modern neurological research has confirmed that meditation increases the levels of DHEAS and melatonin, secretions produced by the pineal and pituitary glands which together are said by occultists to create the Third Eye.

At the age of fifteen Swedenborg was sent to live with his brother-in-law, who for the next seven years would be his mentor, and it was here at his new home that Swedenborg's own researches turned markedly cabalistic.

We have seen how in the Cabala, as in all esoteric traditions, the creation is conceived of in terms of a series of emanations (sephiroth, or servants) from the cosmic mind. In the Cabala, as much as in the myths of the Greeks and Romans, these emanations are thought of as male and female. The En Sof, the unattainable cosmic mind, emanates male and female spirits, and these intertwine in a sexual way as the impulse of creation spirals downwards. In the same way that erotic images in the mind create sperm, the En Sof's acts of loving imagination generate physical effects. *The imagination – and particularly the sexually-fired imagination – is therefore seen to be the root principle of creativity.*

On this cabalistic account, the Fall happened because of an imbalance which occurred between the male and female sephiroth. By imagining balanced and harmonious love-making between the sephiroth, the adept helps set right this primordial cosmic wrong.

In cabalistic lore the Cherubim arching their wings above the Ark of the Holy Covenant in the Holy of Holies in the Jerusalem Temple were seen as an image of the harmonious love-making of the male and female sephiroth. Then when the second Temple was sacked by Antiochus in 168 BC, these erotic images were paraded through the streets to ridicule the Jews. When the Temple was destroyed in AD 70, a great need arose in the heart of the people to rebuild it. Sacred imagery of the love-making of the male and female sephira lay at the heart of a programme to right a *historical* wrong.

Swedenborg also wrote about rhythmic breathing methods relating to the pulse of the genitals. It is evident that, while living with his father's brother-in-law, he began to practise such exercises in breath control in conjunction with the imagining of naked human bodies contorted erotically into the shapes of Hebrew letters already alluded to. These were believed to be powerful magical emblems or sigils. Similar techniques of taking sexual energies and using them as a force for spiritual good are used by some Hasidic groups today. Bob Dylan, who is in some way heir to the poetic tradition of Blake, has explored some of these practices.

The element of control is crucial to these practices and this was emphasized in another esoteric tradition of sexually charged spirituality. The expansion of European empires eastwards had caused rumours of Tantric practices to trickle back in the other direction. Swedenborg explored sexual tantra in detail. Psychological discipline was needed to achieve prolonged arousal. This in turn was needed to redirect sexual energies to the brain and thereby achieve a breakthrough into the spirit worlds, a visionary ecstasy rather than a narrowly sexual one. Swedenborg also mastered what is by all accounts an extremely difficult technique of muscle control known to Indian adepts, whereby at the moment of ejaculation the sperm is diverted to the bladder and therefore not expelled.

Clearly the techniques are dangerous – one of the reasons why they are kept so secret. They risk the sort of nervous breakdown witnessed by Swedenborg's landlord, not to mention madness and death.

The peculiar admixture to his researches that Swedenborg discovered while attending the Moravian church in New Fetter Lane was a specifically Christian version of the arcana of love. At that time Moravians in London were under the sway of the charismatic Count Zizendorf. Members of the congregation were encouraged by him to visualize, smell and touch in imagination the side wound in the body of Christ. This wound was, in Zizendorf's vision, a sweet, luscious vagina oozing a magical juice. The spear of Longinus was to be thrust repeatedly and ecstatically into it.

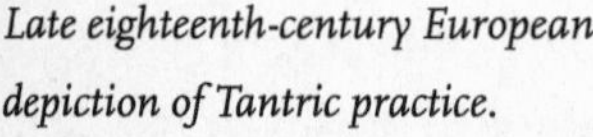

Late eighteenth-century European depiction of Tantric practice.

Zizendorf encouraged sex as a sacramental act and urged his followers to see the divine, spiritual emanations in each other at the moment of climax. A joint mental prayer at this moment has particular magical force. As Swedenborg put it, 'partner sees partner in mind ... each partner has the other in himself' so they 'cohabit in their innermost'. In a visionary trance partners were able to meet, communicate, even make love in their dismembered, spiritual forms.

Marsha Keith Suchard records that Blake's parents were members of this congregation and that Blake absorbed these ideas from his wide reading of Swedenborg. She has shown how the prudish Victorians erased from Blake's drawings much explicitly sexual imagery – including drawing pairs of underpants over genitals. Although there is a popular understanding that Blake was influenced by the esoteric philosophy of Swedenborg and others, we have until now overlooked these very specific techniques of sex magic that were at the root of his imaginative vision.

Blake experienced visions from an early age. At the age of four he saw God looking in through the window, and at four or five, while walking through the countryside, he had a vision of a tree filled with angels 'bespangling every bough like stars'. But it seems that the secret techniques of Zizendorf and Swedenborg gave him a systematic, cabalistic approach to these phenomena.

In *Los* he would write, 'In Beulah the Female lets down her beautiful Tabernacle Which the Male enters magnificent between her Cherubim And becomes One with her mingling ... There's a place where Contraries are equally true, This place is called Beulah.'

In Romanticism the individual interior life has finally expanded to become a vast cosmos of infinite variety. Love is the love of one cosmos for another. Deep calls unto deep. With Romanticism love moves into a new mode and becomes symphonic.

The historical significance of this is that the secret meditations and prayerful practices of a handful of initiates created a popular surge of feeling against materialism. A new way of making love, of re-enacting the creation of the cosmos, was a way of saying that right isn't simply a matter of might, that there are higher ideals than expediency or enlightened egotism, that if you work yourself into the right frame of mind, you can experience the world as meaningful.

If the people make love so that they become illumined, the world will become a world of shadows. When they awake again, meaning will have settled on the world like dew.

THE ROOTS OF ROMANTICISM, therefore, were both sexual and esoteric. The German poet Novalis talked of 'magical idealism'. This magic, this idealism, this volcanic spirit, conjured up the music of Beethoven and Schubert. Beethoven found himself hearing a new musical language, feeling and expressing things that had never been felt or expressed before. Like Alexander the Great he became obsessed with trying to identify this divine influx, the source of his unstoppable genius, reading and rereading Egyptian and Indian esoteric texts. For him his Sonata in D Minor and the Appassionata were his equivalents to Shakespeare's *The Tempest*, the most explicit expressions of his occult ideas.

In France the Martinist Charles Nodier had written of the conspiracies of secret societies in the armies of Napoleon to bring the great man down. Later Nodier introduced the young French Romantics, including Victor Hugo, Honoré de Balzac, Dumas *fils*, Delacroix and Gérard de Nerval, to esoteric philosophy.

Owen Barfield wrote that there is always a great current of Platonic ideas, a current of living meaning that from time to time fine intellects like Shakespeare and Keats can discern. Keats called the ability to do this 'Negative Capability', which he said was when a man is capable of being 'in uncertainties, mysteries and doubtes without any irritable searching after fact and reason'. In other words he was applying to poetry the same deliberate holding off imposing a pattern and waiting for a richer pattern to emerge that Francis Bacon had advocated in the scientific sphere.

'Weave a circle around him thrice ... /For he on honey-dew hath fed, /And drunk the milk, of Paradise.' Samuel Taylor Coleridge carried an aura of the supernatural. He was deeply immersed in the thought of both Boehme and Swedenborg. But it was his friend William Wordsworth who wrote the purest, the most simple and direct expression of the feeling that lies at the heart of idealism as a philosophy of life. When Wordsworth wrote that he 'felt /A presence that disturbs me with the joy/Of elevated thoughts; a sense sublime/Of something far more deeply interfused,/Whose dwelling is the light of setting suns,/And the round ocean, and the living air,/and the blue sky, and in the mind of man,/ A motion and a spirit, that impels,/All thinking things, all objects of all thought,/And rolls through all things ...' he is writing about what it feels like to be an idealist in a way which still feels quite modern.

Even people who on a conscious level would deny the existence of the higher reality Wordsworth is alluding to here, recognize something in this poem, *Lines Written Above Tintern Abbey*. Something, somewhere inside them, calls out in recognition, or it would be completely meaningless to them.

At the time that Wordsworth was writing, people did not have to struggle to discern such feelings. Goethe, Byron and Beethoven led a great popular movement.

So why did it all go wrong? Why did this impulse for freedom end up in the abuse of power?

To understand the roots of this catastrophe it is necessary to trace the infiltration of the secret societies by the proponents of materialism. Chevalier Ramsay had specifically forbidden the discussion of politics in the lodges he founded in 1730, but Freemasonry had a hold on the political leaders of Europe. To anyone who wanted to exert political influence, it must have been a temptation.

26

The Illuminati and the Rise of Unreason

The Illuminati and the Battle for the Soul of Freemasonry • Occult Roots of the French Revolution • Napoleon's Star • Occultism and the Rise of the Novel

THE STORY OF THE ILLUMINATI IS ONE of the darker episodes in the secret history and it has blackened the reputation of secret societies ever since.

In 1776 a Bavarian professor of law, Adam Weishaupt, founded an organization called the Illuminati, recruiting the first brothers from among his students.

Like the Jesuits, the Illuminati brotherhood was run on military lines. Members were requested to surrender individual judgement and will. Like earlier secret societies Weishaupt's Illuminati promised to reveal an ancient wisdom. Higher and more powerful secrets were promised to those who progressed up the ladder of initiations. Initiates worked in small cells. Knowledge was shared between cells on what modern security services call a 'need to know' basis – so dangerous was this newly rediscovered knowledge.

Weishaupt joined the Freemasons in 1777, and soon many of the Illuminati followed, infiltrating the lodges. They quickly rose to positions of seniority.

Then in 1785 it came about that a man called Jacob Lanz, travelling to Silesia, was struck by lightning. When he was laid out in a nearby chapel, the Bavarian authorities found papers on the body revealing the secret plans of the Illuminati. From these papers, including many in Weishaupt's own hand, and together with others seized in raids around the country, a complete picture was built up.

The seized writings revealed that the ancient secret wisdom and the secret supernatural powers promulgated within the Illuminati had always been a cynical invention and a fraud. An aspirant progressed through the grades only to discover that the spiritual element in the teachings were merely a smokescreen. Spirituality was derided, spat upon. Jesus Christ's teachings, it was said, were really purely political in content, calling for the abolition of all property, of the institution of marriage and all family ties, all religion. The aim of Weishaupt and his co-conspirators was to set up a society run on purely materialistic grounds, a revolutionary new society – and the place where they would test their theories, they had decided, would be France.

Finally it was whispered in the candidate's ear that *the ultimate secret was that there was no secret.*

In this way he was inducted into a nihilistic and anarchistic philosophy that appealed to the candidate's worst instincts. Weishaupt gleefully anticipated tearing down, destroying civilization, not to set people free, but for the pleasure of imposing his will upon others.

Weishaupt's writings reveal the extent of his cynicism:

'... in concealment lies a great part of our strength. For this reason we must cover ourselves in the name of another society. The lodges that are under Freemasonry are the most suitable cloak for our high purpose.'

'Seek the society of young people,' he advises one of his co-conspirators. 'Watch them, and if one of them pleases you, lay your hand on him.'

'Do you realize sufficiently what it means to rule – to rule in a secret society? Not only over the more important of the populace, but over the best men, over men of all races, nations and religions, to rule without external force ... the final aim of our Society is nothing less than to win power and riches ... and to obtain mastery of the world.'

Following the discovery of these writings, the order was suppressed – but too late.

By 1789 there were some three hundred lodges in France, including sixty-five in Paris.

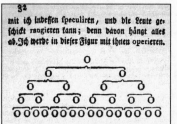

32

mit ich indessen speculiren, und die Leute geschickt rangieren kann; denn davon hängt alles ab. Ich werde in dieser Figur mit ihnen operieren.

Ich habe zwey unmittelbar unter mir, welchen ich meinen ganzen Geist einhauche, und von diesen zweyen hat wieder jeder zwey andere, und so fort. Auf diese Art kann ich auf die einfachste Art tausend Menschen in Bewegung und Flammen setzen. Auf eben diese Art muß man die Ordres ertheilen, und im Politischen operieren.

Es ist ein Kunst dabey, dem Pythagoras etwas aus dem III. min. vorzulesen. Ich habe ihn ja nicht: ich habe keinen einzigen Grad in Handen, nicht einmal meine eigene Aufsätze.

Ich habe auch in des Philo Provinzen eine Art von Eid, Versicherung oder Betheuerung: bey der Ehre des ⊙o: beym ⊙, eingeführt. Man gebraucht sie nur, um sie nicht zu profaniren, bey den wichtigsten Vorfällen.

Wer

Diagram by Weishaupt. He writes to his co-conspirators, 'One must show how easy it would be for one clear mind to direct hundreds and thousands of men.'

According to some French Freemasons today, there were more than seventy thousand Freemasons in France. The original plan had been to impregnate people with hope and will for change, but lodges had been infiltrated to the extent that it has been said that 'the program put into action by the French Constitutional Assembly in 1789 had been put together by German Illuminati in 1776'. Danton, Desmoulins, Mirabeau, Marat, Robespierre, Guillotin and other leaders had been 'illuminated'.

When the king was slow to agree to further reforms, Desmoulins called for an armed uprising. Then, in June 1789, Louis XVI tried to disperse the Assembly and called his troops to Versailles. Mass desertions followed. On 14 July an angry mob stormed the Bastille. Louis XVI went to the guillotine in January 1793. When he tried to speak to the crowd, he was cut short by a roll on the drums. He was heard to say, 'People of France, I am innocent, I forgive those who are responsible for my death. I pray to God that the blood spilled here never falls on France or on you, my unfortunate people ...' That this should happen in the heart of the most civilized nation on earth opened the door to the unthinkable.

It is said that in the melee that followed a man jumped on to the scaffold and yelled, 'Jacques de Moloy, you are avenged!' If this is true, its sentiment was in stark contrast to the king's grace and charity.

In the anarchy that followed France was threatened from within and without. The leaders of the Freemasonic lodges took control. Soon many of their number were accused of being traitors to the Revolution – and so began the Terror.

There are different estimates of the numbers executed. The driving force was the most principled of Freemasons, the austere and incorruptible lawyer Maximilian Robespierre. As head of the Committee of Public Safety and the man in charge of the police department, he was sending to the guillotine hundreds per day, adding up to some 2750 executions. Out of this latter total only 650 were aristocrats, the rest ordinary working people. Robespierre even executed Danton. Saturn was eating his own children.

How could this be? How could the most enlightened and reasonable of men justify this bloodshed? In an idealistic philosophy the ends never justify the means, because, as we have seen, motives affect the outcome, however deeply hidden they may be. Robespierre shed blood as a grim duty, to protect the rights of citizens and their property. From a rational point of view he did what he did for the common good.

Yet in Robespierre's case this yearning to be completely reasonable seems to have driven him mad.

On 8 July 1794 a curious ceremony took place in front of the Louvre. The members of the National Convention sat in a vast, makeshift amphitheatre, each holding an ear of wheat to symbolize the goddess Isis. Facing them was an altar by which stood Robespierre, wrapped in a light blue coat, his hair powdered white. He said, 'The whole Universe is assembled here!' Then, calling upon the Supreme Being, he began a speech which

Napoleon said on more than one occasion that as long as no one else could see his star, visible here in the sky, he would not allow anyone to distract him from following his own destiny.

lasted several hours and ended, 'Tomorrow, when we return to work, we shall again fight against vice and tyrants.'

If members of the Convention had hoped he was going to call an end to bloodshed, they were to be disappointed.

Then he stepped up to a veiled effigy and set light to the cloth, revealing a stone statue of a goddess. The set had been designed by the Illuminated Freemason Jean-Jacques Davide so that the goddess, Sophia, would seem to arise from the flames like a phoenix.

The poet Gérard de Nerval would later claim that Sophia had represented Isis. Yet the ruling spirit of the times was not Isis, the lifting of whose veils leads to the spirit worlds; neither was it Mother Nature, the gentle, nurturing goddess of the vegetable dimension of the cosmos. This was Mother Nature red in tooth and claw.

Robespierre was accused of trying to have himself declared a god by an elderly prophetess called Catherine Théot. Revulsion at the relentless bloodletting reached a pitch, and a crowd laid siege to the Hôtel de Ville. Robespierre was at last cornered. He tried to shoot himself, but only succeeded in blowing away half his jaw. When he went to the guillotine, still wearing his light blue costume, he tried to declaim to the assembled multitude, but could only manage a strangulated cry.

NAPOLEON FAMOUSLY FOLLOWED HIS star. This has been taken as a poetic way of saying that he was destined for great things.

Goethe said of him: 'The daemon ought to lead us every day and tell us what we ought to do on every occasion. But the good spirit leaves us in the lurch, and we grope about in the dark. Napoleon was the man! Always illuminated, always clear and decided and endowed at every hour with energy enough to carry out whatever he considered necessary. His life was the stride of a demi-god, from battle to battle, and from victory to victory. It might be said he was in a state of continual illumination ... In later years this illumination appears to have forsaken him, as well as his fortune and his good star.'

How could Napoleon fail to have sense of destiny? He succeeded at everything he set his mind to, seemingly able to bend the whole world to his will. To himself and many of his contemporaries he was the Alexander the Great of the modern world, uniting East and West by his conquests.

French troops moved into Egypt. It was not a particularly glorious campaign – but it was important to Napoleon from a personal point of view. According to Fouché, the head of the French secret police, Napoleon had a meeting with a man purporting to be St Germain inside the Great Pyramid. It certainly seems to be the case that Napoleon chose the esotericst and astrologer Fabre d'Olivet as one of his advisers, and also arranged to spend a night alone in the Great Pyramid. Did Napoleon meet St Germain in the flesh or in spirit?

Napoleon ordered the making of a catalogue of Egyptian antiquities, *Description de l'Egypt*. It was dedicated to 'Napoleon le Grand', inviting comparison with Alexander the Great. He was portrayed on the front of the catalogue as Sol Invictus, the Sun god.

His empire would expand to include not only Italy and Egypt, but Germany, Austria and Spain. No emperor had been crowned by the Pope since Charlemagne, but in 1804 Napoleon had Charlemagne's crown and sceptre brought to him, and having forced Pope Pius VII to attend, Napoleon symbolically snatched the crown from his hands and crowned himself Emperor.

Napoleon employed a team of scholars to come to the conclusion that Isis was the ancient goddess of Paris, and then decreed that the goddess and her star should be included in Paris's coat of arms. On the Arc de Triomphe Josephine is portrayed kneeling at his feet carrying the laurel of Isis.

We can infer from this that Napoleon did not identify himself with Sirius, he followed it, as Orion follows Sirius across the sky. In Freemasonic initiation ceremonies candidates are reborn – as Osiris was reborn – looking up at a five-pointed star that represents Isis. Osiris/Orion the Hunter is the masculine impulse towards power, action and impregnation, pursuing Isis, the gatekeeper to life's mysteries.

This is how Napoleon thought of Josephine, born of a family deeply immersed in esoteric Freemasonry and already a Freemason herself when he met her. Napoleon could conquer mainland Europe, but he could never quite conquer the sublimely beautiful Josephine. He longed for her as Dante had longed for Beatrice and longing made him aspire higher.

Osiris and Isis are also, of course, associated with the sun and the moon and on one level, as we have seen, this is to do with the cosmos's arranging of itself in order to make human thought possible. In ancient Egypt the heliacal rising of Sirius in the middle of June presaged the rising of the Nile. In some esoteric traditions Sirius is the central sun of the universe around which our sun rotates.

This complex nexus of esoteric thought, combined with his love for Josephine, informed Napoleon's sense of destiny.

But in 1813 the powers guiding and empowering Napoleon left him, as they always leave everyone, quite suddenly, and, as Goethe had described, the powers of reaction rushed in from all sides to destroy him.

We see the same process in the lives of artists. They struggle to find their voice, reach an inspired period during which they cannot put a brushstroke wrong, perhaps leading art into a new era. Then the spirit suddenly leaves them and they are unable to recapture it, no matter how hard they try.

THROUGHOUT THIS HISTORY WE HAVE repeatedly referred to the series of experiences a candidate must go through to achieve initiation, including the experience of *kama loca*, or purgatory, where the soul and spirit, still united, are attacked by demons. Now it is time to touch on the idea taught in the esoteric schools that the whole of humanity was to undergo something like an initiation.

The secret societies were preparing for this event, helping humanity to develop the sense of self and other qualities that would be needed during the ordeal.

In the middle decades of the eighteenth century Freemasonry spread throughout the world – to Austria, Spain, India, Italy, Sweden, Germany, Poland, Russia, Denmark, Norway and China. Following in the footsteps of the American and French brethren, Freemasonry inspired republican revolutions all round the world.

Madame Blavatsky wrote that among the Carbonari – the revolutionary precursors and pioneers of Garibaldi – there was more than one Freemason deeply versed in occult science and Rosicrucianism. Garibaldi himself was a 33rd degree Freemason and Grand Master of Italian Freemasonry.

In Hungary Louis Kossuth, and in South America Simon Bolivar, Francisco de Miranda, Venustiano Carranza, Benito Juarez and Fidel Castro, all fought for freedom.

Today in the USA there are some 13,000 lodges, and in 2001 it was estimated that there were some seven million Freemasons worldwide.

WE HAVE SEEN HOW JESUS CHRIST planted the seed of the interior life, how this interior life was expanded and populated by Shakespeare and Cervantes. In the eighteenth century and, particularly, the nineteenth century the great initiate-novelists forged the sense we all enjoy today that this interior world has its own history, a *narrative* with meaning, highs and lows, reversals of fortune and dilemmas, turning points when life-changing decisions may be made.

The great novelists of the age – we think of the Brontës, of Dickens – were also full of a sense that, just as human consciousness was understood in esoteric thought to have evolved through history, so consciousness also evolves in individual human lives.

John Comenius grew up in the Prague of Rudolf II where he attended the coronation of the Winter King. He knew John Valentine Andrae in Heidelberg, and was then invited by his friend, the occultist Samuel Hartlib, to join him in London 'to help complete the Work'. By his educational reforms Comenius would introduce into the mainstream of history the idea that in childhood we experience a very different state of mind from the one we develop in adulthood.

We see Comenius's influence in, for example, *Jane Eyre* or *David Copperfield* – and we should be aware that it was very new then.

But the area of esoteric thought which would have the biggest effect on the novel would be that of the deeper laws. The novel provided an arena for novelists steeped in esoteric philosophy to show the working out of these laws in individual human lives.

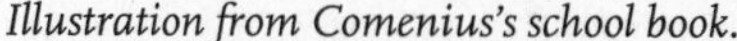
Illustration from Comenius's school book.

THE TIME HAS COME TO GET TO GRIPS with this elusive concept which lies right at the heart of the esoteric view of the cosmos and its history.

We saw how Elijah, working behind the scenes of history, had helped bring about a split in consciousness between the objective Baconian consciousness and the subjective Shakespearean consciousness. We saw, too, how viewing the world as objectively as possible made the laws of physics snap into focus.

But what about subjective experience? What about the structure of experience itself?

In time the science of psychology would arise. But psychology would make the materialistic assumption that matter influences the mind, never the other way around. Psychology, then, turned a blind eye to a universal part of human experience – the experience of meaning.

We have already touched on the way that Rosicrucians had begun to formulate laws in line with oriental esoteric thought on 'the nameless' way, inextricably bound up with notions of human wellbeing. In the East there is an august tradition of tracing the operation of yang and its opposite ying, but in the West this remained an elusive element that slipped between the emerging sciences of physics and psychology.

If the laws that govern these elusive elements are difficult to think about in abstract terms, it is much easier to see them in action. Some of the great novelists of the nineteenth century wrote explicitly occult novels. In addition to Dickens's *A Christmas Carol*, Emily Bronte's *Wuthering Heights* shows a spirit pursue its beloved from beyond the grave. George Eliot's *Lifting the Veil*, the fruit of her passionate investigation of the occult, was suppressed by her publisher. Then, as we shall see shortly, there was Dostoyevsky.

But as well as this explicit occultism, a more widespread influence is implicit in much more fiction. *A great vision of the working out of the deeper laws in individual lives, the complex, irrational patterns that could not occur if science explained everything there is in the universe, can be found in the very greatest novels.*

Jane Eyre, Bleak House, Moby Dick, Middlemarch, War and Peace hold up a mirror to our lives and point up the significant patterns of order and meaning that are our universal experience, even when science tells us not to believe the evidence of our eyes, hearts and minds.

ON ONE LEVEL NOVELS ARE ALL ABOUT egotism. A novel always involves seeing the world from other people's points of view. Reading a novel, therefore, lessens egotism. Also the failings of characters in novels are very often to do with egotism, either in terms of self-interest or, more particularly, the failure to empathize.

But the greater contribution of the novel to the human sense of self is, as we have just suggested, the formation of the sense of an inner narrative, the sense that an individual life seen from the inside has a meaningful shape, a story.

Mother Goose in an eighteenth-century engraving. Mother Goose here reveals her secret identity as Isis, the Moon goddess and priestess of the secret philosophy, not only by her name – in ancient Egypt the goose was one of the traditional attributes of Isis – but also by the crescent shape of her profile. The fairy stories of folk tradition are saturated with the numinous and paradoxical qualities of the ancient and secret philosophy.

Underlying these notions of shape and meaning are beliefs about the ways people's lives are formed by their being tested – the labyrinth that keeps morphing.

What shapes lives in novels is life's paradoxical quality, the fact that it does not run in a straight, predictable line, the fact that appearances are deceptive and that fortunes are reversed. The notions of the meaning of life and the deeper laws here come together.

IF THESE DEEPER LAWS REALLY EXIST AND are universal and so important and powerful, if history really does turn on them, isn't it perhaps surprising that we are not more aware of them? In fact, isn't it odd if we in the West don't even seem to have a name for them?

It is surprising, not least because if these laws come into play when human happiness is at stake it should follow that they could be very useful when it comes to our hopes of living a happy life.

Of course the most common sets of rules for achieving a happy life are the down-to-earth wisdom contained in proverbs and the common-sense cautionary advice traditionally given to children.

But one difference is that both proverbs and the cautionary advice given to children only address the basics – how to avoid physical harm and obtain the bare necessities – while the deeper laws deal in grand notions of destiny, good and evil. As we shall see, they advise us on satisfying our craving for the highest, most ineffable levels of happiness, our deepest needs for fulfilment and meaning.

Compare the proverbial advice to 'look before you leap' with the recommendation contained in this perverse little parable by the proto-Surrealist Guillaume Apollinaire:

> Come to the edge, he said.
> They said, We are afraid.
> Come to the edge, he said.
> They came. He pushed them.
> They flew.

Like Paracelsus, the Brothers Grimm collected esoteric folklore before it died out. Dopey, Happy, Bashful, Sleepy, Grumpy, Sneezy and Doc might seem humorous, child-friendly, made-up names, but in fact they are all literal translations of seven earth demons from Scandinavian esoteric lore: Toki, Skavaerr, Varr, Dun, Orinn, Grerr and Radsvid. Even in the cosy world of Disney the esoteric lies closer to the surface than you might think.

Inspired by the teachings of the secret societies, the Surrealists wanted to destroy entrenched ways of thought, to smash scientific materialism. One of the ways they did this was by promoting irrational acts. Here Apollinaire is saying that *if you act irrationally, you will be rewarded by the irrational forces of the universe.*

If what Apollinaire is saying is true, this is one of the deeper laws of the universe, a law of cause and effect lying outside the laws of probability.

Surrealists were unusually open about their irrational philosophy and its roots in the secret societies, but this same irrational philosophy is also implicit in much more mainstream culture. Take *It's a Wonderful Life,* an old film that on the surface seems homely and comforting, together with its literary forebear *A Christmas Carol,* which Charles Dickens imbued with the philosophy of the secret society of which he was an initiate.

Scrooge is confronted by ghosts that present him with visions showing how his behaviour has caused great misery, together with a vision of what will result if he continues in the same vein. George Bailey, the character played by James Stewart in *It's A Wonderful Life,* believes his life has been a complete failure and he is about to commit suicide when an angel shows him how much unhappier his family, friends, the whole town, would have been were it not for him and his self-sacrificing nature.

So both George Bailey and Scrooge are invited to ask themselves how the world would have been different if they had chosen to live differently. At the end of this process of questioning both characters are asked to go through the same door they were about to go through at the beginning of the story – but this time do the right thing. George Bailey decides not to commit suicide and to face his creditors. Scrooge redeems himself by coming to the aid of Bob Cratchit and his family.

So in a way both *It's a Wonderful Life* and *A Christmas Carol* depict life as having a kind of circular quality and of being a test. They show how life directs us towards crucial decisions and how we may be made to loop round and come back to confront these crucial decisions again if we get it wrong.

I imagine that most of us feel that both *It's a Wonderful Life* and *A Christmas Carol* are in some way *true.* It's difficult to see how anything in science or nature could account for life's being patterned in this insistently testing way, but most of us probably feel that both these very popular works are more than just entertainments, that they say something deep about life.

A few moments consideration may now be enough to convince us that the same sorts of mysterious and irrational patterns also inform the structure of some of the greatest works of literature in the canon: *Oedipus Rex, Hamlet, Don Quixote, Doctor Faustus* and *War and Peace.*

Oedipus somehow draws to himself the thing he fears most, and ends up killing his father and marrying his mother.

Hamlet repeatedly ducks out of his life's challenge – avenging his father's murder – but this challenge returns to confront him in increasingly dire forms.

Don Quixote holds a good-hearted vision of the world as a noble place, and so strong is this vision that by the end of the novel it has in some mysterious way transformed his material surroundings.

In his heart of hearts Faust knows what he ought to do, but because he does not do it, a providential order in the universe punishes him.

Tolstoy's hero, Pierre, is tortured by his love for Natasha. It is only when he lets go of his feelings for her that he wins her.

Imagine if you fed all these great works of literature – in fact *all* literature – into a giant computer and asked it the question: What are the laws that determine whether or not a life is ultimately happy and fulfilled? I suggest the result would be a body of laws that included the following:

If you duck out of a challenge, then that challenge will come round again in a different form.

We always draw towards us what we fear most.

If you choose the immoral path, ultimately you will pay for it.

A good-hearted belief will eventually transform what is believed in.

In order to hold on to what you love, you must let it go.

This, then, is the type of law that gives great narrative literature its structure, and if we read *Oedipus Rex* or *King Lear* or *Doctor Faustus* or *Middlemarch* and feel that in a deep and important sense they are *true*, it is surely because the working out of the laws they portray resonates with our experience. They accurately depict the shape of our lives.

Now imagine what would happen if you fed all the *scientific* data in the world into another gigantic computer and asked it the same question. The results, I suggest, would be very different:

The best way to keep something is to try your hardest to do so and never give up.

You cannot transform the world by wishful thinking – you must do something about it.

If you can avoid being found out and punished by your fellow man, there is no reason to suppose a providential order will punish you.

And so on. The implication is clear and confirms what we suggested earlier. We get very different results, two very different sets of laws, if we try to determine the structure of the world than we do if we try to determine *the structure of experience.*

This is a distinction that Tolstoy wrote about in his essay *On Life*. Though the same laws operate in the outer world of external phenomena and in our inner life with its concern for meaning and fulfilment, they seem very different when we consider them separately. As Abraham Isaac Kook, one of the great Cabalists of the twentieth century and the first Chief Rabbi of Palestine, put it: 'God is revealed in the deep feelings of sensitive souls.'

The deeper laws can be discerned only if we view events in the external world with the deepest subjectivity, as an artist or a mystic might. Is it the subjectivity of these laws, the fact that they work so near to the centre of consciousness, that makes it difficult for us to keep them in focus?

Rainer Maria Rilke, the Central European poet, seems to come close to writing explicitly about these laws in a letter to an aspiring young poet. 'Only the individual who is truly solitary is brought under the deep laws, and when a man steps out into the morning that is just beginning, or looks into the evening that is full of happenings, and when he feels what is coming to pass there, then all rank drops from him as from a dead man, although he is standing in the midst of sheer life.' Rilke is using heightened, poetic language but he seems to be confirming that these deeper laws can only be discerned if we shut out everything else and concentrate on them over a long time with our subtlest and most intense powers of discernment.

IN THE COURSE OF WRITING this book I have met the young Irish mystic Lorna Byrne. She hasn't read any of the literature that lies behind this book, nor even previously met anyone who might have passed its ideas on. Her extraordinary knowledge of the spirit words has come from direct personal experience. She meets Michael, Archangel of the Sun, and has encountered the Archangel Gabriel in the form of the Moon, divided in half yet pressed together and moving, she says, like the turning of pages in a book. She has described to me seeing in the fields near her home the group-spirit of the fox in the form of the fox but with human-like elements. She meets Elijah, who was once a human with the spirit of an angel, and she has seen him walk on water like the Green One of the Sufi tradition. Hers is an alternative method of perception, a parallel dimension that moves things around in our own.

IN THE LATE NINETEENTH CENTURY ANCIENT creatures began to stir in the depths of the earth, to slouch towards the appointed place.

Imprisoned since the first War in Heaven, the consciousness-eaters were on the move again.

27

The Mystic Death of Humanity

Swedenborg and Dostoyevsky • Wagner • Freud, Jung and the Materializing of Esoteric Thought • The Occult Roots of Modernism • Occult Bolshevism • Gandhi

EARLY ROMANTICISM'S JOY IN self-expression, in animal joy at being alive in the natural world, gave way to disquiet. The greatest of the German philosophers of idealism, Hegel, recognized this force in history: 'The spirit cheats us, the spirit intrigues, the spirit lies, the spirit triumphs.'

Taken as an account of humanity's interior life, the literature of the second half of the nineteenth century reveals a terrible darkening, a spiritual crisis. If materialist history explains this crisis as 'alienation', esoteric history sees a spiritual crisis. In other words it sees a crisis caused by spirits – or more particularly by demons.

The great exponent of this view was not someone revered in academia like Hegel or even the more frankly occultist Schopenhauer, but a man who rolled around the mud. Swedenborg saw demonic forces rising up from the depths. He prophesied that humanity would have to come to terms with the demonic in the world and inside himself.

Today the Swedenborg Church is the only esoteric movement admitted to Sweden's National Council of Churches, and Swedenborg's teachings remain influential on exponents of communal living, particularly on American groups such as the Shakers. In his own day, however, he was a rather more dangerous figure. Swedenborg's exceptionally detailed and accurate clairvoyance made him world-famous. The spiritualists tried to claim him as one of their own. Swedenborg repudiated them, saying that his supernatural gifts were unique to him and heralded the dawn of a new age.

It was from his reading of Swedenborg's *Heaven and Hell* that Goethe had derived his sense of the intrusion of evil, supernatural forces that afflicted Faust. It was from

Swedenborg that Baudelaire derived his notion of correspondences, and that Balzac took his notions of the supernatural in *Seraphita*. But perhaps Swedenborg's most important and far-reaching influence was on Dostoyevsky, an influence that would darken the mood of an entire era.

DOSTOYEVSKY'S HEROES ARE POISED over an abyss. There is always a heightened awareness of how much our choices matter – and also that our choices come to us in different disguises.

In Dostoyevsky we encounter the paradoxical notion that those who confront this evil, supernatural dimension, even if they are thieves, prostitute and murderers, are closer to heaven than those whose cosy world-view deliberately shuts evil out and denies it is there.

Eastern, Orthodox Christianity had been less dogmatic than its Western counterpart and it had valued individual spiritual experience more. Raised in this Church, Dostoyevsky felt free to explore the outer limits of spiritual experience, to describe battles between the forces of darkness and the forces of light that were taking place in realms of which most people were barely conscious. Dostoyevsky's journey through Hell, like Dante's, is partly a spiritual journey but it is also a journey through the Hell on Earth that humanity has created. There is in Dostoyevsky a new impulse which would come to characterize the arts in the late nineteenth and early twentieth centuries – the desire to know the worst that can happen.

On Dostoyevsky's death his library was discovered to be well stocked with Swedenborg, including his accounts of the many different hells that people with different capacities for evil fashion for themselves. Swedenborg's accounts of the hells he visited are not fictional. They elude our conventional ontologies, our everyday working assumptions of what is real and what is not. Hell may at first appear no different from the world we live in, but then gradually anomalies show themselves. We might meet a group of genial and amusing men, libertines who love to deflower virgins, but they turn to greet us and we see they are 'like apes with a fierce face ... a horrible countenance'. Non-esoteric schools of literary criticism have missed the way that passages like the following, from *Crime and Punishment*, come straight from Swedenborg:

> 'I don't believe in a future life,' said Raskolnikov.
>
> Svidrigailov sat lost in thought.
>
> 'And what if there are only spiders there, or something of that sort?' he said suddenly.
>
> He is a madman, thought Raskolnikov.
>
> 'We always imagine eternity as something beyond our conception, something vast, vast! But why must it be vast? Instead of that, what if it's one little room, like a bathhouse in the country, black and grimy and spiders in every corner, and that's all eternity is? I sometimes fancy it like that.'

'Can it be you can imagine nothing juster and more comforting than that?' Raskolnikov cried, with a feeling of anguish.

'Juster. And how can we tell, perhaps that is just, and do you know it's what I would certainly have made it,' answered Svidrigailov, with a vague smile.

This horrible answer sent a cold chill through Raskolnikov.

Similarly in *The Brothers Karamazov*, when Ivan has a nightmare in which he is visited by the Devil, neither Ivan nor the reader believes that this is just a delusion. Dostoyevsky is telling his readers that devils may squeeze through into the material dimension. No other single writer so powerfully conveys the undercurrents of evil that welled up in the second half of the nineteenth century. His work is pervaded with a sense of vital contact with other mysterious worlds, some of them hellish. There is, too, the spiritual extremism, the sense that there is no middle way, that if you do not run to embrace the most spiritual, the demonic will fill the vacuum. Those who try to follow the middle way are nowhere.

Like Swedenborg he looked forward to a new age, but in Dostoyevsky's case this grew out of a very Russian sense of history.

'EVERYDAY I GO INTO THE GROVE,' wrote the poet Nikolai Kliuev in a letter to a friend 'and sit there by a little chapel and the age-old pine tree. I think about you. I kiss your eyes and your heart ... O mother wilderness, paradise of the spirit ... How hateful and black seems all the so-called civilized world and what I would give, what Golgotha would I bear so that America should not encroach upon the blue feathered dawn, upon the fairy-tale hut ... Western Christianity among whose heedless gifts to the world we must count rationalism, materialism, a technology that enslaves, an absence of spirit and in its place a vain, sentimental humanism.' This is the Russian perspective.

Orthodox Christianity had taken a different path from Roman Christianity. Orthodoxy preserved and nurtured the esoteric doctrines, some of them pre-Christian, that Rome had discarded or declared heretical. The mystical vision of Dionysius the Aeropagite continued to illumine Orthodox Christianity with its emphasis on direct, personal experience of the spirit worlds. In the seventh century the Byzantine theologian Maximus the Confessor wrote urging disciplined introspection, the monastic or wandering life. 'Illumination must be sought,' he wrote, 'and in extreme cases the whole body will be illumined too.' The same phenomenon was reported by the monks of Mount Athos. Monks deep in prayer would suddenly illuminate their entire cave or cell. This was a vision of God, the *hesychast*, which could be achieved by rhythmic breathing exercises, repetitive prayers and meditation on icons.

In Russia the Church emphasized supernatural powers attainable after severe spiritual discipline. But then in the seventeenth century the Russian Orthodox Patriarch Nikon

Illustration to Wagner's Lohengrin. *No other esoteric artist so conveys that central esoteric doctrine – the sense of impending and overwhelming destiny. Wagner wrote of his ambition to bring a non-existent world into being, and Baudelaire described how watching* Lohengrin *induced in him an altered state of consciousness in which the ordinary world of the senses became dissolved. The occultist Theodor Reuss claimed he had known Wagner and that this gave him special insight into a secret doctrine concealed in* Parsifal. *Reuss saw the closing words of Parsifal at the end of act three, where he stands holding his lance erect, as a glorious deification of the sex drive.*

reformed and centralized the Church. It was left to the Old Believers (*Raskolniki*) to keep the beliefs and spiritual disciplines of the early Christians alive. Their outlawed communities were driven underground, where they survived as a living tradition. Dostoyevsky kept in touch with them throughout his life.

Out of the Old Believer tradition came the Stranniki, or Wanderers, solitary individuals who renounced money, marriage, passports and all official documents as they moved across the country, promising ecstatic visions, healing and prophecy. If caught, they were tortured, sometimes beheaded.

Another later movement which came out of the Old Believer tradition was the Khlysty, the People of God, a persecuted underground society famous for its extreme asceticism and rejection of the world. They were reputed to meet at night, sometimes in a forest clearing lit by banks of candles. Naked under flowing white robes, they danced in two circles, the men in an inner circle in the direction of the sun and the women in an outer circle moving in the other direction, widdershins. The aim of this ceremony was liberation from the material world and ascent into the spirit worlds. They would collapse, speak in tongues, heal the sick and cast out demons.

There were rumours of orgies at these midnight meetings, but more likely they – like the Cathars – were sexual ascetics, practising the sublimation of sexual energies for spiritual and mystical purposes.

The young Rasputin stayed at the Orthodox monastery of Verkhoturye where he met members of the Khlysty. His own doctrine seems to have been a radical development, proposing spiritual ecstasy attained through *sexual exhaustion*. The flesh would be crucified, the little death of orgasm would become the mystic death of initiation.

After a vision of Mary, in which she told him to take up the life of a wanderer, Rasputin walked two thousand miles to Mount Athos. He returned home two years later, exuding a powerful magnetism and displaying miraculous powers of healing.

In 1903 he arrived in St Petersburg. There he was taken up by the personal confessor to the royal family who said, 'It is the voice of the Russian soil which speaks through him.' He introduced Rasputin to a court already fascinated by esoteric ideas and eager for experience.

Martinism was already much discussed in Russia's Freemasonic lodges. Maître de Philippe and Papus had visited the Russian court in 1901. Papus made Nicholas II the head of a Martinist lodge, and acted as the Tsar's healer and spiritual adviser. He is said to have conjured up the spirit of the Tsar's father, Alexander III, who prophesied the death of Nicholas II at the hands of revolutionaries. Papus also warned the Tsar against the evil influence of Rasputin.

Rasputin would be slandered and murdered by Freemasons, but in 1916 his contemporary, the great initiate Rudolf Steiner, said of him, 'the Russian Folk-Spirit can now work through him alone and through no-one else'.

IF, AS WE MOVE TOWARDS THE *FIN DE SIÈCLE*, we look not at the very highest rung of art and literature but at the next rung down, we find a literature of explicit occult themes that would dominate popular culture in the twentieth century. Oscar Wilde was teeped in the lore of the Order of the Golden Dawn. His *The Picture of Dorian Gray*, like Robert Louis Stevenson's *Dr Jekyll and Mr Hyde*, brought the occult notion of the *dopplegänger* into the stream of public consciousness. M.R. James, the Cambridge don who has some claims to be the father of the ghost story, translated many of the Apocryphal gospels into English, gave a lecture on the occult sciences to the Eton Literary Society and wrote a story called *Count Magnus* in which the count, an alchemist, goes on a pilgrimage to the birthplace of the Anti-Christ, a city called Chorazin. The fact that Chorozon is the name of one of the demons who held lengthy conversations with Dee and Kelley suggests James knew what he was talking about.

Earlier in the century Frankenstein's monster had been a fictionalized account of Paracelsus's homunculus. Attending the same house party as Mary Shelley when she conceived of the monster, Byron's friend Polidori wrote an early vampire story. But of course the most famous version is Bram Stoker's, in which the preserved body in the tomb is a sort of demonic version of Christian Rosenkreuz. Stoker himself was a member of the OTO – the Ordo Templi Orientis, a secret society practising ceremonial magic. The Czech theosophist Gustav Meyrink would explore a similar theme in his novel The Golem, which in its turn influenced German expressionist cinema. It was said that in the novel Là-Bas, Huysmans spoke of what had really happened at black magic rituals from personal experience, breaking his oath of secrecy. Aleister Crowley noted with evident approval that he died of cancer of the tongue as result.

In art explicit occult themes can be seen in the symbolism of Gustave Moreau, Arnold Böcklin and Franz von Stuck, in Max Klinger's waking dreams, in the weird erotic-occult art of Felicien Rops, whom a critic of the day dubbed 'a sarcastic Satan'. Odilon Redon wrote of 'surrendering himself to secret laws'.

THROUGHOUT THIS PERIOD THE SPIRIT of materialism was working for victory, devising materialistic versions of esoteric philosophy. We have already touched on the way that esoteric ideas of the evolution of the species appeared in materialistic form in Darwin's theories. We have seen, too, how the ruthless and cynical manipulators of the Freemasons, the Illuminati, provided a methodology for revolutionaries in the late eighteenth and nineteenth centuries. Now Marx's dialectical materialism translated the spiritual ideals of St Germain on to a purely economic plane.

Occultism also played a part in the development of Freud's ideas. His mentor Charcot had in turn been taught by the prominent occultist and inventor of mesmerism Anton Mesmer. The young Freud studied the Cabala and wrote approvingly of telepathy, speculating that it might have been an archaic form of communication used by everyone before the invention of language.

He introduced into mainstream thought an idea that is essentially cabalistic – the idea of consciousness having a structure. For example, the model of the mind that Freud popularized – of super ego, ego and id – can be seen as a materialized version of the tripartite cabalistic model.

Indeed, at an even more basic level the very notion that there are impulses independent of our point of consciousness, but which may impinge upon it from outside, is a secularized, materialistic version of the esoteric account of consciousness. In Freud's scheme of life these hidden forces should be interpreted as sexual rather than spiritual. Freud later reacted against the esoteric roots of his ideas and stigmatized as mad the ancient form of consciousness out of which they had grown.

The esoteric influences on Freud's pupil Jung are even clearer. We have touched on how he interpreted alchemical processes as descriptions of psychological healing, and how

Salome *by*
Gustave Moreau.

he identified what he saw as the seven great archetypes of the collective unconscious with the symbolism of seven planetary gods.

By interpreting the alchemical processes as purely psychological he was denying a level of meaning intended by the alchemical writers – that these mental exercises can influence matter in a supernatural manner. And though Jung saw the seven archetypes as acting independently of the conscious mind, he would have stopped short of seeing them as disembodied centres of consciousness acting completely independently of the human mind. Indeed, when Jung met Rudolf Steiner he dismissed him as a schizophrenic.

But late in life, Jung's work with the experimental physicist Wolfgang Pauli encouraged him to take a few steps beyond the pale. Jung and Pauli came to believe that in addition to the purely physical mechanism of atom knocking against atom there is another network of connections that binds together events not physically connected – non-physical, causal connections brought about by mind. Jung's contemporary, the French anthropologist Henri Corbin, was researching the spiritual practices of the Sufis at this time. Corbin came to the conclusion that the Sufi adepts worked in concert and could communicate with one another in a realm of 'objective imagination'. Jung coined the same phrase independently.

Later in life the materialistic explanations that Freud had been trying to force on to spiritual experiences also sprang back at him, and he became plagued by a sense of what he called the uncanny. Freud wrote his essay on *The Uncanny* when he was sixty-two. By thinking about what he feared most he was trying to stop it happening. A few years earlier he had experienced the number sixty-two coming at him insistently – a hat check ticket, a hotel room number, a train seat number. It had seemed to him that the cosmos was trying to tell him something. Perhaps he would die at the age of sixty-two?

In the same essay he described the experience of walking round a maze of streets in an old Italian town and finding himself in the red light district. He took what he thought would be the most direct route out of this district, but soon found himself back in the middle of it. This seemed to happen to him again and again, no matter which direction he took. The experience can only remind us of Francis Bacon. It was as if a maze were changing shape to keep the wanderer from finding the way. As a result of these experiences Freud began to suspect that there might be some complicity between his psyche and the cosmos. Or perhaps the cosmos was manufacturing meanings independently of any human agency and, as it were, beaming them at him?

If Freud had been forced to admit that either of these had been the case, even if in only one instance, then his whole materialistic world-view would have been smashed into pieces. Freud was naturally anxious to block these promptings. They left him in a disturbed state of mind.

THE EUROPEAN COLONIZATION OF OTHER parts of the world prompted a flow of esoteric ideas in the other direction, a reverse colonization of Europe. The British Empire in India led to the publication in English of esoteric Hindu texts, and as a result oriental esotericism is still better represented in bookshops in the West than its occidental counterpart. Similarly the French colonies in North Africa lent esotericism in French-speaking territories a strong Sufi colouring.

The partition of Poland in the nineteenth century caused the spread of that country's alchemical traditions over the rest of Europe. A genuine Rosicrucian impulse survived in middle Europe in the form of Rudolf Steiner's Anthroposophy. The Russian Revolution caused the occultists who had clustered at the court of the Tsars to flee, helping to introduce a stream of Orthodox esotericism in the West, and the Sufi- and Orthodox-influenced philosophy of Gurdjieff and Ouspensky became very influential in both Europe and America. In the 1950s China's invasion of Tibet would cause the dispersal of Tibetan esotericism all over the world.

At a time when to many in the West the organized religion of the state risks being reduced to mere formalism, and seems to many to be sterile and exhausted, it would perhaps not be surprising if *every* intelligent person reaches a time in life when he or she wants to consider the great questions of life and death and whether or not life and the universe has meaning, and has to cast about for answers. Esoteric philosophy taken as a whole represents the richest, the deepest and the most fascinating body of thought on these questions.

THE VERY GREATEST ARTISTS AND WRITERS find ways of expressing what it *means* to be alive at a moment in history.

The great art at the end of the nineteenth century and the beginning of the twentieth century was on one level the cry of a hurt and puzzled humanity. Some artists and writers, including a few very great ones, looked squarely into the face of existence and decided that it was quite meaningless, that life on earth, human life, is an accident of chemical combinations and that, as Jean-Paul Sartre concluded at the end of *La Nausée*, the only way life can have meanings is if we choose to devise goals for ourselves.

It is true, too, that some artists have taken great pleasure in the material age and its shiny surfaces. Modernism was undoubtedly iconoclastic. However, by the end of the nineteenth century the tyranny of kings, clerical superstitions and stodgy bourgeois morality were pretty soft targets for iconoclasts.

For the majority of great artists of the modern era, the mechanical model of the universe has been the icon they really wanted to smash.

We like to think of Modernism as smart, hip, in tune with the machine age, impatient with the authority and dogma of earlier times. It is all these things, but it is not, as we also sometimes like to think, atheistic, at least not in the radical, modern sense of atheistic. In fact, if you like to see esotericism as the refuge of ancient superstition, then that is what Modernism really is. The great unifying spirit of Modernism – the spirit that unites Picasso, Joyce, Malevich, Gaudí, Beuys, Borges and Calvino is a desire to undermine and subvert the prevailing scientific materialism. It needs a little probing into the lives of these artists and writers to see that they were all deeply involved in the occult, and that esotericism provided them with their core philosophy of life and guiding aesthetic.

If we take Baudelaire and Rimbaud as representative starting points for Modernism, it is all too easy to interpret the derangement of the senses they recommend as ends in themselves. What they really believed was that when the material world is dissolved, the lineaments of the spirit worlds will present themselves. 'The poet makes himself clairvoyant,' said Rimbaud, 'by turning all meaning upside down in a long and reasoned manner.'

Gauguin, Munch, Klee and Mondrian were theosophists. Mondrian's theosophy taught him it was possible to discern a spiritual reality structuring the appearances of the material world. Gauguin saw himself as creating sculptures which – like Golems – could be enlivened by disembodied spirits. Kandinsky, like Franz Marc, was a disciple of Rudolf Steiner's, but the great formative influences on Kandinsky's paintings, leading the way into abstraction, were the 'thought forms' perceived in a trance state and recorded by theosophists Annie Besant and C.W. Leadbetter. Klee depicted himself meditating on the Third Eye. Malevich was in thrall to Ouspensky.

The esoteric roots of Matisse's art may be better hidden, but he said that sometimes he looked at an object such as a plant he intended to paint for weeks, even months, until its spirit began to urge him to give it expression.

Gaudí's Arab-influenced architecture, flamboyantly surging arabesques in which animal and human forms merge and morph into each other, invites the visitor to walk into an altered state of consciousness.

Spain is perhaps the country in Europe where the supernatural lies closest to the surface of the everyday. Picasso, the great artist-magus of Modernism, always had a strong feeling for the intrusions of the spirit worlds. As a boy he was believed by some of his friends to have supernatural abilities, like mind-reading and prophecy. When he travelled to France, Max Jacob, Eric Satie, Apollinaire, Georges Bataille, Jean Cocteau and others initiated him into a sophisticated occult tradition.

Picasso often used esoteric themes in his work. Sometimes he painted himself as the Harlequin. This figure is associated with Hermes and the Underworld, particularly in his native Barcelona, where Harlequin's victory over death is re-enacted annually in street carnivals. His friend Apollinaire sometimes referred to him as 'Harlequin Trismegistus'. At other times he portrayed himself in terms of an image from the Tarot, suspended between the material world and the spirit worlds.

In an analysis of a 1934 drawing of a Spanish bullfight, a long-overlooked work, Mark Harris highlights the theme of *Parsifal*. His essay is an inspiring example of the way that esoteric thought can illuminate dimensions closed to conventional criticism. In his youth Picasso had been a founder member of a group called Valhalla, formed to study the mystical aspects of Wagner. The drawing depicts the scene in Wagner's opera when the black magician hurls the spear of Longinus at Parsifal, but, because Parsifal is now initiated, it only hovers over his head.

Georges Bataille researched Mithraism, and in 1901 Picasso made a series of paintings depicting women wearing a Mithraic cap, a traditional symbol of initiation. The 1934 drawing, Harris convincingly shows, is a portrayal of an underworld initiation. Like Dante and Dostoyevsky before him, he shows that the hell that the candidate must traverse begins with the hell of his own desires. Hell lies the other side of the grave but this life is hellish, too – and hellish according to the temper of the times.

This drawing is a depiction of one of Picasso's grand themes. Our world is being shattered, fragmented by an eruption of evil, subterranean forces. The initiatic artist, Picasso, can remake the world, can be a fertility god reborn, but he will do it not in terms of the conventional canons of beauty. He will recombine the discarded, the shattered, the ugly, in beautiful new ways.

The abstract and conceptual painter Yves Klein discovered esoteric thought when he chanced upon a book by the modern proponent of Rosicrucian philosophy Max Heindel, who had been initiated by Rudolf Steiner but broke away to set up his own Rosicrucian movement. Looking forward to the transfiguration of matter, Klein intended his art to inaugurate a new Age of Space, depicted in canvasses of ultramarine unbroken by line or form. In his new age human spirit free of the restrictions of matter and form would levitate and float.

THE GREAT WRITERS OF THE TWENTIETH century were deeply immersed in esoteric thought, too. Inspired by rumours about William Blake and his sexual religion, W.B. Yeats and his young wife, Georgie, explored first the direct link between sexual and spiritual union to be found in *The Zohar*, then Tantric yoga. Yeats even had a vasectomy in the hope that stemming the flow of semen would help build up the energies needed for a visionary trance. Not only did their experiments produce more than four thousand pages of spirit-inspired automatic writing, but Yeats remained sexually rejuvenated into old age and wrote some of his most magnificent poetry then. He described 'the love that moves the Sun'. Yeats was also a member of both the Order of the Golden Dawn and the Theosophical society, studied the Hermetica, wrote openly about magic and an introduction to a popular edition of the *Yoga Sutras of Pantanjali*. Joyce's *Ulysses* and *Finnegans Wake* show his familiarity with Hindu and Hermetic doctrine, including direct quotes from Swedenborg, Madame Blavatsky and Eliphas Levi. The poetry of T.S. Eliot also uses occult references in an eclectic way. Eliot attended Theosophist meetings and the breakaway Quest group attended by Ezra Pound, Wyndham Lewis and Gershem Scholem, the great scholar of Jewish mysticism. But perhaps the formative influence on his poetic sensibility was the Sufi-inspired philosophy of Ouspensky, whose lectures he also attended. In fact the famous first three lines of perhaps the most influential poem in English in the twentieth century, *Four Quartets* – on time past and time future contained in time present – are a paraphrase of the philosophy of Ouspensky.

Perhaps the most occult writer of the twentieth century and the one who best lived up to Rimbaud's dictum about becoming a medium was Fernando Pessoa. He wrote of holding inside himself all the dreams of the world and wanting to experience the whole of the universe – its reality – inside himself. He awaited the return of the Hidden One, who has himself been waiting since the beginning of time. Meanwhile Pessoa emptied himself like a medium, allowing himself to be taken over by a series of personae, under whose names he wrote different series of poems with very different voices. 'I am the cleverness in the dice', says an ancient Taoist text. 'I am the active in the deeds', says the Gnostic Hymn of the Pearl. Pessoa recognized these sentiments. To move things in space and time, to make the world better, it is not enough to push as hard as we can. We need the spirits to work through us. We need some of that spirit of cleverness.

In the literature of the late twentieth century Borges, Calvino, Salinger and Singer also deal openly with esoteric themes. It is as if they work in accord with Karlheinz Stockhausen's assertion that all genuine creation makes conscious something from the esoteric realm that has not been made conscious before. Rudolf Steiner's Anthroposophy has been extremely influential, not only on Kandinsky, Marc and Beuys, but also on William Golding and Doris Lessing, both of whom lived in Anthroposophical communities.

It is a mark of the strange way that esoteric influences spread that two such different writers as C.S. Lewis and Saul Bellow were both instructed in esoteric philosophy by the same spiritual master, the Anthroposophist Owen Barfield.

Will it always be true to say that the greatest writers of the day are interested in esoteric ideas? We can certainly see the influence of esotericism on both Bellow and John Updike, the two leading novelists writing in English at the turn of the century. Some of Bellow's correspondence with Barfield has been published. Updike has written an overtly occult novel in *The Witches of Eastwick*, but perhaps more telling is this passage from his latest novel, *Villages*: 'Sex is a programmed delirium that rolls back death with death's own substance; it is the black space between the stars given sweet substance in our veins and crevice. The parts of ourselves conventional decency calls shameful are exalted. We are told that we shine, that we are exalted ...'

This passage reaches right to the heart of the issue that lies between the exoteric world view and its opposite. According to esoteric thinkers, life in a mechanized, industrialized, digitalized environment has a deadening effect on our mental processes. The concrete, the plastic, the metal, the electrical impulses bouncing off the screen become internalized, resulting in a sterile wasteland that does not regenerate itself.

A conscious shift in consciousness is needed to open ourselves up again to the free-flowing, revivifying influence of the spirit worlds.

IN 1789 THE ARMIES OF ANGELS LED BY St Michael won a victory in heaven. In order for this victory to be decisive, though, it would have to be fought again on earth.

On 28 June 1914 Rasputin was overtaken by the plot to kill him. On the very same day Archduke Ferdinand of Austria was assassinated.

All hell let loose.

Much has been written about the evil occult influences on Germany in the early twentieth century. Less well known is the story of the occult influences in Russia at the time of the Revolution. We have already touched on St Martin, Papus and Rasputin. What is very little known is the occult influence behind their enemies, the revolutionary communists.

As I have already suggested, Marxism can be seen as a materialistic reframing of the fraternal ideals of Freemasonry. The revolutionary cell structure instigated by Lenin and Trotsky

Like Augustus, like James I, Hitler persecuted occultists because he believed in them, not because he didn't. One of the most learned occultists of the day, Franz Bardon was arrested with one of his disciples by the SS. There is a story that while they were being beaten, the disciple lost control and shouted out a cabalistic formula that froze his torturers. When the spell was broken, the disciple was shot. Bardon worked professionally as a stage magician. The idea of the stage magician who also turns out to be a real occultist was portrayed by Thomas Mann in his story Mario and the Magician *and here in the film* The Cabinet of Dr Caligari.

was closely modelled on the working methods of Weishaupt. Marx, Engels and Trotsky were Freemasons. Lenin was a Freemason of the 31st degree, a member of several lodges including the lodge of the Nine Sisters, the most important lodge to have been infiltrated by the followers and nihilistic philosophy of the Illuminati. Lenin and Trotsky waged war on God.

But there is a deeper mystery here. How was a man like Lenin able to bend millions of people to his will? This seems to go beyond the sinister strategies of a Weishaupt.

The US military research into occult ways of gaining advantage over the Soviet Union has been well documented. Key personnel have given testimony which seems authentic, though the results seem to have been pretty limited.

What is only now beginning to emerge is the much more extreme – and successful – use of the occult by government agencies of the old Soviet Union. Some reluctant initiates have survived to speak of 'the red initiation', of the training to become secret agents which took place in former monasteries. It seems that occult techniques were employed to strengthen the will to a supernatural degree by exploiting the psychic energies of torture victims and sacrificial victims, too. Only someone who had killed in the cause could become a red initiate.

Of course we have seen this form of black magic before – in the pyramid culture of South America. In the secret history Lenin is a reincarnation of a high priest, born again in order to oppose the second coming of the Sun god, and when Trotsky was on the run from his old comrades, hiding in Mexico City, he was returning home.

The image of Lenin, the mummified incarnation of an initiate of the pyramids is both resonant and a little absurd to modern sensibility. Ironically, perhaps, this image seems to encapsulate the very spirit of Modernism, mixing the iconic with the offbeat, of the cheap, banal even tackily up to date with ancient, occult wisdom.

THERE HAS BEEN SOME DEBATE IN occult circles as to how much esoteric wisdom should be made public. How much is useful in the war against materialism – and how much is dangerous?

We return to India, where post-Atlantean history began.

As we approach the end of this history, we are in a good position to see how far humanity has evolved from the communally minded creature of earlier times who had little awareness of the world around him and little sense of an interior life. In Gandhi we see individual free thought, free will and free love. Here is someone who has so expanded his sense of self that he is able to make turning points in his own personal story, his own interior narrative, into turning points in world history.

Gandhi stands as a great embodiment of the new form of consciousness that the secret societies have been working throughout history to help evolve.

It is perhaps a small irony, as well as being a mark of the global reach of the secret societies, that coming from the land of the Rishis, Gandhi first learned esoteric ideas from the Russian/English/Egyptian/American hybrid Theosophy, as taught by Madame Blavatsky.

As a young man Gandhi described himself as 'in love' with the British Empire. Being naturally good-hearted he saw the best in the upright and fair-playing Britons who administered his native country as a colony.

But as he matured, he began to see a deeper reality. Beneath the much-vaunted fair play, he saw, for example, the unfairness of the tax burden from abroad and above all India's lack of freedom to determine her own destiny.

Influenced in part by the philosophy of disobedience of the American Transcendentalist Henry Thoreau and by the art and social critic John Ruskin, Gandhi set about turning the world upside down and inside out.

In 1906, at the age of thirty-six, Gandhi renounced sex with his wife. His spiritual discipline involved daily work on a hand-spun spinning wheel, partly to encourage a method of weaving cloth that would provide employment for the poor, but also because he believed that as he worked on the cloth he was also working on his own vegetable body. If he could master his body in its different dimensions, he could develop what he called *soul force*.

He believed that the cosmos is governed by truth and by the laws of truth and that, by acting in accordance with these laws, an individual would gain Satyagraha, *the force of truth and love*.

For example, if you trust your opponent without fail, you will eventually influence him to act in a trustworthy way – both by means of a psychological influence, but also, crucially, by means of a supernatural one. Similarly, if attacked, you should try to be free from all thoughts of anger and hatred against your assailant. Follow this philosophy, Gandhi taught, and 'you will be free of fear of kings, people, robbers, tigers, even death'.

In the upside down thinking typical of the secret societies, Gandhi blamed Indians not Britons for the occupation of India, pointing out that 100,000 Britons would not be able to control three hundred million Indians unless they went along with it. Indian cotton was being exported to Britain, to the textile mills of Lancashire, then sold back to India at a profit to Britain and a loss to India. Seated at his spinning wheel, he said, 'It's my certain conviction that with every thread I draw, I am spinning the destiny of India.'

On 26 January 1929 he asked people to observe Independence Day in towns and villages throughout India. He asked for the boycotting of law courts, elections and schools. He also chose to challenge the British government's monopoly on salt manufacture, which meant that Indians had to pay the British for salt, even though it lay in open abundance around their own coast. In March 1930 the sixty-year-old Gandhi set off, staff in hand, on a twenty-four-day walk to the sea. Thousands joined him. Finally he waded into the sea for ritual purification, then leaned down and scooped up a small handful of salt. The crowd acclaimed him 'Deliverer!'

Gandhi's soul power was such that when he met armed soldiers, they would lower their weapons. Hindus and Muslims forgave each other in his presence.

The imprisonment of Gandhi and his hunger strikes sapped the moral will of the British government, leading to independence for India in 1947. The largest empire the world had ever seen melted away with an unprecedented lack of bloodshed.

In this history we have followed the lives of great leaders such as Alexander the Great and Napoleon. In a sense Gandhi was greater than any of them. Soul force, he believed, could deflect the greatest military power, because the intention behind an action could have greater and more widespread effects than the action itself.

Gandhi was a devout Hindu but he lived according to the deeper laws as laid out in the Sermon on the Mount. Talking to hostile Hindu and Muslim factions, he argued that someone whose spirit of self-sacrifice did not go beyond his own community eventually became selfish and made his community selfish. The spirit of self-sacrifice, he said, should embrace the whole world.

Like St Francis, he loved the whole world.

28

Wednesday, Thursday, Friday

The Anti-Christ • Re-entering the Ancient Wood • The Maitreya Buddha • The Opening of the Seven Seals • The New Jerusalem

IT IS ONLY IN THIS OBSCURE SUBURB of history, where nothing miraculous ever seems to happen and no great geniuses live, this age when the standards of education of the educated classes is in steep decline – it is only in this time and place that people have held matter-before-mind beliefs. In all other places, at all other times, people believed the contrary. They would have found it just about impossible to imagine how anyone could believe what we do.

According to the secret history this change has been caused by a change in consciousness. In the esoteric account consciousness changes much more quickly and in a much more radical way than in the conventional account. I hope this book has gone some way to showing that if people believed in a mind-before-matter philosophy a few generations ago, it was not because they'd weighed up the arguments on both sides and plumped for idealism. *It was because they experienced the world in an idealistic way.*

Consider, finally, how your consciousness is different from your parents' consciousness. Yours is probably more liberal, more sympathetic, more able to appreciate the point of view of other races, classes, gender, sexual tastes and so on. In some ways you are probably more aware of yourself. Because Freud's ideas have percolated down so thoroughly, you are less likely to remain unaware of underlying sexual motivations for your impulses. Or of commercial motivations – because of Marx. You are probably less repressed, less fearful of authority, more questioning and have less strong family ties. You probably tell lies more readily, have weaker powers of concentration and less determination to stick at boring tasks for the sake of a long-term goal. Although popular culture pays much lip service to romantic love, you, along with most people, probably don't believe in it

The Antichrist by Luca Signorelli, a detail from the San Brizio Chapel in Orvieto Cathedral. Signorelli worked with Botticelli on the Sistine Chapel and was also, like Leonardo, a member of the studio of Verrocchio, whose own work is replete with esoteric references. Mayan astronomer-priests pinpointed the incarnation of Lucifer to 13 August 3114 BC, tying in closely with Hindu traditions of the dawn of the Dark Age. These same priests predicted a similar turning point in history, the closing of one great cycle and the start of another, on 22 December AD 2012.

wholeheartedly any more. Few would want or expect to stay with the same sexual partner for a lifetime. In fact, as Rilke suggested in *The Notebooks of Malte Laurids Brigge*, part of you wants to run from the responsibility that being loved brings.

Our consciousness, then, is different from our parents' consciousness and it is also probably *very* different from our grandparents' consciousness. Project this rate of change back into history and it becomes easy to see how only a few generations ago everyday waking consciousness might have been like the form of consciousness we experience in dreams. It also raises the question:

How will our consciousness change in the near future?

In the mind-before-matter view, mind created the physical universe precisely with the aim of nurturing human consciousness and helping it to evolve.

So what *does* it say about how our consciousness will change?

ACCORDING TO ESOTERIC CHRISTIANITY, Jesus Christ lived on earth in the middle of the history of the cosmos. His life represents the great turning point in history. Everything after it mirrors what happened beforehand. So we are experiencing the great events of pre-Christian times in reverse order and our future development will take us through earlier stages in reverse order.

For example, in AD 2000 our lives mirror the life of Abraham in 2000 BC, walking among the idolatrous skyscrapers of Uruk.

Today's skyscrapers may be taken as representing fundamentalism. On the one hand there are right-wing Christians whom we should bracket with the cruder forms of Islam. Both want to repress human individual free will and intelligence, to lure us into an unenlightening ecstasy. This is the influence of Lucifer.

On the other hand there is the militant scientific materialism that wants to snuff out the human spirit. Machines are making us machine-like. This is the influence of Satan, who wants to go further and squeeze out our spirit altogether and make us mere matter.

And just as Lucifer incarnated so too Satan will incarnate. He will do so as a writer. His aim will be to destroy spirituality by 'explaining it away'. He will have the ability to create supernatural events, but then know how to give them a reductively scientific explanation.

At first he will appear to be a great benefactor on humankind, a genius. To begin with he himself may not realize he is the Anti-Christ, believing he acts only out of love for humanity. He will do away with much dangerous superstition and work to unite the religions of the world. However, there will come a moment of pride when he realizes he is achieving some things that Jesus Christ was, apparently, unable to achieve. He will then become aware of his identity and his mission.

How to recognize Satan? Or any false prophet? Or any false, purportedly spiritual teaching? False teaching usually has little or no moral dimension, the benefits of reawakening the chakras, for example, being recommended merely in terms of selfish 'personal growth'. True spiritual teaching puts love of others and love of humanity at its heart – intelligent love, freely given.

Beware, too, of teaching that doesn't invite questioning, or tolerate mockery. It is telling you, in effect, that God wants you to be stupid.

THIS BOOK HAS ACCUMULATED EVIDENCE to show that throughout history highly intelligent people have immersed themselves in esoteric philosophy.

They have used secret techniques to work themselves into altered states in which they can access an abnormally high level of intelligence.

The evidence shows that the groups involved in these societies were concerned to help forge new, *more highly intelligent* forms of consciousness.

Esoteric thinking has had a great, determining influence on human development that these days is almost wholly overlooked.

ACCORDING TO THIS WAY OF THINKING, humans once had unhindered access to the spirit worlds. Then this access became obscured and dimmed as matter hardened. Now the barrier between ourselves and the spirit worlds is becoming thinner again. The material world is fraying and becoming threadbare.

We may begin to become more aware of the patterns suggested by 'coincidences' and the synchronicities we experience. We may begin to see in these the outline of deeper laws.

We may become less quick to presume that our intuitions, our brilliant ideas are our own – and more open to the suggestion that they might be otherwordly promptings.

As well as becoming aware that we may be prompted by disembodied intelligence, we may realize, too, that we are connected with one another more directly through thinking than we are through speech and physical observation. We may develop a heightened sense that our interaction with other people is a far more mysterious process than we routinely suppose.

In the future we may also learn to look at relationships in terms of reincarnation. We may come to appreciate that relationships in previous incarnations may account for 'subconscious' feelings of liking and disliking which rise up when we meet strangers.

NATURALLY ALL THIS SEEMS MAD FROM a commonsensical point of view. There is no room anywhere in a scientific–materialist universe for these sorts of musings.

But the scientific–materialist view has its limitations, as I've tried to suggest.

When it comes to contemplating such far-flung events as the beginning of the universe, it is inevitable that huge amounts of speculation are mapped on to the smallest conceivable specks of evidence. Leading physicists', cosmologists' and philosophers' speculations on infinite interlocking dimensions, parallel universes and 'soap bubble universes' involve just as much imagination as Aquinas's speculations about angels on a pinhead.

The point is that when it comes to the biggest questions, people are again not necessarily choosing according to the balance of the probabilities, which may be almost too small to measure. The world *is* like the 'perspected' picture that can equally well be seen as a witch or a pretty young girl. People often choose one world-view in preference to another because somewhere in the depths of their being that is what they *want* to believe.

If we can learn to become conscious of this predisposition, we can make a decision which is – to that extent – free, because it is a decision based on knowledge. The part of us, somewhere in our depths, that wants to believe in a mechanical–materialist universe may on reflection not be the part of ourselves we want to determine our fate.

Know Thyself, commanded the Sun god. The techniques taught in ancient times in the Mystery schools and in modern times by groups like the Rosicrucians are intended to help us become aware of the rhythm of our breaths, our hearts, our sexual rhythms, the rhythm of waking, dreaming and dreamless sleep. If we can consciously attune our own individual rhythms to the rhythms of the cosmos measured by Jakim and Boaz, it is suggested we may eventually join our individual evolutions with the evolution of the cosmos. This would be to find meaning in life in meaning's highest sense.

Esoteric philosophy calls for a rediscovery of the spiritual hierarchies ranged *above* us, and, intimately connected with that, a discovery of the divine capabilities ranged *within* us. This was the secret preserved and nurtured by geniuses as diverse as Plato, St Paul, Leonardo, Shakespeare and Newton:

1. If you can think so deeply that you can rediscover the spiritual roots of thought, if you can recognize thoughts as living, spiritual beings ...
2. If you can develop a strong enough sense of your own individuality that you can become aware of your interaction with the Thought-Beings that weave in and out of yourself, yet not be overwhelmed by this reality ...
3. If you can recreate the ancient sense of wonder and use this sense of wonder to help awaken the willpower that lies sleeping in your deep, dark recesses ...
4. If the fire of love for your fellow human beings rises from your heart and causes you to weep tears of compassion ...

... then you have been working on the Four Elements. You have begun the process of their transformation.

This is the mysterious fourfold 'work' also alluded to by St Paul in I Corinthians 13: 'For now we see through a glass darkly; but then face to face; now I know in part but then shall I know even as I am known. And now abideth faith, hope, love, these three, but the greatest of these is love ...'

Intuition is transformed intellect that perceives the spiritual beings as real. Paul calls this faith.

Allegory *by Leonardo da Vinci. As an initiate of the secret philosophy Leonardo understood the spiritual exercises involving work on the Four Elements to which St Paul alludes. The creature on the left is not a wolf, as the catalogue of the Queen's collection states, but a bull.*

Wonder is transformed feeling, feeling that has become aware of the spiritual workings of the cosmos but is not overwhelmed by them. Paul calls this hope.

Conscience is transformed will, when by the exercise of thought and imagination, faith and hope, we have begun to transform that part of ourselves, including the willpower that lives beneath the threshold of consciousness. Paul calls this charity or love.

By applying faith to hope, and by applying faith and hope to love, a human being may then be transformed into an angel.

So the Scorpion is transformed into an Eagle. The Eagle works with the Bull and the Bull grows wings. The winged Bull works on the Lion so that it grows wings in its turn.

And the end of this fourfold process is that the winged Lion works on the Man so that he is transformed into an Angel. This is a great mystery taught in the Mystery centres of the ancient world, which became the great mystery of esoteric Christianity.

The Four Elements play a crucial role in the formation of the physical universe, and to work on them as they weave in and out of us is to transform not just ourselves but the whole universe, even to its outer limits. If an individual cries tears of compassion, his animal nature is to some extent transformed, but so, too, are the Cherubim that occupy and interweave throughout the whole cosmos. Changes in human physiology become seeds of the transfiguration of the entire material universe.

The Cabalist Isaac Luria wrote that, eventually, there will be no single atom that has not been worked on by man.

IN THE EARLY CHAPTERS OF THIS HISTORY we saw how the world and humanity were created in the following order: first the mineral part, second the vegetable, third the animal, and last, as the crown of creation, the distinctly human element. Constituent parts were nurtured one after the other, each providing the conditions for the succeeding stage to develop. As the latter stages of history progress, these parts will be transformed in reverse order: human, animal, vegetable and, lastly, mineral. At the end of time even the very atoms of our material natures will be transformed like the physical body of Jesus Christ in the Transfiguration.

We have seen that according to the secret history humanity is only briefly dipped into matter, that the hardening of the earth and of our skulls has enabled us to evolve a proper sense of self, and so the potential to think, will and love freely. But before this brief sojourn among physical objects, our experience was of *ideas*. The objects of our Imagination, which we conceived of as coming from spirits, angels and gods, were real to us. For the greater part of human history, even long after matter had been formed, what we saw in the mind's eye was still more real to us than material objects. The lesson of *modern* history is that matter is being transformed, dispersed, so that in the not too distant future we will re-enter the realm of Imagination.

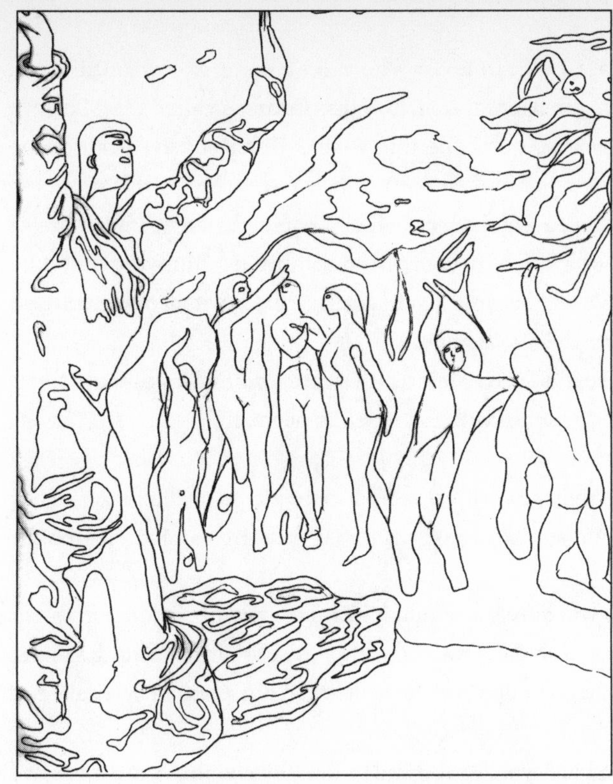

The Opening of the Fifth Seal *by El Greco. This revivifying of the chakras is what is meant in Revelation by the 'opening of the seals'.*

When will this happen? What will happen after the incarnation of Satan? In Chapter 4 we saw that in the mind-before-matter understanding, history is divided into seven 'days'. Saturday was the rule of Saturn, Sunday was the age when the earth was united with the sun, Monday was the age before the moon departed. Tuesday was the age that started with the locking into place of the fixed, material world in 11,145 BC. The death of Jesus Christ marked the halfway point in Tuesday and the Great Week. What will happen in the rest of the week?

In AD 3574 we will enter the age called Philadelphia in Revelation. If the great evolutionary impulses of previous eras have come from India, Persia, Egypt, Greece, Rome and Northern Europe, the next impulse will come from Eastern Europe and Russia. Freemasonic-influenced governments in America and Britain have been keen to involve themselves in this area of the world for this reason. Already it is possible to see extremes emanating from this area, both extremes of spirituality and extremes of evil, such as the Russian 'mafia'.

In future personalities we remember from history, the great personalities who helped lead humanity out of the spirit worlds, will be reborn in order to lead us back into the spirit worlds. There will be a new Shakespeare, a new Moses, a new Zarathustra, a new Hercules. Towards the end of the Philadelphian era, Jesus Pandira, the Teacher of the

Essenes, will incarnate again as 'the Fifth Rider who rides a horse called Faithful and True', referred to in Revelation. In oriental tradition this figure is called the Maitreya Buddha. He will bring great spiritual gifts, opening what St Teresa of Avila called 'the eyes of the soul', the chakras.

We will then re-enter the sacred wood described in Chapter 2. We will be aware of the spirits, then angels and gods, alive in everything around us, but we will not be controlled by them any more. We will become aware again of the spiritual beings ranged on either side of us whenever we *make a decision.*

As good and evil spirits make themselves felt, as everyone communicates more freely with the spirit worlds, organized religion will no longer be needed.

Imagine no religion.

We will regain some of the ability to control animals and plants by the power of our thoughts that Adam enjoyed. We will begin to remember past lives and to foresee the future.

Our waking consciousness will develop so that it bears the same relationship to our present day waking consciousness as today's waking consciousness bears to our dreaming consciousness. We will realize that, although we have believed ourselves to be awake, we have actually been asleep.

These developments will be hard-won. At the end of the Philadelphian era, there will be a catastrophic world war at the end of which the surface of the earth will become a spiritual wasteland, except for America, where the flame of spirituality will be kept alive. This will be the mirror image of the period of the first Zarathustra.

The period AD 5734–7894 is called Laodicea in Revelation. As matter becomes less dense, so our bodies will respond more and more to spiritual impulses. The goodness in good people will shine out of them, while the faces and bodies of evil people will be moulded by the animal passions that dominate them.

Good people will find it increasingly hard to be happy if they are surrounded by people who are miserable. Eventually no one will be happy until *everyone* is happy

If the material world is brief, so too is death. In time we will no longer die but sleep very deeply, and then less and less deeply. Death, as St Paul says, will be swallowed up. As we enter another age of metamorphosis, biological generation too will eventually become unnecessary. We will discover the 'Word that has been lost' of the Freemasons, which is to say we will be able to create by power of the voice.

In the scheme of the Great Week, we'll have moved into 'Thursday', though, of course, time as we understand it today will no longer exist. Our thoughts will take on a life of their own, working on our behalf but independently of us.

As history approaches its end, the forces of evil will assert themselves once more, as the third being in the trinity of evil, Sorath, the Sun demon opposes God's intentions.

This is the beast with two horns like a lamb's, described in Revelation. He will lead the forces of evil in the Last Battle.

Eventually, not only will the sun come up differently as St John Chrysostom predicted, but a sun will rise up inside each of us.

ALL OF THIS WILL HAVE BEEN ACCOMPLISHED by the power of thought!

By and large the people who have most changed history have not been the great generals or politicians, but the artists and thinkers. An individual sitting alone in a room and giving birth to an idea can do more to change the course of history than a general who commands thousands on the field of battle or a political leader who commands the loyalty of millions.

This is the romance and excitement of philosophy. In a mind-before-matter universe there is more than romance and excitement in all thinking – there is magic too. It is not just what I do or say but what I *think* that affects my fellow humans and the whole course of history.

PLATO SAID THAT ALL PHILOSOPHY BEGINS with wonder.

Modern science is killing off wonder, by telling us that we know it all. Modern science is killing off philosophy, by encouraging us not to ask the big Why questions. These questions are strictly meaningless, they say. Just get on with it.

Today's scientists try to insist that theirs is the only way to interpret the basic conditions of human existence. They like to dwell on what they know. In their view, the known is like a vast continent occupying nearly everything there is.

The men and women who have been described making history in this book have preferred to dwell on what they *don't know*. In their view, the known is a tiny island floating on a vast and very strange sea.

Let us sow the seeds of doubt. Let us take Francis Bacon's advice and refrain from rushing to impose a pattern on the world. Let us wait with Keats at our shoulder for a deeper pattern to emerge.

Science is *not* certain. It is a myth like any other, representing what people in the deepest parts of themselves want to believe.

Rudolf Steiner once said that people who don't have the courage to be cruel often develop cruel beliefs. To propose that we don't live in a reciprocal universe is needlessly cruel.

If we accept these cruel views we are allowing the say-so of experts in their own field to take precedence over our own personal experience. We are also denying things that Shakespeare, Cervantes and Dostoyevsky are telling us are true.

The aim of this book, therefore, has been to suggest that if we take a fresh look at the basic conditions of our existence, they may perhaps be seen in a radically new way.

In fact, they may be seen *in a way that is nearly completely the opposite of what we have been brought up to believe.* This is what philosophy does, if it is done well.

The remains of an ancient wisdom lie all around us in the names of the days of the week and the months of the year, in the arrangement of the pips in an apple and in the strangeness of mistletoe, in music, in the stories we tell our children and in the design of many public buildings and statues and in our greatest art and literature.

If we can't *see* this ancient wisdom, it is because we have been conditioned not to. We have been bewitched by materialism.

Science sees idealism as having dominated history up until the seventeenth century when the process of discrediting it began. Science assumes materialism will remain the dominant philosophy until the end of time. In the view of the secret societies, materialism will come to be seen as a mere blip.

THE TEACHINGS OF THE SECRET SOCIETIES have here been pulled out into the light of day for the first time. Readers may find them laughable – but at least on the basis of knowing what they really are. Other readers may sense something in them, even though they seem completely incompatible with the great scientific certainties of our age.

This has been a visionary history, history as it is retained in the human psyche, a night history preserved by adepts able to slip from the material dimension into another one. It might seem incompatible with the history you have been brought up to believe in, but maybe it is true in other dimensions?

Perhaps we should end by considering the musings of a great scientist? The physicist Niels Bohr said, 'The opposite of a correct statement is a false statement, but the opposite of a profound truth may well be another profound truth.'

We have seen that if we try to peer back into the past beyond 11,451 BC there is very little evidence that science can properly count as hard. Vast, airy constructions of interpretation are balanced precariously on the tiniest bits of data. And, of course, the same is true if we try to gaze far into the future, beyond AD 11,451 . The truth is that we must use our imagination. When we travel any distance in either direction, when we leave the confines of this little island of matter, we cannot but enter the realms of imagination.

Of course materialists tend to distrust the imagination, associating it with fantasy and illusion.

But the secret societies hold an especially exalted view of the imagination. Each individual mind is a protrusion into the material world of one vast cosmic mind, and we must use the imagination to reach back into it and to engage with it.

It was using the imagination in this way that made Leonardo, Shakespeare and Mozart god-like.

Imagination is the key.

Acknowledgements

I thank Sarmaurin, Kszil and Aaron. I have been helped in the thinking and writing by Hannah Black, Jane Bradish Ellames, Jamie Buxton, Kevin Jackson, Kate Parkin and Paul Sidey. I am blessed to have such kindred spirits. I have the best agent and the best publisher. Jonny Geller is all deft action like a Zen archer and Anthony Cheetham is a *unique* combination of intellectual clout and commercial nous. As soon as I saw he was setting up a new publishing company, I knew I wanted to be published by it. I wish to thank Sue Freestone, my editor and Publisher of Quercus, and also the exceptionally able Charlotte Clerk. Thanks, too, to Patrick Carpenter, Nicolas Cheetham, Caroline Proud, Lucy Ramsey, Emma Ward, Andrew Sydenham, Doug Kean, Paul Abel and also to Elaine Willis for researching some really obscure pictures. Thank you, Betsy Robbins and Emma Parry for wonderful foreign rights sales, and I'm really glad to have the legendary Peter Mayer as my publisher in the States. Fred Gettings and Lorna Byrne Fitzgerald have, I know, been looking after me from afar. My mother, Cynthia, and Terry provided a peaceful haven when it was needed. My family have had to put up with a lot in the past eighteen months. My daughter Tabitha has also helped by drawing some brilliant illustrations in cases where permissions have been beyond reach, and my son Barnaby is always ready to lighten the mood with his subversive jokes. I thank my wife, Fiona, for all the love and dedication she has shown throughout the writing of this book – and this I now wish to repay.

Illustration Acknowledgements

The publishers would like to thank the following for source material and permission to reproduce copyright material:

Private Collection Pages 15, 21, 23, 34, 36, 37, 38, 43, 48, 49, 50, 52, 54, 57, 58, 59, 60, 61, 62, 65, 66, 67, 68, 69, 71, 72, 73, 74, 76, 79, 82, 84, 85, 86, 91, 92, 96, 97, 100, 101, 103, 104, 105, 111, 114, 116, 119, 124, 125, 126, 131, 133, 134, 136, 138, 140, 144, 145, 148, 155, 156, 158, 160, 162, 165, 166, 171, 172, 173, 179, 181, 184, 187, 188, 193, 195, 196, 197, 198, 199, 205, 207, 213, 216, 218, 220, 221, 222, 223, 225, 233, 235, 244, 249, 252, 253, 256, 261, 264, 267,275, 277, 278, 280, 282, 286, 288, 296, 297, 298, 308, 311, 312, 319, 320, 321, 322, 323, 324, 329, 335, 337, 338, 339, 342, 346, 347, 348, 352, 353, 356, 361, 366, 370, 372, 375, 377, 378, 385, 388, 394, 398, 403, 407
Bridgeman Art Library/Private Collection/Photo Boltin Picture Library © Succession Marcel Duchamp/ADAGP, Paris and DACS, London 2007 Page 24
Bridgeman Art Library/Private Collection Page 56
Bridgeman Art Library/Giraudon/Louvre, Paris Page 284
Tofoto/Fotomas Page 9, 27, 295
Topfoto/Charles Walker Page 55
Topfoto/Picturepoint Page 332
Le Petit Prince by Antoine de Saint-Exupéry, Published in English 1943 Page 141
National Gallery, London Page 212
Corbis/Philadelphia Museum of Art © Succession Marcel Duchamp/ADAGP, Paris and DACS, London 2007 Page 230
Corbis/Alinari Archives Page 401
Martin J Powell © Martin J Powell, Page 131

COLOUR SECTION
Plate 1: Top: The Kobal Collection/Warner Bros, Left: Bridgeman Art Library/Washington University, St. Louis, USA/Lauros/Giraudon © ADAGP, Paris and DACS, London, Right: Bridgeman Art Library / Prado, Madrid, Spain. Plate 2: Top: AKG Images, Bottom: Corbis/ Sygma. Plate 3: Top: Bridgeman Art Library/Peter Willi/Goethe Museum, Frankfurt, Bottom: AKG Images. Plate 4: Top: The National Gallery of Ireland, Bottom: Corbis/Philadelphia Museum of Art © Succession Marcel Duchamp/ADAGP, Paris and DACS, London 2007. Plate 5: Private Collection. Plate 6: Top: Art Archive/Musée du Louvre Paris/Gianni Dagli Orti, Left: Bridgeman Art Library/Musee d'Unterlinden, Colmar, France/Giraudon, Right: Bridgeman Art Library/Prado, Madrid, Spain. Plate 7: Private Collection. Plate 8: Private Collection. Plate 9: Top Left: The British Museum, London, Top Right: Private Collection, Bottom: The Kobal Collection/NERO. Plate 10: Top: Bridgeman Art Library/Musee d'Unterlinden, Colmar, France/Giraudon, Bottom: Private Collection. Plate 11: Top: Bridgeman Art Library/Giraudon/Lauros/Ste. Marie Madeleine, Aix-en-Provence, France, Bottom: Private Collection. Plate 12: Top: Bridgeman Art Library/Giraudon/Louvre, Paris, France, Bottom: Bridgeman Art Library/Graphische Sammlung Albertina, Vienna, Austria. Plate 13: Top: Bridgeman Art Library/Giraudon/Prado, Madrid, Spain. Bottom: Bridgeman Art Library/Alinari/Santa Maria della Vittoria, Rome, Italy. Plate 14: Top: Art Archive/Museum der Stadt Wien/Alfredo Dagli Orti, Bottom: Private Collection. Plate 15: Top: Bridgeman Art Library/ Yale Center for British Art, Paul Mellon Collection, USA, Bottom: Bridgeman Art Library/Duomo, Orvieto, Umbria, Italy. Plate 16: Top: Corbis/Christine Kolisch, Bottom: Corbis/Francis G.Mayer

Every effort has been made to contact copyright holders. However, the publishers will be glad to rectify in future editions any inadvertent omissions brought to their attention.

A Note on Sources and Selective Bibliography

The moment it all came together was when in Hall's second hand bookshop in Tunbridge Wells, I found a copy of Jacob Boehme's *Mysterium Magnum* translated in two volumes by John Sparrow. Written in 1623, before the great influx of esoterica from the East that would result from European empire-building, this book showed me was that there really was a genuine Western esoteric tradition connecting the Mystery schools of Egypt, Greece and Rome with the assertions of modern visionaries like Rudolf Steiner.

Around the same time I also chanced upon Boehme's *The Signature of All Things*, Paracelsus's *The Archidoxes of Magic*, and *Paracelsus: Life and Prophecies*, a collection of his writings edited and with a short biography by Franz Hartmann, and *The Works of Thomas Vaughan*, the English Rosicrucian, edited by A.E. Waite – in a beautiful glowing gold cover. Rich pickings indeed, these books provided further confirmation of this tradition. A modern book, Joscelyn Godwin's *Robert Fludd: Hermetic philosopher and surveyor of two worlds* actually contained a picture of the earth separating from the Sun. I knew there was an esoteric tradition of this as a historical event, but previously I had only read about in Steiner.

Some writers, including Valentine Tomberg and Max Heindel, have been accused of not sufficiently declaring their debt to Steiner. Let me do so now. Steiner is a colossal figure in arcane circles, bestriding the late nineteenth and twentieth centuries, much as Swedenborg bestrode the late eighteenth and nineteenth centuries. He has done more than any other teacher to illumine the difficult and paradoxical world of esoteric philosophy. There are apparently some six hundred volumes of Steiner's work, mostly collections of lectures. I must have read thirty of these, at the very least.

Although he has done so much to illumine, his books are by no means an easy read. Steiner's aim is not to be as clear as possible in the way of Anglo-American academia. His aim is to work on his listeners by a sort of weaving together of themes – the historical with the metaphysical with the moral with the philosophical. There is no structure in the conventional way, and no narrative. Things come round and round again rhythmically, some in larger cycles, some in smaller ones. Many readers will quickly lose patience, but if you persist there are always fascinating nuggets of information – and my own book is as full of these Steinerian nuggets as a plumb pudding.

All idealistic philosophy, (which is to say philosophy that proposes mind came before matter and that matter was precipitated out of a cosmic mind in some way), accounts for this precipitation in terms of a series of emanations from the cosmic mind. The higher science of idealism always – esoteric philosophy in all traditions – relates these emanations to the heavenly bodies in a quite systematic way. The different traditions show some variations, and where they do I have not only simplified for the sake of clarity, I have taken Steiner as my guide. The key texts here are: *Theosophy*, *Occult Science*, *The Evolution of the World and Humanity* and *Universe, Earth and Man*.

(I have stayed away from disputes between different schools of thought, such as the anthroposophists, the theosophists and the followers of Keyserling – about the chronology of these events – because they are abstruse and on the grounds that, as I argue in my text, time as we understand it today did not exist then. I think such discussions sometimes veer dangerously towards the meaningless, but for an intelligent discussion of these issues I recommend the Vermont Sophia web page and the Sophia Foundation website of Robert Powell. Many works by Keyserling are also available online. Incidentally, I have in one instance – on the question of whether or not stories of two Krishnas should be disentangled, preferred Keyserling to Steiner.)

Steiner is a visionary, and rarely sources his teachings. Much of what he says is in principle unverifiable in any academic or scientific sense, but a lot is verifiable and that has almost always checked out. There are only a handful of exceptions, I believe.

I think a problem with Steiner is that he is such a great figure that people who follow in his footsteps find it hard to think freely and independently. Steiner's shadow can inhibit originality. Partly because I have worked for so long in publishing, where a pig-headed certainty that you are right is indispensable if you are to enjoy any success, and partly because my research has ranged so widely that I have been able, to some degree at least, to see Steiner in context, I have not felt him in any way a burden – rather as an inspiration.

Among other modern teachers G.I. Gurdjieff means to tease and bemuse in his writings, but his gigantic, ten volumes *All And Everything* also contain astonishing nuggets that confirm ancient, esoteric teaching. His protégée, Ouspensky, had a gift for reframing ancient wisdom in what we might without being too cute call a modernist idiom in *In Search of the Miraculous* and *Tertium Organon*. Likewise immersed in the Sufi tradition René Guénon is the image of Gallic intellectual rigour, and I have used his *Man and his Becoming*, and *The Lord of the World*, and *Introduction to the Study of Hindu Doctrine*, not only as sources of information but as models of good discipline.

The Secret Wisdom of Qabalah is a wonderfully concise yet illuminating guide. In terms of a specifically Christian esoteric tradition, *The Perfect Way* by Anna Bonus Kingsford and Edward Maitland, written in 1881, is difficult to find, but I chanced upon a ring-bound photocopy. Written by a High Church Anglican, C.G. Harrison, *The Transcendental Universe* was published in 1893, causing a furor in esoteric circles both inside and outside the Church, because it revealed things the secret societies thought better kept secret. From the Orthodox Perspective, the small library of books by Omraam Mikhal Aïvanhov represent a tradition of nurturing the ancient Sun mysteries and Christian esoteric teachings on love and sexuality. Mentioned in the text, *Meditations on the Tarot* was published anonymously in Paris in 1980, it was written by a former disciple of Steiner's, Valentin Tomberg, who later became a Roman Catholic. (For a fascinating account of the fallout, I recommend *The Case of Valentin Tomberg* by Sergei O. Prokofieff.) *Meditations on the Tarot* is a treasure trove of Christian esoteric lore. *The Zelator* by David Ovason is a neglected classic of modern esoteric writing. It draws on the wisdom of several schools but has a Christian message at its heart. Rudolf Steiner's books on Jesus Christ have been invaluable, especially on the Sun-Mystery central to esoteric Christianity: *Christianity as a Mystical Fact and the Mysteries of Antiquity, The Spiritual Beings in the Heavenly Bodies and in the Kingdoms of Nature, Building Stones for an understanding of the Mystery of the Golgotha, the Influences of Lucifer and Ahriman, From Buddha to Christ*, his various commentaries on the gospels, including the so-called fifth gospel and *The Redemption of Thinking* (on Thomas Aquinas). I have also tracked down some works excluded from the various extensive Steiner publishing programmes, including his early, theosophical work on *Atlantis and Lemuria*, and more importantly for my text, *Inner Impulses of Evolution: The Mexican Mysteries and the Knights Templar*. I have made much use of the biblical commentaries of Steiner's friend Emil Bock from *Genesis* to *The Three Years* and *Saint Paul*. I have also used *Lore and Legend of the English Church* by G.S. Tyack, and *Good and Evil Spirits* by Edward Langton.

The great masterpieces of alchemy in twentieth century writing are, of course, *Le Mystère des Cathédrales* and *Les Demeures Philosophales*. Not only do they offer clues to understanding, but they are also brilliant guides to tracking down esoteric sites in France. I recommend Paul Sedir's *History of the Rosicrucian Brotherhood*, which contains an excellent, illuminating account of the greatest flowering of Christianized alchemy. *The Zelator* by David Ovason is good on this subject, as is Steiner's *The Mysteries of the Rosicrucians*. To anyone wishing to research alchemy further, I recommend the writing website of Adam Maclean, a fascinating archive of historical documents.

Steiner's predecessor, Madame Blavatsky, is a bit of a problem, if only because her anti-Christian animus seems in retrospect a bit impish and perverse. I prefer to see Blavatsky as an exemplar of a splendid Victorian tradition – the writing of monstrously large rag bags of books packed with strange ideas and obscure but often fascinating erudition. With the possible exception of Sir James Frazer's *The Golden Bough* – which is at least permanently in print – these books are hardly read at all now. In fact I sometimes wondered whether I was the first person to read some of these pages for perhaps over a hundred years. Their wisdom has become discarded wisdom, but there *is* wisdom to be found, and I have had a lot of fun rummaging around in the following: *The Secret Doctrine* and *Isis Unveiled* by Madame Blavatsky, *Theosophy and Psychological Religion* by F. Max Muller. *Fragments of a Faith Forgotten* and *Orpheus* by G.R.S. Meade, *The Egyptian Book of the Dead* and *Gnostic and Historic Christianity* by George Eliot's friend, Gerald Massey, *Ancient Theories of Revelation and Inspiration* by Edwyn Bevan, *Oedipus Judaicus* by William Drummond, *The Lost Language of Symbolism*, and *Archaic England* by Harold Bayley, *The Canon* by William Stirling, *Architecture: Mysticism and Myth* by William Lethaby, *Pagan and Christian Creeds* by Edward Carpenter, *Introduction to Tantra Sastra* and *The Serpent Power* by Sir John Woodroffe, *The History of Magic* by Eliphas Levi, *The Kabbalah Unveiled* by S.L. Macgregor Mathers, *Mysticism* by Evelyn Underhill, *Studies in Mysticism and Certain Aspects of the Secret Tradition* by A.E. Waite, *Cosmic Consciousness* by Richard Bucke, *The Initiates* by Eduard Schure, *The Eleusian and Bacchic Mysteries* by Thomas Taylor, *The Veil of Isis* by W. Winwood Reade.

Occult physiology is a key part of this book. I have used *The Occult Causes of Disease* by E. Wolfram, *The Encyclopedia of Esoteric Man* by Benjamin Walker, *Occult Principles of Health and Healing* by Max Heindel, *Occult Anatomy and the Bible* by Corinne Heline *and An Occult Physiology, Initiation and its Results, Occult Science and Occult Development* by Steiner. *The Parable of the Beast* by John Bleibtreu, while not framed in esoteric philosophy, has fascinating information, especially on the Third Eye.

Occult art is also key. I have used *Symbolists and Symbolism* by Robert L Delevoy, *Legendary and Mythological Art* by Clara Erskine Clement, *Hieronymus Bosch* by Wilhelm Fraenger, *Symbols in Christian Art* by Edward Hulme, *Three Lectues on Art* by René Huyghe – particularly good on El Greco – *The Occult in Art* by Fred Gettings, *The Two Children* by David Ovason, *Marcel Duchamp* by Octavio Paz on Marcel Duchamp, John Richardson's three volume biography, *A Life of Picasso* and Mark Harris's insightful essay on *Picasso's Lost Masterpiece, The Foundations of Modern Art* by Ozenfant, *Sacred and Legendary Art* by Mrs Jameson, *Surrealism and Painting* by André Breton, *Surrealism and the Occult* by Nadia Choucha.

The books of Albert Pike and A.E. Waite on Freemasonry fall into the baggy Victorian monster category. Together with Manly Hall these men are established as the great writers on the Freemasonic mysteries, and I have used their *Morals and Dogma, History of Freemasonry* and *Secret Teachings of All Ages*, as well as *The Temple Legend* by Rudolf Steiner. I'd like to mention in the same breath, *The Secret Zodiacs of Washington DC* by David Ovason and *The Seven Ordeals of Count Cagliostro* by Ian McCalman. I'd also like to credit the independent-minded research of Robert Lomas, who has co-written with Christopher Knight several best-selling books on the origins of Freemasonry – including *The Hiram Key, The Second Messiah* and *Uriel's Machine*. Like another bestselling writer in the alternative history field, Robert Bauval, Lomas is an engineer, and so able to see things that more theoretically-minded writers have missed. Something I've tried to insist on in my own book is that the fact that esoteric teachings have useful, practical application makes them much more likely to be true. A.E. Waite's *The Hidden Church of the Holy Grail* is the best account of the various sources of the Grail legend.

The great figure in esoteric Egyptology is Schwaller de Lubicz. He represents a major impulse to understand the consciousness of the ancient world. I have taken insights from *The Temple of Man, Sacred Science* and *The Egyptian Miracle*. I have also had the pleasure of sailing up the Nile to visit the major Egyptian sites with many of the most popular modern writers in the field, including Robert Bauval, Graham Hancock, Robert Temple and Colin Wilson. On one occasion I found myself exploring a secret passageway behind the altar of one of the great temples of Egypt in the company of Michael Baigent. Of particular relevance to this work is Bauval's latest book, *The Egypt Code*, referenced in the text. There, I believe, he finally cracks the numerical, astronomical code behind Egyptian architecture. Robert Temple is someone who can certainly access supernatural levels of intelligence. *The Sirius Mystery, The Crytsal Sun* and *Netherworld* are authoritative texts on astronomical symbolism in myth and initiation lore. See also *The Mysteries* by Ita Wegman, *Mystery Knowldege and Mystery Centres* by Rudolf Steiner, *In the Dark Places of Wisdom* by Peter Kingsley. I first read Colin Wilson's *The Outsider* at the right age – 17 years old – and was introduced to Rilke and Sartre. Later my philosophy tutor – sometimes talked of as the cleverest don in Oxford – dismissed Sartre's work as not being real philosophy, and I've no doubt he's say the same of Wilson. But I see Wilson as an intellectual in the highest sense, in that he struggles to understand the great questions of life and death and what it means to be alive now with complete intellectual honesty and remarkable intellectual energy. His intellectual heirs in the next generation were Michael Baigent and Graham Hancock. Baigent co-wrote with Henry Lincoln and Richard Leigh *The Holy Blood and the Holy Grail* the book that created the cultural climate into which any book on the subject of the secret societies must emerge. I explain in my text where I believe it is wrong, giving a materialistic interpretation of a genuine but more spiritual tradition regarding the relationship between Jesus Christ and Mary Magdalene. Like Baigent and Leigh, Hancock is adept at using the techniques of suspense fiction to pull readers through quite difficult ideas. His books, particularly *Fingerprints of the Gods*, have begun to shift the paradigm, to convince a mass readership that they should question the version of history handed down to them by their elders and betters. His latest book, *Supernatural*, takes extraordinary intellectual risks, but is written with all the rigour you would expect from a man who was formerly one of Britain's top financial journalists.

The archeologist David Rohl would perhaps slightly distance himself from some of those I have just mentioned, as he is an academic as well as the bestselling writer of *A Test of Time, Legend: the Genesis of Civilization* and *The Lost Testament*. His arguments on dating, particularly as they relate to the area where Egyptian archeology matches biblical texts, will, I believe, come to be accepted by his elders in the academic establishment over the next ten years.

Something that has struck me during the writing of this book is just how many academics working in their separate fields are coming up with results which are anomalous as regards the ruling paradigm, both in terms of the materialistic hegemony and the conventional view of history. One of the things I've tried to do in this book is to bring together many different groups of anomalies to create a complete, anomalous world-view. Some of the senior academics mentioned in this book I know personally, but most I do not, and I have no way of knowing if they have, or had any private interest in the esoteric. The important point is this: no esoteric allegiances are evident in their texts, but their books bolster the esoteric world-view: *The Origin of Consciousness in the breakdown of the Bi-Cameral Mind* by Julian Jaynes, *The Wandering Scholars* by Helen Waddell, *Les Troubadors et le Sentiment Romanesque* by Robert Briffault, *The Art of Memory, The Occult Philosophy in the Elizabethan Age, Giordano Bruno and the Hermetic Tradition* by Frances Yates, *Shakespeare and the Invention of the Human* and *Where Shall Wisdom be Found?* by Harold Bloom, *Why Mrs Blake Cried* by Marsha Keith Suchard, *Isaac Newton, the Man* by John Maynard Keynes, *Name in the Window* by Margaret Demorest (on John Donne), *The School of Night* by M.C. Cranbrook, *Hamlet's Mill* by Giorgio de Santillana and Hertha von Dechend, *The Roots of Romanticism* by Isaiah Berlin, *Religion and the Decline of Magic* by Keith Thomas, *Church And Gnosis* by F.C. Burkitt, *Emperor of the Earth* by Czeslaw Milosz, *The Double Flame: Love and Eroticism* by Octavio Paz, *John Amos Comenius* by S.S. Laurie, *Meditations on Hunting* by Jose Ortega y Gasset.

Other key sources include:

The Book of the Master by W. Marsham Adams

The Golde Asse of Lucius Apuleius translated by William Adlington

Love and Sexuality by Omraam Mikhael Aivanhov

Francis of Assissi: Canticle of the Creatures by Paul M Allen and Joan de Ris Allen

Through the Eyes of the Masters by David Anrias

The Apocryphal New Testament edited by Wake and Lardner

SSOTBME an Essay on Magic by Anon

Myth, Nature and Individual by Frank Baker

Les Diaboliques by Jules Barbey D'Aurevilly

History in English Words by Owen Barfield

Dark Knights of the Solar Cross by Geoffrey Basil Smith

The Esoteric Path by Luc Benoist

A Rumour of Angels by Peter L Berger*

A Pictorial History of Magic and the Supernatural by Maurice Bessy

The Undergrowth of History by Robert Birley

Radiant Matter Decay and Consecration by Georg Blattmann

The Inner Group Teachings by H.P. Blavatsky

Studies in Occultism by H.P. Blavatsky

A Universal History of Infamy by Jorge Luis Borges

Giordano Bruno and the Embassy Affair by John Bossy

Letters from an Occultist by Marcus Bottomley

The Occult History of the World Vol 1 by J H Brennan

Nadja by André Breton

Egypt Under the Pharaohs by Heinrich Brugsch-Bey
Hermit in the Himalayas by Paul Brunton
A Search for Secret India by Paul Brunton
Egyptian Magic and *Oriris and the Egyptian Resurrection* by E.A. Wallis Budge
Legends of Charlemagne by Thomas Bulfinch
Studies in Comparative Religion by Titus Burckhardt
If on a Winter's Night a Traveller by Italo Calvino*
Hero with a Thousand Faces by Joseph Campbell
Rediscovering Gandhi by Yogesh Chadha
Life Before Birth, Life on Earth, Life After Death by Paul E. Chu
The True Story of the Rosicrucians by Tobias Churton
The Dream of Scipio by Cicero, translated by Percy Bullock
On the Nature of the Gods by Cicero, translated by C.M. Ross
The New Gods by E.M. Cioran
Europe's Inner Demons by Norman Cohn
The Theory of the Celestial Influence by Rodney Collin
Ka by Roberto Calasso
The Marriage of Cadmus and Harmony by Roberto Colasso*
A Road to the Spirit by Paul Coroze
The Mysteries of Mithras by Franz Cumont
The Afterlife in Roman Paganism by Franz Cumont
Valis by Philip K. Dick
The Revelation of Evolutionary Events by Evelynn B. Debusschere
Mystical Theology and Celestial Hierarchy by Dionysius the Aropagite, translated by the editors of the Shrine of Wisdom
Atlantis: the Antediluvian World by Ignatius Donnelly
The Erotic world of Faery by Maureen Duffy
Les Magiciens de Dieu by François Ribadeau Dumas
Chronicles volume One by Bob Dylan*
Foucault's Pendulum by Umberto Eco
The Name of the Rose by Umberto Eco
The Book of Enoch edited by R.H. Charles
The Sacred Magician by Georges Chevalier
Life's Hidden Secrets by Edward G. Collinge
Conversations with Goethe by Eckermann*
A New Chronology of the Gospels by Ormond Edwards
Zodiacs Old and New by Cyril Fagan
On Life after Death by Gustav Theodor Fechner
Ecstasies by Carlo Ginzburg
Once upon a fairy tale by Norbert Glas
Snow-White put right by Norbert Glas
Magic and Divination by Rupert Gleadow
Maxims and Reflections by Johann Wolfgang Von Goethe
Hara: the vital centre of man by Karlfried Graf Dürckheim
The Greek Myths by Robert Graves
M.R. James' Book of the Supernatural by Peter Haining
Cabalistic keys to the Lord's Prayer by Manly P. Hall
Sages and Seers by Manly P. Hall
The Secret Teachings of All Ages by Manly P. Hall
The Roots of Witchcraft by Michael Harrison
The Communion Service and the Ancient Mysteries by Alfred Heidenreich
The Rosicrucian Cosmo-Conception by Max Heindel
The *Hermetica* in the edition edited and translated by Walter Scott
The Kingdom of Faerie by Geoffrey Hodson
The Kingdom of the Gods by Geoffrey Hodson
Myth and Ritual by Samuel H. Hooke
Vicious circles and infinity by Patrick Hughes and George Brecht
The Way of the Sacred by Frances Huxley
La Bas by J.K. Huymans
Vernal Blooms by W.Q. Judge
Eshtetes et Magiciens by Philippe Jullian
The Teachings of Zoroaster by S.A. Kapadia
The Rebirth of Magic by Francis King and Isabel Sutherland
Egyptian Mysteries New Light on Ancient Knowledge by Lucy Lamy
Transcendental Magic by Eliphas Levi
The Invisible College by Robert Lomas
The Book of the Lover and the Beloved by Ramon Lull
Lynch on Lynch, edited by Chris Rodley
An Astrological Key to Biblical Symbolism by Ellen Conroy McCaffrey
Reincarnation in Christianity by Geddes MacGregor
The Great Secret by Maurice Maeterlinck
Experiment in Depth by P.W. Martin
The Western Way by Caitlin and John Matthews
Simon Magus by G.R.S. Mead
The Secret of the West by Dimitri Merezhkovsky
The Ascent of Man by Eleanor Merry
Studies in Symbolism by Marguerite Mertens-Stienon
Ancient Christian Magic by Meyer and Smith
Outline of Metaphysics by L. Furze Morrish
Rudolf Steiner's Vision of Love by Bernard Nesfield-Cookson
The Mark by Maurice Nicoll
The New Man by Maurice Nicoll
Simple explanation of work ideas by Maurice Nicoll
The Idea of the Holy by Rudolf Otto
The Secrets of Nostradamus by David Ovason*
Metamorphoses by Ovid translated by David Raeburn
Gurdjieff by Louis Pauwels
Les Sociétés Secretes by Louis Pauwels and Jacques Bergier
Select works of Plotinus edited by G.R.S Mead
The Double Flame: Essays on Love and Eroticism by Octavio Paz
The Cycle of the Seasons and Seven Liberal Arts by Sergei O. Prokofieff
Prophecy of the Russian Epic by Sergei O. Prokofieff
The Golden Verses of Pythagoras and Other Pythagoran Fragments translated by Florence M. Firth
The Tarot of the Bohemians by Papus
King Arthur: the true story by Graham Philips and Martin Keatman
Freemasonry by Alexander Piatigorsky
Gargantua and Pantagruel by Rabelais, translated by J.M. Cohen
Zen Flesh, Zen Bones by Paul Reps
Letters to a young poet by Rainer Maria Rilke*

The Notebooks of Malte Laurids Brigge by Rainer Maria Rilke
The Followers of Horus by David Rohl
Dionysius the Areopagite by C.E.Rolt
Pan and the Nightmare by Heinrich Roscher and James Hillman*
Lost Civilizations of the Stone Age by Richard Rudgley
The Philosophy of Magic by Eusebe Salverte
The Story of Atlantis and the Lost Lemuria by W. Scott-Elliot
Studies in comparative religion by Frithjof Schuon
The Rings of Saturn by W.G. Sebald
Annotations of the sacred writings of the Hindus by Edward Sellon
Lights Out For The Territory by Iain Sinclair
The Sufis by Idries Shah
Esoteric Buddhism by A.P. Sinnett
Man, creator of forms by V. Wallace Slater
Jesus the Magician by Morton Smith
The Occult Causes of the Present War by Lewis Spence
Egypt, myths and legends by Lewis Spence
Epiphany by Owen St. Victor
The Present Age by W.J. Stein
The principle of reincarnation by W.J. Stein
Tolstoy and Dostoyevsky by George Steiner
Atlantis and Lemuria by Rudolf Steiner
The Book with Fourteen Seals by Rudolf Steiner
The Concepts of Original Sin and Grace by Rudolf Steiner
The Dead Are With Us by Rudolf Steiner
Deeper Secrets of Human History in the Light of the Gospel of St Matthew by Rudolf Steiner
Egyptian myths and mysteries by Rudolf Steiner
The Evolution of Consciousness, and *The Sun Initiation of the Druid Priest and his Moon-Science* by Rudolf Steiner
From Symptom to Reality in Modern History by Rudolf Steiner
Inner Impulses of Evolution by Rudolf Steiner
The Karma of Untruthfulness vols I and II by Rudolf Steiner
Karmic relationships Vols I and II by Rudolf Steiner
Life Between Death and Rebirth by Rudolf Steiner
Manifestations of Karma by Rudolph Steiner
Occult History by Rudolf Steiner
The occult movement in the nineteenth century by Rudolf Steiner*
The Occult Significance of Blood by Rudolf Steiner
The Origins of Natural Science by Rudolf Steiner
Reincarnation and Karma by Rudolf Steiner
Results of spiritual investigation by Rudolf Steiner
The Temple Legend by Rudolf Steiner
Three Streams in Human Evolution by Rudolf Steiner
Verses and Meditations by Rudolph Steiner
Wonders of the World by Rudolf Steiner
The World of the Desert Fathers by Columba Stewart
Witchcraft and Black Magic by Montague Summers
Conjugal Love by Emanuel Swedenborg
Heaven and Hell by Emanuel Swedenborg
Conversations with Eternity by Robert Temple*
He Who Saw Everything – a translation of the Gilgamesh epic by Robert Temple
Mysteries and secrets of magic by C.J.S. Thompson
The Elizabethan World Picture by E.M.W Tillyard
Tracks in the Snow – studies in English science and art by Ruthven Todd
The Tragic Sense of Life by Miguel de Unamuno
Primitive Man by Cesar de Vesme
Reincarnation by Guenther Wachsmuth
Raymund Lully, Illuminated Doctor, Alchemist and Christian Mystic by A.E. Waite
Gnosticism by Benjamin Walker
Madame Blavatsky's Baboon by Peter Washington
Tao, the Watercourse Way by Alan Watts
Secret Societies and Subversive Movements by Nesta Webster
The Serpent in the Sky by John Anthony West
The Secret of the Golden Flower by Richard Wilhelm
Witchcraft by Charles Williams
The Laughing Philosopher: a life of Rabelais by M.P. Willocks
Are These the Words of Jesus? by Ian Wilson
Autobiography of a Yogi by Paramahansa Yogananda *
Mysticism sacred and profane by R.C. Zaehner

This book is the result of some twenty years of reading. Often I've read a book which has yielded only a sentence in my own. So the above is a selective biography. I should perhaps declare a small interest here. In the case of some of these books, I have not only read them, I have commissioned and published them too. I had originally intended that the notes would be almost as long as the text, but then the text is twice as long as intended. Perhaps it's for the best. One more tiny, wafer-thin bit of information and this book might have exploded like Mr Creosote in Monty Python's *Meaning of Life*.

It's a peril of writing a book so wide-ranging that even as you're going to press, new books are published which you need to read and take into account. I'd just like to mention Philip Ball's brilliant *The Devil's Doctor*, a biography of Paracelsus and *The Occult Tradition* by David S. Katz. Both these books show great 'negative capability' when it comes to the question of whether or not occult phenomena are real. Barry Strauss's recent book on *The Trojan War* bolsters the idea that it was a real historical event.

I've put an asterisk by the books – not the obvious ones, not *The Brothers Karamazov*, for example – that I recommend as giving the reader a vertiginous sense of plunging into whole new worlds of thought. I've chosen books that are easy to read – and also, I imagine, relatively easy to find.

Discography: *De Occulta Philosophia*, J.S. Bach is performed by Emma Kirkby and Carlos Mena.

Beethoven spoke of the Appassionata as his most esoteric work, but for me it is his last piano sonata, no. 31 in A flat major opus 110, in the course of which, suddenly he jumps forward to the music of a hundred years later the prophesied jazz.

Esoteric pop music is made by the pataphysicist Robert Wyatt, and the deftest of Donovan. Mountain. No Mountain.

Index

Fama bona
The History